Brazilian Company Law

Dan Wei and Almeida Machava

Brazilian Company Law

PETER LANG
Lausanne • Berlin • Bruxelles • Chennai • New York • Oxford

Library of Congress Cataloging-in-Publication Control Number: 2022037290

Bibliographic information published by the **Deutsche Nationalbibliothek.**
The German National Library lists this publication in the German
National Bibliography; detailed bibliographic data is available
on the Internet at http://dnb.d-nb.de.

Cover design by Peter Lang Group AG

ISBN 978-1-4331-9769-7 (hardcover)
ISBN 978-1-4331-9905-9 (ebook pdf)
ISBN 978-1-4331-9906-6 (epub)
DOI 10.3726/b20098

This edition is an authorized translation from the Chinese language edition
Published by arrangement with Social Sciences Academic Press (China)

Published by Peter Lang Publishing Inc., New York, USA
info@peterlang.com - www.peterlang.com

This publication has been peer reviewed.

Table of Contents

Introduction

In recent years, Brazil has been one of the countries that have introduced maximum number of innovations in their legal system to govern its business activities in both the developing and developed worlds. Indeed, the modernization of Brazilian Law, in particular its Economic Law, has created conditions that warranted unprecedented changes in trade development and business activities in Brazil.

Over a relatively short duration of two centuries of its existence, the Brazilian Company Law, which was originally based on the Roman legal system, later changed its fundamental character to follow the French legal system and eventually settled down for a legal system that had features similar to the Italian legal system. Indeed, its French approach required the Brazilian legal system to classify the nature of country's economic activities into two groups: civil and commercial. In the latter, the approach to company law is based on the theory of acts of commerce as an instrument for objectifying the legal approach to mercantile activity. In the colonial period itself, Brazil was already one of the most attractive places for its development of economic activities, and it was in this context that the development of commercial legislation to respond to the economic vitality of Brazil at that time was urgent, and in order to achieve such a goal the government had to adopt an approach based on the French Code of Commerce whose provisions were marked by the theory of acts of commerce.

Later, already in the 20th century, the Brazilian legislators would embrace the Italian approach, which apparently seeks the unification of the Private Economic Law through the development of the theory of the company to meet the requirements of the so-called superior capitalism. Indeed, with the approval of the Civil Code of 2002, the Brazilian legislators definitively adopted the theory of the company and incorporated the Italian model based on the proven discipline of economic activity.

However, the history of Brazilian Company Law is not only replete with changes in the legal approach to economic activities of a private nature, but also and, mainly, illustrated the innovations that the Brazilian legislators have brought in the country's legal framework, in their efforts to try and keep up with the dynamics of business activity and offer the best legal solutions for various issues in trade and commerce. It is this quest to modernize and, above all, bring innovations in Brazilian Company Law that have inspired many countries, particularly the developing ones, to adopt the Brazilian model of trade and commerce legal system in regulating their legal system to monitor economic and/or trade and commerce activities.

This book highlights the innovative options that the Brazilian legislators have developed in the bid to modernize the legal framework governing the conduct of commercial activities and, at the same time, broaden the horizons on the perception and knowledge of the legal regime governing business in Brazil. The book not only aims to enrich the debate on Brazilian Company Law, and the Corporate Law in general, but can also serve as a source of valuable information on the procedures implemented by the Brazil legislators to govern the conduct of private economic activities in Brazil.

The book is of great importance for academics in the Portuguese-speaking world and will strengthen their efforts in studying and teaching modern Brazilian Company Law, as it discusses key theories and legal features of the Brazilian Company Law. The book it is intended to serve as a reliable source of knowledge for scholars interested in Brazilian Company Law as well as company law in general, as the book can also be used for comparative legal studies. As a matter of fact, this book offers a detailed analysis of the theories and doctrinal debates on Brazilian Company Law by bringing together and presenting contributions from prominent Brazilian Company Law scholars. The book offers a comprehensive analysis and discussion on the legal options adopted by Brazilian legislators in their quest to modernize the domestic business environment in Brazil.

The book provides a comprehensive study of the Brazilian Company Law, and the five chapters together present useful discussion on several key topics in this context, with each of them separately addressing one specific topic: Chapter 1, "General Introduction to Brazilian Company Law," seeks to present the definition, characterization, and the historical evolution of the legal discipline in Brazil and reviews the various stages that the process of construction and modernization of the Brazil's Company Law through, as well as the main features of the company law. Chapter 2, "General Company Law Doctrine," provides an overview of the theory of the acts of commerce as an object of commercial law as well as the classifications of the acts of commerce. Chapter 3, "Objective Perspective of the Company Law," discusses the commercial enterprise, also referred to as "the company," and the commercial premises, also referred to as the "commercial establishment," in addition to exploring the legal nature of these two legal entities, that is, commercial enterprise and commercial establishment. Chapter 4 presents a discussion on the second dimension or perspective of company law and thus deals with the subjective company law, where the focus is on the person who carries out commercial or business activities—that is, the businessperson or commercial entrepreneur, who could either an individual running the business or running the business organization which is a collective of people and a legal entity. This chapter discusses main aspects of business or commercial subjects, such as the requirements for the acquisition of the status of businessperson in Brazil and special obligations imposed on the businessperson. Here, special attention is given to commercial companies, which are regarded as the "collective businessperson" under the Brazilian legal system. Finally, Chapter 5 discusses the laws and regulations in relation to bankruptcy or recovery of commercial entities in Brazil.

As one can see, in terms of content, the book integrates in one single volume the most relevant and important topics that help to comprehensively understand the Brazilian Company Law in its substantive dimensions and presents them in clear and simple language to make it easy for the reader to read and understand the contents presented.

1

Introduction to Brazilian Company Law

1. General Concept of Company Law

Defining Company Law has always proved to be a difficult task for company law scholars, first because it is a discipline that operates in a multifaceted environment where the alignment of different factors that integrate it with the normal course of commerce is not always possible, despite its power to influence the definition of norms that guide commercial activity.[1] In fact, over the years there have emerged differences in how the concept of company law came to be defined given the myriad views and theories proposed in relation to the subject of company law.

On the other hand, the terminology associated with defining the company law is itself presented as a determinant of the concept; that is, the designation of the discipline as *commercial law* or *company law* determines how we understand the definition of the term *company law*. In the present study, we prefer to adopt the terminology of *company law*, in order to respond to the new trends of this legal discipline, which has its focus on the company and no longer on the trader or in the acts of trade; this doesn't mean Commercial Law has disappeared.

1 On this see also Waldo FAZZIO JÚNIOR, *Manual de Direito Comercial*, 11 Edição (São Paulo: Editora Atlas, 2010), 8.

In fact, it is worth to highlight here Soares Hentz's words—"commercial law does not disappear with the new [Civil] Code, but is reborn as Company Law."[2]

According to Fazzio Júnior, there is almost a uniform orientation in the formulation of the tenets comprising the company law, given that one cannot ignore the existence of *an organized professional activity of an economic nature aimed at making products and services available to the consumer.*[3] Thus, continues Fazzio Júnior, in the Brazilian law, company law should be understood as *the positive normative complex that focuses on the legal relations derived from the exercise of business activity [that is] it disciplines the solution of disputes between entrepreneurs, as well as related matters to the organized economic activity of production and circulation of goods* (. . .).[4]

In turn, Fábio Ulhoa Coelho understands that Commercial Law, as a traditional designation of the mercantile legal discipline, *has as its subject the socially structured means of overcoming conflicts of interest among those engaged in the economic activities of production or circulation of goods or services we all need to live.*[5]

A brief analysis of the above definitions reveals a common aspect in addition to its economic content. Indeed, both authors present Business Law in a conciliatory dimension, that is, as an instrument for settlement of disputes between entrepreneurs. We believe that such a consideration can reduce the essence of company law, which, in general, as both authors acknowledge, is the regulation of business activity, that is, the "Law that regulates the relations arising from commercial activities."[6] Indeed, business activity cannot only be seen as conflicting; it has a dimension that goes beyond that. In fact, conflicts between entrepreneurs arise as a result of the exercise of trade; they are not the origin of trade. On the other hand, Fazzio Júnior's consideration of Business Law being *a positive normative complex* ignores not only the origins of Business Law but also one of its main characteristics—*the informalism*—as we will see below. As a matter of fact, not all the rules that make up the company law's normative framework are positive.

Ricardo Negrão looks at the various moments the legal discipline has gone through and to safeguard its origins, concludes that from the point of view of terminology the designation "Company Law" is preferable, as it encompasses the

2 Apud Ricardo NEGRÃO, *Manual de Direito Comercial e de Empresa, Volume 1*, 7ª Edição (São Paulo: SARAIVA, 2010), 34.

3 Waldo FAZZIO JÚNIOR (2010), op. cit., 9.

4 Ricardo NEGRÃO, (2010), op. cit., 10.

5 Fábio Ulhoa COELHO, *Curso de Direito Comercial: Direito de Empresa*, Vol. 1, 13 Edição (São Paulo: Editora Saraiva, 2009), 27.

6 Rubens REQUIÃO, *Curso de Direito Comercial, Volume 1* (Editora Saraiva, 2005), 25.

traditional aspects of Commercial Law and the new institutes of the entrepreneur and will be *"the branch of private law that regulates the activity of the former trader and the modern entrepreneur, as well as their legal relations, established during the professional exercise of commercial and business activities."*[7]

Carvalho Mendonça looked at subjectivist and objectivist approaches and sought to reconcile them in a single concept and conceived Commercial Law as *"the legal discipline that regulates acts of commerce and, at the same time, the rights and obligations of the people who exercise them professionally and their helpers."*[8]

In a more modern approach, Fran Martins says that Commercial Law is a *"set of legal rules that regulate the activities of companies and commercial entrepreneurs, as well as acts considered commercial, even if these acts are not related to the companies' activities."*[9]

In consideration of the foregoing discussion as well as in line with the idea of Fran Martins, we accept the thesis that company law will be a branch of private law constituted by a set of rules that regulate business activity; that is, it takes care of not only the subjects that carry out the commerce but also the relations that they establish in the exercise of the commerce.

2. Origin and Historical Evolution of Brazilian Company Law

Finding an exact moment in which company law would have arisen is not an easy activity, and differences continue to prevail even in contemporary times between scholars. Indeed, some authors refer to the Middle Ages as the period in which the company law emerged. Rubens Requião states categorically that, as a result of the demands of trade, Commercial Law had emerged in the Middle Ages,[10] but others argue that the same thing happened with the emergence of trade, that is, with humanization, because *since the beginning, men have always felt the need to establish commercial exchanges, although at that time there was no universal means of exchange* and that using barter the rules to regulate this activity would soon have emerged; this explains the rules of trade regulation found in Mesopotamia, in the ancient Egypt; in Phoenicia in Palestine; and in the ancient Greece.[11] Other

7 Ricardo NEGRÃO (2010), op. cit., 34.
8 *Apud* Waldo FAZZIO JÚNIOR (2010), op. cit., 9.
9 *Ibid.*
10 Rubens REQUIÃO (2005), op. cit., 10.
11 *Vide*, Manuel Guilherme JÚNIOR, *Manual de Direito Comercial Moçambicano*, Vol. 1 (Escolar Editora, 2013), 31-32.

scholars still ascribe the emergence of company law to the period after the Middle Ages, basing that claim on the *economic ideas and their results in the Western world* during that period.[12] Among the defenders of this idea stands out Tullio Escarelli, who states that

> *"It is in the civilization of the communes that Commercial Law begins to assert itself in opposition to feudal civilization, but also distinguishing itself from common Roman law, which, almost simultaneously, is constituted and imposed. Commercial law appears, therefore, as a historical phenomenon, whose origin is linked to the affirmation of a bourgeois and urban civilization, in which a new entrepreneurial spirit and a new business organization develop. This new civilization appears, precisely, in the Italian communes."*[13]

However, the divergence of views among the authors as to the period in which company law would have appeared does not preclude the almost unanimous view that it developed outside the Roman-based civil law.[14] This general consideration is also in line with the idea that company law has developed in four phases or historical periods. In order to find the origins and history of Brazilian Company Law, we believe it is pertinent to review these four periods.

2.1 First Phase: Second Half of the 12th Century and First Half of the 16th Century

Characterized by a subjective approach to commercial law, in the sense that it applies to merchants associated with arts and crafts corporations,[15] and as the "main and organized class, enriched with resources, merchant corporations obtain great success and political powers, the point of conquering autonomy for some shopping centers, of which the powerful Italian cities of Venice, Florence, Genoa, Amalfi and others are cited as examples."[16]

In this period, the corporations had absolute power since it was up to them to elaborate the regulations from which the commercial uses were established, and the application of rules through their magistrates who, as *mercatorum* consuls, assumed the political-administrative and judicial role, developing and specifying the content and interpretation of the rules.[17] Regarding this absolute power of

12 Ricardo NEGRÃO(2010), op. cit., 25.
13 *Apud* Ricardo NEGRÃO (2010), op. cit., 26.
14 On this Ricardo NEGRÃO (2010), op. cit., 25; and Manuel Guilherme JÚNIOR (2013), op. cit., 31,
15 On this Fábio Ulhoa COELHO (2009), op. cit., 12; e Ricardo NEGRÃO (2010), op. cit., 26.
16 Rubens REQUIÃO (2005), op. cit., 12.
17 Miguel J. A. Pupo CORREIA, *Direito Comercial*, 6ª Edição (Lisboa: Ediforum, 1999), 17.

corporations, Rubens Requião wrote, "merchants, organized in their powerful leagues and corporations, acquire such political and military power that the mercantile cities become autonomous to the point that, in many cases, the statutes of their corporations become confused with the statutes of the city itself."[18]

Describing the first phase of evolution of corporate law, Ricardo Negrão explains that commerce was itinerant, as traders moved from city to city to participate in merchandise fairs. These fairs allowed the old commercial practices to change into uses and standards recognized by all. However, with the decline in fairs from the 18th century onwards, important legal services and institutes have emerged, such as exchange rate, credit securities, banks, and commodity exchanges. It was in the first phase that the insurance contract arose as a result of the itinerant nature of trade, constitution of commercial fund, and distinctive signs and use of trademark and origin of the product. In the corporate domain emerged the first family companies, companies, and their subsidiaries and branches throughout Europe, giving rise to the concept of holding or associated companies. The evolution of maritime companies, which presented themselves as the so-called capital and industry companies, was another important milestone in this phase.[19]

2.2 Second Phase: Second Half of the 16th Century to 18th Century

Influenced by mercantilism, this period was "characterized by colonial expansion and [was] the heyday of the evolution of large societies, always under the authorization of the State."[20] At this stage, the early signs of manifestation of state power appeared. As Ulhoa Coelho writes, in the case of France, "merchants' corporations gradually lose jurisdictional powers to the courts of the gestating state, but there is still a right that is based on the traders' customs and practices and only applicable to them."[21] However, Ulhoa Coelho also writes that the main milestone of this period was the emergence of public limited companies that would prove to be more suitable for the commercial ventures of colonial expansion, demanding large capital contributions and risk limitation.[22]

18 Rubens REQUIÃO (2005), op. cit., 12.
19 Ricardo NEGRÃO (2010), op. cit., 27-32.
20 *Id.*, 32.
21 Fábio Ulhoa COELHO (2009), op. cit., 13.
22 *Id.*, 14.

2.3 Third Phase: 19th Century and First Half of the 20th Century

The Napoleonic Code is presented as inaugurating a new historical phase in company law. The main characteristic of this phase was the "overcoming of the subjective criterion of identification of the scope of incidence of commercial law . . . it is no longer the Law of traders, but of 'acts of commerce' "[23]; that is, with the process of codification initiated by Napoleon, there was an objectification of commercial law that made it a legal discipline applicable to certain acts and not to certain people.[24]

As Ulhoa Coelho explains, the practical significance of adopting the objectivist conception of company law lies in the fact that any citizen can exercise mercantile activity, thus overcoming the corporatism that characterized the previous phases without, however, meaning that the subjectivist dimension has been completely abandoned,[25] even because, as Ricardo Negrão writes,

> "The adoption of the concept of act of commerce, as a central element of mercantile activity and a distinguishing point of mercantile matter, arises as a result of the expansion of the authority and jurisdiction of commerce corporations. Due to the confidence of its decisions by the general public, through practical and summary procedures, the corporation now includes any trader, regardless of previous registration."[26]

Fábio Ulhoa Coelho, at this stage, ascribes the beginning of the history of Brazilian Company Law *with the opening of ports to friendly nations, decreed with the Royal Charter of January 28, 1808* in response to the continental blockade imposed by Napoleon in Europe. In effect, the author adds, the breakdown, from the economic point of view, of colonial dependence with the Portuguese metropolis, due to the strong presence of European powers in Brazilian trade, claimed political independence which, as a consequence, and from the legal point of view, led to the application of the *Law of Good Reason (Lei da Boa Razão)* of 1769 in Brazil. This in the commercial domain led to the application of the Napoleonic Commercial Code in Brazil, of the Portuguese and the Spanish,[27] as laws "of the

23 *Ibid.* On this see also, Ricardo NEGRÃO (2010), op. cit., 33.

24 Tulio Ascarelli *apud* Fábio Ulhoa COELHO (2009), op. cit., 14.

25 Fábio Ulhoa COELHO (2009), op. cit., 14.

26 Ricardo NEGRÃO (2010), op. cit., 33. On this Rubens Requião (cit., p. 13) writes "Such was the success of consular judges, who judged by usages and customs under the inspiration of equity, and the political and social power of the corporation of merchants, that the 'closed' class courts, with exclusive competence to judge and settle disputes between merchants, had attracted to their scope existing demands, very natural, from merchants to non-traders."

27 Fábio Ulhoa COELHO (2009), op. cit., 21-22.

Christian nations, illuminated and polished, with which they were shining in the good, clean and healthy jurisprudence"[28].

It is at this stage that the Brazilian Commercial Code was adopted, in 1850, with a strong influence of the French *Code of Commerce* and the Portuguese and Spanish codes.[29]

2.4 Fourth Phase: Second Half of the 20th Century until Today

The approval of the Italian *Codice Civile* (Civil Code) in 1942 is presented as marking the beginning of the current phase of the history of company law, with the main characteristic of changing the conceptual core of the legal discipline, from the act of commerce to the company.[30] However, it is worth noting here the observation made by Rubens Requião:

> "The first step in building modern Commercial law on the concept of a Company was taken in Germany, in the 1897 Commercial Code, reestablishing and modernizing the subjectivist concept. By the definition of article 343, acts of commerce are all acts of a merchant that pertain to his commercial activity. In view of this definition, both the act of commerce and the merchant only acquire importance for Commercial law when they refer to the exploitation of a company. In it, the preponderance of the isolated act of commerce disappears, as does the figure of the merchant. Thus, the mercantile company appears splendidly, and Commercial law becomes the law of commercial Companies."[31]

Regardless of the exact time and place where modern company law may have started, the fact is that it arises in a context in which its main object—the company—did not have a precise content. In fact, the concept of company was seen from four perspectives: a. in the *subjective sense*, as an entrepreneur, that is, one who carries out an autonomous activity of an organizational nature and with risk-taking; b. in the *functional sense*, in which it is presented as the activity itself, where obtaining profit by offering goods or services on the market is the essential element; c. in the *patrimonial or objective sense*, in which it corresponds to the company property or establishment; and d. in a *corporate sense*, in which

28 Rubens REQUIÃO (2005), op. cit., 17.
29 Ibid.
30 On this Fábio Ulhoa COELHO (2009), op. cit., 18; and Ricardo NEGRÃO (2010), op. cit., 33.
31 Rubens REQUIÃO (2005), op. cit., 16.

the company is presented as an institution, that is, the gathering of people with common purposes.[32]

However, it is in the functional sense that the company is assumed as an autonomous legal concept, that is, as an organized economic activity for the production or circulation of goods or services, and the company does not have the legal nature of a legal subject (entrepreneur) or of a thing (business establishment).[33]

This new approach to company law, in which the theory of acts of commerce is being replaced by that of the company, has also been influencing the Brazilian Company Law, not because of the private legislative evolution that culminated in the adoption of the Civil Code in 2002 thus determined, but because, despite the existence of a Commercial Code that drew its inspiration in the acts of commerce, the other sources of law in general, such as doctrine, jurisprudence, and other loose legislations, have always sought to reorient commercial law in order to guarantee that it fulfills its function of—through standards that and adapted to the economic reality, mainly of the last four of the 20th century—solving the conflicts of interests that could exist between commercial entrepreneurs.[34] The inclusion in Book II of the Special Part of the Civil Code of "Company Law" marks the culmination of the transition from the French system (of acts of commerce) to the Italian system (of the company).

3. General Characteristics of Brazilian Company Law

The company law presents itself as a special private law with its own characteristic features, which allow it to be autonomous from other legal disciplines. Among the various characteristic elements of company law, the doctrine has been unanimous in highlighting the following:

Cosmopolism—it means that company law is generally universal[35]; that is, the construction of company law doesnot look at its recipients as being limited to a social reality since the mercantile phenomenon transcends the boundaries of a given state. In fact, the origins of company law demonstrate this cosmopolitan character, since, in ancient Rome, the law of foreigners, the *jus gentium*, was applied to the merchant; maritime law, universalistic par

32 ASQUINI *apud* Fábio Ulhoa COELHO (2009), op. cit., 18.
33 *Vide* Fábio Ulhoa COELHO (2009), op. cit., 19.
34 Fábio Ulhoa COELHO (2009), op. cit., 25.
35 On this, Manuel Guilherme JÚNIOR (2013), op. cit., 42.

excellence, inspired the creation of several commercial institutes, such as limited partnership, insurance, and, according to some, the limited companies themselves.[36]

Onerosity—the material interest behind the performance of the commercial entrepreneur that translates into the production or obtaining of profit; for this very reason, company law has, by nature, onerosity as one of its main characteristics. Indeed, gratuitousness is not conceived in commercial activity, in such a way that onerosity is presumed[37]; that is, the acts of commercial entrepreneur will not be onerous if it is proven that they are not. However, it must be borne in mind that the profitmaking goal pursued by the entrepreneur does not mean that in his performance he must always have profit, since this will be the result of the combination of several factors pursued by the organization, but that the possibility of obtaining profit must be the basis of entrepreneur's performance.

Dynamism—company law is rapidly evolving,[38] seeking to meet the constant demands of the mercantile phenomenon. This assumes that it is dynamic or flexible, in the sense that its rules can adjust to the requirements of the moment and consequently follow the changes witnessed in the business market. Market rules create new legal figures and institutes, and the company law should be able to welcome them without advocating for creating and implementing any major, radical reforms. Company law must accompany the evolution of trade and market practices.

Informalism—considering the dynamic nature of business activity and the fact that, as a rule, commerce is intended for mass operations, "in which the speed of hiring is a substantial element, the suppression of formalism was forced. On the other hand, good faith prevails in commercial contracts, imposing simpler and more numerous means of evidence than in Civil law."[39]

Fragmentarism—it is justified by the fact that company law is not constituted as a single and complete normative body; it is usually fragmented into several instruments that are also not complete, always leaving a gap to be filled.[40] In fact, this fragmentation supports in a way the analogy that it is a subsidiary source of company law.

36 Rubens REQUIÃO (2005), op. cit., 29.
37 Ibid.
38 Manuel Guilherme JÚNIOR (2013), op. cit., 43.
39 Rubens REQUIÃO (2005), op. cit., 29-30.
40 On this, Rubens REQUIÃO (2005), op. cit., 30.

Individualism—a characteristic of company law—emerges in situations where the entrepreneur pursues selfish objectives; that is, *profit is causally linked to individual interest,* despite *being tempered in modern times by the performance of the state, limiting the freedom of the contract.*[41]

Presumption of solidarity—this is justified by the need for security in the legal trade, due to the celerity or speed with which activities take place that characterize it. Hence, since the beginnings of corporate law, solidarity has always been implicit.[42] However, looking at the Brazilian system, the idea that presumed solidarity can be made autonomous as a characteristic of company law has been refuted, since the rule of Article 896 of the Civil Code, that solidarity is not presumed, resulting either from the law or from the will of the parties; hence, solidarity (except in commercial surety) is never presumed, whether it be for civil or for commercial obligations.[43]

4. Sources of Brazilian Company Law

The expression *source of law* refers to the ways of creating and implementing legal norms[44] or—in the words of Fazzio Júnior, ways of realizing objective law—through which legal rules are established and materialized, to which the individual complies to establish his right or the judge alludes to in order to justify the decision of a certain conflict.[45] Thus, one should seek to understand the "sources of commercial law [in a manner similar to the way] . . . we understand [how] . . . legal norms of a commercial nature arise."[46]

In company law, it is common practice to group sources into *immediate sources* and *mediate sources*, with the former referring to those that in themselves can form the legal order and the latter to those that indirectly contribute to the formation of the legal norms.[47] Added to these two categories is the classification *domestic or internal sources and international or external sources,*[48] depending on whether they are of national or international origin. It is these guidelines that we

41 Rubens REQUIÃO (2005), op. cit., 30.
42 Rubens REQUIÃO (2005), op. cit., 30.
43 *Vide* Rubens REQUIÃO (2005), op. cit., 30.
44 José de Oliveira ASCENSÃO (2005), O Direito – *Introdução e Teoria Geral,* 13ª Edição Refundida, 7ª reimpressão, Coimbra: Edições Almedina.
45 Waldo FAZZIO JÚNIOR (2010), op. cit., 11.
46 Rubens REQUIÃO (2005), op. cit., 25.
47 Ibid.
48 Manuel Guilherme JÚNIOR (2013), op. cit., 38.

will follow; however, we will take the second classification as a standard in which we will analyze the immediate and mediate sources:

4.1. Internal Sources

4.1.1. Immediate Sources

Also called primary sources, they include the normative acts par excellence (the laws). Thus, the immediate sources of Brazilian Company Law include the following:

(a) The Federal Constitution

In modern societies where the rule of law prevails, the constitution presents itself as the fundamental law, for it is the constitution that informs and makes the entire domestic normative system to be in conformance with it; therefore, all normative acts must conform to the constitution. This understanding is not alien to the Brazilian legal context; at the top of the hierarchy of immediate sources is the Federal Constitution, which, "besides proclaiming the supremacy of legality, enunciates norms-principles and norms-rules that infect the entire system, thus claiming the conformation of commercial norms to their major stipulations."[49] Indeed, it is in the Federal Constitution that the general principles of economic activity in Brazil are found, which results, among others, in free competition, in guaranteeing the free exercise of economic activity, in protecting the consumers, as well as in valuing private initiative, as shown in Article 170 et seq. of the Brazilian Federal Constitution.

(b) Commercial Code

Following the tradition of Roman-Germanic systems, Brazil joined the codification process. Thus, in the commercial area, the Commercial Code was approved through Law No. 556 of June 25, 1850. However, Part I, which dealt with commerce in general, was revoked by Law No. 10.406 of January 10, 2002. Therefore, today, the Brazilian Commercial Code, as a source of company law, is valid for its second part—Maritime Commerce, with the exception of Title IX, which was also repealed by Law No. 7.542 of September 26, 1986.

49 Waldo FAZZIO JÚNIOR (2010), op. cit., 11.

(c) Civil Code

The consideration of civil law as a source of company law is ruled out by some Brazilian Company Law scholars, among which Rubens Requião stands out. For him, the fact that the application of civil law to commercial relations does not change the civil nature of the rules to be applied is not enough to consider civil law as a source of company law. He argues thus,

> "If Civil law, as a common law, pre-exists commercial law; if commercial law applies to commercial relations, departing from Civil law, as it constitutes a special law applicable to such relations, it is easy to understand that Civil law does not present itself as one of the sources of Commercial law. When it is invoked, in the absence of a specific rule of special law, to govern certain commercial relations, it is not as Commercial law that is applied, but simply as Civil law. Therefore, it does not lose its civilian nature, integrating itself in Commercial law, when this occurs. Therefore, Civil law is not and cannot be considered as a source of Commercial law when it is invoked by it to fill in the gaps or omissions."[50]

This positioning is understood by the restricted interpretation of the concept of sources of company law that the author presents as mentioned above. In effect, only a restrictive view of that concept will make strict commercial rules and norms as a source of company law. However, we believe that this should not be the understanding. Indeed, as the author himself describes, the application of civil law to commercial relations is not done without conforming its rules to the requirements of company law; that is, civil law must be applied with necessary modifications in order to meet the specificities of the commercial context in which it is applied.

Therefore, we must align ourselves with that group of scholars who are of the firm view that civil law is indeed the source of company law.[51] In fact, today it is in the Civil Code that Brazilian Company Law finds its main basis of normative support, since Book II is dedicated exclusively to company law. It is for this reason that the First Part of the Commercial Code of Brazil was revoked, leaving the regime that was provided for in it and regulated by the Civil Code.

(d) Ordinary Laws

The tradition of jurisdictions that share the Romano-Germanic legal system is to have a commercial code that is the main source of company law and which

50 Rubens REQUIÃO (2005), op. cit., 25.

51 On this see Waldo FAZZIO JÚNIOR (2010), op. cit., 12; and Ricardo NEGRÃO (2010), op. cit., 39.

comprises the various extravagant norms to complement the commercial code. Originally, the Brazilian legal system also shared this tradition. However, today, the Brazilian reality is different due to the residual nature of the commercial code as mentioned above. Currently, Brazilian Company Law, with regard to immediate sources, has in its ordinary laws its main normative framework. In fact, the dynamics of business activity and its rapid evolution led to the emergence of numerous legal instruments to meet the requirements that the merchant imposed each time.

Brazilian Company Law has more than a hundred legal instruments through which it is revealed or carried out, and some of the major ones among them include the following:

- Law 11.101 of February 9, 2005—regulates judicial and extrajudicial recovery and bankruptcy of the entrepreneur and the company.
- Decree 3.708 of January 10, 1919—regulates the formation of limited liability companies.
- Law 6.404 of December 15, 1976—regulates the funding of limited companies by shares.
- Decree-Law 2.627 of September 26, 1940; this was not revoked by Law 6.404 of December 15, 1976, which provides for limited companies by shares.
- Decree 2.044 of December 31, 1908, which defines the bill of exchange and the promissory note and regulates exchange operations.
- Law 9.279 of May 14, 1996, which regulates rights and obligations related to industrial property.

4.1.2. Mediate Sources

(a) Custom or Mercantile Uses

Traditionally, in order to assert themselves as sources of law, customs are presented as all practices repeated with conviction of obligation; that is, it is not enough that we are facing a simple practice to consider it a custom, but that it is necessary that it is not isolated, in the sense that it is repetitive, and that those who practice it do so with the conviction that it is mandatory. It is in this sense that Fazzio Júnior also presents them as sources of company law when he states that "for a uniform and constant practice [the idea of reiteration] to acquire the status of use, it must involve the belief that it is the right that is being observed [this mandatory conviction]"[52] or, as postulated by Rubens Requião, when he writes that use, *after its constant practice and the voluntary recognition of some community of traders, becomes an implicit rule of the legal relationship, for which it was born*. It is pertinent to add here Vivante's views—that *the use must be maintained in a uniform way for a certain time, and it is observed as if it were a rule of law and, therefore, with the conviction that it cannot be violated with impunity.*[53]

The roots of company law per se support the nature of its source for commercial uses. Indeed, as we will see below, company law was born out of commercial practices, that is, from the creations of merchants themselves, who in principle created a series of normative standards to guide their trade exchanges, the so-called *lex mercatoria* or the *law of merchants*, which are nothing more than commercial practices. Indeed, it is worth recalling here Rubens Requião's views on commercial uses here, when he says "commercial uses appear spontaneously. A trader, in his habits, sets a certain standard, which is being adopted by others. The use of individual becomes general. At first, in a particular market, which are local uses, then expanding to others, forming regional or national uses."[54]

Formally, in Brazilian law, the status of the source of company law for commercial uses arises from the regulation of the commercial process—Regulation 737 of November 25, 1850 that in its Article 2 establishes that commercial uses are subsidiary sources of company law and when it comes to social issues, they will even prefer the rules of civil law. On the other hand, several norms of the commercial code established the subsidiary character of the commercial uses.

(b) General Principles of Law

Company law is circumscribed in a normative system and in case of insufficiency of its special rules, it must find in that system the most appropriate legal solutions. It is in this sense that the general principles of law are presented as subsidiary sources of company law, not because they generate norms but because "they only reveal implicit norms, by invoking the superior ideas that rule the order."[55]

(c) Analogy

Traditionally, the analogy is presented as a mechanism for the integration of gaps, through which the legal system is sought to solve a concrete situation that cannot be answered by the special rules. In other words, the analogy assumes that "if

52 Waldo FAZZIO JÚNIOR (2010), op. cit., 14.
53 Rubens REQUIÃO (2005), op. cit., 27.
54 Rubens REQUIÃO (2005), op. cit., 27.
55 Waldo FAZZIO JÚNIOR (2010), op. cit., 16.

two objects of Law or legal situations have similarities, and one of them lacks a legislative solution, the solution already established for the first object or situation that the law contemplated applies"[56] following, in the words of Fazzio Júnior, the idea of equity, in the sense that facts of the same nature must observe identical discipline.[57]

It is precisely the ability to be able to indicate a solution to a situation that originally would not have it that gives analogy the status of a source of law, even if it is not direct. However, as Ricardo Negrão rightly explains, more than a source of law, the analogy must be seen as a process, a method of legislative interpretation[58] that allows for discovering an explicit or implicit legal solution of the existing norm, either in the legal rule (*legis* analogy) or in the legal system (*juris* analogy).[59]

4.2. International Sources: International Conventions

Brazilian Company Law is not realized or revealed only through strictly internal rules. In some situations, the answers to legal situations that arise from it result from international instruments to which Brazil has adhered to or is bound, such as in the case of the Geneva Uniform Law on Bills of Exchange and Promissory Notes, introduced in Brazil through Decree 57.663 of January 24, 1966.

References

- ASCENSÃO, José de Oliveira. 2005. O Direito – *Introdução e Teoria Geral*, 13ª Edição Refundida, 7ª reimpressão, Coimbra: Edições Almedina.
- COELHO, Fábio Ulhoa. 2009. *Curso de Direito Comercial: Direito de Empresa*, Vol. 1, 13 Edição. São Paulo: Editora Saraiva.
- FAZZIO JÚNIOR, Waldo. 2010. *Manual de Direito Comercial*, 11ª Edição. São Paulo: Editora Atlas.
- GUIMARÃES, Márcio. 2013. *Direito das Empresas em dificuldades*. Fundação Gentúlio Vargas: Direito Rio, Graduação.
- JÚNIOR, Manuel Guilherme. 2013. *Manual de Direito Comercial Moçambicano*, Vol. 1. 1ª Edição. Maputo: Escolar Editora.

56 Ricardo NEGRÃO (2010), op. cit., 41.
57 Waldo FAZZIO JÚNIOR (2010), op. cit., 15.
58 Ricardo NEGRÃO (2010), op. cit., 41.
59 On this Waldo FAZZIO JÚNIOR (2010), op. cit., 15.

- NEGRÃO, Ricardo. 2010. *Manual de Direito Comercial e de Empresa, Volume 1*, 7ª Edição, São Paulo: SARAIVA.
- REQUIÃO, Rubens. 2003. *Curso de Direito Comercial*, Vol. I, 25ª ed. São Paulo: Saraiva.
- REQUIÃO, Rubens. 2005. *Curso de Direito Comercial, Volume 1*. São Paulo: Editora Saraiva.

Further Reading

- BARROS, Carla Eugenia Caldas. 2014. *Manual de Direito Empresarial Multifacetado*, Voll. III – Direito Falimentar e Recuperacional. Aracaju: Edição do Autor | PIDCC.
- BULHÕES PEDREIRA, José Luiz and Alfredo LAMY FILHO.1992. *A Lei as S.A. – Pressupostos – Elaboração – Aplicação*. Rio de Janeiro: Renovar.
- BULHÕES PEDREIRA, José Luiz and Alfredo LAMY FILHO. 2017. *Direito das Companhias*, 2ª ed. Rio de Janeiro: Editora Forense.
- CARVALHO FILHO, José dos Santos. 2018. *Manual de Direito Administrativo*; 32ª ed. São Paulo: Atlas.
- CASTRO, Rodrigo R. Monteiro de and Leandro Santos de ARAG ÃO. 2009. *Direito Societário: Desafios Actuais*. São Paulo: Quarier Latin.
- COELHO, Fábio Ulhoa. 2011. *Manual de Direito Comercial: Direito de Empresa*, 23ª ed. São Paulo: Saraiva.
- COELHO, Fábio Ulhoa. 2012. *Curso de Direito Civil*. Parte Geral, Vol. 1, 5ª ed. São Paulo: Editora Saraiva.
- CORREIA, Miguel J. A. Pupo. 1996. *Direito Comercial*, 4ª ed, revista e aumentada. Lisboa: Universidade Lusíada.
- CORREIA, Miguel J. A. Pupo. 1999. *Direito Comercial*, 6ª Edição. Lisboa: Ediforum.
- DINIZ, Maria Helena. 2008. *Curso de Direito Civil brasileiro*, Vol. 8. São Paulo: Editora Saraiva.
- DINIZ, Maria Helena. 2015. Curso de *Direito Civil Brasileiro: Teoria Geral do Direito Civil*. São Paulo: Saraiva.
- MORREIRA, Welliton Luiz. 2016. *A Sociedade Unipessoal e a Limitação da Responsabilidade Patrimonial do Empresário Individual*, Coimbra.
- REQUIÃO, Rubens. 1984. *Curso de direito comercial*; 14ª ed. São Paulo: Saraiva.
- REQUIÃO, Rubens. 1995. *Curso de Direito Comercial*, 22ª ed. São Paulo: Saraiva.
- RIBEIRO, Cláudia and Priscila MENEZES. 2014. *Teoria do Direito Empresarial*, FGV, Direito Rio, Graduação.
- RODRIGUES, Luiz Antonio Barroso. 2016. *Direito Empresarial*, 3 ed. rev. Actual – Florianópolis: Departamento de Ciências da Administração/ UFSC, Brasília: CAPES: UAB, p. 47.
- SILVA ALVES, Itálo Miqueias da. *A Personalidade Jurídica no Direito Civil*, available at https://jus.com.br/artigos/61828/a-personalidade-juridica-no-direito-civil, accessed in 5th July 2019.

2

The Business Doctrine in General

1. Acts of Commerce: General Concept

From the historical review presented in the previous chapter, it was established that the current phase of company law reveals the abandonment of the theory of acts of commerce in order to embrace the doctrine or theory of the company; that is, the acts of commerce tend to lose their value as qualifiers of those engaged in commercial activity.[1] However, as Ricardo Negrão points out, the relevance of studying the acts of commerce will be in its didactic-historical value, in the sense of allowing the evolution of company law to be monitored.[2]

The theory of acts of commerce points to a particularly important stage in the history of company law and, in some legal systems, continues to mark its presence and influence in the legal discipline of company law. However, since its creation, it has always been a concern of company law scholars to find a uniform

1 FAZZIO JÚNIOR (p. 6) denies this idea, as he considers it to be distorting the legal concept of an act of commerce. For this author, "the act of commerce does not confer on the practitioner the quality of a trader. It does not bring commerciality to the productive professional activity. It is just the opposite. Certainly, it is the organization of professional activity that is finalistically directed that gives the acts practiced by the entrepreneur its real specificity."

2 In fact, some contemporary authors have abandoned the acts of commerce approach in their writings.

and universally accepted concept of acts of commerce. In this exercise, two conceptions were developed—one that looks at acts of commerce as possessing the main characteristic of interposition of people in exchange, and another that sees mediation and speculation as the main characteristic features of the acts of commerce.[3]

For the first conception, the Italian jurist Alfredo Rocco is presented as its main precursor. For his thesis, Rocco's premises were, on the one hand, *to abandon the claim to formulate a unitary scientific concept for acts of commerce* and, on the other hand, to determine that *the unitary concept that we want to establish will always be a positive law concept*, departing from the idea that there is no single concept of an act of commerce under positive law.[4] So, it is no wonder that Rocco's work was based on positive law. Indeed, in order to develop his theory, Rocco analyzed the entire list of acts of commerce provided for in the Italian Commercial Code in order to find a unitary and common element in all of them. After this exhausting exercise, Rocco concluded:

> "Now, we saw that the common concept, which is immanent in all four categories of intrinsically commercial acts: in purchase for resale and later resale, in banking, in companies, and in the insurance industry, is the concept of indirect or mediated exchange, of the interposition in effecting the exchange. In the purchase for resale and later resale we have a mediated exchange of goods, and credit and real estate securities against other economic goods, generally against money. In the Banking operations we have a mediated exchange of present money against future money, or money against money on credit. In companies, we have a mediated exchange of the results of work against other economic goods, especially against money. And finally in insurance, a mediated exchange of an individual's risks against a proportional share of a collective risk. Every act of commerce belongs to one of these four categories; it is, therefore, an act in which an indirect exchange is realized or through an interposed person, that is, an interposition functions in the exchange.
>
> The objects of the exchange are diverse: goods, bonds, real estate, money on credit, work products, risks. There are also several ways in which the exchange takes place. But the phenomenon of exchange through the interposed person appears in any of these four categories of acts contemplated in the Law."[5]

3 Ricardo NEGRÃO (2010), op. cit., 54.
4 Rubens REQUIÃO (2005), op. cit., 32.
5 *Apud* Rubens REQUIÃO (2005), op. cit., 33.

With this, Rocco concludes that every act that makes or facilitates an interposition in the exchange will be commercial.[6]

Two notes deserve to be highlighted in view of Rocco's conception. On the one hand, this conception is based on positive law and, therefore, cannot be generalized, since the commercial laws (codes) are not coincident; that is, each legal system has its own rules and list of acts of commerce. On the other hand, by limiting his analysis in positive law, Rocco ignores the other acts specific to mercantile activity and which were not listed in the Italian Commercial Code. In short, the Rocco's conception did not take into account the origins of the commercial law, which had in the commercial practices the main source.

The second conception of acts of commerce has Gaston Lagarde as its main precursor. In essence, the *theory of mediation and speculation* argues that the act of intermediation in the circulation of wealth, with the intermediary (trader) acting for profit, is indeed an act of commerce.[7]

Thus, the theory of mediation and speculation refutes Rocco's view that the idea of profit is not essential for the qualification of an act as mercantile.

Although one can consider the theory of mediation and speculation as the one that would best help to find a uniform concept of acts of commerce, it still raises some criticisms. At the outset, as it happens in Rocco's conception, when defending the idea of mediation, this theory ignores the possibility of direct trade between the producer and the consumer. According to this theory, if there is no intermediation in this relationship, we cannot speak of an act of commerce.

In view of the difficulty in finding a scientific concept of an act of commerce that is unitary and universal, the solution was to leave it to the legislative power of each country to define what could and could not be considered an act of commerce. In this exercise, two legislative systems emerged: *the enumerative system*, in which the commercial legislator lists activities considered as commercial, and *the descriptive system* that summarizes a generic list of activities being considered as commercial.[8]

6 Id, 34.

7 Vide Rubens REQUIÃO (2005), op. cit., 34.

8 Rubens REQUIÃO (2005), op. cit., 34-35 and Ricardo NEGRÃO (2010), op. cit., 54.

2. Acts of Commerce in Brazilian Law: Classification

In Brazilian law, the discussion of acts of commerce also gained space. However, there is a widespread idea that, like all legal systems that were influenced by the Napoleonic Code, an exemplary enumerative system was adopted, in which it is *"permissible for the interpreter, and above all for the courts, to extend them by analogy to other acts not cataloged there."*[9]

One of the concerns of company law scholars has been about how to classify the various of acts of commerce. In effect, given this lack of precise parameters to help define a unitary and universal concept, an alternative was sought that looked for a way to categorize or classify the various acts of commerce. In this exercise, the first conception involved looking at the company law itself and assessing its object, that is, whether the focus would be on the trader (subjectivist approach) or on the acts themselves (objectivist approach).

Thus, it was possible to distinguish:

Subjective acts of commerce —those whose commerciality arises from the action of a commercial entrepreneur in the exercise of his business; that is, the commercial nature of these acts depends on the quality of the subject who practices them.[10]

German and French doctrines also designate these acts as *relative*, given their dependence on practice by a commercial entrepreneur.[11]

Objective acts of commerce, which, in German doctrine, are also considered *absolute* or *by nature*, refer to those acts whose commerciality is defined by law; that is, "they are intrinsically commercial and, as such, defined by law."[12] Unlike subjective acts, objective acts are not dependent on any subject.

Other classifications of acts of commerce include:

Unilateral acts are those whose commerciality refers to one of the subjects of the mercantile relationship.[13] In Brazilian doctrine, these acts are also referred to

9 Rubens REQUIÃO (2005), op. cit., 35.
10 *Vide* Manuel Guilherme JÚNIOR (2013), op. cit., 48.
11 Rubens REQUIÃO (2005), op. cit., 36.
12 Rubens REQUIÃO (2005), op. cit., 37.
13 Manuel Guilherme JÚNIOR (2013), op cit., 49.

as *mixed acts* given their characteristic of being "*bifronts, which on the one hand constitute a civil act and, on the other hand, a commercial act.*"[14]

An example of these acts would be the consumption relationship, where we have, on the one hand, a supplier (commercial entrepreneur in the exercise of the company) and, on the other, the consumer, who purchases the good for his own consumption.

Carvalho Mendonça removes this classification, defending the attractive force (*vis atractiva*) of commercial law, which submits them to his domain[15]; that is, for this author, "we cannot know how the theory of two-way acts acquired city jurisdiction; both civil and commercial acts, when the legal text establishing the unity or integrity of the act of commerce seems clear. The law, it can be said, commercializes the act, which would be civil if the merchant's intervention did not subject him to the provisions of the Code, to commercialize the non-trader who intervenes in it."[16]

Accessory acts—developed in French doctrine, these refer to the "legal acts that are part of the first two categories and that are carried out by traders for the needs of their trade; far from serving to define the trader, they assume, on the contrary, that quality on the part of the one who makes them."[17] An example of these acts would be the purchase of furniture for the entrepreneur to equip his office.

References

- GUIMARÃES, Márcio. 2013. *Direito das Empresas em dificuldades.* Fundação Gentúlio Vargas: Direito Rio, Graduação.
- NEGRÃO, Ricardo. 2010. *Manual de Direito Comercial e de Empresa, Volume 1,* 7ª Edição, São Paulo: SARAIVA.
- REQUIÃO, Rubens. 2005. *Curso de Direito Comercial, Volume 1.* São Paulo: Editora Saraiva.

Further Reading

- ASCENSÃO, José de Oliveira. 2005. O Direito – *Introdução e Teoria Geral,* 13ª Edição Refundida, 7ª reimpressão, Coimbra: Edições Almedina.

14 Rubens REQUIÃO (2005), op. cit., 37.
15 Rubens REQUIÃO (2005), op. cit., 38.
16 *Apud* Ricardo NEGRÃO (2010), op. cit., 57.
17 Rubens REQUIÃO (2005), op. cit., 37.

- BARROS, Carla Eugenia Caldas. 2014. *Manual de Direito Empresarial Multifacetado*, Voll. III – Direito Falimentar e Recuperacional. Aracaju: Edição do Autor | PIDCC.
- BULHÕES PEDREIRA, José Luiz and Alfredo LAMY FILHO.1992. *A Lei as S.A. – Pressupostos – Elaboração – Aplicação*. Rio de Janeiro: Renovar.
- BULHÕES PEDREIRA, José Luiz and Alfredo LAMY FILHO. 2017. *Direito das Companhias*, 2ª ed. Rio de Janeiro: Editora Forense.
- CARVALHO FILHO, José dos Santos. 2018. *Manual de Direito Administrativo*; 32ª ed. São Paulo: Atlas.
- CASTRO, Rodrigo R. Monteiro de and Leandro Santos de ARAGÃO. 2009. *Direito Societário: Desafios Actuais*. São Paulo: Quarier Latin.
- COELHO, Fábio Ulhoa. 2009. *Curso de Direito Comercial: Direito de Empresa*, Vol. 1, 13 Edição. São Paulo: Editora Saraiva.
- COELHO, Fábio Ulhoa. 2011. *Manual de Direito Comercial: Direito de Empresa*, 23ª ed. São Paulo: Saraiva.
- COELHO, Fábio Ulhoa. 2012. *Curso de Direito Civil*. Parte Geral, Vol. 1, 5ª ed. São Paulo: Editora Saraiva.
- CORREIA, Miguel J. A. Pupo. 1996. *Direito Comercial*, 4ª ed, revista e aumentada. Lisboa: Universidade Lusíada.
- CORREIA, Miguel J. A. Pupo. 1999. *Direito Comercial*, 6ª Edição. Lisboa: Ediforum.
- DINIZ, Maria Helena. 2008. *Curso de Direito Civil brasileiro*, Vol. 8. São Paulo: Editora Saraiva.
- DINIZ, Maria Helena. 2015. Curso de *Direito Civil Brasileiro: Teoria Geral do Direito Civil*. São Paulo: Saraiva.
- FAZZIO JÚNIOR, Waldo. 2010. *Manual de Direito Comercial*, 11ª Edição. São Paulo: Editora Atlas.
- JÚNIOR, Manuel Guilherme. 2022. *Manual de Direito Comercial Moçambicano*, Vol. 1. 2ª Edição. Maputo: Escolar Editora.
- MORREIRA, Welliton Luiz. 2016. *A Sociedade Unipessoal e a Limitação da Responsabilidade Patrimonial do Empresário Individual*, Coimbra.
- REQUIÃO, Rubens. 1984. *Curso de direito comercial*; 14ª ed. São Paulo: Saraiva.
- REQUIÃO, Rubens. 1995. *Curso de Direito Comercial*, 22ª ed. São Paulo: Saraiva.
- REQUIÃO, Rubens. 2003. *Curso de Direito Comercial*, Vol. I, 25ª ed. São Paulo: Saraiva.
- RIBEIRO, Cláudia and Priscila MENEZES. 2014. *Teoria do Direito Empresarial*, FGV, Direito Rio, Graduação.
- RODRIGUES, Luiz António Barroso. 2016. *Direito Empresarial*, 3 ed. rev. Actual – Florianópolis: Departamento de Ciências da Administração/ UFSC, Brasília: CAPES: UAB, p. 47.
- SILVA ALVES, Itálo Miqueias da. *A Personalidade Jurídica no Direito Civil*, available at https://jus.com.br/artigos/61828/a-personalidade-juridica-no-direito-civil, accessed in 5th July 2019.

3

Objective Company Law

1. Commercial Enterprise (Company)

1.1 Concept and Elements of Commercial Enterprise (Company)

The concept of enterprise can be approached from both economic and legal points of views.

From an economic point of view, Giuseppe Ferri, quoted by Rubens Requião,[1] maintains that the productive activity of goods and services for the market is not a result of an accidental or improvised activity; it is, therefore, an activity that has a professional and special nature and presupposes the existence of economic entities with a high level of organization and structure and also a constant nature. Such economic entities must be underpinned by factors of production, whose purpose is to pursue the needs or interests of third parties, precisely the demands of the market in general, and which are given in economic science (those entities) the nomenclature of commercial enterprise or company.

1 Giuseppe FERRI, *Traité de Droit Commercial, apud* Rubens REQUIÃO, *Curso de Direito Comercial,* 22ª ed. (São Paulo: Saraiva, 1995), 40.

In this context, the commercial enterprise must be seen as an economic body; that is, it is founded on an organization established on technical principles and economic laws. From an objective point of view, the commercial enterprise is a union of personal and real factors through which it works to achieve an economic purpose. Obviously, since the commercial enterprise is seen as an organized economic activity, some people put it into practice, for example, the businessperson.

The upward understanding is reinforced by the authors Bulhões Pedreira and Lamy Filho,[2] who bring forth three main characteristics to define the conception that the company is a type of collective production unit that differs from others of the same kind[3]:

(i) Manufacturing unit that produces economic goods for sale—the company as a unit producing economic goods accompanies the modern economy, displaying a high level of specialization and potential for trade that enables markets to be interconnected by creating conditions for production intended for sale and not for the social group of producing entities' own consumption.
(ii) Social group composed by the businessperson and the employees—the social group of the company as a dichotomous structure illustrates two clear divisions—the businessperson and the employee; "the businessperson must be seen as the one who organizes production in his name and on his own account and commands the power structure of the production group, and the employees or wage-earners contribute to the productive activity of the group by providing services of their work in exchange for a predetermined payment, and are subordinated to the entrepreneur."
(iii) Risk of activity on behalf of the businessperson—risk is a typical element that must be assumed by those who practice the company or an activity of the company nature, acquiring from third parties resources that are essential for production, against consideration, at a "right price" and then reselling at an "uncertain price"; hence, the selling price of

2 José Luiz BULHÕES PEDREIRA and Alfredo LAMY FILHO, *Direito das Companhias*, 2ª ed. (Rio de Janeiro: Editora Forense, 2017), 41.

3 The company differentiates itself from other production units known in economic history before the Industrial Revolution. In Antiquity and the Middle Ages, the production units were mostly closed economy, in the sense that they produced mainly for the consumption of their human resources (members of family or domestic groups) and not for sale on the market. José Luiz BULHÕES PEDREIRA and Alfredo LAMY FILHO, op. cit., 41.

economic goods resulting from production may not correspond to the recovery of capital injected for the acquisition of resources.

A concept presented by Fabio Ulhoa Coelho[4] leads to the conclusion that the company must be essentially reflected in a profitable activity, insofar as it must be seen as *"an activity whose essential mark is to make a profit by offering goods or services to the market, which are generated through the organization of production factors (labor force, raw material, capital and technology)."*

What previously Bulhões Pedreira and Lamy Filho called as characteristics of the company, Asquini, cited by Ulhoa Coelho,[5] calls them as company profiles, which in our understanding can also be called as elements of the company: (i) Subjective element—the company gets confused with the one that exercises the company activity (the businessperson), or by another one, the one that exercises an economically organized activity, thus assuming the risk on its own account; (ii) functional element—the company is summarized in the activity; (iii) patrimonial/objective element—the company is connoted as a complex of goods disposed of by the businessperson for the exercise of an organized economic activity; and (iv) company element—the company is identified as a social group composed of the businessperson and the employees engaged in achieving the same desideratum and, consequently, covering the business facet of an institution.

On the other hand, Ulhoa Coelho refutes Asquini's position, inasmuch as he believes that, of the four elements listed, only the functional one, indeed, goes within the reach of a proper legal conception; the subjective and objective elements correspond perfectly to a "new name for the well-known institutes of law and commercial premises"; with regard of what the Company characteristic of the company is concerned, it is very far distant from reality, since the "idea of the identity of purposes to be brought in the company proletarians and capitalists, only exists in populist right-wing or totalitarian ideologies (for instance, the fascist regime which dominated in Italy)".[6]

Having seen the concept of a commercial company, it is now opportune to analyze its functions; in this regard, Alfredo Filho and José Pedreira[7] understand that the company has three functions:

4 Fábio Ulhoa COELHO, *Curso de Direito Comercial: Direito de Empresa,* Vol. 1, 13ª ed. (São Paulo: Saraiva, 2009), 18.

5 Alberto ASQUIN, *Revista del Diritto Commerciale*, *apud* Fábio Ulhoa COELHO, *Curso de Direito Comercial: Direito de Empresa,* Vol. 1, 13ª ed. (São Paulo: Saraiva, 2009), 18.

6 Fábio Ulhoa COELHO, *Curso de Direito Comercial: Direito de Empresa*, op. cit., 18, e 19.

7 José Luiz BULHÕES PEDREIRA and Alfredo LAMY FILHO, *Direito da Companhias*, op. cit., 43-44.

(i) Manufacturer function and movement of economic goods—the company as an economic body operates as a mechanism that promotes and drives the movement of economic goods and services; certainly, in modern societies there are diversified companies, which implies the need to adopt a criterion of specialization in the process of production of certain goods because firms do not enjoy the prerogatives of self-sufficiency they incur in the use of third parties' productive services and raw materials produced by other companies.

(ii) Investment and savings organization—the investment function is reflected in the extent to which the businessperson, by spreading or raising his level of production or broadening the horizons of his company activity, gives rise to new production goods and their centers of production that incriminate the amount of capital resources of the company. In the context of this economic phenomenon, the businessperson is seen as an integral subject of a network of production of goods, giving rise to conditions of demand for the possible form of these goods; this presupposes the application of capital by the businessperson—that is, the investment financed by that capital—as financing can also be made by the profit acquired and from the depreciation that is concentrated in his sphere of wealth and with savings from third parties obtained on the capital market.

The savings function can be summarized in two aspects: (i) *"the part of the gross revenue from the sale of products which restores the loss in value of permanent assets employed in production (depreciation, amortization or depletion), accumulates, in the form of gross financial savings, in the assets of the businessperson"*; and (ii) *"at least part of the profit resulting from the activity of the company is not transformed into consumed income (by the individual businessperson) nor distributed to the members of the businessperson group, but remains in the businessperson's assets as savings."*

(iii) Sharing of the income—in the process of selling the goods, the businessperson obtains flows of the financial value that he partly transfers to other producers as the purchase price of the inputs used in production. The point of distinction between the price and sale of the goods and the cost of acquiring the resources is the financial value created by the company's activity. The businessperson distributes this value by means of rent payments (wages, interests, and rent, including royalties and technical assistance) in return for the services provided by the holders of inputs.

In legal doctrine, the concept of company is quite controversial, and attempts to bring a legal approach to company have been profuse. In order to facilitate their work, legal experts have resorted to the economic approach of that body; however, as Rubens Requião states, it is clear that in the universe of the economic physiognomy of the company, not all its components are important to the field of company law. Manufacturing activity, whose purpose is production of goods intended especially for consumption, becomes an object of economic science, thus importing economists and having little interest to the legal field, in particular company law, so its regulation does not fall within this field.[8]

It should be borne in mind that the legal regulation of the company is directly proportional to the regulation of the activity of the businessperson. This understanding leads to the conclusion that, in the field of company law, the legal concept of the company corresponds to an activity carried out by a subject of law (the businessperson) in a professional and habitual manner.

1.2 Legal System and the Nature of Commercial Enterprise (Company)

Legal system is a set of rights, obligations, prohibitions, and penalties applicable to certain social and economic relations qualified by law.[9]

Before talking about the legal system of the company itself, we must dispel certain ambiguities that distort the real understanding of the company in both its legal and economic perspectives. Although usually used synonymously, the terms *"Trading Company"* and *"Company"* represent different legal concepts, and it is crucial to keep in mind their borderline delimitation for the correct application of the legal system of companies, as modalities of trading companies.

From a social point of view, the company is a productive organization composed by a social group comprising the businessperson and the employees and the natural and capital resources put into action for the production of economic goods by these two groups. As the company function is carried out by a company, the company structure occupies the role of a businessperson in the company system and is integrated into it as its subsystem: the social company group becomes a subgroup of a productive organization.

8 Rubens REQUIÃO (1995), op. cit., 41.

9 Maria Helena DINIZ, *Direito Civil Brasileiro: Teoria Geral do Direito Civil* (São Paulo: Saraiva), 47.

On the legal side, the company is represented by the individual businessperson or by the trading company, which are qualified as subjects of the rights and obligations resulting from their creation and operation.

The legal organization of the company involves more than one legal institute, comprising two branches of law—public and private. The laws relating to the economic function of the businessperson require his registration and public registration, impose obligations on him, and define responsibilities, not only in his relations with employees but also in his participation in the markets. Labor law and certain rules of public law strictly regulate the internal relations of the social group (businessperson and employees) that forms the company. In the context of trading companies, relations between partners are regulated by the Civil Code of Brazil and by the Law of Joint Stock Companies (Law No. 6404 of December 15, 1976).

As can be seen, the businessperson is bound to two forms of relations in the conduct of his company's activities, and a better understanding of this can be arrived at through the analysis of the businessperson position, as proposed by Bulhões Pedreira and Lamy Filho; according to them, the subject of the rights and obligations relating to the company is the businessperson (individual or collective): Internal legal relations are established between the businessperson and the employees (as subjects of the rights and obligations of the employment contracts), and external legal relations bind the businessperson and the people in the company's environments.[10]

Internal Legal Relations—internal relations of the social group are mostly regulated by labor law. The law in question encompasses principles and standards considered revolutionary innovations in the law of obligations, which can be explained by the characteristic of the company as a social group, and legally by a structure of benefit exchange systems and not by a system of participation. The bilateral contract for the provision of services is a legal institution specific to exchanges in the markets, and the Brazilian Civil Code regulates (in Article 594) the contract for the provision of services as a legal form of exchange in which the provider (employee) undertakes to provide work and another party (businessperson) pays them retribution.

These peculiarities to the position of the employee as a member of company's production group explain the need for special legal rules and the intervention of the state to regulate and supervise individual employment contracts, ensure

10 José Luiz BULHÕES PEDREIRA and LAMY FILHO. Alfredo *Direito das Companhias,* op. cit., 48.

health and safety conditions, maintain accident insurance, discipline collective employment contracts, and create mechanisms to resolve conflicts between employees and employers. Furthermore, the inclusion of employees in the company's Company group, although without participating directly in the results of its operation, has led to the legal regulation of relations between the employees' community and the company, the creation of employee committees, representation in decision-making bodies of the company, and the modalities for profit sharing in the company.

Rules (some general and some special—for certain types of activity) of civil and criminal law, or rules of special laws, many of them being a part of the public law of the economy also contribute to the internal organization of the company's production group.

External Legal Relations—the external relations resulting from the organization and company's operations are governed, as appropriate, by the rights in rem and obligations, especially by various types of contracts that define the roles of purchaser of productive services (of natural resources and capital) or seller of goods and services. Moreover, labor law and public economic law contain rules that form the legal discipline of the economic function of an entrepreneur.

Labor law disciplines the labor market in which workers and businesspersons participate as well as regulates the internal organization of the company's production group. Equality of power between the parties negotiating in that market is mainly ensured by trade union organizations and the replacement of individual bargaining with collective bargaining, in which professional categories figure as classes represented by trade unions.

The capital markets that organize exchanges of financial capital between savings and investment agents are fundamental to the creation and expansion of companies. They are regulated by general legislation on markets overseen by the Central Bank of Brazil and by a special regime for securities issued by companies that monitors them through the body called the Securities Commission.

The public law of economy comprises many provisions to regulate the behavior of producers, intermediaries, and buyers in the markets of economic goods. Some general laws apply to all, or to a large number of markets (e.g., *antitrust* laws), and others to certain products.

In recent decades, there has been a proliferation of consumer protection laws (to punish malpractices such as disclosure of false information, abuse of power by sellers, or defects in the manufacture of products) as well as laws aimed at protecting the environment against misuse and exploitation, such as liability to compensate for damages (e.g., environmental pollution) caused to the environment by company's operations.

It should be noted from the above explanation that the legal system of the company is vast. We must now take an approach to the legal nature of our subject—that is, the company.

At the outset, we should bear in mind that *"finding the legal nature of an institute of law consists in apprehending the fundamental elements that make up its specific composition, and then setting them against the nearest set of legal figures in order to classify the institute focused on the universe of figures existing in the legal universe."*[11]

There is no consensus about the legal nature of the company in the doctrinal field. There are three doctrinal positions regarding the legal nature of the reality in question. The first states the personification of the company, building a conceptual framework that places the company as a subject of law and thus gives it a legal personality.[12]

The second position is defended by Rubens Requião, who refutes the first, stating that, in the Brazilian systematic normative system, the possibility of the company being seen as a subject of law and obligations is dismissed and, therefore, it cannot enjoy legal personality, fitting the quality as an object of law.[13]

As for the third position, it postulates that fundamentally the company cannot be a sphere of rights and obligations, thus ruling out the possibility of it being a subject of law, and also that it cannot be an object of law. In this position, Ricardo Negrão, for a better understanding of his reasoning, refers to the analysis of objective and functional aspects of the company; regarding the objective/ patrimonial aspect, according to that author, it was contemplated in Articles 1142–1149 of the Brazilian Civil Code and configured as *"every complex of assets organized, for the exercise of the company, by a businessperson, or by a trading company."*

And it is with this logic that he maintains that the conceptual framework adopted by the Civil Code in force in the Brazilian legal system rules out the possibility of subsistence of the company seen as a subject of rights and obligations and as an economically organized activity, without the complex of assets necessary for the development of such activity (that complex is called premises, which corresponds to the object of law). Since the Civil Code provides in Article

11 Maria Helena DINIZ, op. cit., 66.

12 Ricardo NEGRÃO (2010), op. cit., 80.

13 Rubens REQUIÃO, *Curso de Direito Comercial.* op. cit., 49.

1143 that premises may be *"a unitary object of rights and legal transactions, whether translative or constitutive, which are compatible with its nature."* Going through this article must gravitate the understanding that the premises—even they are not composed of tangible things—know the possibility of being constituted by rights that affect no corporeal property; for example, the guarantee of exclusivity of the name, that is, the trademark, by which the businessperson acts in the context of his relations with third parties. As to the functional aspect of the company, that author offers to say it is Article 966 of the Brazilian Civil Code that presents its respective delimitation, which in an objective sense, by the practice of certain acts, qualifies the subject of such acts. The legal provision under analysis, by establishing that *"a businessperson is considered to be one who professionally performs an economic activity organized for the production or circulation of goods or services,"* leads to the conclusion that the elaboration of the concept of businessperson necessarily involves the conception of commercial activity.

For an activity to be considered company, it must have at least three essential requirements: (i) an organized activity; (ii) of an economic nature, producing goods or services for profit; (iii) developed in a professional manner.

Based on the aspects described above, Ricardo Negrão concludes that the functional aspect is useless for the classification of the company, in the sense that the company activity itself cannot be qualified as a subject of law, much less as its object. Speaking of a businessperson, whether an individual or a legal person, as the person who habitually and professionally performs acts and activities of a company nature, on the functional aspect, we would be considering the company as an object of law; on the objective aspect, we would have to classify the company as an object of law, and in this way we would be saying that the company is synonymous with a complex of goods necessary for the pursuit of commercial activity, or to put it another way, it corresponds to the commercial premises.

As explained in the above paragraph, the term "businessperson" is precisely two-dimensional; there is the natural dimension on one hand—natural/human person, who carries out an organized economic activity, and, on the other, the legal dimension—legal person created by positive law. The two dimensions legally exist as subjects of law and, therefore, spheres of rights and obligations. In this context, "legally" is conceived as *"any complex of goods organized, for the exercise of the company by businessperson, or by trading company,"* and the commercial premises are a legal asset protected by law and hence are liable to be the subject of law, both for natural and legal persons.

Ulhoa Coelho adds that *"the company is the economic activity organized for the production or circulation of goods or services."* Since the company is an activity, there is no way to attribute it to any legal nature, and, hence, it cannot be confused with the person of the businessperson, much less with the commercial premise.[14] This is the line taken by Ricardo Negrão, who in turn considers an abstract entity equivalent to the conceptual framework of legal facts attributed to the quality of legal business.[15]

As an activity of an economic nature, with a high level of organization, and carried out with professionalism, the company certainly has the legal statute inherent to it, which allows it to be accepted with abstraction from the businessperson or the complex of goods that make up the company. The separation of company from the complex of goods and from the businessperson himself consists of a technical legal middle ground that should not be applied to justify chimeric points of view.[16]

2. Commercial Premises

2.1 Concept and Its Elements

The doctrine is profuse about the concept of commercial or company premises. Fábio Coelho understands that a commercial premise *"is the set of goods that the businessperson gathers for the exploitation of his economic activity."*[17]

Oscar Barreto Filho (quoted by Ricardo Negrão) states that it is not an easy task to elaborate a concept of company premises, since it is a new concept in Brazilian positive law, which dates back to 1942, the year the Italian Civil Code was ushered into the Brazilian legal system. The company as an entity under the Brazilian law was regarded as the old structural organization of economic activity, which brought only the concept of the figure of the trader—the institute that did not find space in the doctrinal system—who became the object of dissimilar theories that were intended to establish its juridical nature.[18]

From 1942 onwards, in Article 2.555, Italian Civil Law defines a company premises, with *"Azienda"*[19] as the key word, thus defining the premises as *a*

14 Fábio Ulhoa COELHO, *Curso de Direito Comercial: Direito de Empresa*, op. cit., 19.
15 Ricardo NEGRÃO, *Manual de Direito Comercial e de empresa*, op. cit., 81.
16 Fábio Ulhoa COELHO, *Curso de Direito Comercial: Direito de Empresa*, op. cit., 19
17 *Id.*, 49.
18 Oscar BARRETO FILHO, *Teoria do Estabelecimento Comercial, apud* Ricardo NEGRÃO (2010), op. cit., 82.
19 An expression of company under the Brazilian law.

"complex of material and immaterial goods, which constitute the instrument used by the trader for the exploitation of a certain commercial activity."

The legal concept of commercial premises is brought to us by Law No. 10.406 of January 10, 2002[20] (Article 1142), which *"considers premises to be the whole complex of goods organized, for the exercise of the company, by the businessperson or by the trading company."* The consecration of the legal concept of company premises within the Brazilian legal framework is revealed with a new phenomenon, in the sense that the legal diplomas prior to the Civil Code, precisely the Commercial Code of 1850, did not contain any legal consecration concerning the notion of company premises.

An important aspect to be taken into account is that the premises are equivalent to the complex of goods necessary for the development of an economically organized activity. The organization of premises presupposes the organization of goods that can be valued in monetary terms, so the value of the establishment lies in the totality of its assets that the owner has granted to the organization. The aggregation of goods making up the premises is not done spontaneously; it must comply with criteria such as combination, hierarchy, and interdependence in accordance with the specific characteristics and nature of the company activity carried out or to be carried out.[21]

The term *commercial premises* implies bifurcation, in the sense that on one hand it encompasses goods of an intangible nature; here, we are talking about goods lacking a physical body—the name of the company (firm or denomination), trademarks, patents, and so on; on the other, it encompasses goods of a material or tangible nature—goods that have a physical body, for example, machinery, buses, goods, and furniture.

In the doctrinal field, there is heated discussion about Aviation and Clientele; some authors consider them as elements of premises and others see them as a simple attribute (trimming) and a mere fact of the situation (clientele) of the premises.[22]

In the words of Fábio Coelho, *"there are authors who consider trims among the incorporeal elements of the establishment, but this statement is not correct."*[23]

Before presenting in concrete terms the above author's understanding, it is important to bring the concept of trimming that Fazzio Junior[24] provides us

20 Brazilian Civil Code.

21 Miguel J. A. Pupo CORREIA, *Direito Comercial,* 4ª ed, revista e aumentada (Lisboa: Universidade Lusíada, 1996), 157.

22 Ricardo NEGRÃO, op. cit., 107.

23 Fábio Ulhoa COELHO, op. cit., 101.

24 Waldo FAZZIO JÚNIOR (2010), op. cit., 77.

with; he understands that *"trimming (achalandage) is the premises' ability to generate profits, resulting from the good organization of its members. It is the expectation of good results based on several factors, whose prominence can only be diagnosed in each case. It can result either from the personal attributes of the entrepreneur, or from his team of assistants, or it can be from a suitable location of the premises in the geography of the city, among several other factors."*

This is a future probability of profits based on the complex of material goods and rights inherent to the premises—quantity and quality of goods, name of the premises, and point or place where the company's activity takes place. As a result, no form of autonomy can be attributed to the commercial premises because, in material terms, it is strictly linked to the premises and not to the activities taking place for an economic purpose.

It is opportune here to adhere to Ulhoa Coelho's logic, which in this respect understands that the moment that the negotiation of the price that is going be received by the grantor takes place basically corresponds to the trimming; therefore, it is in the probability of generating profit that aviary consists of. However, he adds, we should not assume that trimming is an integral part of the premises or complex of goods to be traded. It simply means that the articulation of goods that compose the premises has added value to them, as a result of the development of an economic activity, and that it is recognized by the market. In short, trimming is, strictly speaking, synonymous with a company fund. That is to say, both terms designate the overvalue added to the assets of the business premises due to their rational organization by the businessperson.

Although it is common to consider customers as one of the elements of commercial premises, such understanding is not correct. The reality in question (customers) must be abstracted from the sphere of company's assets, since it consists of a complex of individuals or persons, who with a considerable degree of regularity acquire services or goods made available by a particular commercial entity. Even if the businessperson enjoys the legal protection of the clientele against legally objectionable behavior of the competition, this does not mean that the clientele is his property, since it is not likely to be appropriate, within the parameters of the current Brazilian legal system.[25]

25 Fábio Ulhoa COELHO, op. cit., 101.

2.2 System and Nature of the Premises

For a better analysis of the legal system of commercial premises, we will take as a starting point the logic of Professor Ricardo Negrão[26]; the concept of commercial premises, from a doctrinal as well as legal point of view, suggests the union of necessary means for the realization of the company, that is, a complex of goods serving the economic basis for the development of the company. By abstracting a specific part of assets, resources, or values, the entrepreneur creates an asset, in this way called a business, intended for the exercise of the company activity.

The separation of a portion of assets from the businessperson's assets for carrying on the company does not necessarily imply the creation of two or more legal spheres of assets; such separation only has effects in the event of the transfer of premises and has no effect on other legal obligations.

This is the rationale of Brazilian law, especially in relation to the individual businessperson, since there is no basis for the existence of two patrimonial masses under the ownership of the same subject of law, thus adopting the *Principle of Patrimonial Unity.*

Ricardo Negrão, considers that though the Brazilian Civil Code adopts this principle, it avoids the use of the word *"patrimony"* and prefers the use of the expression *"complex of legal relations,"* and this distinguishes, in the perspective of the Civil Code in force, the set of assets of a person in two categories, namely: (i) universalities of law—*"complex of legal relations, of a person, having economic value"*—Article 91 and (ii) universalities of fact—*"consists of the plurality of individual assets which, pertinent to the same person, have a unitary destination"*—Article 90.

From this position, each person, whether natural or legal, corresponds to a patrimony, whereby there is no legal effect in the law of obligations to consider abstract universalities, giving rise to assets intended to pay exclusively to a specified category of creditors. When a natural person is a businessperson, his entire complex of legal relationships is liable for the obligations of the undertaking as the sole guarantee of universality of creditors.

In case a legal person is a businessperson, the personal assets of partners and shareholders are separated and a new autonomous asset is formed that is distinct from its founders. The new assets created by partners or shareholders will be used to meet creditors' claims without discriminating between them.[27]

26 Ricardo NEGRÃO, op. cit., 82 ss.

27 Under the terms of Civil Procedural Law, regular companies, like any natural or legal person, are unlimitedly liable for the obligations contracted, in accordance with the provision of Article 591 of the

If the premise is a legal unit, it is capable of being the object of ownership, possession, adverse possession, usufruct, pledge, claims, and possessions. It is pertinent to mention here the need to study the legal transactions relating to the premises: Sale and Leasing of Commercial Premises (Article 1144 of the Civil Code).

Sale of commercial premises consists of the sale of premises; it is a business that is made *inter vivos* whereby there is the definitive transfer of the premises, thus excluding the transfer *mortis causa*. The debts prior to the sale of premises, having been accounted, are the responsibility of the person acquiring the complex of assets; however, the first debtor (transferor) is jointly and severally liable for a period of one year. The length of this period is determined in accordance with the type of credit. In the event of overdue credits, counting begins as soon as the contract is published; in the case of credits that are still within the term (falling due), counting begins from the date set for maturity.[28]

When the contract of sale is published, assignment of seller's credits becomes effective. The provision specified in Article 1149 of the Civil Code read as follows: *"The assignment of claims relating to the transferred premises shall take effect with regard to the respective debtors from the time of publication of the transfer, but the debtor shall be exonerated if he pays the assignor in good faith."* Under Article 1147 of the same legislation, if the contract is silent, the seller of the establishment is prohibited from adopting competing conduct affecting the purchaser within five years of the sale.

It has been said above that the clientele is qualified as a fact situation, and it should be added that it is an essential situation for the survival of commercial activity; by this logic, the purchaser of the company establishment when acquiring it also expects to benefit from that situation (clientele). The positive law was also concerned to ensure that this expectation became effective by creating the *"non-reinstatement clause."*

Fábio Ulhoa Coelho believes that *"the non-reinstatement clause represents a guarantee of the integrity of the value spent by the purchaser, in sale of commercial premises, in remunerating the company fund."*[29] However, it is the prior Article 1147 of the Civil Code that deals with that clause; the period of five years laid

Code of Civil Procedure. *"This is primary patrimonial liability; however the partners shall ordinarily be liable according to the Company structure to which they have submitted themselves, always subsidiarily to the Company assets, or as it has been agreed to be called in procedural language, with secondary patrimonial liability"*—see Ricardo NEGRÃO, op. cit., 85.

28 Waldo FAZZIO JÚNIOR, op. cit., 78.

29 Fábio Ulhoa COELHO, op. cit., 124.

down in the legal provision in question comprises only a general rule, in the sense that it will apply only if the contract of sale of commercial premises does not specify the duration of the noncompetition period.

Leasing of the commercial premises is an agreement of wills whereby the owner (transferor) of the premises assigns them to a third party (transferee) on a temporary basis with the expectation of earning a certain remuneration. The transferor (lessor) waives the exercise of the commercial activity for a certain period, which is then exercised by the lessee or transferee. We need to take into consideration the idea that the purpose of the transfer of the holding is not the property itself, but the premises as a unitary legal asset corresponding to the universality of the components, which give it existence, and the exercise of a given commercial activity.

Generally, the commercial establishment knows its installation in a leased property by the person carrying out the company. If this is the case, the sale of commercial premises implies the assignment of the lease; it is in this line that under Article 13 of Law 8245 of October 18, 1991 (which provides on urban property leases and relevant procedures) *"the assignment of the lease depends on the prior outcome of the lessor"*; another legal provision that can be found in the Civil Code is the rescission of the assignment of lease within 90 days from the date of its publication (Article 1148). The person who eventually acquires the commercial premises installed in a property under lease, in addition to negotiating with the owner of the establishment (tenant), must also negotiate with the owner of the property (lessor).[30]

The property owner's consent to the assignment of the lease can be given in two ways—express consent or tacit consent. The property owner's inertia within 30 days of being notified of the transfer is qualified as tacit inertia. If the propriety owner's conduct does not comply with any of these conditions, the person acquiring the premises may return to the property at any time.[31] In addition, even if the wishes and characteristics of the commercial lease are met, although the lessor has not expressed his formal opposition, the lessor will be deprived of the right to renew the lease.[32]

Even if the lessor is not notified by the lessee of the assignment of the lease or did not respond to it within 90 days of the deposit of the transfer contract in order to advertise it in the official press, the lessor has the option of terminating the

30 Fábio Ulhoa COELHO, op. cit, 121.

31 Paragraph II, Article 9, Law 8245 of October 18, 1991.

32 Paragraph 1, Article 13, Law 8245 of October 18, 1991.

lease; in fact, such an option is subject to verification of just cause. Circumstances characterizing just cause include, for example, economic and financial circumstances, assets that do not meet the minimum conditions required by the lessor, and the occurrence of a plurality of legal actions brought in objection to the purchaser. The alienation shall be bound to indemnify the person acquiring the premises for the resulting losses.[33]

From this perspective, in the process of leasing the property with the intention of setting up a certain company, the businessperson, in order to safeguard the investment made, is bound to proceed with the lessor, negotiating with a view to establishing, in the transfer contract, the express clause concerning subrogation. If such negotiation is not successful in the embryonic phase of establishing the legal relationship between the businessperson and the lessor, there is a greater probability that the businessperson will experience future difficulties in recovering the investment if the lessor determines an excessive monetary value in order to consent to the assignment of the lease.

Now that we have discussed the legal system in relation to commercial premises, what about their legal nature?

To talk about the legal nature of commercial premises, it should be highlighted that it cannot be confused with the nature of the company, since the commercial premises are not an activity and cannot be confused with the businessperson because they are not a personalized entity.

At the doctrinal level, there is a profusion of theories aimed at deciphering the legal nature of the reality in question; even so, three essential elements must be explained in relation to the aforementioned diversity of theories[34]:

(i) **The attribution of Legal Personality to the commercial premises is erroneous**—to affirm that the commercial premises have legal personality is to say that the universality of goods that support the exercise of commercial activity corresponds to a subject of law; however, such an understanding falls apart and contradicts the spirit of Brazilian law. It can only be considered a subject of law if it is responsible for organizing essential assets specifically intended for the exercise of the company—the trading company—which is seen as a center of imputation of obligations and incidence of rights inherent to the company.

33 Article 1148 of the Civil Code.
34 Fábio Ulhoa COELHO, op. cit., 121.

(ii) **The essence of the establishment lies in the universality of goods**—commercial premises cannot be seen as an abstract reality of goods that comprise it; this is because it corresponds to the complex of goods predisposed to the pursuit of the company. The company, on the other hand, cannot be associated with the universality of the goods forming part of the premises, which is an activity of an economic nature carried out in the establishment; in this respect, it should be noted that the establishment may be the object of sale, encumbrance, seizure, or attachment, whereas the company as an activity cannot be the object of the said legal figures.

(iii) **The assets of the trading company are an integral part of the premises**—the composition of establishment is a sum of the assets applied to the development of an economically organized activity; here, we are dealing with the controversy as to whether the estate of the businessperson is separated or not, a controversy that must be overcome. In the case of an individual businessperson who carries on that activity, it is important to make a distinction in the universe of assets that constitute his patrimony—those involved in his company activity and others who are indifferent to it; however, such a distinction is not intended to exempt assets not used in the development of the company activity in the event of the need to hold the individual businessperson responsible; allied to this is the reality that in Brazilian law the principle of unity of patrimony applies except for exceptions expressly enshrined in the law; therefore, all the assets of the person are liable for the obligations contracted by him.

The three points presented above are sufficient for the perfect framing of the company premises in the legal world, or by another, for the definition of its legal nature.

Based on these points, we believe that the commercial establishment consists of a conglomeration of assets that is an integral part of the businessperson's sphere of assets. In turn, conglomeration of assets corresponds to things, whether their nature is singular, simple, or complex, voluntarily brought together by those who own them with the aspiration of carrying out a naturally economic and organized activity.

Ricardo Negrão adds that the perspective of universality of the premises is adopted by Brazilian doctrinarians. By universality, in fact, *"collective things (universitates rerum) are those which, being composed of several singular things, are considered as a whole, forming an economic whole (ex distantibus) and being called a generic (uni nomini subjecta). They are distinguished into conglomeration of assets, which are aggregations of tangible things, such as a flock, a shop, a library; and universalities of law, abstract units of things and rights, such as patrimony, inheritance, dowry, nest-egg."*[35]

The above understanding leads to the conclusion that in addition to being seen as a conglomeration of assets, premises must also be seen as a universality of law. It should not be understood, however, that one of the two universalities should be abstracted from the other; in this regard, the understanding that one covers the other in the sense of giving existence to the premises should be retained, or, in other words, the individual or legal entity is the holder of a certain sphere of property (seen as a set of assets intended for the exercise of the company—universality in fact) that revolves around a complex of legal relations—universality in law.

One should not lose sight of the fact that the establishment corresponds to a single set of assets, which in turn are capable of being the object of legal business. It is a concept whereby it can be inferred as to what conditions are met to qualify premises as one of these universalities. The question to be answered would be which of them would be the company premises, and the following terms would be applied: *"the universality of law depends on a law that recognizes it, and if there is no law that attributes this quality to the premises, of course there would be no alternative left to Brazilian doctrine other than to conceptualize it as a conglomeration of assets."*[36]

On the one hand, Article 90 of the Civil Code states that *"The plurality of singular goods which, pertinent to the same person, have a unitary destination constitutes conglomerations of assets."* And on the other, the same legal provision in Article 1142 states that *"Any complex of assets organized, for the exercise of the company, by a businessperson or by a Company, shall be considered a premise."* In view of the above-mentioned legal provisions, it must be concluded that the unitary allocation of the premises for the development of company activity is subsumed by conglomeration of assets.

35 Ricardo NEGRÃO, op. cit., 94.

36 Oscar BARRETO FILHO, *Teoria do Estabelecimento Comercial, apud,* Ricardo NEGRÃO, *Manual de Direito Comercial e de empresa,* Vol. 1, 7ª edição (São Paulo: Saraiva, 2010), 94.

References

- BULHÕES PEDREIRA, José Luiz and Alfredo LAMY FILHO. 2017. *Direito das Companhias*, 2ª ed. Rio de Janeiro: Editora Forense.
- COELHO, Fábio Ulhoa. 2009. *Curso de Direito Comercial: Direito de Empresa*, Vol. 1, 13 Edição. São Paulo: Editora Saraiva.
- CORREIA, Miguel J. A. Pupo. 1996. *Direito Comercial*, 4ª ed, revista e aumentada. Lisboa: Universidade Lusíada.
- FAZZIO JÚNIOR, Waldo. 2010. *Manual de Direito Comercial*, 11ª Edição. São Paulo: Editora Atlas.
- NEGRÃO, Ricardo. 2010. *Manual de Direito Comercial e de Empresa, Volume 1*, 7ª Edição, São Paulo: SARAIVA.
- REQUIÃO, Rubens. 1995. *Curso de Direito Comercial*, 22ª ed. São Paulo: Saraiva.

Further Reading

- AMANNCIO, A. W. *Cessão de quotas nas Sociedades Limitadas*, available at http ://www.wamancia.com.br/cessao-de-quotas-nas-sociedades-limitadas/ accessed on August 4, 2019.
- ASCENSÃO, José de Oliveira. 2005. O Direito – *Introdução e Teoria Geral*, 13ª Edição Refundida, 7ª reimpressão, Coimbra: Edições Almedina.
- BARROS, Carla Eugenia Caldas. 2014. *Manual de Direito Empresarial Multifacetado*, Voll. III – Direito Falimentar e Recuperacional. Aracaju: Edição do Autor | PIDCC.
- BULHÕES PEDREIRA, José Luiz and Alfredo LAMY FILHO.1992. *A Lei as S.A. – Pressupostos – Elaboração – Aplicação.* Rio de Janeiro: Renovar.
- CARVALHO FILHO, José dos Santos. 2018. *Manual de Direito Administrativo*; 32ª ed. São Paulo: Atlas.
- CARVALHO, Maria Miguel and Sónia MOREIRA. 2013. *Das Sociedades Comerciais (Capítulo I) Sumários desenvolvidos das aulas de Direito para Economia e Gestão*; Universidade do Minho: Escola de Direito.
- CASTRO, Rodrigo R. Monteiro de and Leandro Santos de ARAG Ã O. 2009. *Direito Societário: Desafios Actuais.* São Paulo: Quarier Latin.
- COELHO, Fábio Ulhoa. 2011. *Manual de Direito Comercial: Direito de Empresa*, 23ª ed. São Paulo: Saraiva.
- COELHO, Fábio Ulhoa. 2012. *Curso de Direito Civil.* Parte Geral, Vol. 1, 5ª ed. São Paulo: Editora Saraiva.
- CORREIA, António Arruda Ferrer. 1948. *Sociedades Fictícias e Unipessoais.* Livraria Atlântida, Coimbra.
- CORREIA, Miguel J. A. Pupo. 1999. *Direito Comercial*, 6ª Edição. Lisboa: Ediforum.
- CRUZ, André Santa. *Aquisição de quotas pela própria sociedade*, available at http://genjurid ico.com.br/2016/04.27/aquisicao-de-quatas-pela-propria-sociedade/, accessed in 4th August 2019.

- DAMASCENO, Maria Helena and Silva MEGALE. 1980. *Transformação, Fusão e Cisão de Sociedades*, Revista da Faculdade de Direito, Universidade de Minas Gerais, ISSN: 0304-2340.
- DINIZ, Maria Helena. 2008. *Curso de Direito Civil brasileiro*, Vol. 8. São Paulo: Editora Saraiva.
- DINIZ, Maria Helena. 2015. Curso de *Direito Civil Brasileiro: Teoria Geral do Direito Civil.* São Paulo: Saraiva.
- FRAN MARTINS. 1978. *Comentários à Leis das Sociedades por Acções*, Vol. II. Rio de Janeiro: Forense.
- GARCIA, Mariane Portella. 2005. *Administração da Sociedade Anónima e suas relações jurídicas*, Curitiba.
- JÚNIOR, Manuel Guilherme. 2022. *Manual de Direito Comercial Moçambicano,* Vol. 1. 2ª Edição. Maputo: Escolar Editora.
- MORREIRA, Welliton Luiz. 2016. *A Sociedade Unipessoal e a Limitação da Responsabilidade Patrimonial do Empresário Individual,* Coimbra.
- PAULA, Luiz Gonzaga Modesto de. 2015. *Sociedade Limitada,* 1ª.ed. São Paulo: Saraiva.
- REQUIÃO, Rubens. 1984. *Curso de direito comercial*; 14ª ed. São Paulo: Saraiva.
- REQUIÃO, Rubens. 2003. *Curso de Direito Comercial,* Vol. I, 25ª ed. São Paulo: Saraiva.
- REQUIÃO, Rubens. 2005. *Curso de Direito Comercial, Volume 1.* São Paulo: Editora Saraiva.
- RIBEIRO, Cláudia and Priscila MENEZES. 2014. *Teoria do Direito Empresarial,* FGV, Direito Rio, Graduação.
- WALDEMAR ZVEITER. 1991. *Sociedade por Quotas de Responsabilidade Limitada – Aspectos polémicos;* Conferência dos Advogados Catarinenses – Criciúma –SC.
- RODRIGUES, Luiz António Barroso. 2016. *Direito Empresarial,* 3 ed. rev. Actual – Florianópolis: Departamento de Ciências da Administração/ UFSC, Brasília: CAPES: UAB, p. 47.
- SILVA ALVES, Itálo Miqueias da. *A Personalidade Jurídica no Direito Civil,* available at https://jus.com.br/artigos/61828/a-personalidade-juridica-no-direito-civil, accessed in 5th July 2019.

4

Subjective Company Law

1. Businessperson: Concept and Characterization

It should first be remembered that the company cannot be seen as a duty allocation center, let alone a duty-free center. It consists of activities carried out by a natural or legal person, to whom the name of the businessperson belongs.

In the approach of Bulhões Pedreira and Lamy Filho,

> The meaning of the word businessperson was of chief adventurer, who directs a risky task and takes risks. In France, at the beginning of the 16th century, the word "businessperson" followed to designate the leaders of military expeditions and was then used to mean the head of any adventure. The same word was later used to refer to public works contractors, who contracted the execution at the right price, assuming the risk of construction cost. And when the company gained importance as a modern economic production unit, the word came to refer to the leader of the company's social group, who took on the risks of production activity. The evolution of the word in French highlights the aspects of leadership and willingness to accept risks as characteristic notes of the concept of entrepreneur.[1]

1 José Luiz BULHÕES PEDREIRA and Alfredo LAMY FILHO, *Direito das Companhias*, 2ª ed. (Rio de

It is in this context that Rubens Requião brings the figure of the businessperson closer to that of the capitalist and, based on this approximation, defines the businessperson as the subject who runs the company (economically and technically organized activity). He is, hence, an economic agent of the highest level, who, assuming the status of leader, operates and manages the company through a combination of production factors.[2]

The characteristics of businessperson include two fundamental features: taking initiatives and taking risks; these are the two fundamental, structural components of what constitute the businessperson. For an organized economic activity to become effective, it is crucial that initiative is taken by the person (businessperson) who intends to carry out such an activity; thus, he will have to set out the purpose or aim for which the company is created and which drives and influences the dynamics of its activity.

The businessperson's ability to define the destiny or objective of the company gives him the power to make decisions regarding his employees, and, in the face of a multiplicity of alternatives, the entrepreneur chooses the alternative that is appropriate for the functioning of the economic body that is the company, thus taking risks, in the sense that that choice can lead to advantageous as well as disadvantageous situations.

In company law, it is pertinent to highlight the risk associated with finance, which is likely to occur either in the process of purchasing the resources necessary to produce goods or services, as well as in the sale of economic goods produced, or in the provision of services made available. Whether or not third parties buy goods resulting from production and the degree of prices at which the said products are acquired, we are talking about circumstances on which gross sales revenue depends, and the risks in the process of buying resources and production services especially in relation to their probability of being bought in the market and at the price that the trader needs to pay.

The risk may also be associated with technical aspects, since it already states that the production activity presupposes the combination of technological factors that make possible the materialization of economic goods needed for marketing. The company, when using such technologies, is not exempt from the risk of seeing the goods produced in conditions not suitable for commercialization, thus not achieving the desired degree of profit. Technical risks are not limited to the

Janeiro: Editora Forense, 2017), 45.

2 Rubens REQUIÃO, *Curso de Direito Comercial, Volume 1* (São Paulo: Editora Saraiva, 2005), 62.

technological sphere but can also be linked to the organization of the enterprise, which lacks a healthy, dynamic, and operational structure.[3]

2. Businessperson and Trader

In the words of Rubens Requião, "*the businessperson is the central figure of the company, many authors do not distinguish the commercial entrepreneur from the former figure of a trader.*"[4] As can be seen, in the author's understanding, there is a synonymic relationship between the terms businessperson and trader, but the term trader has been imbued with an egoistic content stemming from the individualistic nature that, in a certain historical context, characterized commercial law, which was formed of a complex set of rules inspired by the exclusively capitalist model of production. Today, seen as an economically organized activity with the aim of producing and circulating goods or services to satisfy the interests of the community, the businessperson is no longer seen as a subject motivated by selfishness but as an economic agent driven by the realization of profit and the pursuit of the needs of the society in which he is inserted.

Brazil had the first regulatory code on commercial matters in 1980, a code inspired by Napoleon's Commercial Code of 1808. This means that the first phase of Brazilian Commercial Law was objective, from the perspective of the theory of commercial acts. The respective acts were listed in Regulation No. 737 of 1850.[5]

The purpose of the above regulation was to remedy the gaps in the said code of 1980, since its normative content was limited to regulating the activity carried out by the trader. The trader was considered the person who habitually performed the acts of trade. Even after its repeal, the regulation still served as a reference to be applied since a law that filled the gaps in the commercial code had not replaced it.

An analysis of the legislation after the regulation leads to the conclusion that the list it contained was not exhaustive since those laws added many other acts to it.

Thus, (a) *"purchase or exchange at wholesale, resale and lease of movable property"; (b) "exchange transactions"*; (c) *"banking transactions"*; (d) *"brokerage"*;

3 José Luiz BULHÕES PEDREIRA and Alfredo LAMY FILHO, *Direito das Companhias,* op. cit., 43.

4 Quoting GIUSPPE VALERI, who states that *"the generic figure of the businessperson coincides today with that of the trader, known under the old law,"* Rubens REQUIÃO, op. cit., 61.

5 Cláudia RIBEIRO and Priscila MENEZES, *Teoria do Direito Empresarial* (Graduação: FGV, Direito Rio, 2014), 3.

(e) *"factories"*; (f) *"commission," "deposit, dispatch, consignment and transport of goods"*; (g) *"public performances"*; (h) *"activities relating to sea and air navigation"*; (i) *"real estate speculation (S. A)"*; and (j) *"charters"* proved to be the most abundant acts. It should be borne in mind that, in addition to the acts listed, *"acts relating to public limited companies and trade companies; operations with public debt securities and any government credit papers; construction companies; those carried out by the commercial representative; bills of exchange; promissory notes; bills of exchange; cheques; warrants; and knowledge of deposits, even if carried out by civilians, are considered commercial by law."*[6]

In addition, some acts, even if civil, when carried out with a certain commonness by the trader, were considered acts of commerce, as part of a contract.

Over time and with the improvement of commercial activities, the legislative framework of many legal systems has tended to change its perspective (no longer concentrating on acts of commerce), focusing on the company as an economically organized activity carried out with professionalism and commonness in order to achieve profit. It is in this context that company theory is being developed to set limits on the content of commercial law. It is the Civil Code of 2002 that in the legislative framework of Brazil has introduced the company theory, a subjective and not objective theory that abandons the use of the term "trader" and instead uses terminologies such as "Company" and "Company Law."

3. Commercial Businessperson in the Brazilian Law

3.1 Requirements and General dogmatic

In the Brazilian legal order, the word businessperson applies not only to the natural person (singular or individual businessman) but also to the legal person created by law (company as a person). These two entities are subject to the practice of economic activity in a way that includes professionalism, commonness, and organization in order to produce goods and services and allow movement of those goods or services with the final purpose of earning profit.[7]

In the wordings of Article 966 of the Brazilian Civil Code of 2002, "a businessperson is considered to be the one who carries out an organized economic activity with professionalism for the production and movement of goods." As we

6 Cláudia RIBEIRO and Priscila MENEZES, op. cit., 3.
7 Waldo FAZZIO JÚNIOR, *Manual de Direito Comercial*, 11 Edição (São Paulo: Editora Atlas, 2010), 17.

can see, the concept of businessperson presented in the cited legal act composes various elements whose analysis becomes pertinent to understand it better:

(1) Professionalism: To engage in an activity in a professional manner implies frequency, only when considering a businessperson as the one commits himself to assume risks that are intrinsic to carrying out activities that are economic and organized in nature. Those who perform the activity in question either occasionally on their own or through the efforts or activities of others cannot be considered a businessperson.
(2) Activity: The activity is the corporation in the proper form; it is not mistaken for the physical space or building where it is performed. As it is already made clear in the previous paragraphs, it cannot be considered a subject or an object of right. It consists of an activity that aims to produce goods and services or allow movement of such as goods or services for commercial purposes in the market and in turn intends to satisfy directly or indirectly the collectivity of needs in general.[8]
(3) Economic: An economic activity is one that generates wealth through goods and services but, at the same time, is liable to pecuniary evaluation. Such goods or services are taken to the market for commercialization and, in turn, generate profit to the businessperson that puts them in the market.
From this, we conclude that an activity cannot be considered economic, in the perspective of the Civil Code, if it involves carrying out work of an artistic, intellectual, literary, or scientific (Article 966), or other associated nature (Article 53) or activities developed by foundations of religious, moral, cultural, and assistance character (Article 62, single section); this is because such activities are not wealth generators and do not serve the ultimate purpose of earning profit.
(4) Organized: Organized because it presupposes a combination of production factors—raw material, labor, capital, and technologic resources. The disposal of these production factors follows some criteria that are predetermined by the businessperson according to the economic nature of the activity to be performed.[9]

8 Tullio ASCARELLI, *Iniciación al Estudio del Direcho Commerciale*, apud, Ricardo NEGRÃO, *Manual de Diretito Comercial e de Empresa*, Vol. 1, 7ª ed. (São Paulo: Saraiva, 2010), 70.

9 Cláudia RIBEIRO and Priscila MENEZES, op. cit., 4.

Based on what has been clarified, the businessperson is understood as the person who functions in a legal capacity and is not infringed by the regular and professional performance of the corporation (activity of an economic nature) working toward the final purpose of earning profit. This understanding comprises the necessary matters for the practice of a business combination. It is important to emphasize that the principles applied in the validity of a legal action (capable person, lawful object, and autonomy) are equally applicable in exercising the business combinations.

According to single section of Article 966 of the Civil Code, "It is not considered to be a businessman, the one who develops an intellectual profession, of scientific nature, literal or artistic, even counting with the procurement of auxiliary, unless the professional performance constitutes a company element."

In line with the legal disposition previously cited, it is important to clarify that, in fact, there are existing cases where regardless of the person possessing the legal capacity, that person is still infringed by the business practice:

Judges and prosecutors: Their restriction results from the constitutional provision in the sub-paragraph of paragraph I, Article 95. Under this article, judges are forbidden to occupy any other position or exercise any other function, even though available, unless in connection with the prosecution. Concerning the prosecution, the prohibition directly results from al. c, II, § 5, Article 128, as a result of which judges and prosecutors cannot participate in the activities of the trading company.

Public Servants: These can be partners in limited liability companies (shareholders, quota holders, and limited partners); however, they cannot perform as subjects of business activity and not even fill administrative or managing positions in a private company (paragraph X, Article 117 of the Act No. 8.112 of December 11, 1990).[10] This prohibition to undertake extends to state ministers and public office holders on commission, as well as to those assuming leading positions in the supreme executive power, at all levels.

The military: Article 29 of the Act No. 6.880, from December 9, 1980—Status of the Military and Armed Forces—expressly forbids military personnel from participating in the undertaking's activities, and this restriction includes the police force as well. On top of the prohibition to

10 Establishes the legal regime of Civil Public Servants of the Union, Municipalities and Federal Public Foundations.

participate in the undertaking, they are equally restricted from participation in the administrative body or the company management or even from assuming a partner position, except as shareholders or quota holders.

The brokerage: Act No. 6.530, from May 12, 1978 prohibits exercising any business activity as well as contracting a company.

The actioners: Article 36 of the Act No. 21.891 of October 19, 1932[11] expressly prohibits the actioners of acting as subjects of an organized economic activity, direct or indirectly, as well as from engaging in acts giving rise to a trading company.

Foreigners with temporary visas: This situation is addressed in the provisions of section II, Article 12 of the Act No. 13.445 from May 24, 2017. In the principles of the law in question, a foreigner found in the Brazilian territory carrying a temporary visa is restrained from installing its company (individual firm), occupy a position or assume administrative functions in management or as a director in a trading company or a simple company. In the eventuality of admission of a foreigner through the modality of the said visa through a contract, he will be restricted to act in the economic body for which he was hired, except if the Ministry of Justice expressly issues an authorization in the opposite sense, that is, giving him permission to act in an economic body after inquiring and in consultation the Minister of Labor.

If by chance those who are legally prohibited to participate in an organized economic activity disregard such a prohibition, they will be assuming a *contra legem* conduct, their acts will have a limited validity before third parties, and there is no denial that violations or acts of fraud under the law will warrant levying penalties against them.

In this regard, the general rule that provides some exceptions cannot be ignored, for example, after "fulfilling the legal requirements (capacity, no legal prohibition, regularity, commonness in the performance of the company activities and the intention to gain profit), nothing prevents the individual trade, i.e., to become a businessperson as a natural person, a sole proprietorship."[12]

If a natural person undertakes (singularly), their patrimonial sphere will be ruled by the principle of the asset's unit, in the sense that their personal assets and company will be considered as one and will respond to the obligation to which

11 Regulates the Actioners Profession.
12 Cláudia RIBEIRO and Priscila MENEZES, op. cit., 8.

he is bound and has unlimited liability for responsibilities. A different situation is when the businessperson is a legal person, the liability is limited (according to the trade company type), and one of the conditions of the company type is the abstraction between the goods of the economic body (company) and the partners' assets, that is, the individual who is a part of the legal person or the company.

4. General Obligations of the Commercial Businessperson

The general obligations of businessperson include the following: (a) business registration in the qualified entities (Board of Trade) prior to the engagement in company activities[13]; (b) provision of regular bookkeeping; and (c) periodical survey of financial statements.

It is a mere matter of formal obligations, but its disregard has serious costs, including criminal charges against failure to fulfill obligations. A key aspect of these formalities to be fulfilled under law by the businessperson is the attentive and thorough verification of the activities performed by them, which are of great importance not only for partners who are economically committed but also for creditors, the State Treasury, and, to some extent, their own economic body (the corporation).

The nonobservance of these obligations attach to the businessperson an unlawful quality, and the businessperson in these conditions will certainly find difficulties in undertaking any commercial enterprise and conclude businesses with its counterparts in a lawful manner; will also find barriers in negotiating with the Public Administration or in assuming debts before financial institutions or will face difficulties in proceeding with an application for judicial reorganization. Included among these violations is the company's failure to comply with tax obligations.[14]

4.1 Company Name

The obligation to register the trading company before the beginning of any act presupposes a prior existence of the name in which the businessperson is known in the sphere of its commercial acts.

13 Cfr. Article 967 of the 2002 Brazilian Civil Code.

14 Fábio Ulhoa COELHO, op. cit., 66.

It is common understanding in the doctrine and in the field of law that the civil name equals the natural person. In this sense, Fazzio Júnior postulates that "the company name distinguishes and points out the type of capital liability of the businessperson or trading company. Every businessperson signs documents under a company name, which constitutes its firm, individualizing it from others."[15]

The regulation of company name in the Brazilian legal system follows the Swiss system. In the mentioned system, it follows that a qualified entity provides legal protection of the name. Once the registration of the name is done in the company register, it can be adjusted; the modification can be voluntary or mandatory or even entailed. The entailed modification will be based on the departure, exclusion, and even the death of a partner whose name was part of the firm or else by the transfer of commercial premises.

In the Brazilian law, the company name is created based on two ways:

(i) **FIRM**—it is the name referring to the businessperson (natural person); however, some company types can be subjected to the use of this nominal kind; it's the case of corporations constituted by contract—general partnership or closed limited partnership— and other company types like limited liability company and limited partnership by shares; all of these are options and ways for a firm to formalize its nominal identification.

(ii) **DENOMINATION**—it consists of the name of the company or public limited company and can be optionally assumed also by a company with limited partnership by shares and a limited liability company.

The general rule is that the firm corresponds to the civil name of the person that engages in the company acts, but nothing prevents the name from being abbreviated or modified with new information that will allow changes in its identification in civil legal relations and also in trade relations.

According to Article 34 of the Act No. 8934 from November 18, 1994—entitled "Public Register of Merchant Companies and Related Activities"—the firm must be structured based on the following principles:

(i) **Veracity**—also known as the principle of accuracy—does not allow the use of pseudonym since it goes against the publication of the name of the person engaging in such activities, something that can jeopardize the interests of third parties. In short, the firm must reflect the reality

15 Waldo FAZZIO JÚNIOR, op. cit., 55.

to which it refers, not mislead with regard to the legal character of the entity; it is in this aspect that they must embrace the truth and not instill error in their identity and the extension of the economic activity that the businessperson intends to pursue.

(ii) **Principle of novelty**—according to this principle, there is no room for simultaneous existence of operating companies in the company field with similar names. In the possibility of adoption of similar firm previously deposited and registered in the company register, there will be a need for alteration of certain information that will allow to establish distinguishing points with the first one registered, or the firm has to manifest the distinction before the ones that are already notarized or registered.

From the principle of novelty emerges the exclusive right to the name, which serves the purpose of prevention of snares and embarrassment as well as warding off unfair competition resulting from the similarity between the names.[16]

The exclusivity lies in the fact that the firm must be private as regards the person concerned after its inclusion in the company register. The company register can be the qualified entity for the registration of the firm and carries the obligation of not proceeding with fulfilling the acts of commercial entities with names similar to the ones already registered; such obligation is based on the protection of the socioeconomic interest and the growth of technology in the Brazilian state.

In the event a company files its name with the company register and the company register fails to fulfill the mandatory obligation of proceeding diligently to confirm whether or not a similar name already exists, such omission can result in judicial enquiry and proceedings about exclusivity of the name and the register will be forced to explain the matter in court.

The same rule applies for the business corporation when it comes to the name that it is likely to adopt, in harmony with the modality of the company, denomination, or company name.

If, hypothetically, the general partnership does not individualize their constituents, it will have to include at least the name of one of the partners (by abbreviation or in full form), adding the expression "company." However, this expression can be replaced by one of equal value like "and son," "and siblings," among many others. The names of the remaining members of the company are subject to the representation in full or abbreviated form, allowing the exclusion of some parts of the names.

16 Waldo FAZZIO JÚNIOR, op. cit., 60.

When it comes to simple limited partnership, the company name must show at least the name of one of the limited partners with addition of the expression "company" in full or abbreviated form. In the situation of limited liability companies' names or when they assume the social grounds or the denomination, it would be enough to add to their names the expression "limited" (Ltd). If they choose the company name, there will have to be at least the name of one of the partners.

For public limited company, there is no space for option; it is mandatory that they adopt the denomination. The expression "public limited company" can or cannot be abbreviated and can be included in the beginning, in the middle, or in the end, mentioning or not mentioning the nature of the economic activity.

If the civil name matches the denomination, it is assumed that it is a made-up expression. When the denomination is based on civil name, there is a rebuttable presumption that the owner of the name expressly authorized its use as a denomination, having given up their legal personality; it is presumed that his heirs issued an authorization to that effect. The civil name of at least one of the directors or managers must coincide with the company name when dealing with the limited-partnership-by-shares company with the addition of expression "company" (by shares) written in full or abbreviated form.

The company name is a crucial right for the execution of company, and in the Brazilian legal order, it is under constitutional protection, as stipulated in Article 5, section XXIX of the Federal Constitution, stating that:

> The law assures to the authors of industrial inventions temporary privileges for the good use of the goods, a protection to the industrial creations, the property of trademarks, the company names and other distinguishing signs, in view of the social interest and the technologic and economic development of the country.

The registration is the sine qua non for the protection of company name, making the formality essential for its legal protection. Such understanding comes from Article 8 of the Paris Convention on Industrial Property, for exempting registration with the National Industrial Property Institute to which other industrial property rights are subject.[17]

Fazzo Júnior calls our attention to the fact that:

17 It is understood that the waiver to the company name registration in the Industrial Property National Institute is against the socioeconomic interest and the technological growth of the mentioned country in the constitutional rule. Waldo FAZZIO JÚNIOR, op. cit., 61.

> The protection of the company name is not in full, since it tries, before the resemblance or the identical names of opposers, to prevent losses for those who hold a registration in their favor. From the decision of the Supreme Court, the right to an exclusive use of the name is subjected to the registration in the National Industrial Property Institute and simply arises with the legal constitution of the company through the filling of its constituent acts in the Register of Mercantile Companies. Being a matter of a firm with the same denomination and Company purpose the prior registration of the company name must prevail.

Another important fact is that although the company name can be disposed, if the principle of accuracy is in effect, it is certain that "in the case of a firm or Company name, the disposal will not be possible if those names are built upon the patronymics of partners, referring to the denomination, nothing prevents the disposal for others, as an integral element of the company, or in an autonomous operation."[18]

The loss of company name is ruled as per conditions stipulated in Act No. 8.934/94, Article 59, where it is stated that after the period for which the company was constituted, if it is for a definitive period, it will lose legal protection of its name. On the other hand, in the event of failure to close down for 10 consecutive years, the company will have to inform the Company Register that it intends to continue operating. If the company does not inform or by any means manifest, even after the notification from the Company Register, the Company Register will have to proceed with deregistration, as is stipulated in Article 60 of the same act.

The company name extinguishes with the cessation of commercial practices (for any cause) or liquidation (in the case of corporation) or change in the company type.

4.2 Bookkeeping

Bookkeeping as an obligation of the businessperson is done for its legal reaffirmation in the Civil Code, Article 1179, where it is stated that the businessperson has the duty to maintain a bookkeeping of the businesses they participate. This means that the continuous execution of the company implies the development of accounting activities to be performed by accountants employed in the company or operating independently.

18 Waldo FAZZIO JÚNIOR, op. cit., 61.

Still in the scope of bookkeeping, exempting the small-scale enterprises, the businessperson or trading company are bound to have the necessary notified books to that effect[19]; "keep to remain, the books, the correspondences and other assets belonging to the turn of the activity before the prescription of the related actions"[20] and "do an annual survey of the balance sheet and the economic results.[21]

The bookkeeping must follow some formalities; that is to say, it is a formal act to the extent that it has to be made in the national currency and language in a compatible way, chronologically stating the day, month, and year, without any blank spaces, following the terms of Article 1183 of the Civil Code.

Therefore, the pioneer instrument was the book. Nowadays, in line with the Civil Code in Articles 1179 and 1180, it is allowed for the businessperson to choose using an "electronic" or "mechanic" accounting system.

The book, in Fábio Ulhoa Coelho's words:

> Still stands the general designation sense of a valuable instrument for the businessperson to fulfillment of the bookkeeping legal duty of its business. Without prejudice to the specific books claimed by the legislation, the daily book (that can be replaced by files) is expendable. It is the only mandatory book, where daily, by direct writing or reproduction, all transactions relevant to the company activity, including the balance sheet and the economic outturn account, both subscribed by the authorized accounting officer and by the manager or representative of the company.[22]

The legal regime of the daily book is described as follows in the first paragraph of Article 1184 of the Civil Code: "the summarized bookkeeping of the diaries is allowed, with totals that do not exceed thirty days relative to accounts whose operations are numerous or carried outside the headquarters of the premises, if regularly authenticated auxiliary books are used for an individualized registration and the documents for its perfect verification are maintained."

In line with Article 1185 of the Civil Code, it is possible to replace the daily book with the daily balance and general balance, as long as the businessperson or trading company adopts a system based on launching files. Such replacement possibility must surround the understanding provided by Article 1186 of the

19 See Article 1.181 Civil Code.
20 See Article 1.194 Civil Code.
21 See Article 1.179 Civil Code.
22 Fábio Ulhoa COELHO, op. cit., 78.

Civil Code where it is stated "the daily balance books and general balance books will be registered in a way that it contains:

(I) the daily position of each of the accountings or accounting titles, the respective balance in the form of daily balance sheets.
(II) the patrimonial balance and the economic results at the closure of the exercise."

The duplicate log is one of the other accounting books that the Ministerial Decree No. 436 of January 27, 1969 rules over. Fazzio Junior[23] adds that the duplicate log will always contain the numerical and chronological sequence of all the duplicates enacted, with the day, month, year, and the value of the primitive invoice, as well as the day, month, and year of the shipment, and the name and habitual residence of the customers of the businessperson or trading company, along other relevant information.

Due to its great importance, the duplicate log cannot be amended, blurred, redacted, or interlined; it is imperative that it is kept in the physical building where the activity is performed. The registration at issue may be moved for an informatics system as long as it is presented according to the conditions described.[24]

According to Ulhoa Coelho, the obligation of the duplicate log is not general since it does not extend to all performers of a commercial activity but only to those who enact "market duplicates" or "Service of provision." The obligation is extended to small-scale enterprises in the event of undertaking a duplicate for collection of debtors or "bank discount."[25]

It is a matter of willingness from the businessperson to enact a duplicate. The businessperson or contractor is not bound to issue his credit by a specific document, but he chooses to issue credit through that title, in meeting the obligation to keep the bookkeeping by means of his title (Duplicate Log).

Among several options, if the businessperson or contractor does not choose the use of the duplicate log, he can choose to document its credits under some other resource, such as "promissory note," "contracts," and "trading cards."

Still under the bookkeeping, the law states that other types of books can be used considering the activity that is developed in the physical building where the premises are situated, and "for this purpose, the commercial premises, the

23 Waldo FAZZIO JÚNIOR, op. cit., 49.
24 Id.
25 Fábio Ulhoa COELHO, op. cit., 80.

wholesalers, the retailers and those who keep the activity under tax payment, overall, they must adopt the following books: (a) Check-in book; (b) Check-out book; (c) Registration of the use of tax documents and events; and (d) Inventory record.[26]

The bookkeeping as a general obligation and encompasses three functions[27]:

(i) Management—it is an instrument that guides the businessperson and the heads of the trading company in the administrative, financial, and commercial matters.
(ii) Documentation—it is a good source of information for the own company as well the third parties related to it; and
(iii) Fiscal—the State Treasure inspects the fulfillment of tax obligation by the company and other legal obligations.

In regards to the fiscal function, tax-related laws provide the fiscal and social security officers the ability to demand the administrative presentation of the books; although bookkeeping is protected by confidentiality, such protection is not relevant when it is related to fiscal matters, and, therefore, the confidentiality is breached.[28]

The Civil Code assures that understanding in Article 1193, determining that "the restriction from the examination of the bookkeeping, in part of in full, does not apply to the tax authorities in the exercise of the inspection towards the payment of taxes in the restricted term of the respective special law." In case where documents related to the bookkeeping are stolen, damaged, or destroyed, it is the company's duty to proceed with the exposition of those acts in the press of the region where those acts took place and will let the Company Register of its jurisdiction know about such accidents in details within 48 hours.

The State Treasury is one such entity that has the prerogative of accessing the bookkeeping, and such power is vested in them as per provisions of Article 1190 of the Civil Code, which states: "except for the cases provided by law, no authority, judge or tribunal, under any excuse can order a measure to verify if the businessperson or trading company follow or not, in their books or files, the legal formalities." It is in this way that it is concluded that beyond the perception of it

26 Waldo FAZZIO JÚNIOR, op. cit., 49.
27 Fábio Ulhoa COELHO, op. cit., 80.
28 On this see, § 1, Article 33 Law 8.212 of July 24, 1991.

as a right, the bookkeeping secrecy is a duty that the businessperson or trading company must fulfill.

The bookkeeping secrecy carries the purpose of removing unfair competition. The businessperson in the undertaking adopts numerous ways to reach profit, and to disclose those ways and means to third parties would bring tremendous losses. Even if the secrecy is important to the success of the corporation, it is not an absolute matter, in the sense that the right to participate and inspect the trading company by the partners is a need that implies its rupture.

The Company by Shares' Act states that the presentation of books to the company can be judicially determined, if the shareholders that carry at least 5 % of the capital stock request in court, basing their request on the violation of the terms of the constitutive act of the company by its members (Article 105). Under this act, and in this company type, the principle of secrecy of bookkeeping is ruptured by the justification of protection of common interest as well as public interest.

Already in the wake of the Civil Code, the court through the judge, with regard to the total presentation of the books and the other bookkeeping documentation, is restricted to authorize it only when its crucial for the resolution of cases dealing with succession, communion or partnership, and administration or management on behalf of others or related to fundamental phenomenon (Article 1191). By clustering of parts, it is understood that the presentation of some parts of the books of bookkeeping will be authorized when there are different circumstances other than those listed in that article.

4.3 Company Registration

According to Article 967 of the Brazilian Civil Code, it is mandatory to carry out the company registration at the Companies Public Registry before starting commercial activities.

The 1850 Commercial Code of Brazil led to the creation of commercial courts, with the competence to interpret and enforce the law in judicial matters involving traders or people who simply practiced commercial acts. Beside commerce-related matters, the courts' competence included a jurisdictional power to deal with registration matters.

The commercial courts had a division called "commercial board," which had the power to conduct the commercial registration and before which the traders had the obligation to perform their registration and maintain all the legal documents required for the exercise of commercial activities.[29]

From the analysis presented in the previous paragraph it can be concluded that the commercial courts accumulated jurisdictional and administrative competences, what was against the principle of separation of powers provided in the 1824 Imperial Constitution. This is the reason why those courts became extinct in 1875 and their competences were attributed to the court judges. The administrative powers were maintained with the commercial boards and inspectorates.

Nowadays, the registration that matters for those exercising organized economic activities is the Company and Related Activities Registration, which came into force by Law 8.934 of November 18, 1994[30] and by Decree 1.800 of January 30, 1996.[31] A commercial board was established in each state and their counties.

According to Article 32 of the Law 8.934/94, three acts are involved in the company registration:

(i) *Registration and cancelation*, mainly for those professionals who are under supervision of the commercial boards, such as the auctioneers, public translators and commercial interpreters, and general stores managers[32];
(ii) *Filling* of (a) documents related to constitution, amendment, dissolution, and extinction of individual commercial names, companies, and cooperatives; (b) acts related to consortium and public companies' groups; (c) acts related to foreign companies authorized to operate in Brazil; (d) micro-enterprises' relations; (e) acts or documents that, by law, are given to Public Registry of Companies and Related Activities, or those that may interest the business operator as the companies.[33]
(iii) *Authentication of bookkeeping documents* of registered companies and auxiliary trade agents, according to the specific law.[34]

Regarding registration, Ricardo Negrão postulates that "The National Commercial Registration Department (DNRC) and the Commercial Boards of each Federative Unity are organs in charge of the public registration of the

29 Fábio Ulhoa COELHO, op. cit., 66.
30 Regulates the Public Registry of Enterprises and Related Activities, and gives other provisions.
31 Regulation of the Law 8.934 of November 18, 1994, on Public Registry of Enterprises and Related Activities, and gives other provisions.
32 See paragraph I, article 32.
33 See sub-paragraphs (a), (b), (c), (d), and (e), paragraph II.
34 See paragraph III.

commercial companies and related activities and are part of the National System of Companies Registration (SINREM). The National Commercial Registration Department has the following competences: (a) supervise, (b) direct, (c) coordinate and create norms in the technical plan, (d) coordinate and supplement in the administrative plan."[35]

The registration has a certain goal, and under Article 1 of the Law No. 8.934/94, its objective is "to give guarantee, publicity, authenticity, security and efficiency to the company legal acts." To achieve those objectives, the registration entities organize the register of all companies that conduct economic activities and those who conduct companies in the Brazilian territory.

In this context, under the Article 1.154 of the Brazilian Civil Code regarding registration, information related to registration, with legally provided exceptions, and when the company has not fulfilled the formally required prerequisites, is not opposable to good-faith third parties. It is justified by the fact that without registration there is no publicity. However, the lack of knowledge does not benefit the third party if the formalities were duly observed; in these cases, the registration is opposable to all.

Another important aspect that matters is the legal nature of registration. Some argue that registration has a declaratory legal nature, but others argue that it has a constitutive nature. The registration would be declaratory if seen as an act whose objective is to recognize the fact of existence or nonexistence and not that of a legal situation, that is, its certification. It is to be noted that such recognition cannot be of the simple fact but of the concrete legal situations that demand the intervention of the National Commercial Registration Department (DNRC) and the commercial boards. In the constitutive perspective, the registration must be seen as an act that has as the objective the creation of a legal situation, in this case the constitution of a company.[36]

Taking into account the two perspectives, it is to be said that, as a rule, the registration has declaratory nature; that is, it only recognizes a *de facto* situation. If someone exercises the commercial activity without the registration, he will be regarded as an irregular entrepreneur. Therefore, the registration is a simple regularity condition.

As mentioned above, Article 967 of the Civil Code foresees the mandatory registration of the company before the business person starts the activity, and the lack of registration of the company prevents him from exercising his activity,

35 Ricardo NEGRÃO, op. cit., 204.
36 Cláudia RIBEIRO and Priscila MENEZES, op. cit., 9.

determining the irregularity of the activity and imposing several restrictions provided in the administrative, procedural, and commercial legislation; for example, under paragraph 1 of the Article 97 combined with the Article 48 of the Bankruptcy Law, the unregistered entrepreneur cannot request the bankruptcy of the other or plead for its own judicial recovery.

It is important to take into consideration the words of Fábio Ulhoa Coelho,[37] who states that "providing the general obligation imposed to the businesspersons to register at the commercial board before starting the economic activity, the law has provided two exceptional situations, of the rural business operators and small business operators."

Regarding rural business operators, under the current system they are defined as equivalent entrepreneur; that is, they will be subject to special law only if he registers before the competent entity. Those who professionally engage in rural economic production have the right to either choose proceeding as rural producer or become an "individual entrepreneur" or create a "business company" through the registration act before the commercial board, according to Article 971 of the Civil Code.

If the rural business operator does not perform the registration in the Company Public Registry, he will not be considered as rural entrepreneur and his activities will be regulated by civil law norms; in case those activities are exercised in a collectivity, it is at the Legal Persons Civil Registry the registration acts for its constitution shall be performed.[38]

Regarding small business operators, Article 179 of Federal Constitution provides that "the Union, the States, the Federal District and the Municipalities will dismiss the micro and small enterprises, defined as such by law, a differentiated legal treatment, aimed at encouraging them by simplifying their administrative, fiscal, providential and creditor obligations, or by their elimination or reduction by law."

The Civil Code has exempted the "small business operator" from registering themselves as one of the general obligations that would apply to the general category of entrepreneurs (Article 970). It is a problematic exemption. It is problematic because (i) the Brazilian legal framework does not provide the conceptual approach of the "small business operator." The absence of a concept provided by law leads to the conclusion that it is a word that refers to micro-entrepreneur and small-sized entrepreneur; (ii) it is also observed that there is exemption for small

37 Fábio Ulhoa COELHO, op. cit., 78.
38 Id., 76.

entrepreneurs under civil laws in relation to the normative complex pertaining to instrumental tax law obligations. Regarding the second problem, what was said means that "for the small-entrepreneur [to] benefit from the civil advantages, [they] should choose the National Simple, taking into account its specific regulation. The solution to the problem depends on the amendment of the law establishing the tax program to promote small business operators, which gives registration in the National Register of the Legal Persons the Commercial Board registration effects."[39]

5. Individual Businessperson in the Brazilian Law

Article 966 of the Brazilian Civil Code defines the concept of businessperson as one "who professionally exercises an organized economic activity for production or circulation of goods or services."

The natural person, who, by their own initiative or own name, takes on risks by deploying convenient resources for the development of an economic activity and commits himself, in an unlimited manner, to respond to the obligations derived from the exercise of such economic activity is named individual businessperson. Thus, there is no legal provision for the limitation of their responsibility. If the enterprise's assets are not enough to respond to the assumed obligations, its private assets which are not used for the commercial activity can be called on to respond to the economic activity debts.[40]

The individual businessperson responds in an unlimited manner for his obligations because the Brazilian legal system adopts the Principle of Patrimonial Unity, according to which to each person corresponds to only one legal patrimony. Therefore, the businessperson's private goods and those assigned for the economic activity constitute one patrimony.

For a certain legal person to be qualified as individual business person, they must meet certain fundamental requirements, namely:

5.1 Legal Capacity

The validity of legal acts depends on the capacity of the agent who performs them, either in civil legal relations or in commercial legal relations.

39 Fábio Ulhoa COELHO, op. cit., 76.
40 Cláudia RIBEIRO and Priscila MENEZES, op. cit., 6.

Generally speaking, the civil majority is obtained at the age of 18, where the natural person gains the legal capacity to perform civil acts.[41] However, there are some legal circumstances that can provide to the minor the legal capacity before they reach 18 years of age. One of those circumstances is legally provided in subparagraph V, Article 5 of the Brazilian Civil Code, where it is stated that the incapacity for minority ceases "for the civil or commercial establishment, or by existing an employment relation, as long as, related to them, the completed 16 years old minor has his/her own economy."

For the exercise of commercial activity, the person must have full civil legal capacity.[42] It is a general rule but has an exception, which is the incapable person can continue to exercise the enterprise that was previously exercised by his parents or by a deceased person, through his assistant or representative.[43]

It is to be kept in mind that such exception is only related to the continuity of economic activity and not to start a new one. From this, one can infer that the supervening disability and/or the disability of the successor in the *mortis causa* succession are the only two circumstances that can allow the incapable person to exercise an organized economic activity, through their assistant or representative.

The continuation of an organized economic activity by an incapable, being an exception, depends on judicial authorization. Therefore, the judge "will provide the judicial permit after examining the circumstances and the risks of the enterprise, as well as the convenience in continuing it, being that the authorization can be revoked by the judge [having] heard the parents, tutors or legal representatives of the minor or the interdict, without prejudicing third parties acquired rights."[44]

If the judge decides to authorize the continuation of the enterprise by the incapable, he will proceed with the nomination of the representative, who, under provisions of Article 875 of the Civil Code, must be capable and not have legal impediments for the exercise of economic activity.

The permit allowing the continuation of business activity must state the fact that the assets the incapable had at the time of succession or interdiction, being different from those constituting the business assets, will be characterized as allocated heritage, according to paragraph 2, Article 974 of the Civil Code.

41 See Article 5, Civil Code.
42 See Article 972, Civil Code.
43 See Article 974, Civil Code.
44 See § 1, article 974 Civil Code.

The permit for continuation of commercial activities by the incapable must be registered or endorsed at the Public Registry of Companies, along with submitting the proofs of emancipation of the incapable, according to Article 976 of the Civil Code. Regarding the emancipated minor, who exercises an organized economic activity, and therefore civilly incapable, can be condemned of bankruptcy crime only when become 18 years old. It is important to highlight that those aged between 16 and 18 years are considered regular businesspersons if they meet the requirements provided in the Articles 966 and 976 of the Civil Code, but such regularity does not count for recovery right if they are not running business regularly for more than two years.[45]

Being a businessperson, and the subject who exploits the enterprise, in these circumstances he cannot be confused with the shareholders of a company. The shareholders of a company can be incapable, as long as they observe the requirements provided by law, namely, to be duly assisted or represented, and have fully paid the social contribution and have not exercised the administration of the company.[46]

It is worth to mention here in this context the rights of the married businessperson. Article 978 of the Civil Code states that "the married businessperson can, without spouse consent, and whenever in the marriage regime, sell the assets that are part of the enterprise patrimony or put on them a real burden."

Article 979 of the Civil Code determines that "besides the Civil Registration, [documentation] will be filled or endorsed at the Public Registry of Companies, [with] the pacts and prenuptial declarations of the businessperson, the donation title, heritage or legacy, the incommunicable or unsellable goods," so that they can be opposable to third parties.

The professional of organized economic activity who has married in community of goods has the ability to involve the couple's assets in the exercise of enterprise. Subject to contrary understanding, the spouses in community of goods benefit from the profits arising from the exercise of the commercial activity, regardless of who exercised the activity. It is presumed that the economic gains derived from the activity of each spouse enter the patrimonial sphere of the couple. If such a thing does not happen, the injured spouse has the ability to, in a casual executive action, make reservation to his summons, by third-party embargo, bringing evidential elements of that circumstance.[47]

45 The Judicial Recovery system was adopted in lieu of the revoked "Preventive Bankruptcy" system provided in the Decree 7661 of June 21, 1945, revoked by the Law 11.101, February 9, 2005.

46 Sub-paragraphs I, II e III, § 3, Article 974, Civil Code.

47 Cláudia RIBEIRO and Priscila MENEZES, op. cit., 22.

5.2 Absence of Legal Impediments

We have briefly discussed this requirement (Section 3). Therefore, it is not worth providing an exhaustive analysis here. It is only worth to remember that, although certain natural persons have full civil capacity, they may be legally prohibited from exercising organized economic activities in their own names or as managers of a company. Under Article 973 of the Brazilian Civil Code, in case a legally prohibited person exercises an economic activity, he will respond to the acquired obligations when it is valid to do so before a good-faith third person.

5.3 Professional Exercise of Enterprise

This is opposed to the occasional or accidental exercise of an activity. The commercial profession presupposes that when the natural person himself in his own name assumes the risks for creation of an economic organism having the goal to produce and circulate goods or services to obtain profit they will not be qualified as businessperson who exercises the enterprise on behalf of others.[48]

As a matter of fact, any person can perform, occasionally, negotiable acts, but that does not bestow upon him the status of businessperson. Professionalism brings the idea that the enterprise must be exercised orderly and periodically. It is not mandatory that the enterprise be an exclusive activity of the businessperson, and the business person can exercise other activities as well.[49]

It is clear that it is not enough that the fortuitous exercise the isolated negotiated acts of the person make them acquire the quality of businessperson. They can be acts of commerce, but if they lack habituality and systematization they cannot effectively attribute to a certain person the quality of businessperson in a professional sense.

5.4 Special Legal Regime of the Insolvent Company

Within the Brazilian normative system, a specific legal regime for the businessperson is in force when he is in an insolvency situation. There is, however, in the Civil Procedure Law an exception related to the creditors contest, which is subject to bankruptcy system.

According to Fazzio Junior, in the special insolvency regulatory framework, one must understand that "the bankruptcy system allows the businessperson to

48 Ricardo NEGRÃO, op. cit., 70.
49 Waldo FAZZIO JÚNIOR, op. cit., 27.

obtain the recovery. He can solve his debts in advantageous conditions than those provided to the civil debtor and, according to the case, even be dismissed from the obligation." Only the debtor businessperson falls under bankruptcy. This, as a universal joint debt solution, is exclusively determined for those who individually or collectively exercise an enterprise. The civil debtor, in same situations, will be subject to execution for a certain amount against the insolvent debtor that is no more than creditors contest in a civil sphere. Depending on the perspective in which it is analyzed, the bankruptcy alternative shows minimum concern for the positive legal order to preserve the enterprise through recovery and shorten the socioeconomic projection of undesirable effects of its extinction.[50]

5.5 Mandatory Registration

Under Article 967 of the Civil Code, the businessperson must register before starting the exploitation of an economically organized activity being, therefore, one of his obligations to be observed since one of the objectives of the registration is to give publicity to the businessperson's acts.[51]

It was mentioned above that the registration is not aimed at characterizing the businessperson as such (those who do not register according to law will be irregular businesspersons; that is, they will not benefit from the legal benefits, as in the case of judicial recovery) but simply gives him regularity.

Under Article 968 of Civil Code, while submitting a request for registration the businessperson is demanded to disclose the following: (a) name, nationality, residence, and marital status; (b) commercial name, including autograph signature; (c) capital; (d) headquarters and object.

It is important to make it clear that in the Brazilian legal order the company registration implies its regularity or its regular status. The above-mentioned article determines the mandatory nature of the company registration before starting the business operations and such obligations as the basis of characterizing the enterprise as a regular profession after its registration.

Legally, the enterprise is qualified as such when it is started according to the legal parameters. As can be noted, registration is not a mere formal procedure. When it is a company that has not fulfilled its obligation to register in the company register will lead to the consequence of it being denied a legal personality,

50 Waldo FAZZIO JÚNIOR, op. cit., 28.

51 Generally, the registration has declarative nature; it will be constitutive only exceptionally, as in the case of rural businessperson.

with the persons leading it forced to bear the burden of having to fulfill unlimited and supportive responsibility when necessary.

6. Business Companies in Brazilian Law

6.1 Introduction to Business Companies Law

We have already said that economic, systematic, and organized activity can be carried out by a natural person for producing or circulating goods or services. It should be underlined that the exercise of business activity is not limited to the individual businessperson; by this we mean that the business company (here after referred to as Company)can also exercise it. The business company is a private law person created by individuals through an agreement of wills (contract); by means of the contract, those individuals are bound to combine assets necessary for the development of a profitable economic activity.[52]

In the words of Ulhoa Coelho, individuals can carry out small economic activities with relative ease. The more the scope of activities broadens, the greater their complexity will be, requiring greater application of capital and skilled labor, which will make it difficult for a single person to carry them out. In this context, the development of these activities will require the combined efforts of various (economic) players, with the aim of achieving a profit-making objective. This combination of efforts is made effective by the formation of a company or business company.[53]

A company is a legal fiction, since it is not a natural or physical person, and it is a person created by law. It can take on various facets. For the present work, we are interested in the social form it will take, since the company may vary according to the interests of its partners, much more with regard to the type of responsibility to which they want to be subject.

The partners make common investments for the exploitation of economic activity and may form a company; this is the object of our study. The company is equivalent to the person created by the law, who in turn carries out economic activity; greater attention should be paid to the expression "Company," which refers only to the company (holder of the economic activity/qualified economic

52 LuizAntonioBarrosoRODRIGUES,*DireitoEmpresarial,*3ed.rev.Actual–Florianópolis:Departamento de Ciências da Administração/ UFSC (Brasília: CAPES: UAB, 2016), p47.

53 Fábio Ulhoa COELHO, *Curso de Direito Comercial: Direito de Empresas: Sociedades,* 13 ed. vol. 2 (São Paulo: Saraiva, 2009), 3.

agent as subject of law) that should be distinguished from the partners who are a part of it.[54]

Under Article 966 of the Civil Code, a company is deemed as a commercial if its objective is to carry out economic activity organized to produce or circulate goods or services. This definition uses economic concepts such as economic activity of production, company, and businessperson. An activity of a productive nature is an action that creates an economic good, from which the individual or social group can extract services used as means or resources employed to achieve a result (profit).[55]

6.2 The Historical Evolution of the Business Company System in Brazilian Law

In order to talk about the historical evolution of the trading company regime in Brazilian law, it is crucial to highlight that commercial/company law has three phases[56]: (i) **subjective phase**—craftsmanship; (ii) **objective phase**—Trade Acts; and (iii) **modern subjective phase**—company theory.[57]

During the Medieval period, the Trade Associations were at the forefront of commercial activities, integrated by the bourgeoisie who were traders of the time. Commercial law, as is generally known, springs from the margins of civil law, which in turn was an instrument regulating commercial relations between the feudalists registered with the associations and that is why it was subjective.

In the early 19th century, the French Revolution immediately after it established itself in France introduced the Commercial Code of 1808 that marked the

54 Id., 5.

55 Alfredo FILHO and José PEDREIRA, *Direito das Companhias,* op. cit.,. 22.

56 Fábio Ulhoa Coelho argues that *"the history of commercial law is usually divided into four periods. (1) In the first, between the second half of the 12th century and the second of the 16th, commercial law is the law applicable to the members of a specific trade corporation, that of traders. A subjective criterion is thus adopted to define its scope of application. Bills of exchange, banks and insurance are examples of institutes existing at that time. (2) The second period begins in the 16th to 18th centuries, commercial law in Continental Europe is still the law of the members of the traders' guild. In England, the development of Common Law contributed to overcoming this characteristic. The most important one at that stage is the public limited company; (3) the third period (19th and first half of the 20th centuries) is characterized by the overcoming of the subjective criterion of identifying the scope of incidence of commercial law. Since the Napoleonic Code of 1808, it has no longer been the law of merchants, but of acts of commerce; (4) the starting point of the fourth and last period in the history of commercial law is the 1942 edition in Italy of the Codice Civile, which integrates into a single law the rules of private law (civil, commercial, and labor). During this period, the conceptual nucleus of commercial law ceased to be the "act of commerce" and became the "company."* Fábio Ulhoa COELHO, op. cit., 13-18.

57 Cláudia RIBEIRO and Priscila MENEZES, op. cit., 3.

beginning of the objective conception of commercial law. It is objectivist because it aimed to list the acts considered as commercial. The acts that were not listed in this context were lacking in commerciality and were marginalized from commercial legal discipline, with their regulation falling within the civil area (by the Civil Code).

The nonexistence of a scientific principle that was taken as a reference to distinguish between an act of commerce and other acts not relevant to commercial relations led to the failure of the objective conception and its consequent replacement by the subjectivist conception (company theory). This theory had its roots in Italian law with the creation of the Civil Code in 1942, thus returning to the subjectivist framework of commercial law.

The historical origins of commercial law in Brazil are closely linked to the decree of the charter (Régia) issued on January 28, 1808 by the Portuguese Regent,[58] which had the objective of allowing access to port areas for the allied peoples. This decree created economic conditions of irreversible events. On the other hand, the return of the king of that time, King João VI, to Portugal in 1821, preceded by pacification in Europe in 1815, proved to be one of the major political factors that led to the birth of the Brazilian state.[59]

Access to port areas for allied peoples accelerated Brazil's economic independence. Brazil as a state was born in 1822, the year in which it became politically independent, an independence that had as one of its consequences the election of a "Legislative and Constituent Assembly" in 1823; this power body issued a command of order according to which all Portuguese norms applied before independence and which did not contradict the principles of the new order would be applied in the new state as well, in order to circumvent the lack of legislation of its own. Among the laws in force in that historical context, the Good Reason Law of 1769, a legal instrument that in the commercial field called for the observance of the laws in force in the so-called civilized "Christian nations," is the most prominent.[60]

The Brazilian state was experiencing an era of economic growth. This period of economic growth required a commercial code of its own, replacing the three legal diplomas (Portuguese, French, and Spanish Civil Code) that had several

58 It must be borne in mind that Brazil was a Portuguese colony at the time.

59 Fábio Ulhoa COELHO, op. cit., 20–26.

60 It is in this context that the Napoleonic, Portuguese, and Spanish codes have become legal instruments regulating the exploitation of the economic activity of the new state.

gaps and were equally contradictory. The Brazilian Commercial Code was only promulgated in 1850 by King Dom Pedro II.[61]

The then-enacted legal diploma had its inspiration in the *Commerce Code*, thus transferring to the Brazilian legal system the legal spirit of France to regulate private activities of an economic nature, which is commerce. Paradoxically, this diploma lacks an expression typical of the French system, *"trade acts"* and therefore does not list them. The introduction of trade acts was made on the basis of Regulation No. 737 of 1850, a procedural document of outstanding technical quality; it is Article 19 of this regulation that defines the activities under the jurisdiction of the competent bodies to analyze commercial causes, for example, the trade courts.

Those courts were extinguished in 1875; even so, the regulation of trade based on an objective concept—trade acts—was maintained, and there were still two systems in force to regulate legal relations—commercial relations, by commercial law; civil relations, by civil law. The enrollment of trade acts by the regulation referred to in the previous paragraph meant that it was seen as an instrument delimiting and indicating the scope of application of the Brazilian commercial normative regulation; it performed as an instrumental function in this logic, such function having lasted beyond its repeal. The year 1960 marks the beginning of the depreciation of the regulation in question, since the Brazilian legal system began to move towards the subjective concept of private regulation of economic activity.

It is the dynamics of society and the development of new areas of company activity that have brought the Brazilian legal system closer to the subjectivist concept—company theory—having its roots in Italian law, which is not limited to the enrollment of trade acts, as happens in the French system.

Ulhoa Coelho is pragmatic in stating that:

> Brazilian commercial law has been a part of company theory since the last quarter of the 20th century. According to Company Theory, any activity can be considered Company. Everything will depend on how it is exercised. There is no longer a list of activities considered commercial or otherwise. This theory also abandons the concept of the trader and starts to use that of the businessperson. In the 1970s, commercialist doctrine studied the Italian system of private discipline of economic activity carefully. In the 1980s, a number of judgments were guided by company theory in order to achieve fairer solutions to conflicts

61 Fábio Ulhoa COELHO, op. cit., 20–26.

of interest between businesspersons. In the early 1990s, at least three laws (Consumer Protection Code, Lease Law and Trade Registration Law) were published without any inspiration from the theory of trade acts.[62]

The authors Monteiro de Castro and Santos de Aragão add that:

> For a number of not only legal but also economic reasons, a substantial increase in Company governance studies can be identified in Brazilian Company law, especially since the late 1990s. Law 10.303 of 31 October 2001, in reforming the Law on Public Limited Companies, had the declared objective of giving greater protection to minorities and thus stimulating the development of the capital market (e.g. limitation of the issuance of preferential shares to 50% of the capital, tag-along to shareholders with voting rights for a price equivalent to 80% of the amount paid to the controlling shareholder).[63]

There is consensus that Law 10.303/2001 was fearful about the attribution of rights to minority shareholders, falling far short of what was expected in terms of introducing principles and rules of good company governance into Brazilian Company Law. The legislator's fear was offset, however, by an important initiative of the market itself, namely, the creation of São Paulo Stock Exchange in 2001 for the newly created market and other special parts of company governance.[64]

The Civil Code of 2002 concludes the transition from the French system to the Italian system by regulating in "Book II" of the Special Part in the "Law of the Company"[65]; that is to say, the Civil Code of 2002 follows the Italian orientation of the company theory, which is the subjective theory. Before the adoption of Civil Code of 2002, the company was regulated primarily by the commercial code (partnerships), by Decree No. 3.708 of January 10, 1919 (limited liability company) and by Civil Code of 1916 (civil companies for economic purposes).

The characteristics of business company as mentioned under the final and transitory provisions of the new Civil Code may be summarized as follows: (a) it is binding on businesspeople and companies, with its adaptation to the dictates of the new code until January 11, 2007, pursuant to Law No. 11.127 June 28, 2005; (b) the said deadline does not extend to modifications of constitutive acts, transformation, incorporation, demerger or split-up, pursuant to Article 2

62 Fábio Ulhoa COELHO, op. cit., 20–26.

63 Rodrigo R. Monteiro de CASTRO and Leandro Santos de ARAGÃO, *Direito Societário: Desafios Actuais* (São Paulo: Quarier Latin, 2009), 102.

64 Rodrigo R. Monteiro de CASTRO and Leandro Santos de ARAGÃO, op. cit., 102.

65 See Article 966 and following.

of the new Civil Code. 033 of the respective law; (c) the winding up and liquidation of business companies, when commenced before the entry into force of the code, comply with the provisions of the previous laws; and (d) the legal rules on trade companies, not revoked by the 2002 Civil Code (e.g., the Public Limited Company Law), continue to apply to Company companies.[66]

6.3 Basic Rules of Business Companies in Brazilian Law

6.3.1 Typicality and Classifications

An important and interesting note is made by Ricardo Negrão with regard to company types. Before the enactment of the Brazilian Civil Code in force, the company entities were regulated by three legal diplomas—"Commercial Code of 1850, Decree no. 3.708, of 10 January 1919, and Law no. 6.404, of 15 December 1976. They are currently regulated by Articles 40 to 52 and 981 to 1141 of the Civil Code of 2002."[67]

In the new legislative order, there are nine types of companies, which we will analyze below. It should be noted that, even though the Civil Code of 2002 mentions the "Public Limited Company" (Articles 1088–1089) and the "Limited Partnership by Shares" (Articles 1090–1092), these company types are regulated by Law 6404/76, and the general regime of Civil Code applies to them in the event that the general regime of Law of Joint Stock Companies proves to be having gaps.[68] The same cooperatives are governed by a special regime, which is Law No. 5764 of December 16, 1971.

The approach to be taken in this section (types of companies) will not include private limited companies, sole proprietorships, and public limited companies; they will be discussed in Section 7, where we will deal with companies in particular.

(a) Simple company—disposed and regulated under Articles 997 and 1038 of the Civil Code. The simple company is considered as the "skeleton" of company law, as many of its provisions are applied to other types of companies. As can be seen from Article 997, the incorporation of this company is by means of a contract (of a public or private nature), whose object is devoid of company conditions. Although it lacks this condition, it has guarantees of protection of its name,

66 Waldo FAZZIO JÚNIOR, op. cit., 109.
67 Ricardo NEGRÃO, op. cit.,. 262.
68 See Article 1.089, Civil Code.

since this is a distinctive element of it from other companies. It follows from the sole paragraph of Article 155 of the Civil Code that, for the purposes of its legal protection, it must use a name.

Depending on what the articles of association provide for, in matters of social responsibility, partners can or cannot be accessorily liable for the obligations contracted.[69] A systematic interpretation of the disciplinary provisions of the simple company contained in the Civil Code suggests that the liability may also be limited or unlimited; this is because Article 1024 of the said legal diploma states that *"The private assets of the partners may not be executed for debts of the company, until after the company assets have been executed."*

The combination of Articles 998 and 1151, sole paragraph 1 and 2, leads to the conclusion that the application for registration of simple companies in the Civil Registry of Legal Persons shall observe the time period of 30 days, the beginning of which is the date on which their acts of incorporation are drawn up. The registration must take into account the necessary data from the company's memorandum of association, the provisions for which are set out in Article 997 of the Civil Code.[70]

From the provisions of Article 1.003 it may be noted that the simple company is a partnership, as opposed to a capital company such as the Public Limited Company (PLC). The partners are linked by *affectio societatis*. A proof that the simple company is a partnership is how the total or partial transfer of shares are dealt with, with the consent of other partners.

(b) Holding Company—is the epigraph of Book II, Chapter II, Article 991 of the Civil Code. In this type of company, the (i) *ostensive partner predominates*, as he is an expert in the business field in which he performs all the activities inherent to it. The most frequent of these activities are the hiring of suppliers of the resources needed to run the company, hiring of labor, and supervision of company's life; (ii) *participating partner*: its function is quite reduced; its function is to inject capital into the company's structure—it is an investor. Under Article 991, however, the sole paragraph of Article 993 does not impose any obligation on third parties, provided, however, that the right to participate in the supervision of management of company's trade relations is safeguarded, and the participating partner must refrain from interfering in the relations of the ostensive

69 See paragraph VIII, Article 997, Civil Code.

70 *"The company shall be formed by means of a written contract, private or public, which, in addition to clauses stipulated by the parties, shall mention: name, nationality, marital status, profession and residence of the partners, if natural persons, and the name or Company name and registered office of the partners, if legal"*; Article 997 of Civil Code.

partner with third parties; otherwise, he will incur joint and several liabilities with the latter.

In this perspective, it is understood that the relations of the participating partner are limited to the ostensive partner, with the latter, in turn, in addition to maintaining relations with third parties through a contractual bond, subjecting himself to unlimited liability for the obligations assumed. In this type of company, the ostensive partner plays a preponderant role, since the act constituting the object of the company is exclusively performed by him in his own name (civil) and responsibility, and as a businessperson (Article 991).

It follows from Article 992 that *"The formation of the holding company is independent of any formality and can be proved by any means of law."* It is a company that waives formalities and waives the deposit of a contract reduced to writing in the Civil Registry of Legal Persons; no matter how much the ostensive partner takes the initiative to register the contract in that entity, the company does not acquire the status of a subject of law (Article 993) and therefore will not enjoy the right to the company name (Article 1162).

In bankruptcy matters, given that the ostensive partner carries on the company activity in his own name, without him the company cannot subsist, in this context, being subject to bankruptcy proceedings, and such submission will result in the winding up of the company and liquidation of the respective account, the balance of which will constitute an unsecured credit (§ 2 of Article 994). When the participating member goes bankrupt, the company may subsist in order to complete any activities in progress, which will enable the bankrupt to earn profits intended to relieve himself of the debts incurred; it is along these lines that § 3 of Article 994 establishes that in the event of the bankruptcy of the participating member, the memorandum of association (contract) shall be governed by the complex rules governing the results of the bankruptcy in the bilateral contracts of the bankrupt (participating member).

(c) General partnership—the general partnership is constituted by a contract. It has its legal provision and regulation in Articles 1039–1044 of the Portuguese Constitution. Natural or nonnatural persons are legally permitted to participate in this type of company; partners are jointly and severally liable for the obligations socially assumed (Article 1039).

As regards the liability of partners, according to the legal provision mentioned above, it may be at the external level–toward creditors, it is always unlimited and joint; at the internal level, it may be configured as limited liability, and the limitation may be made by the members in the instrument by which the company is constituted (in the very act of incorporation) or by means of a last mutual agreement that will limit between them the liability of each of them in the internal relations of the company (sole paragraph, Article 1039).

In administrative matters, the administration of the company concerned is the exclusive competence of partners, and only the partner who has the power to act on behalf of the company (name) may act within the parameters established by the contract (Article 1042). The content of the article under analysis leads us to conclude that we are dealing with a partnership *("affectio societatis")*. The combination of Articles 1041–1157 give rise to the understanding that the company name is the name that the company in question must assume.

When the disciplinary articles (1039–1044) of the general partnership prove to be lacking in a particular area, such gaps will be filled by applying the regulatory system of simple companies (Article 1040).

(d) Limited partnership—provided for and legally regulated in Articles 1045–1051 of the Civil Code.

The instrument of incorporation of this company is a contract and is therefore said to be a contractual company; such instrument includes the distinction between limited partners and unlimited partners (sole paragraph, Article 1045). The following are part of the business partnership: (i) general partners: natural persons, who have joint and unlimited liability; (ii) limited partners: natural or legal persons with limited liability, their obligation being limited to the value of their share (Article 1045). The general partnership regime is subsidiarily applied to the limited partnership with necessary adaptations (Article 1046).

Articles 1047 and 157 stipulate that the name is the nominal form to be adopted by the limited partnership. The provision of Article 1047 is of paramount importance in matters of determining liability in accordance with the conduct of the limited partner or the constancy of his civil name in the company name—*"Without prejudice to the right to participate in the company's deliberations and to supervise its operations, the commander may not perform any act of management, nor have his name on the company's name, under penalty of being subject to the responsibilities of general partner."* It is an article whose interpretation cannot ignore the sole paragraph contained therein, in the sense that it allows the commander to supervise the management of the general partners and makes room for the constitution of the latter as attorney-in-fact of the company entity, under the condition of being vested with private powers.

Without being detrimental to what is established in the memorandum of association of the limited partnership, when the legal personality of the silent partner ceases, the company entity will proceed with its operations ensured by the deceased person's successors, it being incumbent on them to indicate the natural person who will be their representative (Article 1050); in the event of the death of the silent partner, its replacement must occur within 180 days, and if such replacement does not occur the company may be dissolved.

(e) Cooperative Companies—is especially regulated by Law No. 5.764 of December 16, 1971. It has its general system in the Civil Code (Articles 1093–1096). In the wake of the sole paragraph of Article 982, it is a simple company, of persons. This understanding is reinforced by the first part of Article 4 of the Cooperative Companies Law which establishes that *"Cooperatives are person companies."*

According to Article 3 of the Cooperative Law it is possible for cooperative company legal persons to enter into a contract, obliging each other to make a contribution with goods or services intended for the development of an activity of an economic nature, of common benefit, without the purpose of making a profit. In line with the sole paragraph of Article 1155, the name is a nominal form to be used by the cooperative company.

Even if qualified as simple companies, by virtue of Article 18 Cooperative law, cooperative companies do not escape the assumption of compulsory registration to be carried out at the commercial board. And as it is a special rule, it is understood to subsist on the general system (Civil Code).

> The characteristics of cooperative companies are enshrined in both the general law (Article 1094 of the Civil Code) and the special law (Article 4 of the Cooperative law). The two systems have points of convergence with regard to the characteristics of the companies in question, but in order to avoid possible inconveniences, we will use the principle that the special law prevails over the general law; thus, we must present the characteristics on the basis of Article 4 of the special system; see *Ipsis litteris:*
>
> Article 4: Cooperatives are partnerships, with their own legal form and nature, of a civil nature, not subject to bankruptcy, set up to provide for the members, and intended for other companies by the following characteristics:
>
> I—voluntary membership, with an unlimited number of members, unless it is technically impossible to depress services;
> II—variability of the share capital represented by quotes;
> III—limitation of the number of shares of the capital by each member, allowing, however, the establishment of proportionality criteria, if this is more appropriate for the fulfilment of the Company objectives;
> IV—the inaccessibility of capital shares to third parties, outside the company;

V—singularity of voting, with the possibility for central cooperatives, federations and confederations of cooperatives, with the exception of those engaged in credit activity, to opt for the criterion of proportionality;
VI—quorum for the functioning and resolution of the General Assembly in the number of members and not of capital;
VII—return of the net surplus of the financial year, in proportion to the operations carried out by the member, unless the General Meeting decides otherwise;
VIII—indivisibility of the Reserve and Technical Educational and Social Assistance funds;
IX—political neutrality and religious, racial and social indiscrimination;
X—the provision of assistance to the members and, when provided for in the statutes, to the employees of the cooperative;
XI—area of admission of members limited to the possibilities of meeting, control, operations and rendering of services;

It is necessary to make a comparative analysis of Article 1095, paragraph 1 of the Civil Code with Article 11 of the Cooperative Companies Law; these are two legal provisions that vary in regards to the responsibility of the cooperative member. While the cooperative member is liable in a limited way under the general law, they are liable only for the value of their shares and for damages incurred in the company's activities, to the extent they participate in them; this is a form of liability that departs from the traditional criteria of limited liability, now provided for in Article 11 of the special regime, under which the member is liable only for the value of their shares. This means that the liability of the cooperative member at the level of the Civil Code, in addition to being based on the value of the member's quotes, must take into account the level of the cooperative member's participation in the activities of the company and the resulting damage.

(h) Limited partnership by shares—is a company regulated in dual systems, general regulation via Civil Code (Articles 1090–1092), and special regulation under the Law of Joint Stock Companies (Article 280 et seq.). The two systems are unanimous as regards the division of capital share; this division takes the form of shares.[71]

Both Article 282 of the special system and Article 1091 of the general system state that only the partner in shares is responsible for the administration or management of the company and, as a director or manager, is subject to subsidiary liability, in the meantime, on an unlimited and joint basis.

71 See Article 1090 of the Civil Code combined with Article 280 of the Company by Shares Act.

In the limited partnership, it is imperative that the director be a shareholder; a different situation is that in the limited partnership the director may be an individual outside the company.

As for company name, the company can choose between the use of the company name and the name. Only the names of managing partners or managers will be integral parts of the company name or denomination, and they will be jointly and severally liable for the complex of obligations assumed (Article 281 of the LJSC). The name of the director or manager to be used as the firm or denomination shall be supplemented by the expression "Share Command," an expression that may be written in full or in abbreviated form (sole section, Article 281).

The Joint Stock Company Act, even if it is considered the special regime for limited partnerships, does not apply to the whole of these companies. It is Article 284 of the LJSC that determines the inapplicability of the matters governed by it to limited partnership companies, namely: *"board of directors, statutory authorization for capital increase and issue of subscription bonds."*

(i) Joint stock company—is a new term in company law, introduced by Law No. 10.406 of January 16, 2002, replacing the term de facto or irregular company, used in the 1916 Civil Code. It has its legal discipline in Articles 986–990 of the law that introduces it. It is with this in mind that Article 986 of the said law establishes that before the obligation to register the company is fulfilled, it will be disciplined by the rules regulating the common company and in a subsidiary manner by the rules regulating the simple company.

Failure to comply with the obligation to register results in the company not being attributed the status of a legal person (legal personality) and, thus, not being independent in terms of assets. In this scenario, *"the company's assets and debts constitute special assets, of which the partners are the holders in common."*[72] The partners involved in the company shall be jointly and severally liable for the complex of obligations contracted, being exempt from the *"benefit of order,"* as the partner in charge of contracting for the company (Article 990).

In the first stage, the assets destined to the company will be executed; if these prove to be incapable of meeting the obligations, the execution will be extended to the private assets of each of the partners. Only the partner who has entered into a contract on behalf of the company may not invoke Article 1024 of the Civil Code, in order to make use of the "order benefit," or, in other words, the partner who has entered into obligations on behalf of the company is exempt from the

72 See Article 998, Civil Code.

guarantee of demanding that the assets assigned to the company be enforced first and, if insufficient, then the private assets of each of the partners will be utilized.

Having seen the company types, we can now talk about the classification of companies. There are several criteria used in Brazilian doctrine for the classification of business companies, and the criteria vary according to the perception of each author. Fábio Ulhoa Coelho[73] uses three criteria, namely: (1) *"the classification of companies according to the responsibility of the partners for the social obligations"; * (2) *"the classification as to the regime of constitution and dissolution";* and (3) *"the classification as to the conditions for disposal of the Company interest."* Rubens Requião[74] presents four criteria: (i) liability of partners; (ii) personification; (iii) form of capital; and (iv) regime of constitution and dissolution. Ricardo Negrão[75] mentions criteria based on the new Civil Code.

We are interested here in making a classification that in a certain way tries to cover the criteria presented by the authors mentioned above, and such classification will use the following roadmap: (1) according to the object of the company; (2) according to the responsibility of partners; (3) according to the personal characteristics of partners; and (4) according to the constitutive act.

(1) **According to the company's object**: It has to do with the activity carried out by the company[76]:
   (i) *Simple companies* are those that, although they engage in economic activity, do not develop the proper object of business companies.
   (ii) *Business Companies* are those that conveniently predispose the resources necessary to sustain an economic activity aimed at producing or circulating goods or services. Under Article 982 of the Civil Code, they must be subject to registration.

(2) **According to partners' responsibility**: When approaching some criteria, we must take into account that the company is financially autonomous from its partners. Due to this autonomy, as a rule, partners are not liable for the complex of obligations assumed by the company entity.
   Solvency is a state in which a given subject of law has a sufficient patrimonial reserve to satisfy the bond complex to which he is attached. The individual patrimonial sphere of each partner cannot be used to account

73 Fábio Ulhoa COELHO, *Manual de Direito Comercial: Direito de Empresa*, 23ª ed. (São Paulo: Saraiva, 2011), 141.

74 Rubens REQUIÃO, *Curso de Direito Comercial,* 23ª ed. (São Paulo: Saraiva, 1998), 333.

75 Ricardo NEGRÃO, op. cit., 272–281.

76 See Article 982, Civil Code.

for the social debts. In a bankruptcy situation, only after the capital of the company has been completely exhausted can one think of the singular liability of partners.[77] The liability of partners for the complex of obligations contracted by the company entity is of a subsidiary nature.[78] This criterion is used for categorizing the companies as follows:

- (i) Company entities with unlimited liability—they are companies in which the partners' unique complex of assets are called to account for the company's bond complex, and the partners are the guarantor of the company. This is the case of general partnership companies.
- (ii) Limited liability company entities—in this case, each of the partners is called to account for the value of their quotas, but all of them will be jointly and severally liable for the payment of the company capital.
- (iii) Mixed-company entities—the company liability in this type of company is viewed from a two-way perspective; some partners are limited in their liability, and others are unlimitedly liable for the obligations contracted by the company entity (seen as a subject of law), when their company capital is not enough to meet the debts taken from those who have a credit right before the company. An example of a mixed-company entity is the capital and industrial company, where two types of partners can be found: the capitalist partner who comes in with the company capital and is unlimitedly liable for the bond complex contracted by the company, and the industrial partner who comes in with their labor skills or knowhow and not with the company capital and, therefore, is not liable for the bond complex assumed by the company. We can also give the example of the case of limited partnerships and joint-stock partnerships.

(3) According to the personal characteristics of partners:

- (i) Partnership—this type of partnership is regulated in the mutual trust between partners and for this reason it is called *"affectio societatis."* The partners know each other very well, and this is one of the factors that lead to the incorporation of the company; hence, the entry or withdrawal of a member is conditional upon the consent

77 Fábio Ulhoa COELHO, *Manual de Direito Comercial: Direito de Empresa*, 23ª ed. (São Paulo: Saraiva, 2011), 142.

78 See Article 1.024 together with Article 990 of the Civil Code.

of other partners. The nonadherence to such consent, which results in the exit or entry of a new member in the company, will put into question the trust of partners and may lead to a partial or total dissolution of the company. Some examples for such a scenario include **general partnership and limited partnership**.

(ii) Capital company—while in a partnership the trust between partners is counted because they know each other very well, in a partnership it is not preponderant that partners know each other. The capital stock of shareholder is more important than the partner itself; hence, the exit from or entry of one or more members into the company does not necessarily imply the modification of contract (or its memorandum of association). The partner may enter or withdraw from the company by buying or selling shares without the consent of other partners. Examples of companies in this context include: **public limited company and limited partnership by shares.**

Regarding this classification criterion, Ricardo Negrão,[79] quoting Spencer Vampré, considers that "Regarding the greater or lesser importance of affectio societatis in the life of the company. Companies with share capital and persons are distinguished by the criterion of transmissibility of the rights and obligations of each partner, allowing any individual to acquire a share of rights in the company, or to withdraw from it at will. Partnerships do not have the latter characteristic, and, in addition, all partners have no limited liability, except the limited liability for quotes."

(4) **In accordance with the memorandum of association**—this criterion is linked to the types of companies previously seen; thus, what must be retained here is that, of all the company types, some have legal personality and others do not; it is in this perspective that according to that criterion we can find two types of companies: (i) non-personalized companies (governed by Articles 986–996 of the 2002 Civil Code)—the lack of registration does not confer legal personality on them; and (ii) personalized companies (governed by Articles 997–1101)—the registration of their memorandum of association with the competent entity confers legal personality on them.[80]

79 Spencer VAMPRÉ, *Tratado Elementar de Direito Comercial, apud* Ricardo NEGRÃO, *Manual de Direito Comercial e de empresa*, Vol. 1, 7ª ed. (São Paulo: Saraiva, 2010), 273.

80 Ricardo NEGRÃO, op. cit., 273.

6.3.2 General Principles

The matter of business companies must comply with certain principles. Waldo Fazzio Júnior determines two categories of principles—patent and latent. Patent principles are considered crucial as they give rise to other principles.[81]

Patent principles are divided into two types:

(i) Plurality partners principle—the articles of association are an agreement of wills distinct from others in their nature since their purpose is to create a subject of law. The legal person created is intended for the exercise of the business. The assumption of the existence of the company body is an agreement of wills between natural persons motivated by obtaining profit through the exercise of the company (an economic body geared to producing or circulating goods or services).

The multilateral essence of the articles of association must not be confused with the number of participants; it refers to the probability of an undetermined number of parties participating in them. The hypothesis of reducing the number of partners to 2 does not corrupt the essence of the articles of association. In this regard, Cláudia Ribeiro and Priscilla Menezes[82] believe that the formation of articles of association requires the convergence of interests of at least two persons.

The principle of plurality of partners has certain exceptions[83]:

(i) *"The company may be constituted by means of a public deed, with the sole shareholder being a Brazilian company"*—Article 251 of the LSA. This is a wholly owned subsidiary company, which falls within the universe of public limited liability companies and is composed of only one partner. Its unipersonal character is original and uninterrupted.
(ii) The second exception may be identified in Article 37, item XIX of the Constitution of the Federative Republic of Brazil.[84] It is also

81 Waldo FAZZIO JÚNIOR, op. cit., 110.
82 Cláudia RIBEIRO and Priscila MENEZES, op. cit., 21.
83 Id.
84 This is its wording, *"The direct or indirect Public Administration of any of the Powers of the Union, the States, the Federal District and the Municipalities will obey the principles of legality, impersonality, morality, publicity and efficiency and also the following: (Editing given by the Constitutional Amendment No. 19, of 1998). Subparagraph XIX: Only by specific law may an autarchy be created and the institution of a public company, of a mixed economic company and of a foundation be authorized, being the complementary law, in the latter case, responsible for defining areas of its action."*

composed of only one partner: the federative entity that originated it *("Union, State or Municipality").* Holder of an original and constant one-person condition.

(iii) In the shortage of plurality of partners, the company entity remains for a period of 180 days (subsection IV, Article 1.033 of the Civil Code). This is a shortage after the incorporation of the company and, therefore, ephemeral.

(ii) **Principle of Legal Personality**—the filing of the memorandum of association of the company with the competent entity incurs its patrimonial autonomy in relation to the natural persons who originated it, thus becoming a center of imputation of rights and obligations. The registration of the company with the Board of Trade conditions its status as a subject of law (legal personality).[85] When the obligation to register is met, the company becomes independent.

Latent principles. They are guiding principles and exist in a latent form in the legislative context, continuously based on doctrine and accepted by jurisprudence, as parameters for the interpretation and updating of the rules governing business activity:

(i) **The durability of the economic organism**—it refers to the conservation of the company as an economic organism that produces and/or promotes the circulation of goods and/or services to satisfy the interests of human societies. It is a determining principle of the introduction in the legal field of a complex of norms inclined to give priority to the subsistence of the commercial company, accompanied by the intention placed on a higher level in relation to the singular objectives of its members (e.g., complex of norms that deal with the partial dissolution of the company).

(ii) **Contractual freedom / autonomy of will**—the parties materialize their agreement of wills by means of an instrument legally called a contract. In the context of the materialization of such an agreement, they are free to choose the type of company that will serve as a basis for the exploitation of the economic activity they seek, within their capacities and expectations. Their freedom of choice also extends to the modification of the contract that has given life to the company, without detriment to the subsistence of the economic

85 See Articles 45 and 985, Civil Code.

body. Freedom of contract must be exercised taking into account the block of legality so that it does not conflict with it.

(iii) **Legality**—the constitution of the company, its vicissitudes, and its extinction must be through acts that are in conformity with the block of legality or *secundum legem*. It has constitutional consecration in Article 170, Title VII—*"Of the economic and financial order"*; Chapter I—*"Of the general principles of economic activity." "The economic order, based on the valorization of human labour and free initiative, aims at ensuring a dignified existence for all, in accordance with the dictates of social justice, observing the following principles: II—private property; III—social function of property; IV—free competition; V—consumer protection; VIII—pursuit of full employment; IX—favorable treatment for Brazilian companies with small national capital.* Single paragraph. *Everyone is assured the free exercise of any economic activity, regardless of authorization from public bodies, except in the cases provided for by law."*

6.3.3 Collective Legal Personality

It is important to consider the classic division of branches of law, which is intended to be between public law and private law. We are interested in the private branch of the law, since it is in it that the company entities that are the object of our study fall. The Civil Code lists the legal entities considered to be under the purview of private law, and the company does not escape such cataloguing (item II, Article 44).

The legal personality is the result of the registration of the legal instrument that gives life to the company.[86] It is an instrument that can change the form of a contract or statute, and only after it has been filed in the *"Public Register of Business Companies and Related Activities"* does it gain the status of a center of imputation of rights and obligations.

From the moment the company becomes able to exercise its rights and assume obligations itself, it can no longer be confused with the individual personality of each of its partners. As a result, it is necessary to differentiate between the company's assets and the individual assets of partners who make up the legal person; the company gains its own sphere of ownership and becomes responsible for the

86 See Articles 45 and 985, Civil Code.

debts incurred in its own name, in accordance with the form of liability to which it is subject.[87]

The ability to act as a subject of law in the business field, has the corollary of legal personality, which leads to a multiplicity of inferences, from which it is possible to highlight[88]:

(i) *The agent holding its legal business relations*—the exercise of the business activity implies the signing of labor contracts with third parties (to be employees of the company) and the signing of contracts for the purchase of resources necessary for the production of goods and/or services that will be followed by the signing of sales accounts for the respective goods and/or services produced; even if these are business acts carried out through one of the partners legally representing the company, it is on the sphere of the company that the consequences resulting from such acts fall.

(ii) *Procedural capacity*—it is precisely because it is the owner of its legal business relationships that it takes on rights and engages in complex obligations in its negotiations with third parties. In this context, the state guarantees companies' access to the courts against acts that violate their rights, and, in this way, it can give a procedural boost to the restoration of their rights. In the same way that a company can give a procedural impetus for the restoration of its rights, third parties, whether company entities or not, can also do so when it is the company that infringes their rights. The legal representation of the company by one of the partners does not amount to a legal action to be taken against him, but rather against the company, and only the natural person (partner) who authorizes the judicial mandate will be cited.

Disregard of the general ability to assume rights and obligations. In doctrine, this disfigurement is called "disregard of legal entity" or *"teoria da desconsideração da personalidade jurídica."* Within the private branch of the law, legal persons are legally autonomous from the natural persons (partners) who gave rise to it. In some eventualities, partners may use the legal autonomy of the legal

87 Waldo FAZZIO JÚNIOR, op. cit., 110.

88 Fábio Ulhoa COELHO, *Manual de Direito Comercial: Direito de Empresa*, 23ª ed. (São Paulo: Saraiva, 2011), 140.

person (company entity) for the realization of manifestly illegal aspirations, such as the enrichment in question.[89]

The understanding that the attribution of legal personality to company entities should not be seen as a means to sustain unjust enrichment is predominating. The legal system, based on case law, the Civil Code, and the Consumer Code, considers any misuse of the legal personality or the company object of the legal person in favor of partners to be reprehensible. The power conferred on the interpreter and enforcer of the law to disregard the legal personality of the legal person for the purpose of holding the partner or director who uses the autonomy of the company as a shield to get rid of possible obligations or to accumulate wealth without cause is a guarantee of that reprehensibility.[90]

The fraudulent use of the company entity is a presupposition for the implementation of the theory of the disfigurement of the legal personality; there is a tendency to abandon that presupposition, because there are cases in which the application of that theory was verified without establishing that a fraudulent behavior was demonstrated by the legal persons. A paradigmatic case is the *"Osasco Plaza Shopping of 1996"* case, around which a judgment was issued ordering the disfigurement of the personality of this company entity on the grounds that it would constitute an obstacle to compensating consumers for the losses incurred.[91] The main effect of the disfigurement is that the complex of obligations for which the company was to be held liable will become the responsibility of the partners considered individually.

In the Brazilian legal system, there are four predictions of the theory of the disregard of personality, which we now develop as follows[92]:

(i) In Law No. 8.078 of September 11, 1990 (Consumer Protection Code), *"The Judge may disregard the legal personality of the company when, to the detriment of the consumer, there has been an abuse of rights, excess of power, violation of the law, fact or illicit act, or violation of the articles of association. The disregard will also be effective when there is bankruptcy, state of insolvency, closure or inactivity of the legal entity caused by*

89 Luiz António Barroso RODRIGUEZ, op. cit., 62.

90 Miguel REALE, *Lições Preliminares de Direito, apud* Luiz António Barroso RODRIGUES, *Direito Empresarial,* 3ª ed. Rev.actual–Florianópolis: Departamento de Ciências da Administração/ UFSC [Brasília] (CAPES: UAB, 2016), 63.

91 Maria Eugênia FINKELSTEIN, *Direito Empresarial apud* Luiz António Barroso RODRIGUES, *Direito Empresarial,* 3ª ed. Rev.actual–Florianópolis: Departamento de Ciências da Administração/ UFSC [Brasília] (CAPES: UAB, 2016), 64.

92 Cláudia RIBEIRO and Priscila MENEZES, op. cit.,. 22.

mismanagement" (Article 28). *"The legal entity may also be disregarded whenever its personality is in any way an obstacle to the compensation of damages caused to consumers"* (§ 5, Article 28). This is a form of disfigurement provided for in the context of consumer rights.

(ii) On environmental crime—Article. 4, Law No. 9605 of February 12, 1998 (Environmental Crimes Law), "The legal person may be disregarded whenever the personality is an obstacle to compensation for damage to the quality of the environment."

(iii) Article 34, Law No. 12 529 of November 30, 2011 (Antitrust Law) states as follows: "The legal personality of the person responsible for the infringement of the economic order may be disregarded when there is on the part of this abuse of rights, excess of power, infringement of the law, fact or unlawful act, or violation of the articles of association or articles of association."

(iv) Article 50 of the Civil Code—in the context of civil law, the abusive use of legal personality, which is characterized by the practice of acts that are not in accordance with the company object of the company or by *"confusion of assets,"* is presupposed for the implementation of the theory of the disfigurement of legal personality. The judge has the power to issue a decision of lack of characterization and is entitled to request it from private individuals if there is a well-founded motive or from the Public Prosecution Service.

Inverse Legal Personality Disregard. While in the mischaracterization itself, the primary objective is to make partners answer for the obligations that in principle should be fulfilled by the company; in the inverted personality mischaracterization, as the expression itself suggests, the process is reversed, and the company is called to respond by the complex of obligations that in principle would be up to the partners to fulfill. The investment is a mechanism for the recovery of private assets of partners which have been hidden by them within the patrimonial sphere of the company, in order to avoid the fulfillment of certain obligations to which they are attached.

Around the inverted characterization, as a mechanism for recovering the private assets of partners, Fabio Ulhoa Coelho, postulates that *"the inverted disregard especially supports family rights. In the dissolution of the marriage or stable union bond, the sharing of common assets may be defrauded. If one of the spouses or partners, when acquiring goods of greater value, registers them in the name of the legal entity under their control, they do not formally integrate the share to be shared.*

By disregarding the patrimonial autonomy, it will be possible to hold the legal entity responsible for the ex-spouse or ex-partner of the partner, associate or institute."[93]

6.3.4 Legal Capacity

We have focused on the fact that the legal capacity to be studied in this section relates to legal persons. Legal persons, as opposed to natural persons who are natural or human, are those created by law on the initiative of natural persons who wish to develop a larger economic activity.

As a subject of law, the legal person is entitled to hold rights and mandatory complexes. It is a legal fiction of the natural person, being able, therefore, to carry out business acts, from the conclusion of purchase and sale contracts, loan contract, leases agreement, among other business modalities. It is precisely because the legal person is a fictitious person who has limitations in the scope of civil relations, and although he is seen as a subject of law, there are certain acts that they are limited to perform; because they are closely linked to the natural person or human, it is the case of the establishment of a conjugal relationship or a kinship relationship or other gender-based relationship.[94]

Legal capacity is a consequence of legal personality, and this in turn is acquired by filing the constitutive act of the company in the competent entity for this purpose; it is an extensive capacity for all legal areas, and it must be stressed, with due limitations. The exercise of its subjective rights is not restricted to patrimonial relations. The whole of the company, as well as the natural person, is entitled to the name, the domicile, the legal bond that links him to a certain state (nationality), hence the designations national companies and foreign companies.[95]

Under Article 52 of the current Civil Code, "*It applies to legal entities, as appropriate, the protection of the rights of the personality.*" The expression included in the transcribed article—"*as appropriate*"—has the following meaning and scope; the legal person enjoys certain personality rights (and their respective protection) inherent to natural persons, but not all in their universality, since it lacks the standard of human nature (Articles 11–21).

93 Fábio Ulhoa COELHO, *Curso de Direito Comercial: Direito de Empresa*; op. cit., 73–74.
94 Fábio Ulhoa COELHO, *Curso de Direito Civil.* Parte Geral, Vol. 1 5ª ed. (Editora Saraiva, 2012), 152.
95 Id.

To justify what is explained above, let us take as an example "The Superior Court of Justice (STJ), REsp 1032014 RS 2008 / 0033686-0, which deals with trademark infringement, one of the aspects that constitute legal personality"[96]:

> STJ—Special Appeal REsp 1032014 RS 2008/0033686-0; Publication Date: 06/04/2009 Menu: Corporate Law. Brand counterfeiting. Counterfeit product whose quality, compared to the original, could not be verified by the Court of Justice. Violation of the brand that affects the identity of the supplier. Personality Right of legal entities. Recognized moral damage.—Moral damage corresponds, in the Brazilian legal system, to injury to the right to personality, that is, to assets that are not susceptible to monetary evaluation.—In counterfeiting, the consumer is deceived and finds his faculty of choice subtracted. The consumer cannot find out who supplies him with the product and, as a consequence, the manufacturer cannot be identified by a good part of his target audience. Thus, counterfeiting is a real usurpation of part of the manufacturer's identity. The counterfeiter creates confusion of products and, in this step, pretends to be the legitimate manufacturer of goods that circulate in the market.—Certain personality rights are extended to legal entities, under the terms of article 52 of the Civil Code, among which is the identity.—Moral damages are compensated for by the manufacturer whose identity rights were harmed by the counterfeiting of its products. Special feature provided. (STJ—Special Appeal 1032014 RS 2008/0033686-0; Publication Date: 06/04/2009).

From the juridical understanding of the personality emerges the idea of the legal capacity that is equivalent to the faculty of exercising rights related to the human person.

In the Civil Code system, there is no definition of legal capacity, this term being an object of study at the level of doctrine. Interesting is the approach brought to us by the Portuguese Commercial Companies Code.

According to Maria Carvalho[97] and Sónia Moreira, the capacity of a company, in harmony with the provisions of paragraph 1, Article 6, of the aforementioned legal diploma, *"comprises the rights and obligations necessary or convenient for the pursuit of its purpose, except those that are prohibited by law or are inseparable from the singular personality."*[98]

96 Itálo Miqueias da Silva Alves. *A Personalidade Jurídica no Direito Civil*, available at https://jus.com.br/artigos/61828/a-personalidade-juridica-no-direito-civil, accessed on Jully 5, 2019.

97 Maria Miguel CARVALHO and Sónia MOREIRA, *Das Sociedades Comerciais (Capítulo I) Sumários desenvolvidos das aulas de Direito para Economia e Gestão* (Universidade do Minho: Escola de Direito, 2013), 94.

98 A typical example of singular personality rights are family rights based on marriage or adoption.

Thus, the corporate entity is incapable with respect to the practice of acts that are legally prohibited. Take as an example the prohibition resulting from Article 1487 and subsection of the Portuguese Civil Code—right of "Use and Housing," and a second example, in which the company cannot perform acts that are inseparable from the singular personality—receipt of "Public deposit"—Article 8, General Regime of Credit Institutions and Financial Companies.[99]

It is a fact that the ultimate purpose of the corporate entity is the acquisition of profit and its respective distribution among partners. In this logic, by virtue of paragraph 1, Article 6, Commercial Companies Code in conjunction with Article 294, Civil Code, the acts whose essence is distant from the profitable purpose or the corporate object are null and void.

If, by hypothesis, a corporate entity, through the representative partner or its representative body, comes to perform acts incompatible with the corporate purpose or for profit, surely they will be affected by the defect of nullity, and such defect can be evoked at all times for any interested[100] party—for partners and for those who have the right to credit before the company—or even the judge can unofficially issue a declaration of nullity of those acts, in line with the Portuguese Civil Code (Article 266).

The company bodies do not physically exist and therefore acts are represented by their organic structure in accordance with the corporate modality they cover. Under Article 252, No. 6 in conjunction with No. 7, Article 391, both of the Commercial Companies Code, within the respective structure, some bodies have the competence to name the agents to represent the corporate body in which they are inserted; they may also delegate their powers, pursuant to paragraph 2 of Article 261 in conjunction with paragraph 2, Article 408 of the same code.

In the above context, it is imperative to ask the extent to which the corporate entity should be linked to the acts performed by those who represent it.

In order for the company to be linked to them, it is necessary that they are exercised by their representatives, and third parties have not only the probability[101] but also the obligation to delineate whether the one who acts as a representative of the corporate entity really does so within their competences and assignments. And anyone who acts as a representative of the company has the obligation to demonstrate under what circumstances the respective action is continuing. It is in

99 Maria Miguel CARVALHO and MOREIRA, op. cit., 95.

100 Cf. No. 2, Article 6, Code of Commercial Companies combined with Article 294 of the Civil Code (of Portugal).

101 See Article 166 and following of the Commercial Companies Code.

this context that the Supreme Court of Justice issued a Uniformizing Judgment of Jurisprudence (No. 1/2002), in the *Diário da República,*[102] I Series-A, dated January 24, 2002, from which it follows that: "*the indication of quality manager prescribed in paragraph 4 of article 260 of the Commercial Companies Code may be deducted, under art. 217 of the Civil Code, from facts that, in all probability, reveal it.*"[103]

Much can be said about the legal capacity of social corporate bodies at the level of the Portuguese legal system, but we believe that what has already been said is quite evident.

Let us therefore return to legal capacity at the level of Brazilian law. In this regard, Mariane Portella Garcia points out that when the birth of the legal person occurs, the company acquires full ability to execute rights and contract obligations as one of its main effects. Certainly, this action will be faced with legal and conventional delimitations, the latter being imposed by the will of partners, as established in the constitutive act of the company.[104]

These limitations, especially those imposed by law, presuppose the company's activity in line with the purposes for which it was created. Therefore, since the action of the legal entity is outside the objectives preestablished by law or by partners, it is clear that this action should not even be considered as taken by the legal entity, as there was no provision for such action.

The cited author states that this justification is provided by the theory of ultra vires acts, which states that the act practiced by administrators will be characterized by the abuse of power when there is such abuse in relation to the purposes for which the legal entity was created, that is, when it is an action outside the objectives set by the company in its constitutive act. Thus, there will be no connection between the company and the act performed by the administrator outside the scope of the legal entity. Such a rule is implicitly provided for in the Civil Code (Article 47), which provides that the legal entity is only bound to those acts of its administrators practiced within the limits of powers defined by law or in the constitutive act of the company, which, *in Iiteris*, "*oblige[s] the person the acts of the administrators, exercised within the limits of their powers defined in the constitutive act.*"[105]

102 Official Gazette.

103 Maria Miguel CARVALHO and MOREIRA, op. cit., 97.

104 Mariane Portella GARCIA, *Administração da Sociedade Anônima e suas relações jurídicas* (Curitiba, 2005), 12.

105 Id.

It is interesting, in this context, to highlight the theory originating in the English and North American commercial law of the Disregard of Legal Entity, which defines the possibilities of disregarding the legal personality for acts performed by any of its partners, not just by the administrator—which gives rise to their personal accountability, due to the theory of *ultra vires acts*.

Assis Gonçalves, quoted by Mariane Portella Garcia, states that "*The simple practice of an illegal act by the legal entity has nothing to do with the theory of disregard. If the person acts within the purposes for which he was established, but practices an illegal act (he sells goods he does not own, for example), he must respond normally for this act, like any agent who does so. In order to the Disregard of Legal Entity theory to be applied, there must be a deviation from its economic and social function, that is, from the cause of its birth, from the role that the legal entity must fulfill and that justified its creation to act similarly to a natural person.*"[106]

Therefore, there is a need to produce reprehensible effects by the legal system. An example is the case of a shareholder who uses corporate assets to collect goods for personal use, which, in the event of possible payment by the company, which obviously will have the right of return against the partner, has no relation to mischaracterization of the legal entity. However, if the company does not have enough capital to settle the debt effected in its name, it has to be said that, in addition to deviating from the economic and social function for which it was created, there will be repercussions on the company, that is, in relation to the third party you hired with the partner. In this case, the application of the disregard theory will obviously fit, so that only the partner should be held responsible for the contracted obligation.

6.4 Constitution of Business Companies: Articles of Association

The Civil Code determines that the company is constituted by means of a contract reduced to writing, whether of a public or private nature. There is a certain margin of freedom with respect to the elements to be included in the contract, through contractual clauses. Other elements are negative integration; they are the nominal element (company name), domicile, share capital, shares of each partner, corporate purpose, form of administration, term of existence, and liquidation process (Article 997). After the contract is drafted (the corporate entity's

106 ASSIS GONÇALVES, *Lições de Direito Societário*; *Apud*, Mariane Portella GARCIA, *Administração da Sociedade Anónima e suas relações jurídicas* (Curitiba, 2005), 13.

constitutive act), it must be registered with the Commercial Registry or Legal Entities Registry Office within 30 days to acquire legal personality.[107]

The consecration that determines the constitution of the company through the contract is reinforced in the doctrine (Contractual Theory[108]—merit of Tullio Ascarelli) leads to the revitalization of the contractual theory by demonstrating the existence of plurilateral contracts, where several parties coexist and are directed toward a common objective, being that such constitutive acts are characterized as organization contracts, presenting an instrumental function, "not ending with the fulfillment of the basic obligations of the parties, but rather constituting the premise of a further activity." The doctrine of the plurilateral contract is today the majority doctrine.[109]

6.4.1 Form and Nature

Ricardo Negrão defends that the majority of business companies are constituted by written contract, with clauses established by partners, and such companies are called contractual, and in this category the following corporate types are inserted: Joint Partnership, Shareholding Account, Collective Name, Simple Partnership, Capital and Industry, and Limited Partnership.[110]

Classical scholars were of the understanding that the current conception of the business company derives from the conceptual framework of the company, integrated in the Civil Code of 1916 (Law No. 3,071 of January 1, 1916). Under Article 1,363 of the aforementioned legal diploma, it was enshrined that "*Articles of association are celebrated by people who mutually obligate themselves to combine their efforts or resources in order to achieve common ends.*" Therefore, the current Civil Code, limited itself to adding to that concept, the term "*of a commercial nature,*" and thus arriving at the concept of business company.[111]

The Civil Code in force provides in its Article 981 that "*The articles of association are signed by people who reciprocally undertake to contribute, with goods or services, to the exercise of economic activity and the sharing, among themselves, of the results.*" In view of this provision, Fazzio Junior[112] states that this rule in itself is

107 Period set under § 1 of Article 1,151 of the Civil Code.

108 In addition to this theory, there are several others, such as Anticontractualist Theory, Corporate Act Theory, Act of Foundation or Act of Union and Institutional Theory; we believe it is not pertinent to discuss them here.

109 Cláudia RIBEIRO and Priscila MENEZES, op. cit.,. 15.

110 Ricardo NEGRÃO, op. cit., 319.

111 Waldo FAZZIO JÚNIOR, op. cit., 120.

112 Id.

insufficient to be seen as a concept of company contour, since it makes a suggestion that natural persons bring together factors of production and give rise to a corporate entity in order to exercise the company. Perhaps that was one of the reasons that led the Commercial Code to demand that a part of the partners had to qualify as subjects of commerce (traders) and that their commercial activity had to be carried out through a social firm, in the "pre-legal personality" stage. In the current system of Civil Code, this is no longer the case.

It becomes necessary, in that context, to delimit a base of differences. In the foreground, the combination of factors of production by partners is not necessarily focused on the exercise of organized economic activity, but its focus when entering into a partnership agreement is to bring into existence a legal or legal person, so that this, by itself, can exercise the company. It is, therefore, a contract that gives rise to a business entity—the company. In this act of signing the contract, the company is not yet legally constituted. Its creation is in fact and not in law.

The company acquires effective legal personality when its creative instrument is registered or filed with the Civil Registry or the Public Registry of Mercantile Companies. The registration of contract is a crucial condition for the legal existence of the business company. The nonobservance of the principle of mandatory registration of the constitutive act of the company means that the contract is seen as a simple agreement between the parties, which does not give the desired corporate entity the quality of a subject of rights, much less than obligations. Classifying itself this time as an irregular company.

In this context, we understand that it is said to be an effective legal personality because the lack of registration of the instrument creating the company in the competent entity incurs the nonpersonification of the same and its consequent legal inexistence. Keep in mind that a company in these conditions, when carrying out business acts, does so in its supposed capacity as a legal entity, and in this scenario, all assume obligations toward third parties, and certainly it will not be able to invoke its legal inexistence to avoid fulfilling the complex of mandatory obligations. It will be called upon to answer for them, as if it had legal existence. Failure to adopt this solution would put the rights of third parties in danger (in good faith) who maintain legal relations with the irregular company.

The law itself states that "The legal existence of legal entities under private law begins with the inclusion of the constitutive act in the respective registry, preceded, when necessary, by authorization or approval by the Executive Branch, with all changes made to the constitutive act recorded in the registry" (Article 45 of the Civil Code). Analyzing the article in question, Waldo Fazzio Júnior posits that the social contract simply declares the *animus societtatis* (simple will or intention to form a company). In actual terms, the incorporation of company takes place by registering the social contract in the Public Registry of Mercantile Companies.[113]

The company contract form. The entire legal business takes a certain form; therefore, there is no legal business stripped of form. If stripped of the form, the legal business will be like a simple legal consideration without relevance or it does not become known and, therefore, not capable of producing any legal result. The form consists of a middle ground for externalizing the will of the parties to a legal business, and the parties are assisted by the right to freely choose the means they deem convenient for the exteriorization of their negotiating will. On the other hand, in some businesses, the parties are not assisted by free choice of form.[114]

Under Article 302 of the Commercial Code, corporate entities, as a general rule, are constituted by a written contract, either public or private, and, as can be seen, the constitution of business company requires the observance of a formal requirement.

Like the previous system, the current business regime was chosen, as it requires a solemn, written and plural form, and, if the contracting parties prefer, formalization may be in public or private writing. Thus, for the constitution of companies, the law requires a written contract or statutes and its registration with the Civil Registry of Legal Entities where the company is located, depending on whether it is a simple company or a business company (Article 1150 of the Civil Code and Article 53 of the No. 8,934/94).

Nature of the articles of association. Based on what was previously said, it is appropriate to affirm that the company "is a legal business of a contractual nature, it is formed by the contest of coincident wishes of at least two people." This concerns the plurality of parties as a characteristic of articles of association. The plurality of parties to the articles of association is necessary both in their formation and during their existence. Paragraph IV of Article 1.033 of the Civil Code, when regulating the simple partnership, establishes that the partnership may be dissolved due to a lack of multiple partners, if not covered within the 180-day period.[115]

The general rule says that the constitution of the business company has as one of the fundamental assumptions the plurality of partners; it is a presumption

113 Waldo FAZZIO JÚNIOR, op. cit., 123.

114 Ricardo NEGRÃO, op. cit., 325.

115 Alfredo BULHÕES PEDREIRA and LAMY FILHO, op. cit., 25.

that knows a deviation from the rule, in the sense that in some legal situations the "contract" is allowed and the partnership is celebrated by only one party, thus having a nature of unilateralism.[116]

The Brazilian Corporate Law (Article 251) mentions and regulates the formation of a wholly owned subsidiary (composed of only one partner). As much as it revises the facet of the company, the Subsidiary Integral is primarily formed by a unilateral legal business and is transformed into a contract by the supervening adherence of new partners or shareholders. In the past, new members or shareholders joined the corporate entity in question, which contains only one shareholder and the administration (made up of administrators) and the company is equated by the rule of law.[117]

6.4.2 Content

The company becomes legally existing by means of a constitutive act, that is, the contract, which is filed with the competent entity. The drafting of the social contract is an effective mechanism that reflects all the expectations and wishes of the contracting parties (partners). It is during the stage of drafting the contract that the partners examine what matters should be included in the contract (to be framed by means of contractual clauses) and how to best discipline the corporate relationship.

In this regard, Fábio Ulhoa Coelho[118] maintains that the constitutive act of the corporate entity does not dispense with the provision of disciplinary rules for corporate relations. Whatever the matter regarding partners and the corporate entity it is likely to become the subject of an agreement of interests between partners of the company. Of course, not all matters relating to the life of the company may be foreseen and disciplined as a whole, and therefore the parties may seek to include in the contract any matter of their interest, as long as it is not illegal .

The contractual clauses can be of two modalities—essential ones (without these the contract cannot be registered or filed in the Public Register of Mercantile Activities) and indispensable ones.

The indispensable character of a particular group of contractual clauses derives from the law, *in litters*:

116 For further development of this subject, we recommend consulting the general principles of partnership contracts previously seen, in particular the principle of plurality of members.

117 Alfredo BULHÕES PEDREIRA and LAMY FILHO, op. cit., 25.

118 Fábio Ulhoa COELHO, op. cit., 160.

> The company is constituted by written contract, private or public, which, in addition to clauses stipulated by the parties, will mention: (I) name, nationality, state civil, profession and residence of the partners, if natural persons, and the firm or denomination, nationality and headquarters of the partners, if legal; (II) company name, object, headquarters and term; (III) capital of the company, expressed in current currency, being able to include any kind of assets, susceptible to financial evaluation; (IV) the share of each partner in the share capital, and the manner of realizing it; (V) the installments required by the partner, whose contribution consists of services; (VI) the natural persons charged with the administration of the company, and their powers and duties; (VII) the share of each partner in profits and losses; (VIII) if the partners are responsible, or not, in the alternative, for social obligations.[119]

These are extremely important clauses, both in the corporate relations between partners and in their relations with third parties; in short, for the legal security itself. It is in this logic that any abstracted agreement, incompatible with the content of the contract, is not liable to produce any effect whatsoever (sole paragraph, Article 997, Civil Code).

Unnecessary clauses, especially those that do not prevent the filing of the social contract with the registration body and specified by the contracting parties, regulate numerous situations of social life. Some examples of essential clauses are as follows[120]: (i) item I, Article 1.028 of the Civil Code, referring to the provision of nonliquidation and the way of replacing a deceased partner; (ii) pursuant to Article 1.035, "The contract may provide for other causes of dissolution, to be verified by court when challenged." In this case, these are dissolution clauses not provided for by law; (iii) pursuant to Article 1.050 of the Civil Code, "In the event of the death of a limited partner, the company, unless otherwise specified in the contract, will continue with its successors, who will designate who represents them." As can be seen, this nonessential clause consists of the provision on the continuation or noncontinuation of the partnership with the heirs of a partner who died; (iv) the constitutive instrument of the company has the power to provide for the subsidiary discipline of the limited company, using the rules of the limited company (sole paragraph, Article 1.053, Civil Code).

In addition to these examples, there are several situations of accidental clauses that can be found in Brazilian Corporate Law.

119 Cfr. Artigo 997, Código Civil.
120 Ricardo NEGRÃO, op. cit., 332.

6.4.3 Validity of the Contract

In order for the constitutive act of the corporate company to be valid, it must comply with certain requirements, which are clearly preestablished. Failure to comply with these requirements will cause the contract to be terminated by the invalidity defect, which will drag with it the declaration of its nullity or annulment, according to the circumstances of the invalidity. The validity of the articles of association is subject to compliance with two categories of requirements: (i) generic or transversal to all legal businesses and (ii) special ones that refer to the peculiarities of the association contract.[121]

Within the scope of their constitution, contractual companies must observe rules common to contracts in general; we said that the articles of association assumes the nature of a contractual legal business; it is in this perspective that its constitution must take into account Article 104 of the Civil Code, which deals with the necessary requirements for the validity of the legal business.

6.4.4 Generic Requirements

The capable agent[122] is the person who is civilly capable, either by majority or by emancipation, or incapable but properly assisted.

It is of interest now to analyze the "capacity and entry of a minor partner in the Commercial Code regime"—the ability to participate in a partnership of people, as a partner, had a strict rule in the Commercial Code: Article 308 was a prohibitive rule for the participation of nonemancipated minors; successors of a deceased partner, even if the succession of heirs is contractually provided for; and judicial authorization in this regard is prohibited. The purpose of this company, in the absence of major heirs, was extinction; such understanding is brought to us by Ricardo Negrão, substantiating the same based on paragraph 4 of Article 335 of the same legal diploma.[123]

The cited author adds that the commercial law prohibited the participation of minors in the so-called persons companies, established in Articles 311–328. The legal ratio was in the unlimited and joint liability of partners and, consequently, in the necessary participation in the direct administration of company's business. Strictly speaking, any partner with unlimited liability can be a manager of the commercial company.

121 Ricardo NEGRÃO, op. cit., 332.

122 See item I, Article 104 of the Civil Code.

123 Ricardo NEGRÃO, op. cit., 320.

An interesting note is made by Fábio Ulhoa Coelho, when he states that "*the hiring of a limited liability company, duly represented or assisted, has been admitted by the jurisprudence, as long as it does not have management powers and the share capital is fully up paid.*"[124]

Capacity of the minor partner under the Civil Code regime commercial law the current Civil Code has enabled the incapacitated person to continue the exercise of their business activity. Under Article 974 of the aforementioned Legal Diploma, "the incapacitated [can], through a representative or duly assisted, continue the company previously exercised by him while able, by his parents or by the author of inheritance." Permission for this exercise is dependent on judicial supply, after the examination of the state of facts and company risks, as well as the convenience of continuing it (§ 1).

With regard to ensuring the continuity of the company, individual or collective, the Civil Code provides for two situations:

(i) Illustrated in Articles 3 and 4, the owner of the company becomes unable to express their will, transiently or not, due to illness or mental disability, or even their judgment is reduced due to habitual drunkenness, toxic addiction, as well as in cases of incomplete mental development or prodigality.
(ii) Situation in which the owner of the company dies, and the heir is not over 18 years old or emancipated. It seems evident that, by allowing the personal exercise of the individual company, the civil law authorized the minor, or the incapacitated, to participate as a partner in a partnership in the same circumstances. This is because, in the adopted system, there will be no damage to the assets previously gathered by the authorized person. In both legal provisions, civil law protected the assets belonging to the person incapable of the temporal lapse of succession or interdiction from liability to third parties, as long as they are foreign to the assets of the company.

Under the terms of items I and III of Article 1.028, only the succession will not operate, due to death, if the contract does not provide for it and there is no agreement between the heirs and the remaining partners.

Lawful object. Lawfulness presupposes nonviolation of public order and good customs. The Law on the Registration of Public Enterprises and Mercantile

124 Fábio Ulhoa COELHO, op. cit., 158.

Activities includes a prohibitive rule for the archiving of documents that failed to comply with the requirements prescribed by the law or an offensive against good manners or public order (item I, Article 35, Law 8.934/94).

Possible Object—this is a determined or determinable object.[125] In addition to being lawful, the object must be possible, determined, or determinable.

For an object to be regarded as a possible object, one that is under the physical and legal prism, there is the possibility of it being agreed upon as the object of a contract by parties to the contract. If the object is impossible, the legal business tending to form the corporate company incurs frustration. The impossibility occurs when the deal is not possible for any person or cannot be determined. For example, the social contract whose object (economic activity to be exploited by the company) is out of the legal trade by virtue of the law is absolutely impossible.

A determined object is one that is perfectly individualized at the time of the signing of the company's constitutive contract.

Determinable object is one that provides objects necessary for its identification. The absolutely indeterminable object will make the contract void.

Form prescribed or not defended by law (item III, Article 104). The legal transaction whose purpose is the constitution of a corporate entity must be reduced to writing (public or private contract) in **accordance** with the peculiarities of each corporate modality. It is understood that the civil law does not prohibit the oral contract; however, it is imperative to reduce it in writing for the purposes of filing with the Commercial Registry.

Specific requirements. The specific requirements are enshrined in the Civil Code: contribution of partners in the formation of share capital, whether with assets, credit or money[126] and participation of partners in positive or negative results of the company.[127]

Article 1,008 of the Civil Code is a prohibitive rule that does not allow the enshrining of a contractual clause that prevents partners from participating in social profits and losses; a clause in this sense—the Leonine clause—is subject to nullity. Certainly, the right to participate in social gains and losses will be directly proportional to the percentage of partner's participation in the share capital.

It becomes pertinent to mention the factual assumptions, namely: (i) *affectio societatis* or *animus societatis*—it is the intention or will to bring a corporate entity into existence and becoming a partner within it. This is a subjective assumption;

125 See item II, Article 104.
126 See Articles 1004 and 1005.
127 See Articles 1007 and 1008.

(ii) plurality of partners—it is crucial for the beginning of the life of a corporate entity. As a rule, in the Brazilian legal system, at least two people are required to set up companies. This wish is a consequence of the nonexistence, in the Brazilian legal system, of the sole proprietorship, except for two situations—the wholly owned subsidiary and the temporary incidental sole proprietorship.

A common mistake to make is to confuse the assumptions of the creation of the business company with its validity requirements. Therefore, it is necessary to make clear the difference between one reality and the other; the absence of assumptions has the consequence of the nonexistence of the corporate entity and the lack of requirements, which leads to the invalidity of the legal person.[128]

6.5 Registration of Companies

The birth of the company as an autonomous entity or subject to rights and obligations requires compliance with the registration obligation to be carried out with the Legal Entity Registry or with the Commercial Registry of the location where the company is located; all the documentation necessary for registration must be presented within 30 days, a period to be counted from the date of drawing up each of the acts of registration (§ 1, Article 1.151, Civil Code).

As we have referred before, based on items I, IV, and VI, Article 997, Civil Code, the constitutive act of the company must observe certain requirements within the scope of its filing in the Register of Mercantile Companies and Related Activities; they are: capacity of the agent (partner), lawful object, possible object determined or determinable, and form prescribed or not defended by law.

It is opportune to talk about the company and registration acts. The development of activities within the corporate entity is closely linked to the Public Registry of Mercantile Companies; this is because the acts resulting from that development need to be formalized (by registration) in order to be able to produce effects before third parties as well as before partners, in accordance with the specifics of each situation.

The commercial company is legally obliged to register a certain number of acts considered essential for the healthy development of the company and guarantee of legal security for both partners and third parties. An essential and pioneering act that must be followed in the register is the instrument that created the company; in this logic, "*The Company acquires legal personality with the registration, in the proper register and in the form of the law, of its constitutive acts*"

128 Waldo FAZZIO JÚNIOR, op. cit., 127.

(Article 985, Civil Code). What is emphasized here is that the acts of registration must obey, in the path of the **aforementioned** legal diploma, to a preestablished criterion: "*The entrepreneur and the company are linked to the Public Registry of Mercantile Companies in charge of the Commercial Boards and the simple company to the Civil Registry of Legal Entities, which must obey the rules set for that registration, if the simple company adopts one of the types of business company*" (Article 1150).

Thirty days after the corporate legal person is constituted, it has the obligation to request the registration of its legal creative instrument (contract) in the Civil Registry of Legal Persons of the territorial district where it is based.[129] In this context, it is worth mentioning that the simple company that instituted the branch, subsidiary, or agency in the territorial division of another Civil Registry of Legal Entities is also obliged to register it, presenting the evidential elements of the primitive registration.[130]

Taking into consideration the case of assemblies held by business companies, they will have the presidents and secretaries as partners selected from among partners who are present. When the session of the assemblies ends, a minutes of the meeting will be made recording the work conducted and deliberations taken; the minutes will have to be signed by the members of the table and by the association members participating in the meeting in considerable number for resolutions to be considered valid (§ 1, Article 1075, Civil Code). The elaborated minutes must be copied and authenticated by the administrators, or by the members of the board, within 20 days after the meeting, and at the end it will be taken to the Public Registry of Mercantile Companies for filing (§ 2).

In limited companies, "*The reduction of the share capital due to the proportional decrease in the nominal value of the quotas, becomes effective from the registration of the approval minutes in the Public Registry of Mercantile Companies. The same happens with the reduction operated by the refund of part of the value of the shares or the waiver of installments due, which, also result in the proportional reduction of their nominal value, must be registered in the Public Registry of Mercantile Companies.*"[131]

Mandatory books, comprising all appropriate legal documentation and before commencing their use, must be authenticated by the Public Registry of Mercantile Companies (Article 1181, Civil Code).

When a company is resolved, with respect to minority partners, its suppression, deliberated in a meeting or meeting, must be registered, so that the

129 See Article 998, Civil Code.
130 Cfr. Article 1000, Código Civil.
131 Waldo FAZZIO JÚNIOR, op. cit., 127.

liquidation can proceed (Article 1086 in conjunction with Article 1031, all of the Civil Code).

In the context of the above paragraph, it is understood that "*The registration of the company's resolution is a dividing line to mark the responsibility of the ex-partner or his heirs, which lasts up to two years after the withdrawal, exclusion or death. It is also shown with a borderline point to establish the ex-partner's responsibility for obligations after the social bond is undone, since the biennial term is counted from the annotation.*"[132]

6.5.1 Rights and Duties

The *animus societatis,* or the intention to bring a social juridical entity into existence, involves the manifestation of an agreement of wills between two or more persons who enter into a contract between them to carry out that intention. The social contract is capable of creating different corporate types depending on the corporate purpose of each corporate type; in this context, it must be taken into account that the core of rights and obligations assumed by partners will be in accordance with the type of company they create.

The core of rights and obligations assumed by partners may or may not be enshrined in an express way in the act of creating the corporate entity. Partners opting for nonexpress consecration of the rights and obligations, or showing the contract in these matters to be omitted, resort to the law that shapes certain rights and mandatory complexes transversal to all corporate types, and therefore, unsusceptible of suppression.

According to Fazzio Júnior,[133] the rights of partners can be summarized as follows:

(i) *Right to participate in profits*—it is enshrined in Article 1008 of the Civil Code, which establishes a legal provision that states, "*The contractual stipulation that excludes any partner from participating in profits and losses is null.*" The right to share in profits derives from the very purpose of the business company, which consists in the acquisition of profit.

In limited liability companies, it is necessary to distinguish between the equity sphere of the corporate entity and that of partners. The limitation of the liability of partners will depend on the value of the shares that each one securitizes

132 Id.
133 Id, 132.

individually. It is an understanding that results from the law itself—*"In the limited partnership, the responsibility of each partner is restricted to the value of their shares, but all are jointly liable for the payment of Social capital"* (Article 1052, Civil Code).

After the share capital transaction to a corporate entity gets concluded, partners become holders of rights derived from their own status as partners, one of which is the prerogative to participate in the sharing of profits. This is an essential right of partners. As we already know, business activity has risk as one of its basic characteristics, which means that in addition to being successful (profitable), commercial activity can also involve losses, and these also constitute rights in which the partners participate.

(ii) *Right to participate in the inspection of bookkeeping*—the inspection of bookkeeping to which it refers is within the context of a given company. We are facing a right that takes on a double meaning. In the foreground, it consists of assisting the company's administrative activity. In a second sense, partners are faced individually, at all times, with the probability of carrying out an inspection of the ordinary record of facts and administrative or management acts of the company.

The inspection of commercial bookkeeping is a right that gives partners access to economic and financial information regarding the development of activities within the company. In addition, managers and administrators are required to report annually to the meeting. In a period of 30 days after the meeting, the accountability made by the managers and administrators to the meeting must be extended to partners who are outside the administrative structures of the company (Article 1078 and following, Civil Code).

(iii) *Right to the accountability of the administrators*—under Article 1.078 of the Civil Code, "The shareholders' meeting must be held at least once a year, in the four months following the end of the fiscal year, with the objective to (I) take the management accounts and resolve on the balance sheet and the economic result; (II) designate administrators, when applicable; and (III) deal with any other matter on the agenda."

(iv) *Right of withdrawal*—also known as right of withdrawal. The partnership can produce results within or outside the expectations on which the partners entered into the articles of association. As the results are in accordance with the expectations of partners; under normal conditions, the company subsists without major changes of substance. The same cannot be said when the results are far from those expectations; in this situation, the probability of substantial major changes is high. Not being in accordance with such changes, one or more partners may withdraw from the company in order to no longer participate in it or be a part of it. The right to leave or to remain in the corporate entity devolves around the principle of contractual freedom or autonomy of will (already seen in the previous paragraphs).

Choosing to terminate his participation in the company, the partner has the power to negotiate the shares he holds or withdraw from it. It is a break that knows two moments. In the first moment, the partner is bound to make delinquency within the company to find a partner interested in the acquisition of their shares; if there is no intention within the company to acquire the shares, the delinquency may extend outside the company, in the sense of finding interested third parties. In a second moment, also called recess or dissidence, it consists of the prerogative that the partner has to end the ties that link him with the other partners and to the corporate entity by a unilateral act of will.

Articles 1029 serves as an example of the right of withdrawal or withdrawal—in the context of simple companies—and Article 1077, in the context of limited companies, all of the Civil Code. These emphasize that the institute of withdrawal rights applied in the scope of simple companies can be applied in a subsidiary way to limited companies.

(vi) *Right to vote in social deliberations*—it is shown as a core right in persons' companies. In these corporate entities, the will of partners, considered individually, counts for the direction of the life of the company, hence the crucial right to vote. This understanding is based on the Civil Code, when it is determined that in the case of the law or of the constitutive instrument of the company gives competence to partners, the partners then have the power to take decision in relation to the legal business of the company; the matters pertaining to this are deliberated by majority of votes, with the majority determined by the value of the shares of each of the partners.

A different situation occurs in capital companies; let us consider, for example, the Limited Companies by Shares; the right to vote is not crucial. In these companies, the *"capital element"* counts more. In certain situations, holders of preferred shares may be deprived of the right to vote. In this sense, "*The bylaws may cease to grant preferred shares some or some of the rights recognized to common shares, including voting rights, or confer them with restrictions (. . .)*"[134]; they are called preferred shares without voting rights; however, "*Preferred shares without voting rights will acquire the exercise of this right if the company, for the period provided for in the bylaws, does not exceed three (3) consecutive exercises,* [and] *fails to pay the fixed or minimum dividends to which they are entitled, a right that they will retain until payment, if such dividends are not cumulative, or until the cumulative arrears are paid.*"[135] Voting rights are granted to ordinary shareholders, but in some situations they may be suspended.

Obligations of partners. Partners are bound to a certain mandatory nucleus from the moment they sign the contract, unless the contract stipulates an initial term for the assumption of the corporate complex of mandatory obligations (Article 1001, Civil Code).

One of the partners' obligations is to contribute with necessary resources for the company to be able to exploit the economic activity that constitutes its object, in accordance with the contribution modality and within the time period agreed by partners in the articles of association; any partner's failure to comply with their obligation, within 30 days following the date notified by the corporate entity, will incur liability to the company or loss resulting from the delay.[136] As it can be seen, compliance with obligations within the agreed deadlines is law. Failure to meet the deadlines in fulfilling obligations (e.g., payment of the quota) is a factor for the partner to be called a partner in remission.

The figure of the referring partner is precisely described in the Civil Code, Article 1004. In view of that casualty ("default of the referring partner"), there is a diversity of solutions that can be adopted by other partners, such as requesting for compensation for damages caused or for judicial exclusion of the partner or for reduction of the partner's participation in the share capital to the amount already paid (single paragraph).[137]

If the solution adopted is to exclude the remitting member or reduce their shares, there will be a need to reduce the share capital, in case the remaining members do not supplement the missing amount (§ 1, Article 1031, Civil Code).

134 See Article 111, Brazilian Corporate Law.
135 See § 1, Article 111, Brazilian Corporate Law.
136 See Article 1004, Civil Code.
137 Cláudia RIBEIRO and Priscila MENEZES, op. cit., 26.

The obligation to contribution in simple companies can be fulfilled through services. The partner who is attached to this type of contribution, with the exception of a pact in the opposite sense, cannot be employed in an activity foreign to the corporate entity; if he violates this rule, he will incur the sanction of deprivation of profits owed to them or their exclusion from the company (Article 1006). It's a fact that the partner in this situation does not have quotas are limited to contributing in services; obviously, his share in profits will be proportional to the average of the value of the quotas (Article 1007, second part, Civil Code).

In limited companies, if the payment of remittance share has not been paid, without prejudice to the established Article 1004 and its sole paragraph, the other members have the option of appropriating it or alienating it to third parties, which includes exclusion of the original partner and the respective return of what he has paid after deducting the interest resulting from the delay of the installments stipulated in the company's constitutive act, in addition to the expenses.[138]

The complex of mandatory obligations assumed by partners cease with the liquidation of the company and with the extinction of responsibilities of the company (second part, Article 1001, Civil Code).

6.5.2 Obligation to Enter

It is not possible to create a corporate entity without social capital. The patrimonial autonomy of the company is extremely fundamental so that it can develop the economic activity that it is predisposed to explore and to establish legal business relations with third parties. The social capital is a pioneer in the formation of the patrimonial sphere of the company and comprises the total representative contributions sum in monetary values or assets of partners.[139]

For Rubens Requião, "*The capital constitutes the initial patrimony of the commercial company. After the start of activities, the capital remains nominal, expressed in the sum declared in the contract, whereas the social patrimony—social fund—tends to grow, if the company is prosperous, or to decrease, if it fails. This patrimony is what ultimately generates the profit, which is periodically divided among the partners.*"[140]

In any corporate type, the obligation to enter for the generation of social capital is an essential obligation. The indispensable nature of this obligation is associated with the fact that it also constitutes one of the requirements for the

138 See Article 1058, Civil Code.

139 Waldo FAZZIO JÚNIOR, op. cit., 125.

140 Rubens REQUIÃO, *Curso de Direito Comercial,* 23ª ed., actualizada por Rubens Edmundo Requião, v.1 (São Paulo: Saraiva), 358.

validity of the articles of association; in this sense, the contract must indicate the share of each of the partners and their way of realization in the share capital (item IV, Article 97, Civil Code).

In this regard, Fábio Coelho posits as follows: *"commercial company, in order to start its economic activity, evidently needs resources, that is, machines, technology, services, work and other means indispensable to the organization of the company covered by the corporate purpose. It is up to the partners to provide such resources. They do so by transferring, from their assets to that of the legal entity, the ownership of money, good or credit, and receiving, in exchange, shares issued by the company, in a corresponding amount. Once the activity starts, it may happen that the company needs more resources, and the shareholders, by the majority with voting rights of the meeting in a general meeting, understand that it is a case of expanding their contribution to the development of the company. More money, assets or credits are then transferred from the partners' assets to that of the company, in return for receiving new shares. These contributions are appropriated, in the company's accounting, as social capital."*[141]

There are two basic mechanisms used by companies to obtain the necessary resources for the development of their activities: (i) capitalization—it is the process by which the corporate entity collects assets or pecuniary means without any obligation of refund, even if it is in conditions to proceed with the restitution of those, in case certain legal-economic inferences are observed; and (ii) financing—it is a two-dimensional mechanism: bank financing or other financing (issuance of debentures or commercial papers); in this mechanism, the company obtains funds from financiers, thus adhering to the obligation to refund amounts corresponding to those resources with an additional percentage.[142]

Ricardo Negrão uses the Commercial Code's Article 278 as a starting point for discussing the social capital: *"Each partner must contribute to the formation of social capital stock"*; according to this author, the wording of the provision in question is repeated in the Civil Code, precisely in Article 1004.[143] In the systematic definitions of the Commercial Code, the omission regarding the capital formation mechanism was manifest; only the susceptibility of a partner to enter its industry was indicated specifically (Article 917); this article (of the Commercial Code) referred to partners providing services in the capital and industrial company, a susceptibility that ceased with the adoption of the 2002 Civil Code.

141 Fábio Ulhoa COELHO, op. cit., 206.
142 Fábio Ulhoa COELHO, op. cit., 206.
143 Ricardo NEGRÃO, op. cit., 327.

In the perspective of the Civil Code, the expression of the social capital must be made in current currency; however, partners can contribute to the formation of social capital in monetary values or any other assets subject to monetary appreciation[144]; the assets can revise several facets, from the material to the immaterial, from the movable to immovable. In simple companies whose object is lacking in the entrepreneurial spirit, partners are allowed to contribute to the formation of social capital by performing services[145]; such a contribution is expressly prohibited in the limited partnership (§ 2, Article 1.055).

Law No. 18,833 of July 4, 2019,[146] in its Article 35, in relation to this theme introduces a new aspect; in addition to the designation of capital, the contract brought to the register must contain "the description and identification of the property, its area, data related to their title, as well as the registration number in the Real Estate Registry" (para. a, item VII) and "the urgent or marital grant when necessary" (para. b, item VII), in the event of incorporation of properties into the company.

The Brazilian Corporate Law (Law No. 6,404 of December 15, 1976) in Article 80 presents preliminary requirements to be fulfilled for the creation of the company. *"The constitution of the company depends on the fulfillment of the following preliminary requirements: (I) subscription, at least by 2 (two) people, of all shares in which the social capital established in the bylaws is divided; (II) "realization, as a down payment, of at least 10 % (ten percent) of the issue price of the shares subscribed in cash; (III) deposit, at Banco do Brasil S/A., or at another banking establishment authorized by the Securities and Exchange Commission, of the part of the paid-up capital in cash."*[147] Much attention needs to be paid to the sole paragraph of the legal provision in question, as it determines the nonapplicability of the content contained in item II to companies for which there is a legal requirement to enter a percentage exceeding 10 %. The transfer of goods in favor of the company is subject to appraisal by specialists (Articles 7–9 of the law in question).

The aforementioned precautions, in the legislation in force, they are not rules for the other types of companies; this creates difficulties in determining the real value of the capital of the incorporated company, allowing the inclusion of unreal

144 See item III of Article 997, Civil Code.

145 See Article 1.006 in conjunction with Article 997, all of the Civil Code.

146 Law providing for the transfer of Union to the Federal District of activities of public registration of mercantile companies and similar activities in the Federal District amends Law No. 8,934 of November 18, 1994, which provides for Public Registry of Mercantile Companies and related activities.

147 See Article 80 of Law No. 6.404/76.

and fantastic values and, with that, all kinds of credit fraud from suppliers and banks. Even if such a practice is considered criminal, it is only verified in situation of failure; it is only verified in case of bankruptcy or judicial or extrajudicial[148] recovery, when partners become involved and, probably, have failed to render correct accounts.

The Civil Code in force does not expand requirements, allowing only the mere indication of company's capital in currency. The only ones listed are limited to imposing on the partner who transmits the right of possession or usufruct of property the responsibility for eviction and, in the case of credit transfer, the debtor's solvency. The provision of Article 1005 in this context is as follows: "*The partner who, by way of social share, transmits dominion, possession or use, is responsible for eviction; and the debtor's solvency, whoever transfers credit*" is reflected in a norm of general application to all corporate modalities. In the case of limited liability companies, however, the joint and several liabilities of partners were imposed for the precise estimation of the assets granted to the capital of the company, within a period of five years, whose counting starts from the date of registration of the corporate entity.[149]

It is common, but not correct, to confuse between social capital and the heritage of the company. A distinction is needed between the two realities. Generally, social capital is unreal (nominal) and invariable (intangible), whereas the company's assets are real and variable. The invariability of capital lies in the fact that it remains fixed in the constitutive act of the corporate entity, and the assets are likely to proliferate or decrease, depending on the oscillation in the importance of social assets and the level of profitability of the corporate entity. Equity is used to satisfy the company's complex of mandatory obligations and must exceed the company's capital.[150]

6.5.3 Conservation of Capital

The social capital must be included in the charter of the corporate entity, and this, in turn, must be properly registered with the Commercial Registry, in accordance with the type of corporate (in the universe of companies with a business condition—business companies, and in needy companies, that is, simple companies).

It is the duty of the administrator, in line with the Brazilian Corporate Law (Article 153), in the context of carrying out the functions under their competence,

148 See item IV of Article 168 of Law No. 11.101/2005 (Bankruptcy and Corporate Recovery Law).

149 See Article 1.055, Civil Code.

150 Waldo FAZZIO JÚNIOR, op. cit., 126.

to act carefully and deliberately or as a *bonus pater familiae*. This way of proceeding, which must be observed by the administrator, aims to guarantee the integrity of the share capital, especially because it is the managers' obligation to keep the capital intangible and report any damage whose effects affect it, since its allocation is only admitted in case of losses and changes in the company's activities (al. E), § 1, Article 157).

Social capital, seen as a sum of the company's assets, cannot be used by partners or shareholders for their benefit, because it serves as a guarantee for third parties who are entitled to credit before the company. The subsidiary application[151] of the rule contained in Article 1059 of the Civil Code to public limited companies establishes that *"The partners will be obliged to reimburse the profits and amounts withdrawn, in any capacity, even if authorized by the contract, when such profits or amount are distributed at a loss of capital."* It is an indisputable fact that the content of this rule has the ultimate aim of guaranteeing the conservation of the company's capital.

For capital conservation to become effective, it must be guided by a set of principles[152]:

(i) ***Principle of determination***—the social capital goes through the precise indication in the social contract; since it is in the nature of a structural element of the company, the nondetermination of the social capital in the constitutive act of the company invalidates the respective contract due to source.

(ii) ***Principle of Unity***—it is a principle that precludes any possibility that in the constitutive act of the company—contract—in the case of contractual companies and bylaws—for example, in the case of statutory companies—mention should be made of two or more partner capitals; under this logic, each corporate entity must develop its activities on the basis of a single capital. In public limited companies, this unit is reflected in a single inventory, in a single balance sheet, even though the company may have several branches or subsidiaries, projecting itself in the guarantee unit that the company's assets are represented in relation to creditors.

(iii) *Advertising Principle*—on the one hand, the constitutive act of the company must comply with the requirement of mandatory registration

151 See Article 1089, Civil Code.

152 José Luiz BULHÕES PEDREIRA and Alfredo LAMY FILHO, op. cit., 145–147.

with the competent entities (in accordance with each corporate type); the observance of this obligation drags the public capital's publicity, since third parties are assisted by the right to request access to information about the social capital of corporate entities registered with the Commercial Registry or the Registry. On the other hand, it is the duty of the administrative structures of the corporate body to proceed with the publication of capital.

(iv) ***Principle of Stability or Fixity***—it is a principle that aims to protect those who before the corporate entity have credit rights against arbitrary changes of capital at the initiative of partners or shareholders; under this logic, once the share capital is established in the contract or the statute it cannot be changed, except in the cases provided for by law. The fixed or stable nature of capital, recommended by the principle in question, is not of an absolute nature, since, provided the legal dictates are observed, it can be altered by a deliberative act of partners or shareholders and will have the consequence of modifying the contract or the statute. Although the protection of social creditors is the essence of this principle, it cannot be ignored that its field of projection reaches the partners or shareholders themselves, guaranteeing their rights and obligations, since these are directly proportional to the level of participation of each one in regards to their social capital.

(v) ***Principle of Reality***—the difference between the company's capital and its assets was excluded in the previous paragraphs. It has been made clear that social capital is nominal and intangible and equity, in turn, is real and variable. Capital is said to be nominal because it is unreal and is previously established in the constitutive act of the company. Once the capital is fixed in the charter, the process of its payment follows and this in turn will be affected by the individual contribution of each of the partners or shareholders. The principle we are dealing with presupposes that the amount of assets that constitute the company's capital under the terms of the constitutive act must be perfectly adjusted to the totality of contributions that contribute to the real formation of capital. The process of paying in diversified assets must be carefully evaluated by specialists (Article 8, Brazilian Corporate Law).

Projected in the law, this principle explains the existence of a large number of articles. Thus, item I of Article 80 of the aforementioned law requires the full subscription of capital for the constitution of a company; the sole paragraph of

Article 10 establishes the responsibility of the subscriber in the event of incorporation of credits, stipulating a minimum capital increase (item II of Article 80) for the creation of the corporate entity. Article 13 prohibits the issuance of shares below the nominal value (if any). Article 107 grants permission for the company to collect in installments the subscribed and unregulated capital. Article 170 allows for only a capital increase after the payment of three-quarters of the capital already subscribed.

vi) ***Principle of Integrity***—the essence of this principle is to protect capital in opposition to acts emanating from the administrative structures of the corporate entity, whose purpose is to benefit the partners or shareholders. Once the contributions (whether for monetary values or for goods subject to monetary evaluation) have been made by partners/shareholders for the payment of the company's capital, those values or assets can no longer be disengaged and reallocated in the individual assets of each of the partners. If this happens, then shareholders are subjected to penalty for jeopardizing the normal development of the company's activities. The law presents certain exceptions to this understanding, such as reduction of share capital (Article 1082, Civil Code) and corporate vicissitudes (liquidation, merger, and extinction—Articles 206–219, Brazilian Corporate Law).

(vii) ***Principle of effectiveness***—refers mainly to limited liability companies and aims to guarantee the rights of social creditors. In these circumstances, the assets that make up the company's capital must make the guarantee of those rights effective. In the event of insufficient capital to answer for the mandatory complex of partners/shareholders or to satisfy the rights of third parties who before the company enjoy the right to credit, the individual assets of partners cannot be used due to the limitation of liability regime.

Now, according to Article 50 of the Civil Code, "In case of abuse of legal personality, characterized by misuse of purpose, or by confusion in property, the judge may decide, at the request of the party, or the Public Prosecutor when it is up to him to intervene in the process, that the effects of certain and certain relationships of obligations be extended to the private assets of the administrators or partners of the legal entity." This is to say, the regime of limitation of social responsibility is inapplicable in the context of the aforementioned article; when the social capital is not sufficient to answer for the social obligations, one can resort to the private assets of partners/shareholders.

(viii) **Principle of intangibility**—the principle of unity and that of the reality of capital must be solidified at the moment when the company is constituted. The irrevocable nature of the contributions made constitutes the guarantee of the social creditors and requires that the fund resulting from the contributions be lifelong and intangible at the time when the corporate entity operates its activities and there are social creditors whose rights have not yet been satisfied.

Intangibility has multiple projections in the law, which include the following: the rigor in verifying the existence of profits to admit the distribution of dividends, the rules that preside over audits and preparation of balance sheets, the advertising to which the company's financial life is subject, the prohibition of reciprocal participation of companies (which would defraud the concept of capital), the inability of the company to buy[153] or receive as collateral for its own shares,[154] the obligation to constitute a legal reserve, and the imperative to promote the annual monetary correction of capital.

To conclude the topic of conservation of social capital, its importance cannot be seen at the same level as in people's companies with unlimited liability. In the companies that adopt the limitation of liability (responsibilities), the social capital is an element that ensures the rights of third parties who have a credit right before the company; when social capital is insufficient to satisfy those rights, creditors will not be assisted by the right to utilize the private assets of partners/shareholders for the satisfaction of their credit rights (except for the situation provided for in Article 50 of the Civil Code).

6.6 *Structure and Functioning of Business Companies under Brazilian Law*

The legal person brought into existence by the articles of association or by the statute is reflected in an economic body made up of a diversity of bodies, each exercising its function; it is the constitutive act of the corporate entity that establishes the functions of each of the organs or existing bodies in the company.[155]

153 See Article 30 of Brazilian Corporate Law.

154 See Article 193 of Brazilian Corporate Law.

155 José Luiz BULHÕES PEDREIRA and Alfredo LAMY FILHO, op. cit., 563.

Structure is the disposition and order of the elements of a system, which are perceived through their interrelations and refer to the disposition of the company's bodies as a structure.

Hierarchical Structure: The structure of a business company, as can another social group in which the members' action is oriented towards the common purpose, is hierarchical—it is a system of organs and normatively organized social roles, which includes subordination relations—the holders of some bodies or positions exercise power over those of others who have an obligation to carry out the orders received. Enterprise and Company Structure: the organization created by the company includes, in addition to partners and members of the governing bodies, the employees who are part of the company's social group, and the structure of the business company becomes a segment of the company structure from the moment the company hires an employee.[156]

6.6.1 General Meeting

Within the organic structure of corporate entities existing under Brazilian law, the general meeting is the highest body; it is said to be the highest body because in addition to it there are others who are in lower position (in relation to it; for example, the board—the insertion of this body in the company's organic structure is not mandatory; it depends on the will of the partners or shareholders; depending on social needs, it is more frequent in larger companies, which adopt the limitation regime responsibility, and the articles pertinent to this situation include Article 1066 in conjunction with Article 1070, all of the Civil Code).

The individual will of each partner or shareholder is crucial for the formation of the will of the company, and the manifestation of the individual will of those becomes effective at the general meeting. In the process of expressing individual wishes, there is a greater likelihood of opposing interests, depending on the matters to be discussed; therefore, the general meeting is not a simple consultation of the opinions of partners/shareholders, as is the case with postal voting. It is an efficient mechanism at the disposal of partners/shareholders to jointly map the destiny of the corporate entity through the exchange of opinions; it also allows the intervention of minority partners/shareholders. Even though they are considered to be minority shareholders due to the social capital, their opinions have a very high persuasive value and can influence social deliberations. The deliberations at the general meeting are the result of a joint will of partners/shareholders;

156 Id.

a different situation is that which occurs in the vote by consultation where the isolation of those is verified.[157]

6.6.1.1 Composition and Functioning

The general meeting consists of a congregation of partners/shareholders at the head office of the company, conveniently promoted and installed with regulation *quorum*, defined by the percentage of shareholders or quota holders who have the right to vote; such right is the corollary of the deliberative power that they hold, which is carried out by an absolute majority of the votes of those who attend the meeting. The status of partner or shareholder is the prerequisite for participation in the general meeting. The validity of this is conditioned to the predetermination of the place where the general meeting is to be held and to a preliminary convocation of partners/shareholders; this last condition will only be waived if there are partners/shareholders in the assembly who represent the totality of the share capital. The installation of the meeting is subject to different procedures and becomes effective with a *minimum quorum*, which is configured by the capital of partners/shareholders who have the right to vote in regards to the matter to be resolved.[158]

On the one hand, there is the installation *quorum* and, on the other, the deliberation *quorum*, which consists of the absolute majority of votes of partners/shareholders who participate in the meeting. The law itself took care to list matters that fall under the exclusive competence of the general meeting.

Skills. In the case of joint stock companies, the general meeting, as a sovereign decision-making body with powers to issue the corporate will and decide its main matters, has the following exclusive powers: to proceed with the reform of the constitutive act of the company (in this case, bylaws)[159]; to elect or remove holders with power to govern the administrative and fiscal bodies of the company, at all times, with the exception enshrined the provisions of item II of Article 142[160]; to take, annually, the management accounts and deliberate on the financial statements presented by them[161]; to give authorization to issue debentures, without prejudice to the provisions of paragraphs 1, 2, and 4 of Article 59[162]; to proceed with the suspension of the practice of shareholder rights (Article 120)[163]; to issue

157 Elisabeth Maria PEREIRA, op. cit., 79.
158 Id.
159 See item I, Article 122 of Brazilian Corporate Law.
160 See item II, Article 122.
161 See item III, Article 122.
162 See item IV, Article 122.
163 See item V, Article 122.

a resolution to evaluate the assets presented by the shareholder in the context of competition for the formation of social capital[164]; to issue authorization for the issue of beneficiary parties[165]; to issue a resolution on the transformation, merger, incorporation, and spin-off of the company, including its dissolution and liquidation, and proceed with the election and dismissal of liquidators and judge their accounts[166]; to grant authorization to the holders of administrative bodies to declare bankruptcy and file for bankruptcy.[167]

In order to set up the meeting and gather the votes of participating shareholders, certain acts must be observed: First, there is a call to be made by shareholders or by governing bodies, as provided by law; second, under Article 127 of the Brazilian Corporate Law, prior to the start of the meeting, shareholders are required to sign the "Attendance Book," which must include the name, nationality, residence, quantity, and the type and class of shares they hold. In line with Article 128 of the aforementioned law, the activities of the assembly are directed by a compound table and may not be composed if the statute provides otherwise; the said composition includes the president and secretary who are selected by the shareholders attending the meeting.

The following step is the verification of the installation *quorum*, in accordance with the circumstances[168] and the quality and representation of the shareholder, under Article 126, considering that the meeting is installed; the meeting then proceeds with a discussion on the agenda of the meeting; votes are collected; and the meeting is concluded with the declaration of the closing of the meeting, minutes are drawn up, and signatures are obtained from members of the board and by those present, in accordance with Article 131.

Requirements upon convening the general meeting. The effectiveness of the general meeting depends on the observance of two essential requirements.

On the one hand, the propulsion of the assembly must be done by the body or person competent to do so. Pursuant to Article 123 of the Brazilian Corporate Law, "*It is incumbent upon the board of directors, if any, or the directors, subject to the provisions of the bylaws, to call the general meeting.*" Still in the sole paragraph of the aforementioned article, the fiscal council has equal competence in

164 See item VI, Article 122.

165 See item VII, Article 122.

166 See item VIII, Article 122.

167 See item X, Article 122.

168 See Article 125 of Brazilian Corporate Law: "*Except for the exceptions provided by law, general meeting will be installed, on first call, with the presence of shareholders representing at least ¼ (one quarter) of the voting share capital; on second call it will be installed with any number. Articles 71, § 3,* 135, or 221 can also be checked."

the situations established in number V of Article 163[169]; the same competence is extended to the shareholder (without discrimination), provided that the holders of administrative bodies are slow in taking decisions, for a period of time greater than 60 days, with regard to the calling of the meeting in the positive situations indicated by law or enshrined in the statute[170]; the same competence is extended to shareholders who hold a minimum representation of 5 % of the social capital, provided that the holders of administrative bodies do not comply, within a period of 8 days, with the request they present, suitably substantiated and accompanied by a statement of the matters they intend to address[171] and to shareholders with a minimum representation of 5 % of the capital with voting rights; shareholders with the same minimum percentage representation but lacking the right to vote are also competent, as long the holders of administrative bodies do not attend, within a period of 8 days, the meeting for requesting the installation of the fiscal council.[172]

On the other hand, the second requirement advocates strict compliance with the acts aimed at making the assembly public and the others legally consecrated. The meeting will be convened by means of a public announcement, with a minimum publication of three periods, and must contain the following elements: the place; the day, month, and year; the time of the meeting; and the meeting's agenda; the amendment to the bylaws being the object of the meeting, the mention of the matter is mandatory (Article 124 of the Brazilian Corporate Law).

The ratio of the legal imperiousness of the convening of the meeting consists of guaranteeing the participation of shareholders interested in company's business; in the case of controllers, holders of preferred shares without right to vote, and holders of ordinary shares, the law holds that their attendance is not mandatory since they do not have the rights enjoyed by shareholders who are mandatorily obliged to attend the meeting.

Kinds of Assembly. Two types of assembly can be identified—ordinary and extraordinary, in accordance with the material references to be treated.[173]

Ordinary General Meeting—under the law, this meeting is held once a year; if the company's constitutive act contains a contradictory clause in that sense, it will be void. Its purpose is to assess the following matters: taking the accounts of administrative bodies into account; follow up on examination,

169 See al. (a) of single section of Article 123.
170 See al. (b) of single section of Article 123.
171 See al. (c), single section of Article 123.
172 See al. (d), single section of Article 123.
173 Ricardo NEGRÃO, op. cit., 485–486.

discussion, and profit-sharing among shareholders; promote the election of members of administrative bodies and members of the fiscal council; and approval and correction of the monetary expression of the social capital.[174]

As it can be seen, the time of holding and objectives of the ordinary general meeting are determined based on the provisions of the law; it is called ordinary because it is transversal and binding in the universe of corporations.

Extraordinary General Meeting—the diversity of matters that fall outside the scope of the ordinary general meeting (those listed in Article 132 and previously described) are the responsibility of the extraordinary general meeting. The extraordinary character makes the field of matters to be deliberated by the meeting broader; due to such breadth, there is no legal command that sets the number of times and the date on which the meeting must be held; in these terms, it can be called to at all times, as long as there is a basis for such a call.[175]

It is clear from the sole paragraph of Article 131 of the Brazilian Corporate Law that "The ordinary general meeting and the extraordinary general meeting may be cumulatively called and held at the same place, date and time, instrumented in a single act." In practical terms, a single meeting will be held, and this in turn will deal with matters from a holistic perspective, without detriment to the observance of the specific rules of procedure of each assembly.

The two kinds of assemblies have low points of distraction with regard to the legal regime applicable to them. In this sense, even if the points in question are reduced, it is necessary to present them for better clarification: (a) the installation *quorum* of the ordinary general meeting whose agenda aims to change the company's constitutive act (bylaws) will be different from the general rule of Article 125; (b) the difference will also drag on to the *quorum* for deliberation in the context of provisions made in Article 129, in the event of addressing the matters enshrined in Article 136. In addition to these differences, it should be added that in relation to the holding of the meeting, the ordinary general meeting is mandatory, but the extraordinary general meeting is not.

According to teacher Ricardo Negrão,[176]

> "in some cases the legislation requires a qualified quorum, due to the importance of the issue to be voted, as is the case of provided for in article 136 of the Brazilian Corporate Law, which claim the adhesion of shareholders representing

174 See items I, II, III, and IV, Article 132 of the Brazilian Corporate Law.

175 João Pedro Barroso DO NASCIMENTO, *Direito Societário Avançado* (FGV DIREITO, Rio, Graduação, 2015), p. 101.

176 Ricardo NEGRÃO, op. cit., 486.

at least half of the voting shares, if a larger quorum is not required by the company's by-laws: (I) creation of preferred shares or increase class of existing preferred shares, without being proportionate to the other classes of preferred shares, unless already provided for or authorized by the bylaws; (II) changes in preferences, advantages and conditions for redemption or amortization of one or more classes of preferred shares, or creation of a new, more favored class; (III) reduction of the mandatory dividend; (IV) merger of the company, or its incorporation in another; (V) participation in a group of companies (article 265); (VI) changing the object of the company; (VII) termination of the company's liquidation status; (VIII) creation of beneficiary parties; (IX) spin-off of the company; (X) dissolution of the company."

6.6.1.2 Social Resolutions

In the Brazilian legal system, precisely in the legislation referring to business companies, in matters of social deliberations, the field of requirements pertaining to the *quorum* for the installation of the general meeting is vast, which applies as well for the effectiveness of the deliberations made. It is in this perspective that Lacerda Texeira, mentioned by Ricardo Negrão, affirms that a distinction must be made in relation to the number of participants required for the installation and deliberation of matters in assembly. The implementation and the validity of the resolutions issued by the meeting are subject to the observance of an essential requirement—the installation *quorum*.[177]

According to Article 125 of the Brazilian Corporate Law, it appears that the installation *quorum* corresponds to the minimum number of shareholders whose attendance at the place of the meeting is essential to the validity of the work carried out during the meeting. Without prejudice to the legally enshrined exceptions, the general meeting will be installed, in a primary call, with the attendance of shareholders with a minimum representation of one-quarter of the social capital with voting rights. In this way, shareholders holding shares that represent 25 % of the voting capital (represented by the total number of shares that confer voting rights) must physically be present in the meeting, so that the resolutions adopted therein are valid.

The nonappearance of shareholders whose capital corresponds to 25 % of the voting capital will lead to a second call for the meeting, with a greater probability

177 Egberto Lacerda TEXEIRA e José Alexandre Tavares GUERREIRO, *Das Sociedades Anónimas no Direito Brasileiro. Apud* Ricardo NEGRÃO, *Manual de Direito Comercial e Empresa: Teoria Geral de Empresa,* Vol. 1, 7ªed. (São Paulo: Saraiva, 2010), 488.

of changing the *quorum* to an undetermined number. In these circumstances, the summons at the second instance, aiming at a new meeting, may confer its validity only by the appearance of a single shareholder holding a single share. Pursuant to Article 135 of the Brazilian Corporate Law, the matter being resolved by the extraordinary general meeting regarding the modification of the company's constitutive act (bylaws), the installation in the primary call will only be carried out with the attendance of shareholders whose minimum representation of voting capital corresponds to two-thirds; however, it can be installed in second instance in a proportion lower or higher than that, and it will count in this context only the number of those who are present at the meeting.

Shareholders deliberations. There is an intrinsic relationship between the shareholders' deliberations and the deliberative *quorum*, which in turn concerns the fraction of votes in favor of a certain proposal; if the proposal does not gather the number of votes necessary for its approval, it cannot be ratified. Under Article 129 of the Brazilian Corporate Law, *"The deliberations of the general meeting, with the exception of the exceptions provided for by law, will be taken by an absolute majority of votes, blank votes not being counted."* For this reason, for matters in general, the proposal that meets the bisection of blank votes is ratified.

For deliberations, the Brazilian Corporate Law has five *quorum* orders: (i) the ordinary, enshrined in Article 129, more than half the votes of those present, without counting the blank votes; qualified *quorum*, provided for in Article 136, advocates the approval of shareholders, with minimal representation, of the bisection of voting shares; (iii) qualified special *quorum*, presupposes a minimum approval of the bisection of debentures in motion at the time the matter of the special meeting intends to consent to the change in the conditions of the debentures (§ 5, Article 71); (iv) the statutory *quorum*, in closed corporate entities, is beyond what is legally enshrined; (v) the unanimous character at the time of the matter making reference, in the constituent assembly, to the amendment of the draft statute (§ 2, Article 87); and in the event of a change in the corporate entity.[178]

6.6.2. Administration

The corporate entity management is carried out by the respective board of directors, which is a body of a deliberative and supervisory nature; with a minimum composition of three shareholders, it is competent to appreciate the universe of

178 Ricardo NEGRÃO, op. cit., 489.

matters of relevance to the company, without detriment to exclusive competences of the general meeting, in the context of Article 122 of the Brazilian Corporate Law. Its functional essence is to promote the speed of the process of issuing resolutions within the corporate entity.

The insertion of the board of directors in the company's organic structure is mandatory in publicly held companies and mixed-capital companies and is optional in closed public limited companies. It consists of a collegial body of a deliberative nature, whose insertion in the organic structure of the company is between the general meeting and the management; some of its functions include the orientation of company's negotiations, and election, monitoring, and inspection of the directors, and the pursuit of such functions is vested with executive power (Article 142 of the Brazilian Corporate Law).

One of the fundamentals for the insertion of board of directors in the organic structure of the company results from the restricted nature of the meeting, in the sense that, under the law, it meets once a year, which is not enough time to deal with company's negotiations. The board of directors allows an efficient exercise of the guiding and controlling functions of the management of the corporate entity. The bylaws establish the number of members who must be members of the board, which cannot be less than three members. It is a legal requirement, the establishment in the statute, of the time lapse of management, whose maximum limit cannot exceed three executions and the way in which the directors are switched and the method of convening, installing, and operating the board (items I and IV of Article 140 of the Brazilian Corporate Law).[179]

It is precisely because it is a collegial body that the continuation of most of its duties becomes effective through deliberations. Article 140, in its item IV, establishes the *quorum* indispensable for the consent; by a number corresponding to most of the votes, the statute requires a qualified quorum in certain circumstances.

The board of directors is essential to assist the general meeting in the management of the company; such assistance becomes effective through the delegation of certain duties, from the second body to the first. Attention needs to be paid, since the powers contained in Article 122 of the Brazilian Corporate Law are exclusively the responsibility of the general meeting; therefore, they are not subject to delegation. The range of powers of the board of directors is listed in Article 142 of the aforementioned law.

179 João Pedro Barroso DO NASCIMENTO, op. cit., 142.

6.6.2.1 The Legal Situation of the Directors

Within the structure and functioning of the companies, there is the figure of administrator, and the conceptual framework of this figure includes members of two bodies: board of administrators and board of directors, who are management bodies par excellence. The applicability of rules regarding claims, impediments, investiture, remuneration, duties, and responsibilities to the members of administrative bodies (administrators) is equally valid for the board of directors.

Who can be an administrator? The answer to this question is found in the law. In legal parameters, only the natural (natural) persons can be holders of administrative bodies (administrators) and acquire such status by election. For operational reasons, only natural persons can be administrators; this means that the operation of administrative activities becomes simpler and more efficient when performed by those persons. If the law allowed the management bodies to be held by legal persons, they would certainly lack natural person(s) to act on them. The natural person domiciled outside the Brazilian state (abroad) who is elected to the position of administrator must constitute a public prosecutor domiciled in Brazil, and the latter must be empowered to be summoned in actions brought against the person of the administrator.[180]

Impediments. From the combination of Article 147, § 1, Law 13.833 of July 4, 2019,[181] with Article 11, item II and Article 35, item II, of the respective law, it is understood that a person *"cannot be elected to the board of directors, administration or to the directory* [if they are] *legally prevented by special law, condemned for the practice of bankruptcy, prevarication, bribery, concussion, embezzlement, against the popular economy, public faith or property; or even, one who serves the sentence, even if temporarily, access to public offices, functions or jobs."* An impediment in the same context can still be found in the Brazilian Corporate Law, in the wake of § 2 of Article 147—*"They are still ineligible for management positions Publicly held persons declared disabled by an act of the Securities and Exchange Commission."*

Investiture. The investiture of the members of the council and directory for the respective positions takes place by signing the term of investiture in the minute's book.[182] If the signature of the investiture term is not verified within 30 days after the appointment, it will be ineffective, unless the nominee presents a justification accepted by the administrative body for which he was elected.[183] The

180 See § 2 of Article 146 of the Brazilian Corporate Law.
181 See § 2 of Article 146 of the Brazilian Corporate Law.
182 See Article 149 of the Brazilian Corporate Law.
183 See § 1 of Article 149 of the Brazilian Corporate Law.

domicile is one of the essential elements that must appear in the *term of possession*; its non-consistency can lead to the nullity of the term. As an element of the term, the domicile serves as a point where the administrator will be mentioned or summoned in the event that an administrative or judicial proceeding is initiated against its management acts; the change of domicile by the administrator must be communicated through a written document to the company.[184]

Remuneration. The company's highest body is responsible for setting the remuneration of the members of administrative bodies, as well as other prerogatives, considering their positions, the time lapse within which they exercise their functions, their professional category, and the quality of their services in the market.[185] About profit-sharing, "*The company's statute that fix the mandatory dividend at 25 % (twenty-five percent) or more of the net profit, can attribute to the managers a share in the company's profit, as long as its total does not exceed the remuneration of directors' annual fee or 0.1 (one tenth) of profits (article 190), whichever is the lower limit.*"[186] "*The directors will only be entitled to profit sharing for the fiscal year in relation to which the mandatory dividend is attributed to shareholders, as referred to in article 202.*"[187]

Duties of administrators. The shareholders of a certain corporate entity are responsible for electing the directors. These in turn have a duty to exercise their functions driven by social interest, and it is in this sense that they are bound to observe the mandatory complex of responsibilities resulting from their positions and those legally provided for. A mixed criterion adopted by the Brazilian legislator for the categorization of the duties of the members of the administrative bodies is evident, listing them concretely in some circumstances and in others making an abstract inventory.[188]

The Brazilian Corporate Law establishes the duties of directors in Articles 153–157, which we now analyze.

(i) **Duty of diligence**—provided for in Article 153 of the Brazilian Corporate Law; the manager of the corporate entity fulfills the functions inherent to his position, acting as a bonus pater family. We are faced with a duty characterized by abstraction because the law does not make a clear and delimited approach to what should be understood by diligence, leaving

184 See § 2 of Article 149 of the Brazilian Corporate Law.
185 See Article 152 of the Brazilian Corporate Law.
186 See § 1 of Article 152 of the Brazilian Corporate Law.
187 See § 2 of Article 152 of the Brazilian Corporate Law.
188 João Pedro Barroso DO NASCIMENTO, op. cit., 114.

that task to doctrine and jurisprudence. Since the law is silent on these terms, a theory was developed in the USA with the aim to make a clear delimitation of what should be understood by the duty of investigation and thus promoting legal certainty: the business judgment theory rule.

It is a theory that results from the assessment of a diversity of cases by the courts to assess whether or not, in the scope of the exercise of their functions, the administrators do so in observance of their duties. In this context, the decisions taken by administrators, as long as they are independent, disinterested, and informed and aim to defend the interest of the company (company), they have to be approved through a review process by the courts, and the administrators will not incur any responsibility even if the respective decisions do not produce desired results.

(ii) ***Duty of loyalty***—foreseen in Article 155; here, the administrator manages the company's business in the interests of social interest and cannot therefore make such management for the pursuit of individual interests. As a result, there is an express prohibition on the administrator to make use of the commercial opportunities resulting from the exercise of their functions to their own advantage or to third parties, thus creating damages to the company. The duty under analysis is considered violated, only, and only if, the company has a real and potential interest in the commercial advantage that the administrator may eventually benefit from. Therefore, in the context of managing the company's business life, the administrator must do so based on social interest and good faith.

Paragraph 1 of the Article in question establishes that, "In addition, it is up to the manager of a publicly-held company, to keep confidentiality about any information that has not yet been disclosed to the market, obtained due to the position and capable of influencing in a considerable way in the quotation of securities, being forbidden to use the information to obtain, for yourself or for others, an advantage through the purchase or sale of securities." The administrator's failure to comply with this stipulation is revealed as the most frequent means of breach of duty under consideration, especially in open companies, in the form of insider trading: use of privileged information, which may create changes in the price of shares, or lead to actions to the advantage of third parties.

(iii) ***Duty to avoid conflicts of interest***—enshrined in Article 156, it prohibits the administrator from getting involved in legal situations that are essentially contradictory to the company's social interest or from getting involved in the social decisions taken by the other directors, whose essence is incompatible with its functions; in these situations, it is the duty of the administrator to invoke the respective incompatibility before the other administrators and to reduce it to writing in the minutes of the meeting of the board of directors or management.

(iv) ***Duty to inform***—from Article 157, it is inferred that the duty in question aims to guarantee the equality of shareholders in accessing information related to the life of the company; under these conditions, the use of privileged information for the advantage is expressly prohibited for a small number of shareholders at the expense of the others. What for the administrator is the duty to inform, for the shareholder it translates as the right to be informed; it is shown as a very crucial right since it provides subsidies that influence social deliberations. For third parties, information is a major factor that leads them to decide whether or not to invest in a certain commercial company. It is in this context that paragraph 4 of the same article establishes that "The managers of the publicly-held company are obliged to immediately communicate to the stock exchange and to disclose in the press any resolution of the general meeting or of the company's management bodies, or relevant fact occurred in their businesses, which may have a significant influence on the decision of market investors to sell or buy securities issued by the company."

6.6.2.2 The Content of the Administration

It should be noted that since the board of directors is a collegial body, most of its duties are carried out by deliberation. The minimum number of members of the board of directors is 3, and it is incumbent upon the general meeting to elect and dismiss them at all times, and the bylaws are responsible for determining the rules regarding the calling, installation, and operation of the board and the latter will take its decisions by an absolute majority of votes; the statute may also determine a qualified *quorum* for certain resolutions, subject to the specification of matters covered (Article 140, item IV, Brazilian Corporate Law).

The content of administration is limited to the competences that it has and are clearly enshrined in Article 142 of the Brazilian Corporate Law. In the direction of the aforementioned article, the board is responsible for: (I) establishing general guidelines for the company's legal business relations; (II) proceeding with the election and dismissal of the company's directors and establish their duties taking into account the provisions of the bylaws; (III) carrying out the inspection of the management activities of the directors and the examination, at all times, including the books and other documentation of the company, and requesting information regarding the contracts in the process of being signed or already signed, among various acts; (IV) encouraging the convening of general meeting at the time it deems necessary or in situations provided for in Article 132; (V) commenting on the reports and accounts of the board; (VI) taking a position in advance on acts or contracts, within the probable requirements of the bylaws; (VII) issuing a resolution regarding the issue of shares or subscription bonuses, when the statute authorizes; (VIII) proceeding with the authorization of the sale of noncurrent assets, constitution of real liens, and provision of guarantees and obligations of third parties, except as otherwise provided in the bylaws; (IX) choosing and removing the auditors where necessary.

6.6.2.3 Directors' Civil Liability

The directors are guided by the principle of legality and competence in the exercise of their functions; it is precisely because they act within the legal parameters they are not responsible for their actions, even if such actions result in damage to the corporate entity. However, they will be held responsible if they act intentionally or with guilt, even if they are pursuing their duties and/or when their acts substantiate the violation of the law or the constitutive act of the company. Liability is the legal virtue by which the director is obliged to respond for damages that his acts caused to the corporate entity, to the shareholders, or to third parties.[189]

The civil liability of administrators is capable of assuming different modalities, taking into account the subject of law on whom the damage caused by that person falls[190]:

(i) ***Civil liability to the company***—its intention is to ensure that all activities exercised by the administrators contribute to the pursuit of social or company interest. Illegal acts are those that can lead the civil liability of administrators to the company, including in the following situations: (i) execution of acts of a lavish nature, creating unnecessary and unfounded expenditures for the company[191]; (ii) adoption of behavior that is clearly

189 João Pedro Barroso DO NASCIMENTO, op. cit., 118.
190 João Pedro Barroso DO NASCIMENTO, op. cit., 118.
191 See § 20, Article 154 of the Brazilian Corporate Law.

offensive to the duty of loyalty[192]; (ii) sale of company assets at low prices in relation to the market or without due authorization, and inconvenient distribution of dividends, an act that gives rise to joint and several liabilities.[193]

(ii) ***Civil liability to shareholders***—there will be room for civil liability to shareholders if the administrator violates the duties arising from the law; such violations include the following: (i) illicit prohibition of shareholders or attorneys from entering the general meeting[194]; (ii) fraudulent exemption of shareholders in the distribution of dividends[195]; (iii) prohibition on the enjoyment of preemptive rights.

(iii) ***Civil liability to third parties in general***—the term *third* in this context refers to those who maintain legal relationships with the corporate entity, as is the case of those who have credit rights with the company (creditors), contractors, employees, and those who provide any resources to the company. If one of these suffers any damage resulting from illegal or unlawful behavior on the part of the administrator, there will be room for compensation; some of the behaviors that can give rise to compensation include the following: (i) improper use of information before its publication, resulting in damage to capital market investors[196]; (ii) publication of a fraudulent balance sheet that will serve as a basis for inducing third parties to subscribe for the value about a shareholder or third person; there is talk of individual action, and it is up to the holder of the same who suffered the loss. Social action aims at restoring property damage to the company. The object of the individual action is the reimbursement of damages that directly affected third parties or shareholders. The interposition of social action does not rule out the likelihood of filing an individual action, since the holders and the object of the action are different.

6.6.3. Oversight

We have already talked about the general meeting and the board of directors as corporate bodies; in addition to these, there is another one – the supervisory board – whose insertion in the organic structure of the company is mandatory in

192 See items I, II, and III, Article 155 of the Brazilian Corporate Law.
193 See Article 201 of the Brazilian Corporate Law.
194 See single paragraph of Article 126 of the Brazilian Corporate Law.
195 See item IV, Article 109 of the Brazilian Corporate Law.
196 See paragraph 3 of Article 155 of the Brazilian Corporate Law.

corporate entities that take the form of a company and which aims to promote the supervision of administrators. To this end, it is bound to monitor the life of the company, from the verification of regular aspects of procedures and legal business situations, to issue opinions on the official reports of company's financial situation, as well as on possible operations; and bring changes to capital, issue of debentures, and distribution of dividends.[197]

The functions of the supervisory board, the supervision of the board of directors, and the board of directors are also constituted. The supervisory function of the body in question is not applicable to the general meeting, as this is an organ that is at the top of the hierarchy of the organic structure of the company and therefore in a superior position in relation to the others. Its composition requires a minimum number of three members and a maximum of five, and an equal number of alternates, whether they be shareholders or not.[198] The right to participate in the general meeting is granted to all shareholders.[199] The participation of members of the board of directors in the directory corresponds to a third of the total number of members of that board (this is because the two bodies are inserted in the administrative structure of the company). Members of the administrative bodies cannot be part of the fiscal council.[200]

6.7. Vicissitudes of Business Companies

As a rule, once the share capital is established in the company's charter, it cannot be changed. However, its alteration is likely to occur in the act of reforming the statute, on the initiative of the general assembly; as for bylaws, including a clause that authorizes the increase/reduction of the social capital through a deliberative act of the meeting or of the board of directors, there will be no need to reform the bylaws. Within the universe of the prerogatives of corporate legal persons, there is the right to modify the organizational structure of the company at all times; such a right can be exercised for meeting or dissociation of assets between two or more corporate entities or for changing the type or object of the company and the modality of accountability of shareholders. Among the possible corporate vicissitudes in the Brazilian legal system are *transformation*, *incorporation*, *merger*, and *spin-off*.[201]

197 See Articles 161 and 163 of the Brazilian Corporate Law.
198 See § 1, Article 161 of Brazilian Corporate Law.
199 See § 2, Article 12 of the Brazilian Corporate Law.
200 See § 2, Article 12 of the Brazilian Corporate Law.
201 Ricardo NEGRÃO, op. cit., 499.

6.7.1 Capital Increase

The legal transaction whose object is the modification of articles of association—whether unilateral ("capitalization of profits or reserves") or bilateral in nature (has the assumption and issuance of the collective will of the company, deliberating in the sense of creating shares and informing the people who can acquire them)—is called a capital increase.[202]

Modes of capital increase. As a legal business, the capital increase can become effective in a variety of ways.[203]

(i) **By a share-subscribing act**—for its capital increase, the company launches an offer for the acquisition of shares by contributing in monetary values or goods or by capitalizing credit against the company, which the acquirer (underwriter) simply accepts.
(ii) *Conversion of Debentures into Shares*—this is a modality provided for in Article 57 of the Brazilian Corporate Law. The convertible nature of debentures into shares gives the debenture holder the alternative to stop investing in debt securities and start to do so in shares of the issuing company. Such conversion process presupposes the capital increase of the respective company, with the purpose of guaranteeing the creation of shares that will fall to the holder of the debentures that execute the transformation right, with the termination of the credit included in the debenture of which he was the holder.
(iii) *Exercise of Subscription Bonus and Call Option*—the subscription contract related to the issue of security is effective when the execution of the right to purchase and pay the issue price of the shares is verified and the capital of the company is increased by exercise (item III, Article 166 of the Brazilian Corporate Law). In the purchase and sale alternative, a legal business relationship through which the company consents to the right to obtain shares from other people, the company's capital is increased when the shares targeted by the option are transferred, in which case there is business modification of the company's contract.
(iv) *Act to capitalize profits and reserves*—the legal provision in the Brazilian Corporate Law, in Article 169, states as follows: "*The increase through capitalization of profits or reserves will imply a change in the nominal value of shares or distributions of new shares, corresponding to the increase,*

202 José Luiz BULHÕES PEDREIRA and Alfredo LAMY FILHO, op. cit., 997.
203 João Pedro Barroso DO NASCIMENTO, op. cit., 90.

among shareholders, in proportion to the number of shares they own." In the company (company) where the nominal value does not exist, the act of capitalizing profits or reserves is likely to be consummated without changing the number of shares (§ 1 of the referred article).

(v) *Repercussions of other operations*—here it is necessary to bear in mind that in the process of incorporation of companies, there is, on the one hand, the incorporating company and, on the other side, the incorporated company, which in turn subscribes to the increase in the capital of that company, with the purpose of giving rise to shares that will replace the shares terminated therein, and the incorporator's capital increase is due to the transfer of the merged company's net assets. A similar phenomenon occurs in the process of spin-off of companies with the transfer of part of the merged company's net assets.

The increase in capital in publicly held companies is effective without changing the number of shares but with a change in their nominal value. It therefore consists of a simply nominal increase as opposed to an increase in valuation. The purpose of this rule is to guarantee the prevention of the exacerbated distribution of subsidized shares, "*which is equivalent to the annual subdivision of the shares in circulation on the market, preventing quotations from serving as a reference to measure the evolution of their real value, and encouraging, in the investing public, illusion of gains that contribute to hinder the normal functioning of the market.*"[204]

The Brazilian Corporate Law, in its Article 166, for the purpose of distinguishing the increases, whose corporate acts are filed in the Public Register of Mercantile Companies, from those registered therein, establishes that the capital increase can occur by: (I) deliberative act of the ordinary general meeting, in order to correct the way in which the corresponding monetary value is expressed; (II) deliberative act of the meeting or of the board of directors, in compliance with the provisions contained in the constitutive act of the company, in situations where it is authorized to issue shares within the statutory limitations; (III) conversion of **debentures** or founders' shares into shares and the implementation of rights granted through subscription bonuses or an alternative to purchase shares; (IV) deliberative act of the extraordinary general meeting propelled to deal with the matter related to the reform of the constitutive act of the company, in the event that the statute does not authorize the increase of the capital or if the authorization limit has been reached. Due to the stipulation mentioned in paragraph

204 Waldo FAZZIO JÚNIOR, op. cit., 210.

1 of the aforementioned article, within the time lapse of 30 days after the consummation of the capital increase, the company will request its registration in the trade register or the filing of the minutes of the statute reform meeting.

Let us now see how the Civil Code of 2002 regulates the increase of capital in limited company.

In Article 1081 of the aforementioned statutory instrument, it is enshrined that: "Except for the provisions of a special law, when the quotas are paid in, the capital may be increased, with the corresponding amendment to the contract. There are those who believe that two fundamental concepts of capital increase can be extracted from this article: (i) Being that in the limited partnership the share capital is configured by quotas and partners issue a deliberative act to increase the capital when the payment of the capital is complete; (ii) the increase in the company's capital does not dispense with the modification of the company's articles of incorporation (articles of association).

The implementation of increase in company's capital is likely to occur through granting of new values to preexisting quotas or through segmentation of new importance into new quotas. The segmentation into new quotas knows the preemptive right, since it facilitates the entry of third parties in the corporate entity, in the event that the primitive partners choose not to exercise that right[205] or decide to assign it.[206]

Primitive partners, in the capital increase process, are guaranteed the right to continue participating in the share capital through the preemptive right, and it is in this context that they can proceed with the subscription of capital to the extent of its social contingents. Once the deliberative act regarding the capital increase has been issued, partners have a 30-day period to exercise the preemptive right in the same proportion of the shares they hold. It is a well-known fact that in the face of the company's capital increases process, two alternatives assist the partners: The first consists of the right to participate in the capital increase, and, the second, to assign the respective right to third parties.[207]

After preference has elapsed the time limit set, if opted for by partners or if third parties were given the full amount of the increase, it will be necessary to hold the general meeting of partners, whose purpose will be to approve the amendment of company's charter (articles of association).[208] The shareholders'

205 See § 1, Article 1.081 of the Civil Code.
206 See § 2, Article 1.081 of the Civil Code.
207 Id.
208 See § 3, Article 1.081 of the Civil Code.

deliberative act, referring to the amendment of the articles of association, will be carried out by voting by a minimum number of votes equivalent to three-quarters of the company's capital.[209]

6.7.2 Capital Reduction

The Brazilian Corporate Law establishes in its Article 173 the following content: "The general meeting may decide to reduce the share capital if there is a loss, up to the amount of accumulated losses, or if it deems it excessive."

In the first event ("loss up to the amount of accumulated losses"), the shareholders have the intention of decreasing the figure of the company's capital in order to remedy the losses recorded and to accommodate the amount of the company's capital, under the principle of reality of social capital. The ultimate goal is to clean up the company's accounts to give it the legitimacy to proceed with the promotion of profit-sharing resulting from the date of the reduction, a situation that would prove impossible without the respective reduction of capital, due to the principle of decomposition of the company's capital.[210]

In the second eventuality ("excessive capital reduction in relation to the corporate purpose"), the shareholders projected the company's capital disproportionately in relation to the corporate object, being offensive to the economic principles to continue with the business activity within such disproportionality, for several reasons, whether of an accounting or operational nature. In this situation of a decrease in the capital of the company, two possible solutions can be adopted: (i) to return to the shareholders a portion of the amount invested in the investment or (ii) to dispense with the amounts that, until then, have not been contributed. In the wake of paragraph 1 of Article 174 of the Brazilian Corporate Law, the decrease in the capital of the company can only be effected if those who are not entitled to credit before the company are not opposed; the creditors have a term of 60 days to express their opposition, which is counted from the date on which the minutes of the meeting approving the capital decrease are published. The effectiveness of the minutes of the meeting in this sense recognizes a suspense condition: no opposition from creditors in the 60-day period.[211]

Being inserted within the organic structure of the company and exercising its functions, the fiscal council has a fundamental role in the process of decreasing the share capital, since the issuance of an opinion by this body, around the

209 See item I, Article 1.081 of the Civil Code.

210 João Pedro Barroso DO NASCIMENTO, op. cit., 90.

211 Waldo FAZZIO JÚNIOR, op. cit., 209.

proposal of the administrators who wish to propel the referred process, is an essential formality for the proposal to be presented at the general meeting.

The reality that the capital decrease process goes through three procedural phases is undeniable: (i) Management's proposal for the reduction; (ii) issuance of the opinion of the fiscal council; and (iii) issuance of the resolution by the general meeting regarding the reduction proposal (§ 1, Article 173 of the Brazilian Corporate Law). Once the deliberative act regarding the reduction has been issued, the rights inherent to the shares whose certificates have been issued will be suspended until they are presented to the company for necessary replacement.

Article 174 of the Brazilian Corporate Law establishes that, "*Except for the provisions of articles 45 and 107, the reduction of the share capital with a refund to shareholders of part of the value of the shares, or by the decrease in the value of these, when not paid, to the importance of the entries, will only become effective 60 (sixty) days after the publication of the minutes of the general meeting that decided on it.*" The exceptions referred to in Articles 45 and 107 relate to the possibility of redemption and shareholder remission. The 60 days are summarized in a period of decay, within which the unsecured creditors for securities preceding the date, on which the minutes are published, by means of notification, may express their opposition to the capital decrease, communicating the same to the Company Registry of Company's headquarters.

On the one hand, if creditors do not express their opposition within the legally established timeframe, the deliberative act of the general meeting regarding the reduction of capital continues to be filed in the Register of Mercantile Companies. On the other hand, if opposition is expressed by those who have a right to credit before the company, the minutes of the reduction can only be filed after the presentation of evidence of the payment of credit or the judicial deposit of the respective amount.

6.7.3 Merger of Companies

When two or more corporate entities are involved in an operation on the basis of which they unify to form a new company, or even in an operation through which one or more corporate entities are absorbed by an existing one, such an act is called the merger of companies. At the first stage of operation, the authors usually call fusion itself as fusion by constitution, fusion by creation of a new company, fusion by integration, fusion in the strict sense or union, or simply fusion and in the second stage of operation, they call merger as merger by absorption and merger by incorporation, annexation, or incorporation.[212]

212 Maria Helena DAMASCENO and Silva MEGALE, *Transformação, Fusão e Cisão de Sociedades*, Revista da Faculdade de Direito, Universidade de Minas Gerasi, ISSN: 0304-2340, 1980, 284.

From a legal point of view, Brazilian legislators, both those of 1940 and 1976, perhaps with a view to presenting the institute under a more accessible legal structure, followed a different technique from that which dominates foreign legislation; that is, it did not formulate a broad concept of fusion; on the contrary, he defined the two fusion species for creating a new company and incorporating them into separate articles. These two figures, incorporation and merger, are respectively provided for in Articles 227 and 228 of the Brazilian Corporate Law (Law No. 6,404, of December 15, 1976).

Although, with this, both have not ceased to be aspects of the same phenomenon; in both, there is a merger of companies, as this occurs when two or more companies are integrated to form a new one, as when one or more companies are integrated into one that subsists. What changes in either mode is the procedure.[213]

Even though regulated by the law of public limited companies, the merger is not an exclusive institution of these types and can be applied to any corporate type as well as operated between companies of different types. For example, a limited liability company, one limited liability company, and one jointly owned company may participate in the same merger agreement. This understanding is based on Article 223, which states that "*The merger, merger or spin-off can be operated between companies of the same or different types and must be resolved in the manner provided for the amendment of the respective articles of association or articles of association.*"

Characteristics of the Merger. The merger has certain characteristics that allow it to be distinguished from other phenomena that occur in the context of the vicissitudes of business companies, which are as follows[214]:

(i) Legal economic unity and extinction of at least one company—the merger of companies is one of the forms that serve to carry out the concentration of companies, constituting among the various concentration operations the one that carries out the corporate integration in a more intimate way, since the economic and legal aspects coincide. The merger results not only from an economic unit but also from a single legal person; this means that, in the merger, with the economic-legal union of the companies, at least one of them renounces its condition of subject of rights and obligations, which is to say, it loses its legal personality. Of all the legal entities involved in the merger process, only one remains: the

213 Id.
214 Maria Helena DAMASCENO and Silva MEGALE, op. cit., 287.

one that arises from the creation of the new company or the one that remains in the incorporating company.

In the case of a merger to form a new company, all those that merge are extinguished; also, when a company incorporates one or more companies, the incorporated company or companies are extinguished. It is in this context that the Brazilian Corporate Law, in its Article 219, establishes that the company is extinguished by the end of the liquidation (item I) and by incorporation or merger and by the spin-off with the transfer of all assets in other companies (item II).

(ii) Universal succession of rights and obligations—in the merger, there is a succession of all rights and obligations of at least one company: In the merger to form a new company, this happens to the merged companies; in the merger, the developer succeeds the final form of the merged companies, that is, the new company.

Special attention needs to be paid to Articles 227 and 228 of the Brazilian Corporate Law. "It being convenient to remember that in the merger and incorporation, the figure of the wholly-owned subsidiary, an innovation introduced in the positive Brazilian law by the new law of public limited companies, and that consists of the company constituted by a single shareholder, which legally must be a Brazilian company. When a company incorporates the wholly-owned subsidiary of which it is the sole shareholder, under the economic aspect there is no succession for the incorporator in the rights and obligations of the merged company, since the incorporation of the wholly-owned subsidiary, from the outset, the incorporator owns the company's equity. There is only a transfer of rights."

This is a universal succession, with the transmission of the social heritage *uno actu*. As it can be seen in Article 234 of the Brazilian Corporate Law, "*The certificate, issued by the registry of trade, incorporation, merger or spin-off, is a suitable document for the registration, in the competent public registers, of the succession, resulting from the operation, in assets, rights and obligations.*" With the merger, all rights and obligations arising from ongoing contracts are transferred to the new company or the incorporator, as the case may be, unless they are contracts entered into *intuitu personae*, in which case the merger ends. Due to the universal succession, which leads to the confusion of two or more assets, the successor responds ultra vires, except for the separation of assets, as provided for in paragraph 3 of Article 232 of the new law on public limited companies.

(iii) Entry of partners of the merged companies or of the merged companies into the new company or the merging company—as a general rule, with the merger, partners of the merged companies and of the merged companies that approved the merger become partners of the new company or of the merging company, receiving directly from the issuing company the shares that fit them, which will correspond to the net assets transferred and will be distributed to partners in proportion to the participation of each one in the transferring company.

The law provides for exceptions to this rule: the wholly-owned subsidiary, of which the incorporating company is the sole shareholder, and that of the incorporating company, which, when participating in the merged company, owns shares in it whose value corresponds to the net assets to be merged.

Protocol and Justification. Protocol—the interpretation of Article 224 of the current Brazilian Corporate Law implies that the Protocol is a document, the elaboration of which falls to administrative bodies or to partners/associates who show an interest in the operation, which contains all the requirements of the negotiation of incorporation, merger, or spin-off with incorporation and is submitted to the competent corporate bodies to form the business.[215]

Under Article 223 of the aforementioned law, the decision of these bodies in the process of incorporation, merger, or spin-off follows the formalities that guide the modification of the respective acts that constitute the company (contract or statute). In companies, it is the private responsibility of the general meeting to issue a deliberative act regarding their merger, incorporation, and spin-off; as a result of item VIII of Article 122 and of items IV and IX of Article 136 of the Brazilian Corporate Law that require the merger and division of the company or their incorporation into another, and all of this are deliberated only during the general meeting with the consent of shareholders with a minimum representation of half of the voting shares, if the constitutive act of the company does not require a greater quorum and the negotiation of the company's shares is prohibited on the stock exchange or on the over-the-counter market.

The content of the Protocol is enshrined in Article 224 of the Brazilian Corporate Law and is presented in the following terms, "*which will include: (I) the number, type and class of shares that will be assigned in lieu of the rights of shareholders to be extinguished and the criteria used to determine the replacement relationships; (II) the active and passive elements that will form each portion of the assets, in the event of a spin-off; (III) the criteria for valuing the net worth, the date*

215 José Luiz BULHÕES PEDREIRA and Alfredo LAMY FILHO, op. cit., 1270.

to which the valuation will be referred, and the treatment of subsequent changes in equity; (IV) the solution to be adopted regarding the shares or quotas of the capital of one of the companies owned by another; (V) the value of the capital of the companies to be created or of the increase or reduction of the capital of the companies that are parties to the operation; (VI) the statute project or projects, or statutory amendments, which must be approved to complete the operation; and (VII) all other conditions to which the operation is subject."

Keep in mind the sole paragraph of the article in question, which provides the following—"*the values subject to determination will be indicated by estimate.*"

Justification—it is a legal requirement, under Article 225, Brazilian Corporate Law, that in incorporation, merger, and spin-off operations with merger, the protocol must be presented to the general meetings of interested companies accompanied by justification, which will expose the following elements: (i) reasons or objectives of the operation and the company's interest in its execution; (ii) the shares that will be received by the shareholders with preemptive rights and the reasons for the change in the rights they held, if there is provision; (iii) the composition—after the operation, according to types and classes of shares—of the capital of the companies that should issue shares in replacement of those that should be extinguished; (iv) the amount of the return/refund of the shares that will constitute the right of the dissenting shareholders.

The function of justification is to provide the general meetings of the interested companies with information that allows shareholders to assess whether the transaction is in the company's interest and whether there is justification for modifying the rights of the preferred shares when provided for.

6.7.4 Spin-off of Companies

It is Article 229 of the Brazilian Corporate Law that provides the legal definition of the spin-off. "A spin-off is the operation by which the company transfers portions of its assets to one or more companies, constituted for that purpose or already existing, extinguishing the spin-off company, if there is a version of all its assets, or dividing the its capital, if the version is partial. " It should be noted that the spin-off, under Article 223, can be applied to any corporate type, as well as operated between companies of different types.

In accordance with the new law on public limited liability companies, the following hypotheses (modalities) occur[216]:

216 Maria Helena DAMASCENO and Silva MEGALE, op. cit., 300.

(i) **When a company allocates part of its assets to an existing company**. In this case, (i) the first company divides its assets, transmitting part of them to another existing company, and continues to develop its activities, although in a different way. (ii) When a company transfers portions of its assets to more than one existing company—here the figure changes because a company divides its assets, transmitting not only a portion of them to an existing company but transmits two or more equity shares, respectively, to two or more existing companies. As in the previous hypothesis, the spin-off company continues to develop its activities. (iii) When a company divides its assets into parcels that are destined for two or more existing companies, and, in this case, due to the total transfer of its assets, the spin-off company is extinguished. (iv) When a company divides its assets and moves part or parts of it to create one or more companies. This spin-off modality operates for the creation of a company called a wholly owned subsidiary, which, according to the provisions of Article 251 of the Brazilian Corporate Law, may only be constituted by a Brazilian company, which will be its sole shareholder. In this case, the spin-off company remains. (v) When a company divides its assets into portions that will be used to form two or more new companies.

Characteristics of the Company Spin-off.[217] (i) Division of social assets—in any modality of division, there is a division of social assets. The company divides its assets to highlight a portion or parcels that will integrate the assets of another company or other companies. When the equity version is partial, the spin-off company remains. When, however, it is total, it is extinguished.

(ii) *Succession of rights and obligations*—the corporate entity absorbing the equity fragment of the spin-off corporate entity will succeed the latter in the rights and obligations related to the legal phenomenon of the spin-off, if the spin-off corporate entity is still present. However, in the situation of split-up with extinction, the corporate entities absorbing the equity fragments of the spin-off corporate entity will succeed it, in proportion to the transferred net assets, in unrelated rights and obligations (§ 5 of Article 229 of the Corporate Law by Actions).

(iii) Allocation of shares or quotas to the partners of the spin-off company—as a result of the spin-off—the partners of the spin-off company who

217 Id., 302.

approve the transaction will receive shares or quotas of the companies resulting from the spin-off or who have absorbed portions of the spin-off company's equity, as appropriate. The shares or quotas will be attributed to partners in replacement of the shares or quotas they owned and in proportion to their interests in the spin-off company.

Legal Procedure for the Company Spin-off.[218] The legal spin-off procedure comprises acts that can be classified into three stages: (i) The first stage consists of defining the business stipulations, and the managers of the spin-off company or its shareholders prepare and sign justification to be submitted to the company's general meeting, which must comply with the provisions of Articles 224 and 225 on Protocol and Justification; (ii) the second stage corresponds to the formation of the legal business; the general meeting deliberates on the justification and its approval forms the legal business of spin-off; and (iii) the third stage consists of executing the legal transaction; after approval of the justification, the general meeting (a) appoints the experts who will evaluate the portion of the assets to be transferred; (b) when the appraisal report is completed, it will decide on the report; and (c) if approved, it will function as the general meeting for the constitution of the new company, following the terms stipulated in § 2 of Article 229 of the Brazilian Corporate Law.

Effects of the legal business of spin-off. The spin-off legal business has its effects, according to each case, in accordance with the Brazilian Corporate Law[219]:

(i) **In the case of total spin-off**—there is the creation of new corporate entities that absorb the equity fragments of the spin-off corporate entity and its extinction; subrogation of the shares of the created companies; the corporate entities absorbing the assets fragments of the spin-off will succeed it in the rights and obligations forming part of the assets portion of the absorbed and in proportion to the net assets transferred in the unrelated rights and obligations (§ 1 of Article 229); and consolidation of the shareholder's equity shares in the new companies and the formation of social groups and social organizations in the new companies.

(ii) **In the case of partial spin-off**—the constitution of the company or companies that will absorb portions of the spin-off's assets, which will

218 José Luiz BULHÕES PEDREIRA and Alfredo LAMY FILHO, op. cit., 1305.
219 Id.

> remain with the rest of its assets; the shares of the spin-off company that are extinguished will be subrogated to the shares of the new or newly incorporated companies, and these will jointly and severally respond to the spin-off, for their obligations prior to the spin-off, under the terms of Article 233; the formation of the assets of the new companies with a portion of the spin-off's assets and of the social groups of the new companies with the shareholders of the spin-off and the social organizations of the new companies.

Under the sole paragraph of Article 233 of the Brazilian Corporate Law, "*the act of partial spin-off may stipulate that companies that absorb portions of the spin-off company's assets will be responsible only for the obligations transferred to them, without solidarity with each other or with the spin-off company, but, in this case, any previous creditor may object to the stipulation, in relation to its credit, provided that it notifies the company within 90 (ninety) days from the date of publication of the demerger acts.*"

Right of withdrawal. The shareholders of the spin-off company dissenting from the spin-off resolution will be assisted by the right of withdrawal when the spin-off is initiated: (i) alteration of the object of the company, except if the spin-off assets are transferred to the corporate entity whose dominant activity coincides with the object resulting in the spin-off corporate entity; (ii) reduction of the mandatory dividend; or (iii) as recommended in Section III, Article 137 of the Brazilian Corporate Law, participation in a group of companies.

Creditors' Rights. The Brazilian legal system, aiming to protect the interests of creditors in the spin-off, offers them the guarantee of joint and several liabilities of the companies involved in the operation. Raul Ventura, mentioned by Maria Damasceno, affirms that "*the reason for the creditor's complaint is the reduction of the debtor's assets; as long as it is maintained, assets to be transferred; (b) when the appraisal report is completed, it will go away with different holders, the reason for the complaint ceases; it is enough, therefore, for all liabilities to be responsible, through solidarity, all societies, old and new.*"[220]

Pursuant to Article 233 of the Brazilian Corporate Law in force, "*With the disruption of the company, the companies that absorb portions of its assets will be jointly liable for the obligations of the extinguished company. The spin-off company*

220 Raul VENTURA, *Cisão de sociedades. apud* Maria Helena DAMASCENO and Silva MEGALE, *Transformação, Fusão e Cisão de Sociedades*. Revista da Faculdade de Direito, Universidade de Minas Gerais. ISSSN: 0304–2340, 1981, 304.

that survives and those that absorb portions of its assets will jointly and severally answer for the obligations of the former prior to the spin-off." It is in this context that it is understood that solidarity between companies is constituted in favor of creditors of any kind.

With regard to debenture holders, of paragraph 2 of Article 231, they are assured of the redemption of the debentures, and the spin-off corporate entity and the absorbers of their equity fragments will respond jointly for the redemption of debentures.

The law allows that in the act of partial spin-off; solidarity between the absorbing corporate entities is removed from the patrimonial fragments of the spin-off corporate entity and between it and those.

If there is no prior creditor to the transaction and within the ninety-day period, counted from the date on which the acts are published, a creditor opposes the stipulation that removes solidarity, the corporate entities absorbing the patrimonial fragments of the spin-off the company will only answer for the complex mandatory transfer to them. It should be noted that in the wake of the sole paragraph of Article 233 of the Brazilian Corporate Law, the opposition of each creditor only benefits him.

6.7.5 Transformation of Companies

The concept of transformation can be presented both from a doctrinal point of view and from a legal point of view.

In the doctrinal point of view, Maria Damasceno understands that the transformation consists in the operation by which a given company leaves its original legal structure to submit to the legal norms of another type of commercial company. For this to operate, it is necessary that the company that until then had been dressed in a certain way adopts a new guise, thus changing from one corporate type to another.[221]

In the law, precisely in the Brazilian Corporate Law, "*Transformation is the operation that the company undergoes, regardless of dissolution and liquidation, from one type to another.*" This concept follows from Article 220; under the terms of the sole paragraph thereof, the legal figure in question will comply with the rules governing the constitution and registration of the corporate modality to be adopted and assets to be transferred; (b) consummation of the appraisal report leads to a change in the corporate type; it is a practical process that meets the evolution

221 Maria Helena DAMASCENO and Silva MEGALE, op. cit., 276.

of the company, since it allows the transition from one form to another without interruption of social life. It is around this passage that the legal nature of the transformation is discussed.

As Ricardo Negrão[222] postulates, there are two theories that contribute to clarify the legal nature of transformation: (i) the theory of novation; according to this, transformation is a kind of dissolution of the corporate entity, which has the consequence of creating a new and different legal person; (ii) the theory of identity or continuation (subsistence of legal personality); based on this theory, it is understood that the transformation does not equate to dissolution; what occurs in the transformation is the alteration of the constitutive act of the company (contract/statute) by partners/shareholders based on the law that assists them in this sense.

In this regard, Bulhões Pedreira and Lamy Filho posit that "*transformation is a unilateral legal business, which only modifies the particular legal system that organizes the company: the legal person, the assets and the partners that form the corporate body remain the same. There is no succession of assets—which presupposes different legal entities. What is modified is the legal system of the transformed company, which was stipulated according to one type of company and becomes that of another type, with the consequent modification of the rights and obligations of the partners and the social organization created by the company.*" The transformation business is linked to that of incorporation, merger, and spin-off, if the type of incorporating company that results from the merger, or to which part of the assets of the spin-off is transferred, is different from that of the merged and merged or spin-off company.[223]

As can be seen, the authors in question defend the theory of subsistence of legal personality; they justify their position in legal terms, stating that Article 220 of the Brazilian Corporate Law and Article 1,113 of the Civil Code expressly state that the transformation does not imply the dissolution and liquidation of the corporate entity.

Defending the same position, Ricardo Negrão, claims that under the Civil Code, as the Brazilian Corporate Law did, transformation is merely a continuation of the company under a new legal guise, having established that the transformation does not depend on the dissolution or sale-off. However, the transformation can bring about a substantial change in the partner's responsibility, a situation he did not aim for when he entered the original corporate entity.

222 Ricardo NEGRÃO, op. cit., 508.

223 José Luiz BULHÕES PEDREIRA and Alfredo LAMY FILHO, op. cit., 1261.

Therefore, the law requires unanimous consent, unless something else stipulates the contract or its bylaws (Article 1,114 of the Civil Code and Article 221 of the Brazilian Corporate Law).[224]

The first theory referred argued that in the transformation of companies there was a substitution of legal entities. One of the defenders of this notion was Miranda Valverde, and he understood that

> The preservation of the legal personality in the transition from one type of company to another does not mean, therefore, permanence of the same person legal. It results from the very process of transformation, and consists precisely in the transition, without intermediate status, from one type of legal entity to the other. The previous legal entity remains until the moment it is transformed or transformed into another legal entity. In the transformation of one company into another, there is always the constitution of a new legal entity, without; however, the parts that were part of the former legal entity completely disappear.[225]

Nowadays it is a peaceful opinion that in the transformation there is no substitution of a legal person: The transformed legal person is the same one that existed before the transformation. The legal personality of the company does not vary with its type, and changing the type does not cause the extinction of one legal person and the constitution of another.

Requirements. In order to verify the legal transformation phenomenon, it is necessary to comply with legally established requirements, namely[226]:

(i) *Resolution*—it is clear from Article 221 of the Brazilian Corporate Law that the transformation may be provided for in the bylaws or articles of association, in which case there is silence regarding the *quorum* for the resolution; this will be taken by an absolute majority of votes, pursuant to the provisions of Article 129 of the same law. If it is not foreseen, the law requires that it be approved unanimously by partners.

Deliberation as a requirement or general rule for the transformation of companies has an exception, which is based on its transitory nature. This is the company

224 Ricardo NEGRÃO, op. cit., 508–509.

225 Trajano de Miranda VALVERDE, *Sociedades por Acções: Comentários ao Decreto-Lei nº 2.627 de 26 de Stembro de 1940. Apud* José Luiz BULHÕES PEDREIRA and Alfredo LAMY FILHO, *Direito das Companhias,* 2ª ed. (Rio de Janeiro: Forense, 2017), 1261.

226 Maria Helena DAMASCENO and Silva MEGALE, op. cit., 279.

created before the new law on public limited companies, with capital not exceeding 5 million cruzeiros, which may, up to one year after the entry into force of Law No. 6,404 of December 15, 1976, regardless of statutory authorization, issue a resolution, by voting by shareholders representing two-thirds of the share capital, transforming it into a limited liability company, with limited liability (Article 298 of the Brazilian Corporate Law).

Pursuant to Article 135 of the Brazilian Corporate Law, in any event the extraordinary general meeting whose object is the transformation of the company will be installed in a primary convocation, with shareholders with a minimum representation of two-thirds of the voting capital attending; the call at second instance may be installed without observing a maximum or maximum representation of the shareholders.

(ii) **Archiving and publicity**—under the terms of paragraph 1 of Article 135 of the Brazilian Corporate Law, "*Acts relating to changes in the corporate type, must obey the filing and publication formalities. However, the failure to comply with these formalities cannot be opposed, by the company or its partners, to third parties in good faith.*"

(iii) Requirements' proper for the constitution and registration of the company whose form is to be adopted—since the purpose of the transformation is the adoption of a new corporate type, it is not possible to stop observing the set of requirements established by law for the constitution and registration of the company that revises the desired form. The requirements for constitution and registration vary according to the respective assumptions. So, the company that wants to adopt the form of a public limited company must obey all the requirements established by law for the constitution and registration of that corporate type as required.

Right of withdrawal. Article 221 of the Brazilian Corporate Law establishes that "*The transformation requires the unanimous consent of the partners or shareholders, unless provided for in the bylaws or in the articles of association, in which case the dissenting partner will have the right to withdraw from the company.*" However, the respective article establishes that the partners have the option to waive, in the constitutive act of the company, the right of withdrawal in the situation of transformation of the company.

Creditors' Law. The legal phenomenon of transformation will not, under any circumstances, jeopardize the creditors' rights before the company; the same rights will remain until their complete satisfaction is verified, under the exact guarantees that the previous corporate entity granted them.[227] The phenomenon that affects the transformed corporate entity will only produce effects in relation to partners that, in the previous corporate modality, would be subject to them, in the event that the holders of credits prior to the transformation request it, and only these will benefit.[228]

According to the principle of the intangibility of the creditors' rights, the rights that they acquired before the transformation of the company, that is, under the validity of the previous corporate type, cannot be altered as a result of that operation. The company that is transformed retains the same responsibility in relation to creditors established before the transformation under the old corporate form. In other words, the transformation of the company can never be opposed to creditors prior to the change of the corporate type, since otherwise it would be the best means of harming social creditors.[229]

6.8. *Extinction of companies*

6.8.1 Dissolution

Fábio Ulhoa Coelho posits that

> Dissolution is an ambiguous concept in corporate law. In a broad sense, it means the procedure for terminating the legal personality of the company, that is, the set of acts necessary for its elimination, as a subject of law. As of the dissolution, understood in this first sense, the business company no longer secures rights, is it not debtor of provision. In a strict sense, the dissolution refers to the act, judicial or extrajudicial, that triggers the procedure for extinction of the legal entity. The acts of closure of the legal personality of the company (the dissolution, in a broad sense) are distributed in the phases of dissolution (strict sense), liquidation and sharing.[230]

In the context of the Brazilian legal system, precisely in corporate law, there is a duality of rigidities applicable to the legal phenomenon of the dissolution of

227 See Article 222 of the Brazilian Corporate Law.

228 See single section, Article 222 of the Brazilian Corporate Law.

229 José Manuel Adriasola NAVARRETE, *La transformacion de la empresa, apud* Maria Helena DAMASCENO and Silva MEGALE, *Transformação, Fusão e Cisão de Sociedade,* Revista da Faculdade de Direito (Universidade de Minas Gerais, 1921), 282. ISSN: 0304-2340.

230 Fábio Ulhoa COELHO, *Curso de Direito Comercial: Sociedades*, op. cit., 569.

companies. One of the regimes refers us to the Brazilian Corporate Law (Article 206 and subsections), and its applicability extends to institutional companies, and the other provisions of the Civil Code (Articles 1033–1038) applicable to companies brought into existence through the social contract, therefore, are contractual.

The difference between the two regimental systems is quite small. The basic conceptual framework is the same: (i) the dissolution procedure starts with a solemn act by shareholders/partners or the judge; (ii) the liquidation phase follows, in which the company has its assets in order to make the final adjustment of its accounts, distributing the net assets or losses that occur to partners/shareholders; and (iii) as a last step, we proceed with the distribution of remaining assets among partners/shareholders. Although the field of distinction between the two regimes is reduced, it is important to clarify it; the same refers to the nature of the corporate bonds that cease to exist, or on the other hand, the contractual corporate entities in the dissolution process, in part, are based on contractual rules and principles, a particularity that does not exist in the dissolution of institutional societies.[231]

Causes of dissolution in the systematic of the Civil Code. Under Article 1.033, "*The company is dissolved when: (I) the expiration of the term expires, unless, once this has expired and without opposition from a partner, the company does not go into liquidation, in which case it will be extended for a period of time indeterminate; (II) the unanimous consensus of the partners; (III) the resolution of the partners, by absolute majority, in the company for an indefinite period; (IV) the lack of plurality of partners, not reconstituted within 180 (one hundred and eighty) days; (V) the extinction, as provided by law, of authorization to operate*."

The provision of item IV does not apply if the remaining partner, including in the event of concentration of all the shares of the company under their ownership, requires, in the Public Register of Mercantile Companies, to transform the registration of the company to an individual entrepreneur or to an individual limited liability company, subject, where applicable, to the provisions of Articles 1,113–1,115 of the Civil Code.[232]

Dissolution of the company under the Brazilian Corporate Law. In the situation of public limited company, the reasons for the total dissolution of full rights are: the termination of the preestablished lapse time for the existence of the corporate entity[233] in the situations provided in the bylaws[234]; by deliberative

231 Fábio Ulhoa COELHO, *Curso de Direito Comercial: Sociedades*, op. cit., 569.
232 See single section, Article 1.033.
233 See al (a), item I, Article 206.
234 See al (b), item I, Article 206.

act of the assembly[235] for the existence of one single shareholder, verified in the ordinary general meeting, if the minimum of 2 is not reconstituted until that of the following year, except as provided in Article 251[236]; by the extinction, in the form of the law, of the authorization to operate.[237]

The dissolution by the end of the period provided for in paragraph (a), item I, Article 206 of the Brazilian Corporate Law coincides with that enshrined in the civil code (item I, Article 1.033): This is the hypothesis in which the company was constituted for a determined period fixed in the bylaws, which, once elapsed, does not extend. It is a fact that it does not need any administrative or judicial declaration, resulting only from the will of the shareholders established in the articles of association. It is crucial that until the date of the term stipulated in the contract it is possible to decide on the extension, leading to the decision to be registered with the Board of Trade. However, under the terms of item IV, Article 35 of Law 8.934 of November 18, 1994,[238] after the expiry of the period, the registration bodies can no longer proceed with the filing.[239]

About the second hypothesis, it concerns the cases provided for in the articles of association, as per paragraph (b), item I, with due regard for the will of the shareholders. The occurrence of those causes *ipso facto* the dissolution of the corporate entity. The Civil Code limited itself, in Article 1.035, to reproducing the text of the Brazilian Corporate Law.

The third situation results from the resolution of the general meeting al. (c), item I, Article 206 of the Brazilian Corporate Law. As provided for in item III, Article 1.033 of the Civil Code, shareholders in an extraordinary general meeting specially convened for this purpose decide the dissolution by the majority—the consent is made by shareholders with a minimum representation of half of the voting shares—unless a larger *quorum* is required by the company's articles of association; this follows from item X, Article 136 of the Brazilian Corporate Law.

The fourth eventuality, provided for in Article 1.033 of the Civil Code, refers to "*the existence of a single shareholder, verified at an annual general meeting, if the minimum of two is not reconstituted by the following year*" (al. [D], item I, Article 206 of the Brazilian Corporate Law), except as enshrined in Article 251, which deals with the wholly owned subsidiary, the one in which the Brazilian corporate entity is created by public deed or by the acquisition of all the shares of another

235 See al (b), item I, Article 206.
236 Cfr. al (d), item I, Article 206.
237 See al (e), item I, Article 206.
238 Law as amended by Law No. 13.833, July 4, 2019.
239 See al. (b), item I, Article 206.

Brazilian company. The requirement of plurality of partners is at stake, without which there cannot be a company under Brazilian law, a principle mitigated by the possibility of restructuring the company within the period established by law.

The Civil Code, in item V of Article 1.033, provides for the "*extinction, in the form of the law, of the authorization to operate.*" In some cases, the state has reserved for itself authorization for the operation and inspection of certain commercial companies, aimed at controlling public credit and thus avoiding negative effects on the national financial system or areas considered to be of great strategic interest by the state. They are the official or private banking establishments and credit societies, among others.

Once the authorization for the operation of these institutions in the country is canceled, the dissolution of the company will take place, immediately after the governmental act.

Dissolution by judicial decision. "*Judicial dissolution is dissolution by sentence. The judicial path will be followed whenever there is a conflict of intentions between the partners about the dissolution or when the bankruptcy of the company occurs.*"[240]

The cases of dissolution by sentence at the level of the Civil Code are enshrined in Article 1.034. Here are its wordings—"*The company may be dissolved in court, at the request of any partner, when: (I) its constitution is annulled; (II) the social purpose is exhausted, or its feasibility is verified.*"

It is necessary to consider that the causes of the dissolution listed in the aforementioned article are not exhaustive; in this logic, the partner has the power to invoke other grounds for the merit of the dissolution by sentence, provided that their individual rights are at stake.

In the universe of public limited companies, the following are reasons for dissolution by sentence: the declaration of the annulment of the creation of the corporate entity, by means of an action brought by one of the shareholders (al. [a], item II, Article 206); when evidencing elements of its inability to fulfill its objective, by means of an action brought by shareholders with a minimum representation of 5 % of the share capital (item [b], item II, Article 2) and bankruptcy, al [c] (item II, Article 206).

Any shareholder is entitled to bring an action for annulment of the company due to a procedural defect in its constitution. The Brazilian Corporate Law prescribes a procedure for the formation of the company's contract, which comprises

240 Waldo FAZZIO JÚNIOR, op. cit., 144.

formal acts and in which requirements must be satisfied, under penalty of any shareholder deducting in court a claim for annulment of the constitution. In the wordings of Article 285 of the Brazilian Corporate Law, "*The action to annul the constitution of the company, due to defect or defect, expires in 1 (one) year, counted from the publication of the articles of incorporation.*" Even after the filing of the action, the possibility of the company, by means of a deliberative act of the general meeting, creating measures to remedy the respective defect (sole paragraph) is not ruled out.[241]

The legitimacy for filing the company's annulment action is also extended to the Public Ministry. In this context, the processing of the liquidation by sentence may be requested by the Public Prosecution Service, if the company, within 30 days after dissolution, does not trigger the liquidation or, if after doing so, suspend it for a period greater than 15 days, in the case of dissolution by extinction, in the form of the law, of the authorization to operate (item II of Article 209 of the Brazilian Corporate Law). The procedural legitimacy of the Public Ministry is restricted to that cause of dissolution.

Dissolution by administrative decision. It is a form of dissolution provided for in item III of Article 206 of the Brazilian Corporate Law; it refers to administrative decisions, such as those for the extrajudicial liquidation of a financial system company (Law No. 6,024 of March 13, 1974).[242] Liquidation is the administrative procedure that has the same purpose as the bankruptcy institute: collecting assets and paying them and selling them for the payment of those who are entitled to credit before the company. Sometimes in the interest of preserving public credit, the state prefers to liquidate a business company administratively, rather than allowing it to be subjected to the common bankruptcy process.[243]

In the case of financial institutions, the extrajudicial decree of the liquidation can be verified in the present situations: (i) depending on the occurrences, its economic or financial status, or by the verification of the necessary requirements to be authorized for the decree of the bankruptcy; (ii) violation of legal or statutory rules that govern institutional activities by the administrators; and (iii) the occurrence of damage to the institution, which entails subjecting its unsecured creditors to unusual risk.[244]

241 José Luiz BULHÕES PEDREIRA and Alfredo LAMY FILHO, op. cit., 1323.
242 Law providing for extrajudicial intervention and liquidation of financial institutions.
243 Ricardo NEGRÃO, op. cit., 526.
244 Id.

6.8.2 Settlement

Pursuant to Article 207 of the Brazilian Corporate Law, "*The dissolved company retains its legal personality, until extinction, in order to proceed with liquidation." And under article 51 of the Civil Code, "In the case of dissolution of the legal entity or the authorization for its operation is revoked, it will remain for the purposes of liquidation, until it is concluded.*" Consequently, the corporate entity dissolved through acts of partners/shareholders or judicial decision, does not immediately cease its legal personality. Its personality remains only for the purpose of liquidating the mandatory complex to which the company is attached.

It is in this perspective that Ulhoa Coelho[245] maintains that the corporate entity comes to know about a significant limitation of its personality, in the sense that it cannot perform acts whose purpose is not the liquidation. This pertains to all legal transactions entered into on behalf of the dissolved corporate entity that does have a purpose of being responsible for the complex of pending mandatory obligations attributable to the legal person. This has lost the legal substance to be a center for the imputation of rights and obligations, with the exception of the imputation of the essential acts to the course of liquidation. In these circumstances, if the effects of the business acts are not attributable to the legal person, they can only be attributed to the natural person who executed them on behalf of the dissolved corporate entity.

Fazzio Júnior affirms that

> The peculiar procedure to the execution of the dissolutory sentence, the liquidation is the final phase of the extinction of the company, consisting of realizing the asset and resolving the social liability, being able to be sued in court or not. Once the dissolution is verified, the administrators must promote the liquidator's investiture and limit the proper management to urgent business, new operations are forbidden, which if carried out will lead to their joint and several liability.[246]

As the constitutive act of the corporate entity does not include the appointment of the liquidator, the members are granted the option of appointing a third party outside the company. In the legal dissolution phenomenon of full right, the partner can issue a request, in any case, for settlement by sentence.

In the situation of the dissolution phenomenon resulting from the extinction of the governmental authorization to operate the corporate entity, the Public

245 Fábio Ulhoa COELHO, *Manual de Direido Comercial: Sociedades*. 578.

246 Waldo FAZZIO JÚNIOR, op. cit., 145.

Prosecutor's Office is assisted by the subsidiary legitimacy to file a lawsuit aiming at liquidation, if the administrators do not file the action, within a period of 30 days following the extinction. If the partner also fails to bring an action, the person representing the parquet has an obligation to take it to court. In the event that the Public Prosecutor's Office does not exercise its legitimacy, the authoritarian entity empowered to grant authorization will appoint an intervener to proceed with the liquidation request and with the provisional administration of the corporate entity, until the liquidator is appointed.[247]

As a result of the position, the judge who issues a dissolution sentence must still indicate the liquidator in accordance with that enshrined in the articles of association or in the legal provisions regulating the corporate modality that will be in question. Because the judge has powers to appoint the liquidator, the judge also has the power to remove the liquidator; the liquidator can also be removed on the initiative of one of the partners, provided that the liquidator does not observe the legal duties to which he is attached, or without foundation, makes the liquidation process slow, or practice incompatible acts with the liquidation interests, among several other behaviors.

From § 1, item I of Article 1.038 of the Civil Code, it appears that if the liquidator elected by partners is a third party outside the membership, he is likely to be removed by partners at all times.

Liquidator's duties in the Civil Code—Article 1,103 (contractual companies) and in the Brazilian Corporate Law—Article 210. Under the mentioned articles, the liquidator's duties are:

(I) to register and publish the minutes, sentence or dissolution instrument of the company;
(II) collect the company's assets, books and documents, wherever they are;
(III) proceed, in the 15 (fifteen) days following its investiture and assistance, whenever possible, of the administrators, in the preparation of the inventory and the general balance of assets and liabilities;
(IV) finalize the company's business, realize the asset, pay the liability and share the remainder between the partners or shareholders;
(V) to demand from the quota holders, when the asset is insufficient to solve the liability, the payment of their shares and, if applicable, the necessary amounts, within the limits of the responsibility of each one and in proportion to the respective participation in losses, sharing,

247 Waldo FAZZIO JÚNIOR, op. cit., 145.

among the solvent partners and in the same proportion, the due by the insolvent;

(VI) call the shareholders' meeting, every 6 (six) months, to present a report and balance of the settlement status, reporting on the acts performed during the semester, or whenever necessary;

(VII) confess the company's bankruptcy and file for bankruptcy, according to the formalities prescribed for the type of liquidating company;

(VIII) after the liquidation ends, present the liquidation report and its final accounts to the partners;

(IX) to record the minutes of the meeting or the assembly, or the instrument signed by the partners, that it considers the liquidation closed.

In all activities, documentation, or publications, the liquidator will use the firm or company name always followed by the "in liquidation" clause and its individual signature, with the declaration of its quality (sole paragraph, Article 1,103 of the Civil Code). The general meeting is responsible for expressly authorizing the liquidator to record assets or assumes debts. Such authorization is subject to reservations when it comes to a situation in which a company needs essential conditions to satisfy imperative complex of mandatory obligations.[248]

In the process of liquidation, for the purpose of identifying the corporate entity, the signature of the same (represented by the liquidator) must be accompanied by the expression liquidation; the representative is limited to performing essential acts for the termination of irresolute businesses, moving forward with the settlement of the terminated. Every six months, it is necessary to call the meeting, by the liquidator, for the purpose of rendering accounts of the activities and operations performed by him, presentation of a report, and balance of the liquidation situation. The meeting is empowered to establish periods of not less than 3 months and not more than 12 months, for the said rendering of accounts.

During the holding of general meetings at companies, in the context of liquidation, regardless of their type, the shares have equal voting rights; therefore, restrictions are not allowed under any circumstances, regarding preferred or common shares, any limitation being ineffective. When the state of liquidation reaches its end, the effective character of the limitations relating to the right to vote is restored. In the course of liquidation by sentence, the judge will convene and be the chairman of the general meetings essential for the deliberation of the interests of the corporate entity, briefly resolving the disputes and clarifying the

248 Waldo FAZZIO JÚNIOR, op. cit., 146.

doubts raised. The minutes of the meeting will be multiplied in certified copies and then attached to the judicial process.

7 Companies in Particular

7.1. Private Companies

The roots of private limited companies are found in the German legal system. It was specifically on April 20, 1892, in Germany, that the creation of companies essentially characterized by the limitation of liability took place. The limitation of liability within the scope of corporate entities was designed under Brazilian law and was preferably adopted by businessmen and non-businessmen for the development of small, medium, and large-scale activities.[249]

Before the enactment of the Civil Code of 2002, Decree No. 3,708 of January 10, 1919 (as a result of the project by Ingles De Souza[250]) was the only legal instrument that disciplined the creation of private limited companies characterized by limiting the liability of their partners to the total social capital, jointly and severally. With the validity of the Civil Code of 2002, the company started to be called Limited Liability Company.

As it can be seen, in a first stage, the private limited company was regulated by Decree No. 3.708/19, nowadays by the Civil Code, in Articles 1.052–1.087. Several factors drove the incorporation of the limitation of liability in business, but the two main factors that led to the origin of limited companies in the European continent (specifically in Germany and England), in the last phase of the 19th century are: (i) *"Guarantees the partners against undesirable equity effects that may occur in unlimited companies"* and (ii) *"at the same time, it dispenses the complex structuring stock companies, which may, in certain situations, translate into a simplified capital company."*[251]

In this regard, Ulhoa Coelho says that limitation of liability is the most prevalent characteristic in corporate societies that operate in the context of the

249 Ricardo NEGRÃO, op. cit., 385.

250 It is in 1912, with the Commercial Code Project of INGLES DE SOUZA, that the company's origins by quotas, of limited liability, under the name of "limited company," Ingles de Souza booked Chapter II of his five-article project to consider the issue. Such a company would turn under a social firm; the partners would be responsible for the total importance of the subscribed capital for the formation of the company. This distanced itself, in some points, from Portuguese law, because it only admitted the development of its activities.

251 Waldo FAZZIO JÚNIOR, op. cit., 148.

Brazilian economy. The introduction of this feature dates back to 1919, and today it has a percentage representation above 90 % (of the corporate entities that have completed the registration formalities with the competent entities—commercial boards). Its greater predominance in the Brazilian legal system is strictly linked to two fundamental characters[252]:

(i) *Limited nature of the liability of partners*—protection of the individual patrimonial sphere of partners against those who have credit rights before the company, in case it is unable to answer for the complex mandatory to which it is attached. From such protection it follows that the social creditors are prevented from requesting the execution of their credits in the individual assets of partners.

(ii) *Contractuality*—the creation of the corporate entity presupposes the establishment of social legal relationships, which can be legally disciplined by contract (in the case of contractual companies) and by statute (in the case of statutory or institutional companies). In contractual societies in which liability is limited, the field of freedom of negotiation between partners is vast, a different situation from which occurs in institutional societies, as is the case of public limited companies that have a preestablished legal regime.

Limited membership concept. Having made the introduction of the outstanding aspects of limited company, it is now interesting to look for its concept.

Fazzio Júnior posits that the elaboration of any concept of the limited company must be based on the elementary aspects provided by its legal regime. This perspective is not dissociated from the concepts presented in Brazilian business law and allows the formulation of a synthesis concept—contemplating the limited company as a legal person brought into existence "*for the shareholders with limited liability to the payment of social capital, individualized by corporate name that integrates the limited adjunct.*" The starting point, according to that author, for the elaboration of the concept of limited company, in the doctrinal field "*is to know if the limited company is a person or capital commercial company.*" It is in this path that the doctrine itself knows asymmetric positions.[253]

As noticed by Fazzio Júnior, for Rubens Requião and Pontes Miranda, it is a person company, while Waldirio Bulgarelli sees it as a capital company. On the

252 Fábio Ulhoa COELHO, *Manual de Direito Comercial: Direito de Empresa*, op. cit., 180.

253 Waldo FAZZIO JÚNIOR, op. cit., 150.

other hand, he defends that neither one nor another position is consistent, since all corporate entities are made up of people and do not exist without capital. The classifying criterion operates according to the hegemony of one or another element, aiming to make it easy to understand the specific organization of each type of company.[254]

A single analysis, with regard to the secondary applicability of the normative complex disciplinary of the simple company to the limited company, is likely to attribute a "*personal*" character to it; even so, there is nothing to prevent its configuration as a capital company, since the introduction of the Civil Code; the partners allow the disciplinary rules of the anonymous company to be applied to the limited company: "*The articles of association may provide for the supplementary regulation of the limited company by the rules of the anonymous company*" (sole paragraph of Article 1053). According to this, the alternative, in the middle term of the secondary discipline of the normative complex pertaining to simple companies or subsidiary regency by the regulatory rules of the companies, opens space for the limited company to be confused between the two types of companies (person and capital).

Without advancing with any positioning, it will be interesting to bring up the person company and capital company characteristics.

The limited company will be considered an *intuito personae* corporate entity if (i) the constitutive act of the company includes in its systematization a provision that makes the alienation of social quotas by one of the partners subject to the consent of the other quota holders; (ii) if the constitutive act of the company (contract) highlights the assignment of quotas, and in the meantime make a declaration of unseizability; or (iii) even if it misses in relation to the two points already mentioned, it will still be personal, if the creative act of the corporate entity determines that, in the event of the death of one of the quota holders, the surviving members will decide on the calculation of the its patrimonial collection.

In the capital company, on the other hand, there is a situation different from that of the people—while in the person company the trust among shareholders counts for knowing each other; in the capital company, it is not a fundamental necessity that the partners know each other. The social capital of the shareholder is more important, not the shareholder himself, and for this reason their departure from the company or entry of one or more members into the company does not require the consent of other shareholders.

254 Id.

Waldo Fazzio Júnior concludes that, outside the previously described hypotheses, where the element "*person of the partner*" is shown to be predominant, the corporate entity under analysis is closer to capital companies. It is crucial to keep in mind that the hybrid nature of the limited company and its insufficient legal discipline make it to be in constant oscillation in the middle of the person company (*intuitu personae*) and capital companies (*intention pecuniae*).[255]

Legal regime—the limited liability company is regulated in a specific chapter of the Civil Code, precisely in Articles 1,052–1,087. However, this normative complex is insufficient to regulate the vastness of legal matters pertaining to limited liability companies; therefore, the code itself allows other legal instruments to be applied to this corporate modality.

It is in this context that Article 1.053 of the Civil Code establishes that "*The limited liability company is governed, in the omissions of this Chapter, by the rules of the simple partnership.*" It is a case of supplementary regulation that aims to solve the problem of the insufficiency of the articles mentioned above for the discipline of limited liability companies.

The Brazilian Corporate Law can supplement the limited liability company; for that, it is essential that the constitutive act of the corporate entity insert in its systematics a provision that authorizes the secondary applicability of the normative complex of corporations to situations whose discipline does not fit in the proper chapter of the Civil Code that deals with limited companies; if the social contract so disposes, consequently, the regulatory rules of simple companies will be inapplicable to limited companies. In other words, "*if the limited company's social contract is silent or defines the discipline of simple companies as its subsidiary application legal regime, articles 997 to 1,032 of the Civil Code apply, whenever the matter is not disciplined in the articles. 1,052 to 1,087 of the same Code. However, if the partners stipulate in the articles of association that the limited liability regime of their limited liability company will be anonymous companies, in matters not regulated by the articles 1,052 to 1,087 of the Civil Code, the rules of the Brazilian Corporate Law will be applied.*"[256]

Due to the fact that the limited companies are brought into existence through the association articles, their incorporation and dissolution comply with the rules of the Civil Code. Even if the limited liability company is supplemented by the Brazilian Corporate Law, by virtue of the contractual provision, with regard to its constitution and dissolution, the legal regime of contractual corporate entities

255 Waldo FAZZIO JÚNIOR, op. cit., 150.

256 Fábio Ulhoa COELHO, *Manual de Direito Comercial: Direito de Empresa*, op. cit., 180.

will be applied, in compliance with Articles 1.033–1.038 and 1,102–1,112, all of the Civil Code.

Social capital—under Article 1.052 of the Civil Code, "*In the limited partnership, the liability of each partner is restricted to the value of their shares, but all respond jointly and severally for the payment of the share capital.*" This means that the universal set of partners in the limited liability company is jointly responsible for the payment of the share capital. Still from the perspective of the code "*Contributions that consist of service provision are prohibited*" (§ 2 of Article 1.055). Interpreting this legal precept, Fazzio Júnior,[257] states that the individual responsibility of partners will be determined according to the value of the shares that they hold and the industry partner is not allowed to participate in the share capital of the company.

There are important points to take into consideration in the context of social capital: (i) The company's incorporation (articles of association) must be written down and can be of a public or private nature; it will not only contain the provisions established by the contracting parties but will also contain: "*the share of each partner in the share capital, and how to do it*"[258]; (ii) "*Contributions consisting of rendered services are prohibited*"[259]; and (iii) the partners, when contributing to the formation of the share capital, must do so in compliance with the lapse time and form established in the articles of association; (iv) the limitation of the liability of partners is based on the full value of the company's capital.

Share capital is liable to be increased or reduced, provided that intangibility is taken into account as a principle of social capital.

Increase in social capital—in the act of incorporation of the limited liability company, the fixing of share capital is imperative. This, once paid, may undergo modifications, with the intention of being increased. Having verified the resolution of capital increase by partners, in a meeting or assembly, whose decision will be made by the vote with a minimum correspondence of three-quarters of the share capital (item I, Article 1.076 of the Civil Code), partners will exercise within a period of 30 days their preemptive rights in obtaining new shares, in proportion to their ownership. Thus, in the event that the partner holds 30 % of the paid-up share capital, it is likely to enjoy the preemptive right of up to 30 % of the deliberate increase.[260]

257 Waldo FAZZIO JÚNIOR, op. cit., 151.
258 See Article 997 of the Civil Code and its item IV.
259 See Article 1.055, § 2, Civil Code.
260 Ricardo NEGRÃO, op. cit., 408.

About the preemptive right, Ricardo Negrão posits as follows:

> It is possible that third parties who are not partners participate in the preemptive right due to the assignment made by a partner. In this case, there can be no opposition from holders of more than a quarter of the share capital. The law does not specify the form of opposition, but it is crucial that other partners can only exercise the right to object when they become aware of the assignment agreement. Therefore, it is the responsibility of the assigning partner or the third assignee to take the necessary steps to notify all the partners or obtain the consent of at least three quarters of the shareholders of the share capital in the assignment instrument.[261]

Two situations may occur, after 30 days of deliberated increase: (i) Partners or third persons with preemptive rights acquire the universality of the increase, and in this situation an assembly or meeting will be held with the purpose of agreeing to the alteration of the constitutive act of the company, so that it can be deposited in the entity with competence for its registration; and (ii) a portion of partners or third persons have refrained from exercising the preemptive right; there will be freedom among partners to subscribe to the increase; thus, it will be up to those who have an interest in the subscription to execute it, being able, in this case, to add its participation in the total capital.

Continuing after the installments are paid off, the share capital is likely to be increased through a deliberative act of partners; consequently, the constitutive act of private limited companies will be changed. Certainly, the quota holders are assisted by the preemptive right in the withdrawal of new quotas, to the extent of the shares they hold in their equity sphere. The interest in exercising the preemptive right must be manifested within a period of 30 days after the deliberative act of the addition has been issued. After the aforementioned lapse of time, and after the totality of the increase by partners or third parties has been canceled, a meeting or assembly of partners will take place, which will have the purpose of agreeing to amend the company's charter.[262]

Capital reduction—there are situations that can lead to a decrease in capital, which may occur before or after the payment of capital:

(i) **Reduction of capital due to the default of a remission partner or its exclusion**—Article 1,004 of the Civil Code regulates the situation of the

261 Id.
262 Waldo FAZZIO JÚNIOR, op. cit., 152.

remission partner. Any partner who fails to comply with the obligation to pay in the approved share capital is thus called, even though it has been notified in due terms. It is a case of default by the defaulting partner; in view of this delay, the remaining partners have the option to take the following actions: (a) claim compensation for the losses verified; (b) proceed with the exclusion of the referring partner from the corporate entity; and (c) proceed with the reduction of the shareholder's interest in the social capital to the amount already contributed.

If the actions taken by the other partners consist of excluding the remitting member or reducing their shares, and those (partners) do not complete the missing amount, there will be a need to reduce the share capital, in line with Article 1.031, § 1 of Civil Code. In this sense, Article 1.058 of the same legal diploma must be taken into account "*If the share of a remission partner is not paid, the other partners may, without prejudice to the provisions of art. 1.004 and its sole paragraph take it for yourself or transfer it to third parties, excluding the original holder and returning to him what he has paid, less the interest on arrears, the installments established in the contract plus expenses.*"

(ii) **Capital reduction due to irreparable losses**—the corporate entity has the power to reduce the share capital, when its payment is verified; such reduction implies a change in the constitutive act of the respective entity, as long as there are damages without repair. Under Article 1.083 of the Civil Code, the reduction for damages without redress will be directly proportional to the nominal value of the quotas, and the minutes of the meeting that approves it should be recorded in the Public Registry of Mercantile Companies.

(iii) **Reduction based on the disproportionality between the capital and the corporate purpose**—in the wake of Article 1.082, item II of the Civil Code, the corporate entity is likely to decrease its capital, through the respective amendment of its constitutive act, if there is any disproportionality between capital and the corporate purpose and when the latter is excellent in relation to this. It is in this context that Article 1.084 establishes that, "*In the case of item II of Article 1.082, the capital reduction will be made by refunding part of the value of the shares to the partners, or by dispensing the debt justification, with proportional decrease, in both cases, the nominal value of the shares.*"

The effectiveness of the capital decrease for showing itself to be excellent to the corporate object is conditioned to the registration of the minutes of deliberation in the Public Registry of Mercantile Companies, within 90 days, and in case there is no challenge by those who have the right to credit before the company or if there is evidence of the settlement of the debt or the judicial deposit of the respective amount. Within that period, the unsecured creditor who holds a liquid and certain title has the power to oppose the reduction (§ 1, 2, and 3, Article 1.084 of the Civil Code).

(iv) **Reduction due to withdrawal of partner**—in this modality of capital reduction Ricardo Negrão[263] states that, in the numerous cases of withdrawal of partner, it is always possible to provide for contractual clauses that regulate payments and the status of capital. Meanwhile, if no prediction is made, the capital may suffer a decrease, except if the other partners proceed with the suppression of the value of the withdrawn quota (§ 1, Article 1.031, Civil Code). "*The payment to the withdrawing partners, their heirs or creditors, according to the case, will be made in cash, within ninety days from the settlement of their quota, based on the company's equity situation at the date of resolution, verified in a special balance sheet.*"

Shareholders Liability—the characteristic of private limited companies is the limitation of liability for the assumed complex obligation. The emphasis here is that those who respond in a limited way for that complex are the partners and not the corporate entity itself. The implies the absolute limitation of the liability of members to third parties.

However, if the equity of the corporate entity proves to be insufficient to satisfy the debts to which it is assigned, those in the company who have credit rights can only request the execution of the private equity assets of the quota holders up to a certain amount. This means, the essence of the social modality in question consists of limiting the subsidiary responsibility of the quota holders to the payment of the social capital (partners, individually, respond in solidarity with the act of paying the universality of the shares of the company).

Once the capital is fully paid, the shareholders' equity sphere cannot be called upon to answer for the debts of the corporate entity. In this case, the corporate entity will now respond unlimitedly, using its assets, for the complex mandatory

263 Ricardo NEGRÃO, op. cit., 411.

to which it is linked. *The limit of the partners' liability, in the limited partnership, is the total subscribed and unpaid share capital. Subscribed capital is the amount of resources that the partners commit to deliver for the formation of the company; paid-in is the part of the social capital that they actually deliver.*[264]

It is not too important that the company has been brought into existence by public or private scribes. The important thing is that its constitutive act establishes a provision according to which the limitation of partners' liability will be made according to the total value of the social capital. If such a provision doesn't exist, the corporate entity will be referred to as a corporate entity in name of the collectivity. Of course, the absence of a clause in this regard means that the partners are held jointly and severally liable.

In this regard, Fazzio Júnior, adds that "*When dealing with a company formed by limited liability shares, the partners respond up to the limit of the social capital in full, only being released when the social capital is paid in, that is, the share capital is not paid in, the pledge that falls on the assets of partners by debt of the company for limited liability shares is valid, if there are no social assets that are responsible for the obligation.*"[265]

Exceptions to the rule of limitation of liability—it is essential to state that limitation, as one of the properties of liability in private limited companies, has reservations; in some situations, partners are called upon to respond in a subsidiary way, however unlimitedly, by the obligatory complex of the company. Here are the situations:

(i) The first exception results from Article 1,080 of the Civil Code; such a legal provision establishes that "*Decisions that violate the contract or the law make the liability of those who expressly approved them unlimited.*" The meaning and scope of this legal precept is as follows: Partners who decide against *legem* or against the social contract will answer, in an unlimited way, for the resulting social obligations, and partners who formalize their disagreement will be exempt from this unlimited nature of liability.

(ii) According to Article 50 of the Civil Code, in a situation where those who have the right of credit to the company find themselves defrauded by the partner, having used the prerogative of the abstraction/separation of assets, based on the referred fraud, which drags the legal personality

264 Fábio Ulhoa COELHO, *Manual de Direito Comercial: Direito de Empresa*, op. cit., 183.
265 Waldo FAZZIO JÚNIOR, op. cit., 153.

of the legal person, will be the partner obliged to answer unlimitedly for social obligations.

Fábio Ulhoa Coelho presents a situation of unlimited liability that occurs in the context of marital companies[266]:

> "*The marital company, that is, the one composed exclusively of husband and wife, irrespective of settled case law in the STF, has sometimes been understood as null, because it would, according to certain lessons, imply fraud against family law. The Civil Code prohibits marital company if the regime of goods in marriage is that of universal communion or mandatory separation (art. 977). Thus, if, in spite of the legal prohibition, a company composed exclusively of husband and wife is registered with the Commercial Registry, its partners would be responsible for unlimited social obligations.*"

Number of shares—the starting point, as recommended by Fazzio Júnior, for the study of the number of shares, is the Limited Company Law, Decree No. 3,708 of January 10, 1919. The aforementioned author understands that Article 5 of the aforementioned decree—by establishing that "*for all purposes, the original share of a partner and those that* [are] *subsequently acquire*[d] *will be considered as separate accounts*"—adopted the German system of initial single share, and consequently, in Article 6 of the same legal diploma, which establishes that "*The co-owners of the undivided quota, who shall designate among themselves one who represents them in the exercise of the rights of partner, must exercise in common their respective rights. In the absence of such a representative, the acts practiced by the company in relation to any of the owners produce effects against everyone, including the heirs of the partners. The co-owners of the undivided quota are jointly liable for the installments that are missing to contemplate the payment of the same quota*," he tried to discipline communion in the undivided quota.[267]

Meanwhile, although the intent of the aforementioned decree was not to discipline communion in the undivided quota, the current practices and customs entail dividing share capital into quotas of equal value. In practical terms, the French system of plurality of quotas was in place. This is because it is a system that makes it possible to negotiate quotas and make division more comfortable, which means that the shares of corporate entities with limited liability assume the facet of the companies' shares. Therefore, nowadays, the system is adopted

266 Fábio Ulhoa COELHO, *Manual de Direito Comercial: Direito de Empresa*, op. cit., 186.
267 Waldo FAZZIO JUNIOR, op. cit., 157.

that divides the share capital into quotas of equal value, which are allocated in different quantities, individually to partners, in accordance with the fraction that will have been realized.

In view of the what was presented before, the provisions modeled in precepts 5 and 6 of the Limited Liability Company Law ("*as each partner would have an initial share of a different value, according to his participation, article 5 provided that the shares he acquired first, they would be distinct from the primitive one. In turn, article 6 stipulated the condominium of quotas and their representation*") fall to the ground.

However, Article 1.055 of the Brazilian Civil Code by stating that "*The share capital is divided into quotas, equal or unequal, with one or several shares belonging to each partner*" admits, as can be inferred, unequal quotas and, in § 1 of Article 1.056, the quota condominium, for the purposes of transfer. In this situation, the rights relating to the condominium quota will be exercised by the representative condominium. When dealing with a deceased partner, by the estate intervener, paragraph 2 of Article 1.056 establishes that the representative condominiums of undivided shares are jointly liable for their payment. In view of the company, the quota is not divisible and payment must be observed.

As noted in the last paragraph, in the *regímen* prior to the current one, the system of initial single quota applied to Portuguese law was adopted and transferred to Brazilian law by means of the decree under analysis, a system distinguishing the original quota from the derivative, or acquired later, not to consider remission of the partner who, having paid in the first (original quota), would delay the payment of those subsequently acquired. Meanwhile, the original single-share system does not present any utilitarian justification, which led to its abolition and consequent replacement by the shareholding mode: The partners individually acquire a certain number of shares or quotas.[268]

Ricardo Negrão, in face of such scenario, concludes that the custom of adopting multiple quotas, in disagreement with the legal dictates, dragged with it practical repercussions, since some thought that it was the result of a law that the multiplicity of quotas subscribed by partner actually corresponded to only one quota and, in view of that, the sale of the fraction of the respective portion made the assignee associated with the selling partner and not a partner of the company. The purchaser of part of the share of the partner (who originally had only one share), having not acquired all of it, became a mere condominium, under the

268 Ricardo NEGRÃO, op. cit., 399.

terms of Article 334 of the Commercial Code. The legal diploma that ended this strange solution is the Brazilian Civil Code in force; under the terms of this, *the shares can be conferred in single or in multiple units to each partner. They are said to be the same or unequal because one partner may acquire a different number than another one may acquire.*"[269]

Acquisition of quotas—Article 8 of the lately Limited Former Companies Law provides that "*It is lawful for companies referred in this law to acquire released quotas, as long as they do so with available funds and without offending the capital stipulated in the contract. The acquisition will take place by agreement of the partners, or the exclusion of a remitted partner is verified, keeping the capital intact during the term of the company.*"

The aforementioned legal provision expressly authorized the acquisition of shares by the limited liability company. The corporate entity would become a partner of its own, since the acquisition of quotas by the corporate entity itself was carried out or with the purpose of being placed in treasury, to be transferred to third parties later or to be canceled. In both alternatives, the rights and duties relating to quotas incurred suspension. For a corporate entity to acquire its own shares, it must observe certain assumptions: (i) the payment of shares must be rigorously carried out; (ii) the act of acquiring the shares had to be carried out with reserve funds ("balance of profits not distributed to the partners in previous years"); and (iii) the acquisition of shares had to be approved by unanimous decision.[270]

Now, the Brazilian Civil Code of 2002 has no rule in the same sense; it doesn't say anything about the acquisition of quotas in such a way that its entry into force caused debate about the continuity or rupture of that practice.

As a consequence of what was said above, André Santa Cruz states that the doctrine is divided as to the continuity or rupture of the acquisition of quotas by the company itself. Some doctrines understands that, although the Civil Code does not contain a rule in this regard, that practice continues to operate, subject to its provision expressed in the constitutive act of the corporate entity, or that it is supplemented by the Brazilian Corporate Law; this is because this legal instrument opens space for the company to acquire its own shares, "*to remain in treasury or cancellation, provided that even the value of the balance of profits or reserves, except the legal one, and without decreasing the share capital, or Donation.*"[271]

269 Ricardo NEGRÃO, op. cit., 399.

270 Waldo FAZZIO JÚNIOR, op. cit., 160.

271 André Santa Cruz: *Aquisição de quotas pela própria sociedade,* available at http://genjuridico.com.br/2016/04.27/aquisicao-de-quatas-pela-propria-sociedade/, accessed on August 4, 2019.

Other doctrines defend that in the current regime the reality of the limited liability corporate entity acquiring its own quotas has become inoperative, as it is a contractual company and therefore would be incompatible with that reality. Such doctrinalists are of view that Article 1.057 of the Civil Code, by providing that "*In the omission of the contract, the partner may assign his share, totally or partially, to anyone who is a partner, regardless of the audience of the others, or to a stranger, if not there is opposition from holders of more than 1/4 (one quarter) of the share capital*" gives permission only for the transfer of the quota by the partner to another partner or to third parties; however, it does not allow the corporate entity to assign its own shares to itself.[272]

With regard to Article 1.058 of the same legal diploma, which provides that "*If the share of the remission partner is not paid, the other partners may, without prejudice to the provisions of art. 1.004 and its sole paragraph, take it for itself or transfer it to third parties, excluding the original holder and returning to him what he has paid, less the interest on the arrears, the installments established in the contract plus the expenses*," it should be understood that this is a precept that gives partners permission to take the shares of the referring partner for themselves or assign them to third parties, with no reference to the transfer of shares to the corporate entity itself.

The aforementioned author posits that the Department of Business Registration and Integration (DREI), in Annex II of Normative Instruction 10/2013, provides in item 3.2.10.2 that "*the acquisition of quotas by the company itself is not authorized by the new Civil Code.*" The Department of Business Registration and Integration joined the second doctrinal current mentioned above.

Even so, that author does not agree with such positioning, because Article 1.057 of the Civil Code, when considering the initial phase of its wording "in the omission of the contract," opens space for the constitutive act of the company to make provision, through clauses, which makes other situations operative, in addition to those enshrined in the law. Especially because the practice says that the propensity to use the Brazilian Corporate Law to discipline the limited liability companies, under the sole paragraph of Article 1.053 of the Civil Code, results in that the company can acquires its shares.[273]

André Santa Cruz strengthens his understanding in the following terms—

272 Id.
273 André Santa Cruz, cit.

"*with the entry into force of the new Civil Procedure Code, it seems that DREI will be obliged to review its understanding, since the aforementioned procedural law expressly provides for the possibility of the company to acquire shares when they are pledged and no partner wants to acquire them*"; he cites Article 861 of the Civil Procedure Code—"*Once the quotas or shares of a partner in a simple company or business are pledged, the judge will sign a reasonable term, not exceeding 3 (three) months, for the company to: especially in the form of law; (II) offer the shares or quotas to the other partners, with due regard for the legal or contractual preemptive right; (III) if there is no interest from the partners in the acquisition of shares, the calculated amount will be deposited in court, in cash; (§ Sole). To avoid the settlement of quotas or shares, the company may acquire them without reducing the share capital and using reserves, to be held in treasury.*"[274]

Assignment of quotas—the Civil Code, Law No. 10,406 of January 10, 2002, regulates the assignment of quotas through its Article 1,057, which reads as follows: "*In the omission of the contract, the partner may assign its quota, wholly or partially, to anyone who is a partner, regardless of the audience of others, or to a stranger, if there is no opposition from holders of more than 1/4 (a quarter) of the share capital.*"

Interpreting the aforementioned legal provision, Fazzio Júnior posits that the one to deal with the issue of the assignment of shares takes as a starting point the possibility that the constitutive act of the corporate entity may be omitted with respect to the aforementioned subject. The emphasis here is that, with the entry into force of the Civil Code of 2002, the solution to this issue is conditioned to what the constitutive act of the corporate entity has to provide. In the event of omission of the initial pact, the subsidiarity rule cannot be applied, since the hypothesis is provided for in the Civil Code.[275]

The legal transaction that has the object of assigning quotas will only produce *erga omnes* effects, before the company and third parties, if the instrument that formalized it is duly registered with the Commercial Registry for the purposes of its publication.[276]

There are two mechanisms that can make the transfer of quotas effective: (i) legal business of assigning rights (contractual mechanism—*inter vivo*) and (ii) by succession phenomenon (hereditary universal succession—*mortis causa*). In both mechanisms, the transfer is likely to be total or partial. There is no space for the merger between the sale of the business establishment and the transfer

274 Id.
275 Waldo FAZZIO JÚNIOR, op. cit., 160.
276 See single section, of the Article 1.057, Civil Code.

or assignment of quotas, and this in turn does not include the extinction of the corporate entity.

"*The transfer or assignment of quotas is an operation through which the transferor transfers to the transferee quotas of a company.*" Within the scope of the assignment of quotas, the main corporate aspects in the Civil Code line can be highlighted, which are listed as follows[277]:

(i) **Right of first refusal**—the constitutive act of the company is the contract, which, in addition to the clauses established by the contracting parties, is capable of presenting the optional clauses. In the path of Article 997 of the Civil Code, matters relating to the assignment of quotas are clauses lacking mandatory conditions, which may or not be included in the articles of association; it is in this perspective that Article 1.057 determines that "*In the omission of the contract, a partner may assign his share, totally or partially, to anyone who is a partner, regardless of the audience of others, or to a stranger, if there is no opposition from holders of more than 1/4 (one quarter) of the share capital.*" As can be inferred, the precept in question grants partners the option of making the use of the articles of association to establish specific rules governing the transfer of quotas of the limited company.

In the process of transferring shares, there is no consecration resulting from the law, which gives the other members the right of first refusal; it is a situation that the law reserved to its members, its regulation, obviously, in the articles of association, or in another convention among quota holders, which requires its filing in the company. This is because in the transfer of shares that belongs to other partners, the shareholding of others that are not involved in the business remains intact, a situation that does not happen in the process of adding capital, where new shares are subscribed.

Even if it was understood that there is legal support for the preemptive right in the process of assigning quotas, with the articles of association being omitted, the other partners with representation corresponding to more than a quarter of the share capital have the power to express their opposition regarding the entry of a new partner. The reality is that there is no preemptive right, but there is a

277 A. W. AMANNCIO (Consultoria Empresarial), *Cessão de quotas nas Sociedades Limitadas*, available at http://www.wamancia.com.br/cessao-de-quotas-nas-sociedades-limitadas/ accessed on August 4, 2019.

likelihood of interdicting a certain partner to transfer their shares to a third person who is not a partner (Article 1.057 of the Civil Code).

In this way, the transfer of shares by the partner is likely to occur in two different cases: (a) transfer of shares from one to another partner; here, the transfer may occur without the consent of the other partners, because the Civil Code opens space for the assignment of quotas, the assignee also being a partner in the same corporate entity; (b) transfer of shares to third parties outside the corporate entity; the transfer is conditional on the absence of opposition from the other partners representing 25 % of the share capital and subject to the consent of other partners representing three quarters of the capital, where there will be a need to sign the instrument of assignment by the respective partners.

(ii) **Total or partial assignment**—legally provided and regulated in accordance with Article 1.057 of the Civil Code; the assignment of quotas is the operation through which a certain partner formalizes the transfer of their quotas, in whole or in part to another partner or to a third person who is not a partner. The transfer of quotas as a whole is said to be a total assignment and has the consequence of leaving the partner who assigned them from the corporate entity; the transfer of part of the quotas is called partial assignment, and the partner who assigned them remains in the company, but the level of their participation in the company is reduced.

(iii) **Modification of the articles of association**—the validity of the legal business of assigning quotas is subject to changes in the articles of association with the consent of other partners (Article 1003 of the Civil Code). From Article 1.057 it is inferred that, in order to have effects before the corporate entity and third parties, it requires the registration of the instrument (containing the subscription of partners who announced it) through which it was carried out.

(iv) **Modality of social responsibility**—the assignor and the assignee respond jointly to the corporate entity and third parties; this joint responsibility is based on the complex mandatory to which the assignor was attached and which starts to link the,assignee and it has two years as a lapse time of its duration, to be counted from the date on which the modification of the constitutive act of the corporate entity is verified.

Attachment of the social quota—with regard to whether or not the attachment of the social quota is valid, it is noteworthy that neither the Commercial Code nor Decree No. 3,708/19 provided for it.

The pledge admission of the quota, as stated by Ricardo Negrão, was supported by the Superior Court of Justice, which in turn concludes that it may be attached even if the company is under a preventive bankruptcy regime.[278] The question of *affectio societatis*, which could be an impediment, is answered with absolute propriety by Minister Cláudio Santos:

> The problem of the breakdown of **affectio societatis** is not of such a magnitude that it results in an unengagedness not prescribed by law. On the other hand, there is no question of covering up forever debtors who would carry all their assets to a limited company, getting rid of debts. The issue of the breach of affectio societatis can be resolved with the acquisition of the other partners and payment of the amount corresponding to the quota or, with the dissolution of the company, in the absence of an alternative.[279]

The author Waldemar Zveiter adds that the Supreme Federal Court, compassionate with the question, proceeds with the admission of the pledge of the share of the partner based on the individual debts of the quota holder, in private limited companies, when the constitutive act of the corporate entity is permissive regarding the assignment and transfer of shares without the preliminary approval of other partners. The commercial company created in this way does not have the essence of the person company and is therefore inclined toward capital companies. The quotas subject to attachment (or pledged) would be reasonably likely to be sold by public auction, making room for free entry into the corporate entity.[280]

There are those who admit the seizure of quota in the following terms: The seizure of quota becomes possible when the constitutive act of the corporate entity through a precept allows its assignment without the approval of other partners. In this perspective, the company would be lacking in *affectio societatis* and would be forged to be configured as a capital company. The same occurs, in the doctrine, with the closed corporation, whose statute is limited to the negotiability of its shares, subjecting the ceding shareholder to give preference to the acquisition to

278 *"BRASIL, Superior Tribunal de Justiça, Recurso Especial nº 114.130–MG, Rel. Min. César Asfor Rocha, j. 23-11-1999." Apud* Ricardo NEGRÃO, op. cit., 402.

279 *"BRASIL, Superior Tribunal de Justiça, Recurso Especial nº 21.223–PR," apud* Ricardo NEGRÃO, op. cit., 402.

280 WALDEMAR ZVEITER, *Sociedade por Quotas de Responsabilidade Limitada–Aspectos polémicos;* Conferência dos Advogados Catarinenses–Criciúma–SC, 1991, 101.

the other shareholders, in order to avoid entering the corporate group of strangers. Such statutory rule gives the anonymous company the appearance of a *cum Intunu penonae* company. Rescuing the issue, if the entry of third persons outside the corporate entity by quotas is not conditioned by the approval of other partners, the attachment is proven to be valid, because the acquirer can freely enter the corporate entity.

Rubens Requião, mentioned by Waldemar Zveiter, maintains that:

> Admitting, to argue, that the private creditor partner can obtain the attachment of social funds in the process of executing the partner's private debt, with the fundament that they belong to him, and, at the same time, that the social contract prohibits transferring them to strangers, in which situation would the bidder [be] who acquired them? It is clear that, under these conditions, the quota would have no corporate value for the acquirer, who could not, with it, enter the company: he would, at most, have to wait for the dissolution and liquidation of the company in order to have his credit.[281]

What should be kept in mind is the belief that the company's funds are not owned by the quota holder, however, by the corporate entity. To advocate an understanding in an opposite sense would be to invalidate the theory of legal personification and the consequent denial of the patrimonial autonomy of the company. The concern of a considerable number of Judicial Magistrates, who were impelled by the parties, to admit that, in the absence of other assets of the quota holder debtor, he is exempt from the execution process, configuring himself as an alleged debtor in the state of insolvency. Such a claim is erroneous. And it is prudent to reason in the following terms:

> The attachment must fall on the credits that the debtor has in the company's current account, or on the profits that the company [declares] after the balance sheet. If these do not occur, the attachment can only be made in the liquidation of the company, on the net product that can be paid in payment to the debtor. If, however, there is a misuse of legal entities, and the debtor has maliciously or fraudulently transferred his assets to the limited liability company, the Judge will have the right to, examining the fraud, disregard the legal personality, ordering the pledge of the shareholder's asset in the company. It would be a perfect application of the disregard doctrine.[282]

281 Rubens REQUIÃO, *Curso de Direio Comercial, apud* WALDEMAR ZVEITER, *Sociedade por Quotas de Responsabilidade Limitada–Aspectos polêmicos;* Conferencia dos Advogados Catarinenses–Criciúma–SC (1991), 100.

282 Id., 102.

The Brazilian Civil Code of 2002, in the field of limited liability companies, does not pronounce on the seizure or social quotas as a basis for executing the partner for individual debts or auction based on the state of bankruptcy; however, it tried to discipline this matter within the scope of the simple partnership, making room for the debtor partner holding the right to participate in the profits of the partnership or in the portion that may fall into liquidation.

It is in this context that Article 1.026 of the Civil Code establishes that *the private creditor of a partner may, in the absence of other assets of the debtor, cause the execution to fall on what falls to him in the company's profits, or the part that touches him in liquidation*. As it can be inferred in Articles 1.026, sole paragraph and 1.031, in simple companies, the private creditor of each partner is guaranteed the right to proceed with the application for the settlement of its quota. Such a solution applies in its entirety in limited companies, not only based on the omissive attitude of the legislator, when disciplining the matter in question in the correlative chapter, but based on the fact that there is legal admission expressly for the execution of part of the capital in persons societies—which is also the case in simple societies—there is no prohibition on the application of the same rule in corporate capital or mixed arrangements, as well as in limited liability companies.

The quota holder—the validity of any legal transaction requires the observance of certain preestablished requirements in the law. It is in this context that, Article 104 of the Civil Code, determines that the validity of the legal business requires: (I) cable agent; (II) lawful, possible, determined, or determinable object; and (III) prescribed form or non-defense itself.

As the social contract is a legal business, for its effectiveness it must observe the requirements listed above, and the nonobservance of these incurs its nullity. Meanwhile, Maria Helena Diniz,[283] affirms that, in the specific case of the creation of the limited liability corporate entity, there are certain peculiarities legally imposed and that cannot be marginalized, in terms of the capacity of the contracting parties; coupled with this is the fact that the principal capacity is configured as a general rule and disability is the exception.

Article 1.134 of the Civil Code states the following: "*Foreign companies, whatever their object, cannot, without authorization from the Executive Branch, operate in the country, even though they are subordinate establishments, however, except in the cases expressed in law, to be a shareholder of a Brazilian limited company.*" This means that, just like natural persons, with capacity and without impediments,

283 Maria Helena DINIZ, *Curso de direito civil brasileiro*, Vol. 8 (São Paulo: Editora Saraiva, 2008), 67.

have the faculty to enter into contractual legal business (articles of association), in the same way, there is no impediment for legal persons, regular, under representation, to celebrate articles of association to bring a limited liability company into existence. The signing of articles of association can take place between a natural person and a legal person, and this person must have Brazilian nationality, as a foreign person needs to be authorized by the Executive Power.

Minors and the disabled—an interpretation of the letter of the law in Article 104 of the Civil Code implies that minors, who are incapable or relatively capable, are not susceptible to celebrating establishment of any legal business relationship and, consequently, are not susceptible to being included in the corporate purpose of limited liability as partners.

In 1976, due to the end of the legal personality (death) of a partner in a limited liability company, the São Paulo State Board of Trade refused to proceed with the filing of the modification of the constitutive act of the company; the change focused on the replacement of one *de cujos* by his heir, civilly incapable due to minority. "*The question went to the Judiciary, through a writ of mandamus, and after having been granted in all instances, the Supreme Federal Court, which in a memorable Judgment, rendered in Extraordinary Appeal no. 82.433-SP, from 1982, by the then Minister Xavier de Albuquerque, established the possibility of the entry of a minor, by succession, in the limited company, as long as duly represented or assisted* ."[284]

Waldo Fazzio Júnior adds that there is no legal basis that prevents the participation of the minor in the limited liability company due to lack of assistance, if the capital has been paid up. The successors of the partner of *de cujus*, even though they are minors, may hold quotas in limited liability companies, which may be shareholders of the limited liability companies. According to "*Normative Instruction No. 46/96, of the National Department for the Registration of Commerce*," these are presuppositions for archiving the acts of a limited company, such as participation of the minor partner, payment of share capital, and nonattribution of management or administrative powers to the minor.[285]

In this context, the jurisprudential order issued by the Supreme Federal Court started to make it possible for minors to become partners and to sensitize the "*National Department of Trade Registration*" to guide the commercial

284 See *"RT. 478/96 e RTJ. 70/608: 'EMENTA: Sociedade por quotas de responsabilidade limitada. Participação de menores, com capital integralizado e sem poderes de gerência e administração, como quotistas. Admissibilidade reconhecida, sem ofensa ao artigo 1'. do Código Comercial."* According to Luiz Gonzaga Modesto de PAULA, *Sociedade Limitada* 1ª.ed. (São Paulo: Saraiva, 2015), 16.

285 Waldo FAZZIO JÚNIOR, op. cit., 162.

boards to consent to the filing of acts constituting the corporate entities in which minors participate and the respective contractual modifications, subject to the observance of three assumptions: (i) The minor cannot exercise management or administrative acts; (ii) full payment of capital stock; (iii) participation of the incapacitated by minority as a partner requires that he is duly assisted or represented, in accordance with each situation.[286]

Let's say, however, still today, except for Article 974 of the Civil Code, a legally expressed rule isn't available regarding the participation of the disabled by minority as partners in corporate entities under a limitation of liability regime. The development of business activity by the incapacitated, under representation or assistance, is only valid in situations of supervening incapacity or of the successor in the *mortis causa* succession. It is in this line that the aforementioned legal provision provides that "*Can the incapable person, through a representative or duly assisted, continue the company previously exercised by him while able, by his parents or by the author of inheritance*." The interpretation of this legal concept must not, however, ignore its § 1, which reads as follows—"*In the cases of this article, authorization shall precede after examining the circumstances and risks of the company, as well as the convenience of continuing it, and the authorization may be revoked by the judge, after hearing the parents, guardians or legal representatives of the minor or the interdict, without prejudice to the rights acquired by third parties.*"

Deliberation of Partners—it was previously said that, in the first phase, the limited liability company was regulated by Decree No. 3,708 of January 10, 1919. It must be said that such decree, within the scope of its regency, was not pronounced around the assembly's or shareholders' or directors' meeting to decide on the interests of the corporate entity in the context of pursuing the purpose of the company.[287]

In the omission of the constitutive act of the company with regard to the matter of corporate resolutions, the aforementioned decree, in its Article 18, allowed the normative complex of public limited companies to be applied in a supplementary manner: "*They will be observed as regards limited liability companies, in that is not regulated in the bylaws, and in the applicable part, the provisions of the Corporate law.*"

In turn, the Brazilian Civil Code of 2002 came to introduce limitations to the powers of administrators, in determining in its Article 999 that "*The amendments to the articles of association, which have as their subject matter indicated in*

286 Luiz Gonzaga Modesto de PAULA, *Sociedade Limitada* 1ª.ed. (São Paulo: Saraiva, 2015), 17.
287 Luiz Gonzaga Modesto de PAULA, op. cit., 69.

art. 997 depend on the consent of all members; the others can be decided by an absolute majority of votes, if the contract does not determine the need for unanimous deliberation." Any alteration to the constitutive act of the corporate entity must undergo registration and compliance with the requirements set forth in Article 998 (sole paragraph of Article 999).

In view of this, the Civil Code requires deliberative unanimity for the validity of the decision to change the matters listed in its Article 997: "*(I) name, nationality, marital status, profession and residence of the partners, if natural persons, and firm or name, nationality and headquarters of the partners, if legal; (II) name, object, headquarters and term of the company; (III) capital of the company, expressed in current currency, being able to comprise any kind of assets, susceptible of pecuniary valuation; (IV) the share of each partner in the share capital, and the manner of realizing it; (V) the installments required by the partner, whose contribution consists of services; (VI) the natural persons charged with the administration of the company, and their powers and duties; (VII) the share of each partner in profits and losses; (VIII) if the partners are responsible, or not, in the alternative, for social obligations.*"

Deliberative unanimity for the decision of certain matters is also required in addition to those contained in Article 997; these are the matters listed in Article 1.071 of the same law. In this context, the following are subject to the deliberative act of partners, in addition to the matters listed in the articles of association or listed in the law: "*(I) the approval of the management accounts; (II) the appointment of the managers, when made in a separate act; (III) the dismissal of the administrators; (IV) the method of remuneration, when not established in the contract; (V) the amendment to the articles of association; (VI) the incorporation, merger and dissolution of the company, or the termination of the liquidation status; (VII) the appointment and dismissal of liquidators and the judgment of their accounts; and (VIII) the recovery request.*"

The corporate resolutions must take into account the principle of legality and the contractual provisions, since if they are directly or indirectly offensive to the law and to the articles of association, the partners who issued them will be boundlessly liable for the resulting damages, in such a way that the evocation of mischaracterization of the legal personality as a mechanism of accountability of the offending partners becomes unnecessary (Article 1.080 of the Civil Code).

Matter subject to the Meeting of the Assembly—the meeting is configured as the most preponderant organ within the organic structure of limited companies. The Brazilian Civil Code of 2002, unlike Decree No. 3,078 of January 10, 1919, provides for the meeting or assembly of quota holders in order to deliberate on certain matters listed in Article 1.071 of the Code.

The matters listed in the aforementioned Article 1.071 are merely exemplary and nonexhaustive and are the exclusive competence of the assembly; their exemplary character stems from the fact that the same legal precept recognizes the existence of other matters possibly arising from the law or of the constitutive act of the company. In limited companies with a number of partners below 10, the form used for the resolution is the meeting, being composed of a number of more than 10 shareholders; the form of resolution will be the assembly.

The number of shareholders is one of the criteria used to distinguish one assembly from the other; in addition to this, it also serves as a distinction criterion required for its continuation; the holding of the assembly obeys the legally established commands and the meetings taking place according to the commands resulting from the articles of association and will only observe the legal commands in cases of omission of the respective contract (Article 1.079 of the Civil Code). Ulhoa Coelho[288] adds that "*the difference between the two types of meeting is not only in the designation. The articles of association are free to provide for the frequency, convocation, holding and registration of the shareholders' meeting. As the law says that the rules on the assembly only apply to meetings, in the omissions of the social contract, it is understood that it can freely discipline the installation, operation and settlement of the meeting.*"

Mandatory Annual Meeting or Meeting—also called ordinary general meeting. The legal basis for the mandatory annual assembly or meeting is found in the Civil Code. It is in this context that Article 1.078 of the respective legal diploma establishes that "*The shareholders' meeting must be held at least once a year, in the four months following the end of the fiscal year, in order to: (I) take the management accounts and resolve on the balance sheet and the economic result; (II) designate administrators, when applicable; (III) deal with any other matter on the agenda.*"

The legal provision in question has three paragraphs relating to the procedure and method of operation of the assembly or meeting:

> Up to 30 (thirty) days before the date set for the meeting, the documents referred to in item I of this article must be made available, in writing, and with receipt proof, to the partners who do not exercise management[289]; Once the meeting is installed, the documents referred to in the preceding paragraph will be read, which will be submitted, by the president, for discussion and voting, in which the members of the administration and, if any, of those council fiscal

288 Fábio Ulhoa COELHO, *Manual de Direito Comercial: Direito de Empresa*, op. cit., 188.

289 See § 1, Article 1.078 of the Civil Code.

may not take part.[290] The approval, without reservation, of the balance sheet and of the economic result, except for error, intent or simulation, exonerates the members of the management and, if any, of those fiscal council[291]; The right to cancel the approval referred to in the preceding paragraph is extinguished in 2 (two) years.[292]

Administration of the limited liability company—provided and disciplined in Articles 1.060 and related sections of the Civil Code. In line with the aforementioned article, the management of the corporate entity in question is pursued by a minimum number of one person and a maximum not determined ("*or more people*") whose designation must be included in the company's articles of incorporation (articles of association) or in a document that is not to be confused with the social contract. However, under the sole section of the article in question (Article 1060), the administrative powers conferred on the universality of partners/quota holders in the social contract are not fully extended to supervening members.

It may also be a director who is not a partner of the company, but the appointment of director in these conditions is subject to the unanimous consent of partners, before the verification of payment of share capital, and if the appointment occurs after payment of capital, then consent will require a minimum number corresponding to two-thirds of members (Article 1.061).

The appointment of administrator in a separate act is invested in the position by means of a term of office in the minutes of the administration (Article 106); if the designated administrator does not sign the term within 30 days after their appointment, this will be ineffective (§ 1). In a period of 10 days following their investiture, the administrator must make a request to register their appointment with the competent entity, mentioning their name, nationality, marital status, residence, with the presentation of an identity document, the act and the date of appointment, and the period of time within which the administration will exercise (§ 2).

The limited liability company operates under a specific corporate name, which may be a firm or denomination, and the use of one of these is exclusively granted to the administrators empowered to do so (Article 1064).

The assumption of administrator *status* must take into account the rigidity of impediments, whether this means that certain people are legally prevented from acquiring administrator status and whether or not there is a special law that

290 See § 2, Article 1.078 of the Civil Code.
291 See § 3, Article 1.078 of the Civil Code.
292 See § 4, Article 1.078 of the Civil Code.

enforces restriction on according administrator status. The Civil Code was in charge of listing those who are affected by the impediment regime, namely, those sentenced to the penalty that prohibits access to public offices; those convicted of bankruptcy crime; prevarication, bruising (active corruption or passive) or bribery, concussion, embezzlement; or acting against popular economy, national financial system, rules of competition defense, consumer relations, and public faith or property, while the effects of condemnation endure (§ 1 of Article 1.011).

In the scope of exercise of administrative activities, administrator must observe the duty of investigation; in this way, he must act as a *bonus pater familias* or as a person of normal investigation. The administration of company's business by the director must contribute to the pursuit of its object and for that purpose the director must act within the limits of their mandate (Article 1.011).

If the administrator acts outside the limits of their mandate, as a rule, their acts cannot be opposed to third parties, but, exceptionally, the opposite can be true in certain situations: (i) The limits of the powers resulting from the mandate have passed through enrollment or registration in the registration of the corporate entity itself; (ii) evidence was provided that the limitation was known to the third person; and (iii) it is an operation notoriously incompatible with social businesses.[293]

The application of credits or assets of the company by the administrator, without the written consent of partners, for their own benefit or that of third parties, incurs the obligation of restitution by that person to the corporate entity or the payment of the corresponding amount, with all the resulting profits, and, if there is a damage, he/she will also respond for it.[294] Interpreting this article, Waldo Fazzio Júnior states that this is a situation where the administrator acts outside their powers and in disagreement with the interests of the corporate entity.[295] By acting so, the administrator should be subject to sanctions (sole paragraph of Article 1.017).

During the fulfillment of their mandate, the administrator cannot be substituted; however, he has the power to proceed with the social mandatory constitution, the document by which the mandatory is constituted must specify the acts to be performed by him (Article 1.018). Obviously, we are facing a situation of the "*trustee of the trustee*"; therefore, the mandate regime is applicable to directors.

293 Waldo FAZZIO JÚNIOR, op. cit., 166.
294 See Article 1.017 of the Civil Code.
295 Waldo FAZZIO JÚNIOR, op. cit., 166.

Irrevocability is an essential characteristic of the powers vested in the partner in the administration, by a clause expressed in the constitutive act of the company; it is a characteristic that has reservations, in the sense that that irrevocable character can be removed by the court, upon the request of partners, and if there is a just cause judicially considered valid (Article 1.019). However, the powers vested in the partner in the administration, or the non-partner administrator, by a separate act, may be revoked at any time (sole paragraph, Article 1.019).

The obligations of administrator, before partners, include the justified accountability of their administrative activities, such as annual presentation of the inventory, balance sheet, and economic result (Article 1.020). It serves as the foundation of the legal precept in question; given the reality that the execution of administrative activities does not presuppose their irresponsibility, the administrator is not exempt from certain responsibilities inherent to the exercise of their functions.

The conditions leading to the end of occupation of the position of administrator are set out as follows in the Civil Code:

> The exercise of the position of administrator ceases by the dismissal, at any time, of the holder, or by the end of the term if, fixed in the contract or in a separate act, there is no renewal.[296] In the case of a partner appointed as administrator in the contract, his removal is only effected by the approval of holders of quotas corresponding, at least, to 2/3 (two thirds) of the share capital, unless otherwise provided in a different contractual provision.[297] The cessation of the exercise of the administrator position must be registered in the competent registry, by means of a request submitted within 10 (ten) days after the occurrence.[298] The resignation of an administrator becomes effective, in relation to the company, from the moment that it becomes aware of the written communication of the waiver; and, in relation to third parties, after registration and publication.[299]

Fiscal Council of the Limited Company—it is an optional body, foreseen and regulated in accordance with Article 1.066 and subsections of the Civil Code.

The constitutive act of the corporate entity may provide for the insertion of the fiscal council in the organic structure of the company, and the powers to be conferred on this supervisory body should not conflict with the exclusive powers of the shareholders' meeting; the minimum composition required for that body is

296 See Article 1.063 of the Civil Code.
297 See § 1, Article 1.063 of the Civil Code.
298 See § 2, Article 1.063 of the Civil Code.
299 See § 3, Article 1.063 of the Civil Code.

three members, and when the maximum composition as required by the law does not rule, it is necessary to have alternates, partners or not, residing in Brazilian territory and acquire the status of fiscal councilors through the election to be held at the ordinary general meeting (Article 1.066).

The acquisition of the *status* of fiscal director is susceptible to impediments; in this sense, such people are prevented from being directors, in addition to conditions of ineligibility listed in § 1 of Article 1.011, who are members of other corporate bodies or others under their supervision, employees of any of them or of the respective administrators, and the spouse or relative of the latter up to the third degree.[300]

Pursuant to paragraph 2 of Article 1.066, minority shareholders with a minimum representation corresponding to one-fifth of the share capital are entitled to elect a member of the fiscal council and the corresponding alternate in a separate act. It is relevant here to present the interpretation offered by Waldo Fazzio Júnior around the referred paragraph, in order to understand that:

> The legislators intended that the representation of the majority in the fiscal council should be 1/3 of the collegiate. Because the body can be composed of more than three members, it seems that the majority may elect two members of the Fiscal Council with their respective alternates. If this is not the case, that is, the majority is always represented by a fiscal councilor, whatever the number of members of the body, the protection of the corporate minority may become mere rhetoric.[301]

Article 1.068 recognizes other attributions that may arise from the law of the constitutive act of the company, and in its systematic progress, it enshrines these duties to be observed individually or collectively:

> (I) examine, at least on a quarterly basis, the books and papers of the company and the state of the cash and portfolio, with the administrators or liquidators providing the requested information; (II) draw up the results of the examinations carried out in the minutes and opinions of the fiscal council; (III) record in the same book and present to the annual shareholders' meeting an opinion on the business and social operations of the year in which they serve, based on the balance sheet and the economic result; (IV) denounce the errors, fraud or crimes they discover, suggesting useful measures to the company; (V) call

300 See § 1, Article 1.066, Civil Code.
301 Waldo FAZZIO JÚNIOR, op. cit., 170.

> the shareholders' meeting if the board delays its annual call by more than 30 (thirty) days, or whenever there are serious and urgent reasons; (VI) to carry out, during the liquidation period of the company, the acts referred to in this article, in view of the special liquidation regulatory provisions.

The range of attributions and powers legally attributed to the fiscal council cannot be extended to other corporate bodies (1,070). The accountability parameters of the fiscal council members obey the rules applied to the administrators; in turn, their responsibility is regulated according to Article 1.016, under the terms of this, to the administrators, due to poor performance of their functions, and they are jointly and severally liable before the company and third parties suffering damage.

7.2. One-Person Company

In the Portuguese doctrine, according to Ferrer Correia,[302] the sole proprietors face the problem of their acceptance; over the years, the practical existence of this corporate modality was not accepted, and the challenge to any argument that defended the possible consummation of the company was done based on the conceptual framework of the company. In this way, the accumulation of quotas/shares in the legal sphere of a single shareholder would result in the dissolution of the corporate entity; in this scenario, the doctrine did not reach a unanimous consensus, with some defending the dissolution *ipso jure* and others contesting this understanding, proclaiming that the dissolution did not occur and that the presence of a single shareholder made the company lose its essence.

In view of the aforementioned situation, Ferrer Correia concluded that the problem of whether or not to accept the possibility of the existence of a sole proprietorship had as its starting point the analysis of the conceptual framework of a commercial company, the concepts seen as determinants in prejudice to the increasingly emerging socioeconomic requirements and which in turn do not dispense the legal regulation.

The situation that was reported in the first paragraph of this section, in a certain way, portrays the supervening sole proprietorship; as for the original sole proprietorship, the author emphasizes that this possibility was null, based on the assumption that the constitution of a corporate entity requires an agreement between two or more legal subjects. On the other hand, he

302 António Arruda Ferrer CORREIA, *Sociedades Fictícias e Unipessoais* (Coimbra: Livraria Atlântida), 195 and ss.

> admitted the permanence and existence of companies that, during their life, had their shareholdings reduced to just one shareholder, taking into account that the collectivity, although essential for the constitution of the company, would not be, equally, for its legal persistence. However, the subsistence and existence of these companies would depend on the social type that they chose in their origin. The gathering of shareholdings in the hands of just one person would be a cause of dissolution; however, such dissolution would not occur automatically. Furthermore, the main virtue in the subsistence of that company that had reduced its social participation to just one shareholder would be the possibility of reconstituting the collectivity.[303]

The author in question, when addressing the legal situation of the corporate entity in which the existence of a single partner is verified, identifies it as an "*autonomous asset to which a legal subjectivity corresponds.*" In this perspective, the corporate entity that was previously characterized by the multiplicity of partners, at the time of its reduction to a single partner, would result in its extinction; however, its legal personality and the patrimonial complex related to the development of business activity will remain.

Brazilian legislation, tied to the contractual principle, took a long time to regulate the situations in which a single proprietor develops the business activity based on a corporate entity. Nowadays, the contractualist principle has known derogations, in the sense that there is the institution of some sole proprietorship in Brazilian law. The sole proprietorship of companies exists in two types: original and supervening (in this case, the deadline established for the reestablishment of its plurilaterality must be taken into account, at the end of which the dissolution of the corporate entity will take place, within the law). There are, therefore, points of disagreement between the Portuguese and Brazilian laws; while the Portuguese law demands the reinstatement period and a judicial sentence, the Brazilian law imposes sanctions, in the event that the accumulation of quotas in the legal sphere of one within a period stipulated in the law has elapsed, with the dissolution of the social entity. A significant and daring advance in the Brazilian legal system is evident, which consists of the establishment of the limited liability of the individual entrepreneur through the institution of the Individual Limited Liability Company (EIRL).[304]

303 António Arruda Ferrer CORREIA, op. cit., 195 and ss.

304 Welliton Luiz MORREIRA, *A Sociedade Unipessoal e a Limitação da Responsabilidade Patrimonial do Empresário Individual* (Coimbra, 2016), 42.

A superficial analysis of comparative law shows that the establishment of the original sole proprietorship, specifically in the type of quotas, is not linear. In the context of the German legal system, by means of a legislative act, the existence of limited companies consisting of one or more persons is allowed. In the French and Spanish legislative fields, the corporate entity is allowed to be brought into existence through the articles of association (presupposes the legal involvement of at least two people), as well as there is permission for the company to be constituted through a unilateral act. In the Portuguese legal system, the permission for the creation of a company composed of a single person is only valid in the cases legally provided for.[305]

Under Brazilian law, in the Article 980-A of the Civil Code, it is stated that "*The individual limited liability company shall consist of a single person holding the entire share capital, properly integrated, which shall not be less than 100 (one hundred) times of the highest minimum wage in force in the country.*" As it can be seen, the existence of a sole proprietorship is recognized: EIRELI (Individual Limited Liability Company). It is an incomplete legal provision in its content, in the sense that it does not comment on the nature of the act that will give it legal existence. It is understood that the interpretation of the current legal precept must be made taking into consideration the Brazilian legal system as a whole (systematic interpretation). For this, it is important to evoke Article 981 of the same legal diploma: "*Celebrate the association contract people who reciprocally contribute, with goods or services, to the exercise of economic activity and the sharing, among themselves, of the results.*" This provision makes the inclination of corporate law to contractual theory notorious.

The idea of the contractual conception of the company is also manifested in the Brazilian Corporate Law, which in its Article 80 provides that "*The constitution of the company depends on the fulfillment of the following preliminary requirements: (I) subscription, at least by 2 (two) persons, from all shares into which the share capital established in the bylaws is divided.*"

The reality that Brazilian law has strong contractual traits is undeniable, in such a way that, based on the corporate nature of a model lacking in the multiplicity of shareholders, a specific case of sole proprietorship becomes an equation of difficult resolution. Although with strong features of the contractual theory, the Brazilian legal system itself recognizes the existence of unilaterally constituted companies, based on the need to follow the dynamics of the current

305 Welliton Luiz MORREIRA, op. cit., 42.

socioeconomic situation; it is a foundation essentially covered by the need to abandon the dogma according to which the constitution of a corporate entity lacking the plurality of partners cannot be conceived. The recognition of sole proprietorship covers the legal aspect of a public company, wholly owned subsidiary[306]; temporary supervening sole proprietorship[307]; exclusion from the dissolution of the full right of the company, when it becomes personal and the remaining partner chooses, within the legality,[308] to continue with the exercise of the company without restoring the plurality of members.[309]

Rubens Requião, even though he defended the plurality of shareholders as an essential requirement for the formation of a company, joining in this way the classic contractual theory, which is summarized in the conception that the constitutive act of the social entity is without reservation the social contract, recognizes and posits "*that the principle that a company must be constituted by at least two people is no longer uncontroversial*"; such an understanding is based on the fact that currently there are modern theories that underlie the phenomenon.[310]

In addition, the aforementioned author confesses that the drafting of the Brazilian Corporate Law was inspired by the institutionalist doctrine[311] because it allows the creation of the wholly owned subsidiary submitted in this condition to a sudden change. It also known that the Brazilian legal system had a long tradition of connoting company with the contract; however, the aforementioned author argues that the inadmissibility of the sole proprietorship phenomenon stems from a traditional practice according to which the corporate entity is constituted exclusively through the contract; sole proprietorship can only be admitted, provided that it is maintained that the commercial company, as a legal entity, is liable to be constituted by an act that is not necessarily a contract.

306 See Article 251 of the Brazilian Corporate Law.

307 See item IV, Article 1.033 of the Brazilian Civil Code.

308 See item I, subparagraph (a) of Article 206 of the Brazilian Civil Law; item I, Article 1.033 of the Civil Code and item IV, Article 35 of Law No. 8.934, November 18, 1994.

309 Welliton Luiz MORREIRA, op. cit., 44.

310 Rubens REQUIÃO, *Curso de Direito Comercial,* Vol. I, 25ª ed. (São Paulo: Saraiva, 2003), 366–68.

311 "Institutionalist theory—it is a theory that emerges to support the constitution of public institutions, and later be incorporated into corporate law to explain public limited companies. According to this thesis, the constitutive act of the company would not definitively fix the socio-political rights; they would only accept the discipline imposed on the corporate type. The prosperity of the company and its purpose would not be conditioned to the interest of the partners. Once the institution was created, it would have its own interests, different from its founders, which is why the lack of execution of the obligations by the partners or by the simple will of one of them would not imply the dissolution of the company." It is understood that this is the theory adopted predominantly by the Brazilian legislature when regulating the public limited company." In this regard, see Wellinton Luiz MORREIRA, op. cit., 47.

Calisto Salomão Filho, referred by Luiz Morreira,[312] suggests that neither the contractual theory nor the institutionalist theory is capable of sufficiently explaining the sole partnership phenomenon, since the argument presented by the traditional contractual doctrine of commercial company goes against the existence of a sole proprietorship entity, and the pure and simple application of the institutionalist doctrine raises certain blind spots. For example, it is unable to define in real terms the dimension of the interest of the company and shareholders. It is in this context that the same author proposes that the most convenient mechanism for explaining the nuances brought about by sole proprietorships is the theory of the organization contract.

The organization contract theory has as its starting point the differentiation between *the associative contract and the exchange contract*, and its essence is far removed from the classical current, which promotes the differentiation between the figures based on the existence or nonexistence of a common end. The proposed solution is the nature of the rights managed by the two contractual figures, with the exchange giving rise to subjective rights; on the other hand, associative contracts are the creators of an organization. The act that brings into existence an organization that lacks the convergence of interests of a multiplicity of people allows the admission of sole proprietorship even in the presence of a strongly contractual doctrine of company.[313]

In this theoretical perspective, considering the theory of the organization contract, the social interest is no longer justified on the basis of the interests of partners, since the constitutive act does not create subjective rights for a certain universe of members. The corporate entity created is characterized by the organization and not the unity or multiplicity of parts. The definition of the social interest would be made according to the will of the party and the legal commands; in this sense, the interest of the organization would be forged and shaped by the profitable purpose of the company and the self-preservation interest. Therefore, the business activity would be directed in a way to promote the balance of the interests of the organization that would present itself as an autonomous decision-making entity.

312 Calixto SALOMÃO FILHO, *A Sociedade Unipessoal*; apud, Welliton Luiz MORRERIA, *A Sociedade Unipessoal e a Limitação da Responsabilidade Patrimonial do Empresário Individual* (Coimbra, 2016), 51.

313 Id., 52.

7.2.1 Unipersonality in the Brazilian Legal System: Individual Limited Liability Company

Entrepreneurs, natural and legal persons, are both legal subjects capable of exercising the company in the Brazilian legal system. As subjects of law, they share a certain normative complex that disciplines them, which includes rules regarding registration, business name, accounting, protection of the establishment, bookkeeping, judicial recovery, and bankruptcy. One cannot talk about commonality among those subjects with regard to structural training and liability limitation regime.

In this perspective, the main point of distinction lies specifically in the liability regime for debts that result from the exercise of the company.[314] The individual entrepreneur is responsible for unlimited liability; the universality of his assets is called upon to answer for the mandatory complex assumed by him, while the corporate juridical person continues his activities under the limited liability regime (it is his partners who respond in a limited way, except in cases of mischaracterization of the legal personality).

The EIRELI was introduced by Law No. 12,441 of July 11, 2011, seen as a new type of legal entity under private law.[315] This law added Article 980-A to the Civil Code. In the meantime, it is important to note that EIRELI has not extinguished the figure of the individual entrepreneur; quite the contrary, it is configured as an intermediary between him and the corporate entities governed by the Code.[316]

For the constitution of the sole proprietorship, Individual Limited Liability Company, certain legally established requirements must be observed, which we will now discuss[317]:

(i) ***Unipersonality*** means that the business entity will have only one holder (natural or legal person) and will operate under the liability limitation regime (limitation will be made taking into account the paid-in capital). In the case of a human person, it will be configured as an EIREL under § 2, Article 980-A of the Civil Code.

(ii) *Capital stock duly paid up and representing the minimum of 100 times the highest minimum wage in force in the country*[318]—there is no division of

314 In this regard, see the criteria of the classification of companies, in particular the criterion of liability of partners.

315 See item VI, Article 44 of the Civil Code.

316 Cláudia RIBEIRO and Priscila MENEZES, op. cit., 8.

317 Cláudia RIBEIRO and Priscila MENEZES, op. cit., 8.

318 Cláudia RIBEIRO and Priscila MENEZES, op. cit., 8.

share capital by quotas, and this in turn must be properly paid up at the time of its constitution. Contributions in services are prohibited (§ 6 of Article 980-A in conjunction with Article 1.055, all of the Civil Code).

The formation of the corporate name does not dispense with the expression "EIRELI" to be added at the end of the company name or the name of the "*Individual Limited Liability Company*" (§ 1 of Article 980-A). Both the firm and the denomination, when one of them chooses "EIRELI," can be registered both in the Commercial Registry and in the Civil Registry of Legal Persons (RCPJ). A third party who is not the holder of the EIRELI may exercise administrative functions, since this business modality, in cases in which Article 980-A is shown to be omitted, will be governed by the limited partnership regime (§ 6 of the aforementioned article).[319]

EIRELI aimed, in principle, to remove from the irregularity a large number of irregular entrepreneurs and to discourage the formation of companies with fictitious partners, such as those where one of the partners has 99 % of the shares and the other only 1 %. However, there was a mistake on the part of the legislator who could have chosen between two legal figures: (a) individual entrepreneur with limited liability or (b) sole proprietorship. However, we opted for the institution of the Individual Limited Liability Company, which, due to its technical imprecision, generated several criticisms by the specialized doctrine; after all, as we know, a company is an activity.[320]

Although the adoption of EIRELI has generated several criticisms by the specialized doctrine, it cannot be denied that its introduction in Brazilian law made possible the individual exercise of the company under the regime of limitation of liability. It also served as a means of protecting the individual patrimonial sphere by allowing the limitation of liability in the individual company, a phenomenon that did not exist in Brazilian law but that was already quite common in other legal systems.[321]

Sole Proprietorship Company: **Full subsidiary**. It is a fact that the sole proprietorship under Brazilian law is not limited to the Individual Limited Liability Company; there is another means of primitive manifestation of the sole proprietorship; it is the denominated wholly owned subsidiary, provided for and regulated under the Brazilian Corporate Law, in Articles 251–253.

319 For a better understanding of the process of the administration of limited company, we recommend reading Articles 1.060 and subsections of the Civil Code.

320 Cláudia RIBEIRO and Priscila MENEZES, op. cit., 10.

321 Welliton Luiz MORREIRA, op. cit., 58.

From Article 251 of the aforementioned law, it follows that "*The Company may be incorporated, by means of a public deed, with the sole shareholder of Brazilian legal person.*" This corporate modality, in the Brazilian legal system, must be configured as a public limited company.

Pursuant to paragraph 2 of Article 251 of the Brazilian Corporate Law (Law No. 6,404 of December 15, 1976), the existence of the wholly owned subsidiary may be effected in a derivative manner through the conversion of another public limited company, through the acquisition, by Brazilian corporate entity, of the total number of preexisting shares; it may also become effective under the terms of Article 252, through the incorporation of all the shares of the share capital to the equity of another Brazilian company.

The phenomenon of corporate unilateralism may be of a supervening nature, in addition to being original. It is in this context that Brazilian law provides for situations in which the company during its existence will be composed of one partner. The emphasis here is that the admission of these companies is temporary, so there is a determined time lag for the restoration of the plurality of partners, and the nonobservance of the respective time lapse incurs the dissolution of that company's full right. In a first stage, the survival of the previously plural entity, reduced to a single shareholder, was legally disciplined for public limited companies and limited by shares within the scope of the al. (d), item I of Article 206 of the Brazilian Corporate Law; it was permissible for the corporations to survive with a single shareholder, until the ordinary general meeting of the following year, when the minimum number of two partners will be replaced.

With regard to other corporate types, before the current Brazilian Civil Code came into force, the subsistence of the company made up of one partner due to death, recess, exclusion, or other reason incurred the dissolution of the corporate entity, with no deadline for its reestablishment. In this event, if the remaining partner preferred to continue the exercise of the company, he would continue as an individual entrepreneur or would have to create a new company. However, at the doctrinal and jurisprudential level, the need for subsistence of the corporate entity reduced to a single partner for the preservation of the business entity was allowed.

The Civil Code in force has made it possible for the companies governed by it, in the event of supervening sole proprietorship, to continue to operate regularly within the period of 180 days, which starts from the date of the occurrence of the fact that gave rise to sole proprietorship. Within the aforementioned period of time, the plurality of partners must be restored; otherwise, the company will be dissolved in its own right (item IV of Article 1.033).

Law No. 12,441 of July 11, 2011 changed the regime relating to the reduction to one partner. Among other changes, it inserted the sole paragraph of Article 1.033, item IV of the Civil Code, thus modifying the dissolution regime when the existence of a single partner occurs. *In verbis*:

> Sole Paragraph. "The provisions of item IV do not apply if the remaining partner, including in the event of concentration of all the shares of the company under his ownership, requires, in the Public Register of Mercantile Companies, to transform the registration of the company to an individual entrepreneur or to an individual company limited liability, subject, where applicable, to the provisions of articles 1.113 to 1.115 of this Code."

The founding law of the *individual limited liability company* made it possible that, when the reduction in the remaining membership is observed, as long as the legal requirements are met, the remaining partner can continue with the business activity, as an individual entrepreneur of a limited company; in this way, the consequences of not reestablishing the plurality of partners fall to the ground.

Sole Proprietorship Company: Public Company. It finds its constitutional basis in Article 37, item XIX, of the Federal Constitution of the Brazil Federal Republic. It is a corporate modality made up of only one partner, and the federative entity that brought it into existence by law (Union, State, or Municipality) may appear as a partner. Its one-person nature is primitive and constant.

Public company means an "*entity with private legal personality, with its own assets and exclusive capital of the Union, created by law for the exploitation of economic activity that the Government is required to exercise due to contingency or administrative convenience being able to take on any of the forms admitted by law.*"[322]

Although it is denominated as a public company, the legal regime that applies to it, as can be seen in the definition above, is that of business entities of a private nature, even with regard to civil, commercial, labor, and tax rights and obligations. It is not allowed to grant benefits that cannot be granted to individuals, as can be seen in Articles 172 and 173 of the Federal Constitution of the Federative Republic of Brazil.

In this perspective, the public companies have the condition of entrepreneurship and are an instrument at the service of the state for the development of economic activity because of its dynamism. The expression "*Public*" refers to the controller, being pluripersonal—where the capital belongs to more than one

322 Cfr. Inciso II, artigo 5 do Decreto-Lei nº 200, de 25 de Fevereiro de 1967 ("*Dispõe sobre a organização da Administração Federal, estabelece directrizes para a Reforma Administrativa e dá outras providências*").

entity of the Public Administration (direct or indirect) or sole proprietorship—the capital is exclusively owned by an institution integrated in the public administration, directly or indirectly.

7.3. Public Limited Companies

Public limited companies are part of a group of joint stock companies,[323] whose most outstanding feature is the organization of partners in sets of shares. In accordance with the provisions of Law No. 6,404 of December 15, 1976, it is possible to arrive at the concept of a public limited company as being the corporate type of business because it is framed in the concept of a business company, in which there is capital in shares called shares, and the limitation of the liability of shareholders is made according to the issue value of the shares acquired or subscribed by them.

Certainly, public limited companies are governed by the rules of the Brazilian Corporate Law, Law No. 6,404 of December 15, 1976. This understanding is based on Article 1,089 of the Brazilian Civil Code of 2002, which provides as follows: "*The limited liability company is governed by a special law,*[324] *the provisions of this Code being applied to the omitted cases.*"

The purpose of limited liability company is essentially to move capital, regardless of who are its partners, so that its character of stability and longevity is much more visible, mainly due to the fact that the involvement of partners in the constitutive act is waived, avoiding small personal problems that could eventually compromise the social enterprise. Thus, it is quite common to find in the doctrine the approximation between the concepts of company and institution, considering the company as the very personification of social capital. As a result of this, it is the characteristic of the pecuniary nature of public limited companies, since it is a capital company, marked by the attraction of individuals with the purpose of investing resources for the common enterprise and with a view to obtaining good results. However, it is possible to find that some public limited companies are also characterized as *personae intent*, commonly seen in privately held companies,

323 Share companies are classified into two types of institutional nature: the public limited company and the limited liability company. In the systematic Law on Companies by Shares, the public limited company (company), whose rules are transversal to the universality of companies by shares, is disciplined in a specific way, and in the background the limited liability company by shares is disciplined. On this, Fábio Ulhoa COELHO, *Manual de Direito Comercial: direito de empresa;* op. cit., 212.

324 Please note that the special law referred to in this article is Law No. 6,404 of December 15, 1976, the Brazilian Corporate Law.

despite the fact that they also have the scope of capital movements, as will be seen below.[325]

Within the scope of the creation of public limited company, there are two essential phases related to the formation of share capital, namely, subscription and payment. The subscription "*guarantees the individual the right to acquire shares, through payment, which is the act of effective equity disposition.*"[326]

There are two facets that can be covered by subscription: (i) **private**—also called simultaneous constitution. In this facet, those who found the company hold the precise capital[327]; (ii) **public**—also called successive constitution. In this regard, those who intend to found the corporate entity do not have the necessary capital to do so, making it necessary to resort to attracting investors. In this event, an early CVM (Securities and Exchange Commission)[328] registration is essential. Article 82 of the LSA requires that such share subscription is mandatory and that it be interceded by a financial institution.

Much attention needs to be paid to social capital, since at least 10 % of social capital must have been realized as a means of entry. In the case of financial institutions, the minimum percentage must correspond to 50 %. The bank deposit of amounts corresponding to the referred percentages takes place at Banco do Brasil or at another banking institution authorized by the Securities and Exchange Commission.[329]

After the subscription process is completed and all the share capital has been subscribed, the general meeting will be convened by the founders, and the latter should proceed with the promotion of the valuation of the assets and issue a resolution regarding the constitution of the company.[330] The call for meeting will be made through announcements that indicate the time, date, and place for the meeting to be held; this information will be published in the newspapers in which the subscription offer has been made.[331] The combination of Articles 95 and 96 of the LSA leads to the conclusion that assembly or public deeds are two possible means of constituting the company.

After the holding of the meeting whose purpose consisted of constituting the public limited company, the company is registered with the Commercial

325 Mariane Portella GARCIA, op. cit., 23.

326 Cláudia RIBEIRO and Priscila MENEZES, op. cit., 37.

327 See Article 88 of the Brazilian Corporate Law.

328 The Securities and Exchange Commission is a federal authority promoting the supervision of the Securities Market and the performance of publicly held companies (only).

329 See items I, II, and III of Article 80 of the Brazilian Corporate Law.

330 See Article 86, items I and II of the Brazilian Corporate Law.

331 See single section, Article 86 of the Brazilian Corporate Law.

Registry, as provided for in Article 97 of the LSA, as well as if in the statute there are contrary clauses to the law, public order, and good customs.

The payment of subscribed shares consists of the second period in which the share capital is not formed. It can be carried out with money or through other economically evaluable resources; in this context, Article 7 of the LSA provides that "*the share capital may be formed with contributions in cash or in any kind of assets that can be valued in cash.*"

It should be noted that, unlike what happens in limited companies, in companies, the formalities for valuing assets listed in Article 8 of the LSA are more rigorous than is required for the former. Under the provisions of Article 1.055, § 1, Civil Code, in the limited liability company, once the payment of shares by its partner is verified, there are no procedural assessment formalities; the valuation of the good or assets is made by its respective owner and needs approval from the other partners; and due to the precise valuation of assets granted to the share capital, the universality of partners responds in solidarity, within the limit of the timespan of each year from the date of registration of the company.

General features. It is convenient to include the public limited company in the universe of legal entities of private law,[332] essentially commercial, in which the share capital is divided into freely negotiable shares and the limitation of the liability of subscribers or shareholders is done in a judicious way, a criterion that consists of limited liability according to the issue price of shares by those purchased or subscribed. The incorporation of public limited liability companies in the universe of legal entities implies accepting that it is a subject of law and therefore vested with legal capacity (Articles 16 and 20 of the Civil Code).[333]

The recognition of legal personality of the public limited company goes through the filing of the act that brought it into existence in the register of trade and prevails for a period scheduled for its operation; its prevalence is extended until the time of its liquidation, and the extinction of the respective personality can only be verified in the legal cases provided.[334] The condition for subscribers to shares in public limited companies to be considered shareholders is registration. A characteristic that is transversal to other corporate types, from which the

332 Please note that Brazilian law, based on the Civil Code, distinguishes between Legal Entities of Public Law and Legal Entities of Private Law (Article 40 and subsections of the Legal Diploma in question); it is from this perspective that under Article 40, item II, it is established that companies are legal entities under private law, and it is therefore inferable that the public limited company has the legal nature of a legal entity under private law.

333 Elisabeth Maria PEREIRA, op. cit., 40.

334 See Article 21 of the Civil Code and Article 219 of the Brazilian Corporate Law.

limited liability company is not exempt, it has a different legal personality or is autonomous from that of its partners.

Specific features. The characteristics of public limited companies are likely to vary according to the understanding of different authors.

In Fábio Ulhoa Coelho's[335] view, the limited company is essentially characterized by its capitalist nature (capital company). The partners participate in the company by means of securities called shares, and these in turn are guided by the principle of free negotiability. It is a principle that entails the entry of any person (interested in acquiring the shares) in the corporate entity without impediment to the shareholders. In the corporate mode, the pledge of shares is always valid for the purposes of the proposed execution against the shareholder's person.

In case of death of the shareholder, nothing prevents the successors of the deceased from joining the association. Allied to this, as it is an institutional corporate entity, there is no need or legal basis for the successors of the *de cujus* (shareholder) to enter into litigation in order to ascertain its assets. The heir or legatee of action in a certain company, regardless of his will, becomes a shareholder within the respective company.

We are facing a corporate modality in which the share capital is divided into portions whose representation is made by shares. It is in this perspective that the norm of Article 1 of the Brazilian Corporate Law is presented in the following ways: "*The company or public limited company will have its capital divided into shares, and the liability of the partners or shareholders will be limited to the issue price of the subscribed shares or acquired.*" It must be stressed that there should be no confusion between the price at which the share is issued and its negotiable or nominal value, so if, perhaps, a question arises about the value of the share of a certain company, the answer will depend on an explanation "*about what value the question is being asked.*" The value of a company's share is determined according to the objectives of the valuation.

From what was stated in the paragraph above, the following are deduced[336]:

(i) **Nominal value**—is the quotient that results from dividing the value of the share capital by the number of shares. The company's creative act (bylaws) may (and at times may not) contain in its systematics the expression of that value. If the constitutive act of the company expresses the aforementioned value, there will be an action with a nominal value;

335 Fábio Ulhoa COELHO, *Manual de Direito Comercial: Direito de Empresa*; op. cit., 211.
336 Id., 212-15.

otherwise, there will be an action lacking a nominal value. It is relevant to affirm that the expression or absence of expression of the nominal value brings benefits of a certain order, in accordance with the specificities of each situation, as will be seen later.

(ii) **Equity value**—this type of value represents the shareholder's share in the net equity of the company (company). It is the quotient resulting from the division of the net assets by the number of shares in which the capital of the company is divided. In the event of a liquidation of the corporate entity or amortization of the share, the equity owed will be due to the shareholder, due to the verification of the referred phenomena.

The prediction of the nominal value, in case of its existence, is effective in the statute that creates the company. As for the equity value, it can be known through financial statements that are configured as one of the obligations of the company to be fulfilled in the final phase of social exercise.

(iii) **Dealing value**—during the process of divesting shares by their respective holder, a certain value is fixed at which the share will be acquired; at the end of the sale, this value is called negotiation value. The definition of the amount to be paid for acquiring the shares is made in function of a conjuncture of factors of an economic nature, of which the profit production expectations can be highlighted, along with highlighting the net equity sphere of the corporate entity, the level of profitability of the corporate sector in which the company operates, among other factors.

(iv) **Economic value**—the calculation of economic value of the share is based on the absence of specific technical means applied in the valuation of assets (e.g., the "*discounted cash flow*"); this is a representative value of weighted amount for the payment of a share, considering the profitability expectations of the public limited company that issues the respective share.

(v) **Issue price**—consists of the price whose payment is made by the person who subscribes for the share, and payment can be made in full or in installments. Its purpose is to measure the assets of the shareholder which are allocated to the formation of share capital (and, occasionally, for the purpose of reserving capital) of the limited company, and the value of share capital serves as a criterion for limiting the shareholder's subsidiary liability. "*The issue price must be fixed, without unjustified dilution of the participation of the former shareholders, even if they have*

> *preemptive rights to subscribe them, considering, alternatively or jointly: (I) the company's profitability perspective; (II) the value of the share's net worth; (III) the quotation of its shares on the Stock Exchange or on the organized over-the-counter market, with goodwill or negative goodwill on account of market conditions*" (Article 170 of the Brazilian Corporate Law).

From the perspective of Mariane Portella Garcia, the most striking feature of the limited liability company concerns the complexity of its administration, which has a large normative apparatus to be observed, starting with the requirement for the tripartition of its powers in the general assembly—responsible for the manifestation of social will; directorate—executor of deliberate wills; and fiscal council—whose function is to control the company.[337]

About the corporate name, the public limited company must adopt the name. It is in this context that in the path of Article 295 Brazilian Commercial Code, the attribution of the corporate name to the public limited company must take into account its object, but it does not fit the attribution of Civil Code—"*The public limited company operates under the name of the corporate object, integrated by the terms limited company or anonymous company, in full or abbreviated*" (Article 1160). In the wake of the sole paragraph of that article, the name of the individual who founded the company or the shareholder or the person who has made a significant contribution to the creation of the company can be included in the denomination.

It is pertinent to emphasize that it is optional to use one of the following expressions—"*Anonymous company*" *or* "*company*"—to appear in the name; however, their simultaneous use is not allowed. The corporate name of the company (in this case, denomination) should also include the name of the founder or mentor of the limited company, shareholder, or other subjects who have brought the company to a prominent position in the business sector in which is inserted. The basis of the denomination is to turn the anonymous company into individual one; it is this foundation that makes it necessary to include (in the denomination) the fancy name or civil name that will serve as an element of distinction from other corporate entities.[338]

From the provisions made in the rule of Article 982 of the Civil Code in conjunction with the rule of Article 2, paragraph 1, of the Brazilian Corporate Law, it follows that, independently of its object, the public limited company is

337 Mariane Portella GARCIA, op. cit., 24.
338 Elisabeth Maria PEREIRA, op. cit., 41.

classified as an entrepreneur. One of its most notable milestones is the pursuit of profit to be shared among shareholders who compose it. Such a notable landmark is legally grounded by the mandatory dividend distribution, to be enshrined in bylaws or in the law, in case of omission of bylaws (Article 202 of the Brazilian Corporate Law).

Classification of public limited company: The classification of company allows identifying different forms that it can take, according to the interests for which its social purpose is destined. The classification that stands out the most is that which distinguishes between a publicly traded company and a privately held company. The classification according to the capital criterion has two foundations[339]:

(i) **In accordance with whether or not their shares are** common or preferred, and common or fruition. Ordinary shares assure holders the common rights of members, while preferred shares confer more privileges; they are given primacy in the distribution of dividends; primacy in the return of capital; fruition shares are derived from the amortization of ordinary or preferred shares, with amortization being understood as the advance distribution to shareholders of amounts that would be distributed to them in the event of dissolution.

As can be seen from the previous paragraph, the author who bases that understanding does not present an exhaustive approach to the actions he mentioned; thus, it is necessary, for a better understanding, to resort to other authors and the law itself.

Ordinary shares—in principle, all shares of the company are ordinary: If the bylaws only provide for the number of shares by which the share capital is divided but do not mention their respective type, then such shares are considered common, of a single class and confer the same rights. Under Article 16 of the Brazilian Corporate Law, in the closed company the law allows the bylaws to divide ordinary shares into classes, but allows it only for the following reasons: *convertibility into preferred shares*[340]; *Brazilian nationality requirement of the shareholder*[341]; or *the right to vote separately to fill certain positions of organs of administrative bodies.*[342]

339 Id.
340 See item I, Article 16 of the Brazilian Corporate Law.
341 See item II, Article 16 of the Brazilian Corporate Law.
342 See item III, Article 16 of the Brazilian Corporate Law.

Conversion of ordinary shares into preferred shares and the right to occupy certain positions in administrative bodies are legally permitted mechanisms for forming the interests of different groups of shareholders in the private limited company; Brazilian nationality as a requirement for the acquisition of ordinary shares of a certain class can be useful for the preservation of balance of power in a closed corporation with foreign partners.[343]

The exhaustive enumeration of the law of differences in rights between classes of ordinary shares precludes the possibility that the constitutive act of the company makes other distinctions between ordinary shares of different classes. In legal terms, no more than one class of ordinary shares is allowed in the public limited company because the difference in rights conferred by classes would imply the flow of different securities, with different prices, to the detriment of the efficient functioning of the market and the liquidity of shares.

Preferred Shares. Preferred shares are those that grant their holders special benefits to the detriment of certain common rights, such as the right to vote. In accordance with Article 17 of the Brazilian Corporate Law, the following rights are granted by preference shares: priority in the distribution of dividends, fixed or minimum[344] and priority in the reimbursement of capital, with or without a premium[345] or in the accumulation of the listed benefits.[346]

From the rights listed by the aforementioned article, "***priority in the distribution of dividends***" must be understood as the probability of sharing profits, having these at the end of each year (each year corresponds to a calendar year); the distribution will be made in the first line to the holders the preferred shares, taking into account the limits established in the constitutive act of the company, and in this case, the bylaws. Other shareholders will receive dividends in the event of the existence of surplus profits to be distributed. Dividends earmarked for preference shares are likely to have a fixed, minimum or cumulative aspect.[347]

It is Article 17 of the Brazilian Corporate Law that mentions fixed, minimum and cumulative dividends.

Dividends consisting of the determined or determinable value are fixed, which, if there are profits, the holder of the preferred shares will receive with priority, even if other shareholders do not receive them. In compensation, without prejudice to the provisions of the company's charter, the holder of preferred

343 Alfredo FILHO and José PEDREIRA, op. cit., 147.
344 See item I, Article 17 of the Brazilian Corporate Law.
345 See item II, Article 17 of the Brazilian Corporate Law.
346 See item III, Article 17 of the Brazilian Corporate Law.
347 Elisabeth Maria PEREIRA, op. cit., 17.

shares will receive nothing more in this case. If there are remaining profits, their distribution will be made only among other partners, even if these will, in this way, obtain higher dividends than the fixed one, due to the high profits of the company.[348]

Minimum dividends are considered to consist of the determined or determinable value that, if there are profits, the holder of preferred shares will receive on a priority basis, even if other shareholders do not receive them. "*Except that, unless otherwise provided in the bylaws, the treatment reserved for the remaining profits is different, since, if these allow the payment, to the other shareholders, of dividends equal to the minimum, the rest, if any, will be distributed in equal parts—but proportionally to the number of shares of each one—among all shareholders of the company.*"[349]

We are facing the cumulative dividend when the statute expressly provides for the accumulation of the following year, in the event of not having been paid in a certain year, due to insufficient profits. It means that when the dividend is cumulative, the fixed or minimum dividend not paid in a given year must be paid twice in the following year, and thrice in another year, and so on until the profits are sufficient to cover the payment of dividends. In the absence of profits in a certain year, however, if there is reserved capital, it can be used to pay the cumulative dividend.[350]

It is necessary to take into consideration that the preferred shares do not only confer advantages, but also confer certain disadvantages, as can be seen in the wordings of Article 111 of the LSA: "*The bylaws may cease to confer to the preferred shares . . . some of the rights recognized* [for] *common shares, including voting rights, or to confer it with restrictions.*"[351] However, the holder of preferred shares has to abide by these restrictions because he receives financial benefits (preferential dividends) in compensation. If the preferred shareholder stays in the company for three successive years without receiving dividends, he will acquire the right to vote, and that right will only cease when the payment of dividends in arrears is verified.[352]

Under the provisions of § 2 of Article 15 of the LSA, the proportion of preferred shares without voting rights, or subject to restrictions on the exercise of that right, cannot exceed 50 % of the total issued shares.

348 Id.
349 Elisabeth Maria PEREIRA, op. cit., 17–18.
350 Id.
351 The statute may not restrict the essential rights listed in Article 109 of the Brazilian Corporate Law.
352 See § 1 of Article 111 of the Brazilian Corporate Law.

Fruition actions. Paragraph 5 of Article 44 of the LSA provides as follows:

> The fully amortized shares may be replaced by fruition shares, with the restrictions set by the bylaws or by the general meeting that decides on the amortization; in any case, if the company is liquidated, the amortized shares will only compete for the net assets after the non-amortized shares are guaranteed an amount equal to the amortization, monetarily restated.

For Bulhões Pedreira and Lamy Filho, the stipulations of the paragraph in question imply but do not impose that the law authorizes the replacement of amortized shares with fruition shares. Such substitution and restrictions to which the fruition actions will be subject, if not established in the constitutive act of the company, will be deliberated by the general meeting, and the deliberation questions the competence of general meeting to replace, without agreement of the interested shareholders, substituted shares with fruition and restrict the rights of the latter.[353]

The aforementioned authors draw attention to the fact that the Brazilian Corporate Law does not reproduce the reservation of § 3 of Article 18 of Decree-Law 2,627 /1940 that the rights recognized to fruition actions should observe the provisions of Article 78, corresponding to Article 109 of the Brazilian Corporate Law, which prohibits the act of creating the company (bylaws) and the general meeting to prevent the shareholder from exercising fundamental rights. Meanwhile, Article 109, being a general rule that applies to all shares, Article 44 (paragraph 5) authorizing the creation of fruition shares with limitations established by the constitutive act or by the general meeting that issues the amortization resolution must, being a special rule, prevail over Article 109, since the new law does not contain the limitation of Decree-Law No. 2,627 of September 26, 1940.

The process of amortizing fruition shares does not undo the inherent rights. In other words, if, prior to the said process, the fruition action was an ordinary or preferential action, it will retain the rights of its primitive species; if ordinary, it will retain the respective rights, say the same in the case of a preferred share. The existing difference occurs in the event of future liquidation of the company in which the amortization process takes place, in principle; the fruition action receives nothing, since there has already been anticipation. Subsequent to the receipt of amounts that were due to the holders of the shares of fruition, for these,

353 José Luiz BULHÕES PEDREIRA and Alfredo LAMY FILHO, *Direito das Companhias*, op. cit., 197.

they could still receive something, similar to the other shareholders. The purpose of the fruition actions is to return the investment made to the shareholder.[354]

About the right to "*priority in the repayment of capital*," it occurs in the process of liquidation of the company, after making payment of those who have a credit right to the company, the remaining assets will have to be distributed to the shareholders, in proportion to the shares of each one, and in the following terms: "*the common shares will receive nothing until the preferred shares are fully repaid, at their nominal value, with or without a premium*."[355]

In accordance with Article 18 of the Brazilian Corporate Law, the constitutive act of the company may ensure that one or more classes of preferred shares have the right to elect, in a separate vote, one or more members of the management bodies and may also, in accordance with the sole paragraph of the aforementioned article, subject the statutory amendments that it specifies to the approval, at a special meeting, of the holders of one or more classes of preferred shares.

(ii) **Other securities issued for business on the stock exchange or on the stock market**—there are securities issued by public limited companies, in addition to shares, through other modalities such as ***beneficiary parties***, ***debentures***, and subscription bonuses. The beneficiary parties aim to establish an advantage in a part of the profits for the founders of the company or third parties that have contributed to its formation. Debentures are securities with a fixed term that the company issues to third parties that want to invest in it, without necessarily being shareholders, and that in relation to the company will be holders of credit rights. The subscription bonus, finally, gives its holder the right to subscribe for shares in a future capital increase.[356]

Beneficiary Parties. The company can create, at any time, negotiable securities, with no par value and foreign to the social capital, called "beneficiary parties."[357] The beneficiary parties give their holder the right to participate in the annual social profits. It must be borne in mind that the holders of these papers are not shareholders, as they do not receive dividends. The emission limit of beneficiary parties is one-tenth of the profits (§ 2, Article 46). The creation of more than one

354 Cláudia RIBEIRO and Priscila MENEZES, op. cit., 42.
355 Id.
356 Elisabeth Maria PEREIRA, op. cit., 41.
357 See Article 46 of the Brazilian Corporate Law.

class or series of beneficiary parties is prohibited (§ 4, Article 46). The bylaws may provide for the conversion of beneficiary parties into shares, by capitalizing the reserve created for that purpose (§ 2 of Article 48 of the LSA). They may be granted for a fee or free of charge (these, if they are not intended for companies or charitable foundations of the employees of the company, may not exceed 10 years).[358] Publicly held companies are prohibited from issuing founders' shares (sole section of Article 47 of the LSA).

Debentures. Article 52 of the LSA provides that "*The company may issue debentures that will grant its holders the right to credit against it, under the conditions set out in the deed of issue and, if any, the certificate.*"

The figure of debentures corresponds to credit securities that the public limited company issues in the event it needs funds; however, it does not choose to request pecuniary values in financial institutions or is not yet interested in increasing its share capital through subscription, which would imply new members joining the company or change in the participation of primitive partners. Since debentures are credit instruments, they are issued in series or in bulk. In the case of credit securities of the same series, they will have the same nominal value and will grant the respective holders equal rights; on the other hand, they are representatives of equal installments of the same loan. In general terms, they are traded on the Exchanges Stock.[359]

Subscription bonus. Regulated in accordance with Articles 75–79 of the LSA (Law No. 6,404 December 15, 1976). In consideration of the aforementioned articles, it is common to define subscription bonuses that are subject to negotiability, endorsable to the bearer, but strange and eccentric, to the share capital. The bonus grants its holders the right to subscribe for shares of the same capital, within the parameters of the increase authorized by the bylaws.

The term subscription bonus implies that this credit security is configured as a guarantee by its respective holder, since it guarantees its holder the right to subscribe for shares in the event of a capital increase (Article 75). The general meeting is responsible for deliberating the issue of the subscription bonus, in the absence of a statutory provision that confers such competence on the board of directors (Article 76). The granting of subscription bonus may take two forms—free grant and onerous grant (Article 77).

Having seen the foundations ("*In accordance with the fact that they are or not their shares*"; "*Or other securities issued by companies admitted to business on the stock*

358 See § 10, Article 48 of the Brazilian Corporate Law.

359 Elisabeth Maria PEREIRA, op. cit., 24.

exchange or on the stock market") of the classification that divides companies into publicly and privately held companies, see now the concept of the two figures.

Depending on the legal definition of the Brazilian Corporate Law, enshrined in Article 4, *"(. . .) the company is open or closed depending on whether the securities issued by it are admitted to trading on the securities market."* Only securities issued by a company registered with the Securities and Exchange Commission may be traded on the securities market.[360] What characterizes the publicly held company is the distribution of the issue or trading of its securities in organized markets, and any company that does not participate in the capital markets in this way is, in the legal definition, is a closed company.

The distinction between publicly and privately held companies stems from the fact that, although the company model was invented as an instrument for capturing savings in the market, from the 20th century onwards the use of the type of company without values traded on the capital markets was recognized by the law, after the state's intervention in the capital markets to regulate the distribution of securities through public offerings and circulation of securities markets.[361]

The classification of public limited companies can also be made according to the form of capital increase, which results in *public limited companies with authorized capital and unauthorized capital.* Public limited companies with authorized capital have a statutory provision admitting the capital increase, whether or not the constitutive act of the company is reformed.[362]

With regard to authorized capital, Waldo Fazzio Júnior[363] posits that, as there is a statutory provision that allows for the increase of capital, the increase must be made taking into account a certain limit; such limit is the nominal value of the share capital. The capital increase in these situations does not require the amendment of bylaws and can only be preceded by a previous agreement between shareholders through the general meeting or the board of directors.

The authorized capital is regulated in accordance with Article 168 of the Brazilian Corporate Law, from which it follows that "*The bylaws may contain authorization to increase the capital regardless of statutory reform." Under the 1st of the aforementioned article, "The authorization must specify: a) the increase limit, in capital value or in number of shares, and the types and classes of shares that may be*

360 See § 1, Article 4 of the Brazilian Corporate Law.
361 José Luiz BULHÕES PEDREIRA and Alfredo LAMY FILHO, op. cit., 97.
362 Mariane Portella GARCIA, op. cit., 25.
363 Waldo FAZZIO JÚNIOR, op. cit., 211.

issued; b) the competent body to deliberate on the issues, which may be the general meeting or the directors board; c) the conditions to which the issues are subject; d) whether or not there is a preemptive right to subscribe, or whether there is no such right."

The constitutive act of the public limited company (bylaws), being a publicly held company in which the permission for the increase of the share capital is patent, does not exclude the possibility of bylaws making provision for the issue, lacking the preemptive right for former shareholders to shares, debentures, or beneficiary parts convertible into shares and subscription bonuses, which can be disposed of through sale on the stock exchange or public subscription, or even through exchange for shares, in the event of a public offer for acquisition of control. It is reflected in a compensatory gesture or incentive for people who contribute to the success of the anonymous company.[364]

The controlling shareholder can be used as a criterion for the classification of companies or public limited companies, which results in mixed-capital companies or private companies.[365]

Mixed-capital companies are legally constituted or they depend on prior legislative authorization and have as a controlling shareholder any public entity, representing the Indirect Public Administration; that is, it is controlled by a legal entity of public law. They are created by combining public and private capital, as a way of guaranteeing assistance to public interests, provided that the paid-in capital by the state represents the majority of the shares. In turn, private companies are those constituted mainly by private capital, which does not mean that there can be no participation of public capital; it just will not be in the majority.

Structure of the Public Limited Company and Its Internal Organization. Public limited companies, as well as other types of companies, depend on an organization to carry out their efficient operation and, these having a more complex structure, a need arises in such cases for better distribution of powers.

According to Ricardo Negrão,[366] there are four corporate bodies foreseen for corporations,[367] which are responsible for directing the business: the board of directors, the supervisory board, the general meeting, and the executive board. The first two bodies mentioned are optional for most incorporated companies.

364 Waldo FAZZIO JÚNIOR, op. cit., 212.

365 Mariane Portella GARCIA, op. cit., 26.

366 Ricardo NEGRÃO, op. cit., 480.

367 It has been said before that there are two companies per share, also classified as institutional: the public limited company and the limited liability company.

Rubens Requião posits that the bodies that make up the public limited company establish a democratic structure, being formed in three different spheres, namely, the deliberative body, responsible for expressing the company's will; the executive body, charged with pursuing the will of the social will; and, finally, the controlling body, which monitors the punctual fulfillment of the social will.[368] In this context, the essential bodies that constitute the public limited company are the general meeting, the board of directors, and the supervisory board.

Still within the scope of the organic structure of public limited companies, it is possible to meet the board of directors, which as a rule is optional; however, in some circumstances, it is mandatory and must be part of the body of authorized capital companies, mixed and open economy, or by virtue of Article 160 of the Brazilian Corporate Law, which provides for bodies and consultation for the guidance of directors in relation to certain matters of their own competence.

Giuseppe Ferri, quoted by Mariene Portella Garcia, argues that the organs of the company are linked to the legal person in an intersubjective relationship, what he calls an organic rapport, and not merely an internal relationship. He further posts that "*similarly to the state organization, there is, in public limited companies, a division of functions between three spheres, namely, the Assembly, with deliberative functions; the Directors, with executive functions; and the Supervisory Board (collegio sindacale), with control functions.*"[369]

General Assembly—it is an organ that is inserted at the top of the organic structure of public limited companies, and its essential function is to express its respective will through deliberations; in this line, the discussion, voting, and deliberation pertain to all matters related to the company (Article 121 of the Brazilian Corporate Law). The aforementioned legal precept implies that the general meeting "*is the shareholders' meeting at the company's headquarters, duly convened and installed with a regulatory quorum, determined by the percentage of voting shares, to deliberate by an absolute majority of the votes present on the matter of its competence.*"[370]

In turn, Fran Martins, presents the concept of the general meeting having as legal basis Article 122 of the Brazilian Corporate Law; it is in this sense that he conceptualizes it as being the body whose responsibility consists in expressing the will of the company, in a way that has great influence on the administration.

368 Rubens REQUIÃO, *Curso de Direito Comercial,* 23ª ed.; Vol. II (São Paulo: Saraiva, 2003), 166.

369 Giuseppe FERRI, *Manuale de Dirrito Comerciale,* apud, Mariene Portella GARCIA, *Administração das Sociedade Anónima e suas Relações Jurídicas* (Curitiba, 2005), 27.

370 Elisabeth Maria PEREIRA, op. cit., 79.

Since its functions are enshrined in the aforementioned, and it has absolute powers to decide the business relating to the corporate purpose, in addition to making the decisions it deems convenient in order to defend and promote the development of the company.[371]

On the one hand, Cláudia Ribeiro and Priscila Menezes argue that the general assembly is the supreme, "*sovereign*" body of the limited company and that its insertion in the organic structure of the company is essential and therefore mandatory. Participation in the general meeting is a right that assists all shareholders, even those who do not have the right to vote, because, even though they do not have the right to vote, they are likely to express points of view that may influence social deliberations.[372]

In a different circumstance, Fran Martins does not deny that the general assembly is a supreme organ of the company under analysis; however, he says that contrary to what it may at first appear, the general assembly "*is not a sovereign orga*n" of the limited company. There are numerous restrictions on its activities, since it cannot, for example, deliberate on certain matters without respecting a *quorum* established by the statute or the law or suppress or modify essential rights as a shareholder.[373]

According to Fábio Ulhoa Coelho, in the Brazilian legal system, a situation that differs from that found in other regulations occurs, in which the interference of shareholders in matters of administrative nature is prohibited, this in the context of the meeting. In the Italian legal system, by way of example, the general meeting can only issue a resolution on matters pertaining to the management of the company with statutory provisions in this regard, or even if the meeting is requested by administrative organs or bodies. In the United Kingdom, it is also the constitutive act of the corporate entity (bylaws) that should cover in its systematics the matter concerning the division of power between the "*general meeting" and the "board of directors*" and the respective delimitation of matters whose exclusive competence is of the latter. In the United States, guidelines from the judiciary maintain that the establishment of essentially business policies is the exclusive competence of the "*board of directors, therefore, they cannot be analyzed at the 'annual meeting'*"; nevertheless, such support may vary depending on the rules of the statutory state law.[374]

371 FRAN MARTINS, Comentários à Leis das Sociedades por Acções, Vol. II (Rio de Janeiro: Forense, 1978), 137.

372 Cláudia RIBEIRO and Priscila MENEZES, op. cit., 44.

373 FRAN MARTINS, op. cit., 137.

374 Fábio Ulhoa COELHO, *Curso de Direito Comercial: Sociedades*; op. cit., 255.

It is, therefore,

> an anachronistic comparison, since the organization of power, in corporate law, is based on the measure of the contribution of each shareholder to the formation of social capital, that is, it is a parameter of the economic strength of participating in the organ. Now, contemporary democracy vehemently repels any census formula for organizing political power. If, in the origins of the modern state, ideology favored the opinion of the wealthiest citizens, because they had contributed more to the existence and maintenance of the bureaucratic apparatus (the figure of the census vote in the Brazilian Imperial Constitution of 1824 is a late manifestation of this ideology), for a long time the correct thing, politically speaking, is the disregard of the unequal economic contribution to the state in the discipline of citizenship rights. The memory of the organs of the democratic state is, therefore, nothing useful for understanding corporate law.[375]

Although the general meeting is considered to be the supreme decision-making entity of the public limited company, with the prerogative of addressing the universality of matters that interest the company, it is usually convened as exclusivity in legally determined eventualities. Article 122 of the Brazilian Corporate Law determines that a certain range of matters are the exclusive competence of the general meeting and its convocation will be based on the need to analyze the respective matters. When the matter is liable to be the subject of a valid decision by another body of the company, not the meeting, no matter how important the matter is to the interests of partners, the meeting is not called.[376]

The paragraph written by Fábio Ulha Coelho certainly goes against Fran Martins' position, in the sense that he does not deny that the general assembly is a supreme organ of the public limited company; however, he states that contrary to how it may appear, in principle, the general assembly "is not a sovereign body" of the limited company. There are numerous restrictions on its activities, since it cannot, for example, deliberate on certain matters without respecting a *quorum* established by the statute or the law or suppress or modify essential rights as a shareholder. And he also agrees that the general assembly is a higher deliberative body to address the universality of matters of interest to the company but recognizes at the same time that when the subject is susceptible of valid deliberation by another body of the company, however preeminent the subject may be, it should

375 Id., 255–56.

376 Fábio Ulhoa COELHO, op. cit., 255.

still be allowed for review by the other body for the greater good or collective interests of company.

Board of Directors—to manage the public limited company, the creation of board of directors is allowed, which will receive delegations from the general meeting. The body in question is elected by the general meeting and removed by it and has competence determined by Article 142 of the Brazilian Corporate Law, which gives it power to carry out administrative and supervisory functions. It is to the Supervisory Body to which the directors are subordinate in the practice of management acts, so that it can, by determination of the same Article 142, item III, at any time, "*supervise the management of the directors, examine at any time, the company books and papers, request information on contracts signed or about to be signed, and any other acts.*"

It is important to bear in mind that the powers contained in Article 122 of the Brazilian Corporate Law are the exclusive competence of the general meeting or they cannot be delegated to another body. It deals with the powers of the board of directors in accordance with Article 142 of the aforementioned law.[377]

As a general rule, the insertion of the board of directors in the company's organic structure is optional. It consists of a collegial body of a deliberative nature that is responsible for the attribution of a part of the competences of the general meeting, with the purpose of making the process of decision-making in the interests of the company's dynamic. In the path of § 2, article 138 of the Brazilian Corporate Law, "*Publicly-held companies and those with authorized capital must have a board of directors.*" The same law, in Article 239, establishes that "*The mixed-capital companies must have a Board of Directors, guaranteeing the minority the right to elect one of the directors, if a greater number does not belong to them through the multiple voting processes.*" As can be seen, the mandatory inclusion of the board is required in public limited companies (publicly held companies), those with authorized capital and those with mixed capital.[378]

Articles 153–159 of the Brazilian Corporate Law deal with the rights and duties of company directors. Mariane Portella Garcia points out that the directors do not represent the company, do not practice acts of external management, and do not contract obligations in its name. And to support this understanding, the author mentions Arnoldo Wald; the referred author understands that the board of directors "*is a Collegiate Deliberation Body, without powers of representation, of mandatory existence in Publicly-Held Companies, mixed-capital companies and*

377 Cláudia RIBEIRO and Priscila MENEZES, op. cit., 45.

378 Fábio Ulhoa COELHO, *Manual de Direito Comercial: Direito de Empresa*; op. cit., 233.

those with authorized capital. The members of the Board of Directors must deliberate together; therefore, they do not have individual competence and cannot, moreover, represent the company."[379]

Such an understanding does imply that the members of the board of directors have no liability to the company. Evidently, their responsibility is distinct from that of the directors who are individually expressing their will and are also individually responsible for the unfounded exercise of the powers conferred on them. However, the board members are responsible for the decisions taken on behalf of the board. Even so, it is important to emphasize that, due to the repercussions caused by the deliberations taken by only one director, with intent or guilt, or that offend the statute or the law, only such a person or an entity and those who are conniving with them will be held personally responsible.[380]

Management—the management is the body responsible for exercising the executive powers of the public limited company; proceeding with the execution of guidelines issued by the board of directors, which is inserted in the organic structure of the company; and it can also execute the guidelines from the general meeting. The insertion of the board of directors in the organic structure of the current corporate entity is essentially mandatory, and a new person or entity seeking a place in it must be selected by the board of directors; if this is not included in the organic structure of the company, the meeting will do it (Article 143 of the Brazilian Corporate Law).

In the perception of Lamy Filho and Bulhões Pedreira, the board of directors is a body created by law, with the statute regulating its composition, lapse time in management and the method of replacing the directors, duties and powers corresponding to each of the directors, and their functioning as a collegiate organic entity.[381]

It is in this context that Fábio Ulhoa Coelho posits that the board is an organic entity that legally represents the public limited company and executes the deliberative acts of the assembly and the council. The act of creating the company (bylaws) must make the forecast, in the context of the board, with the number of members limited to two or the maximum numbers allowed; the timespan of the mandate, with a maximum limit of three years; substitution modality of the

379 ARNOLDO WALD, *Da Responsabilidade dos Membros do Conselho de Administração no Regime da Lei 6.024/74*; *Apud* Mariene Portella GARCIA, *Administração das Sociedade Anónima e suas Relações Jurídicas* (Curitiba, 2005), 29–30.

380 Mariene Portella GARCIA, op. cit., 31.

381 José Luiz BULHÕES PEDREIRA and Alfredo LAMY FILHO, op. cit., 771.

directors; and the delimitation of the attributions and powers to be conferred individually to each director (Article 143 of the Brazilian Corporate Law).[382]

As the board of directors is a body that performs executive functions of the public limited company, Lamy Filho and Bulhões Pedreira are of the view that the body in question will represent the company before third parties in all its legal relationships, whether or not the board of directors is included in the organic structure of the company (Article 138, paragraph 1 and Article 144 of the Brazilian Corporate Law). Therefore, the board of directors is the body that executes and externalizes social wills and must be composed exclusively of natural persons, shareholders or not, with fixed residence in Brazil, these members being submitted to election and their respective removal at all times by the Administrative Council. Thus, it appears that the executive board, except in the absence of a board of directors, will not be subject to the general meeting.[383]

The members to be elected as directors of the public limited company may or may not be shareholders of the public limited company, and their election is made by the board of directors, existing in the company; in case of its nonexistence, they will carry out their respective election to the general meeting; the removal of directors occurs at all times by the body with competence for their election; up to a third of the members of the board of directors may compose the board (Article 143 of the Brazilian Corporate Law). Still in the same law, Article 144, the director who is assigned competence in a specific manner for that purpose will be legally represented by the constitutive act of the company, the social statute being omitted in this sense; such omission, by means of a deliberative act, if the board of directors does not already exist, gives rise to a situation where any director of the company may represent the board.

The management of company is a function of the board of directors, and it is this body that legally represents the public limited company, with such representation having its exclusive competence; therefore, it cannot be delegated to another body (Corporate Law, Article 138, § 1). The non-permission of the delegation of said competence concerns ordinary representation (which cannot be delegated to the general meeting or the board of directors). Nevertheless, there are situations of extraordinary representation. Take as an example of extraordinary representation, a situation in which there is a vacancy in all positions of the management bodies; in this case, the shareholder holding the largest number of

382 Fábio Ulhoa COELHO, *Manual de Direito Comercial: Direito de Empresa*; op. cit.,. 235.

383 José Luiz BULHÕES PEDREIRA and Alfredo LAMY FILHO, *A Lei as S.A.—Pressupostos—Elaboração—Aplicação* (Rio de Janeiro: Renovar, 1992), 241.

shares will be appointed as a representative of the company to carry out urgent acts of management (Article 150, § 2).[384]

The rights and responsibilities of the board of directors are in line with those of the other directors, and these are established in the same articles, Articles 153–159. The director of the company also has the duties of loyalty in the performance of his function, to safeguard the secrecy about information of facts by him known due to the exercise of the position (e.g., a violation in this case is usually insider trading) and provide information about the deliberations of the general meeting or of the management bodies (disclosure), in addition to fulfilling the ethical-social duty toward the company and the duty of diligence, employing in practice of the functions that are responsible for all care and probity.[385]

The directors, as well as administrators, may be held personally responsible, if they act in bad faith, willfulness, or guilt, deviating from the functions entrusted to them, thereby causing damage to the company, to any shareholder, or to third parties. Evidently, the administrator or the director will be held responsible, in isolation, as long as there is no collusion on the part of the other administrative members, which presupposes an express mention of the attitude that may cause losses to the company.

In this context, Lamy Filho and Bulhões Pedreira explain that the members of the administrative bodies of the companies—board members and directors—are subject to the same legal regime comprising statutory requirements to be fulfilled as well as to attend to important aspects such as investiture, impediments, remuneration, and duties and responsibilities. The authors cited take as an example what happens in other jurisdictions, for example, United States and England, where the duties and responsibilities of administrators are provided for in the law in the form of somewhat broad standards of conduct. Likewise, the Brazilian legislature chose, in the name of the normative economy, to establish, in Articles 145–159, the rules that make up the common regime of administrators.[386]

On the other hand, while contemplating the rules of general application to both categories of directors, the corporate law system disciplines the actions of directors and board members with attention to what is specific to them. The roles of the board of directors and the board—the first, a strategic, supervisory body, and the second, eminently executive, of a more accentuated professional nature—require specific rules, which are present in the legal system. It should

384 Fábio Ulhoa COELHO, *Curso de Direito Comercial: Direito de Empresa*; op. cit., 296.

385 Mariene Portella GARCIA, op. cit., 30.

386 José Luiz BULHÕES PEDREIRA and Alfredo LAMY FILHO, op. cit., 775–76.

be said that even common standards reflect the different treatment of directors and officers. To serve as an example, Article 150 of the Brazilian Corporate Law, which deals with the replacement and termination of the management of directors, provides for the vacancies of different categories of directors in different ways, in recognition of the differences between one position and another.[387]

Supervisory Board—the inclusion of the supervisory board in the organic structure of the public limited company is mandatory. The powers of this body are listed in Article 163 of the Brazilian Corporate Law.

Under the aforementioned article, the audit committee is responsible for the following functions:

> (I) inspect, by any of its members, the acts of the administrators and verify the fulfillment of their legal and statutory duties; (II) opine on the management's annual report, stating in its opinion the complementary information deemed necessary or useful for the resolution of the general meeting; (III) opine on the proposals of the management bodies, to be submitted to the general meeting, regarding the modification of the capital stock, issuance of debentures or subscription bonuses, investment plans or capital budgets, distribution of dividends, transformation, incorporation , merger or split; (IV) denounce, by any of its members, to the management bodies and, if they do not take the necessary measures to protect the interests of the company, to the general meeting, the errors, fraud or crimes they discover, and suggest useful measures the company; (V) call the annual general meeting, if the management bodies delay this call for more than 1 (one) month, and the extraordinary, whenever serious or urgent reasons occur, including in the agenda of the meetings the matters deemed necessary; (VI) analyze, at least quarterly, the balance sheet and other financial statements prepared periodically by the company; (VII) examine the financial statements for the fiscal year and give an opinion on them; and (VIII) exercise these powers, during the liquidation, in view of the special provisions that regulate it.

As it was noted from the above statement, the supervisory board has its attributions listed in Article 163 of the Brazilian Corporate Law and includes inspection and consultation activities, allowing a more effective control of social management, as it reveals to shareholders the behavior of administrators and the progress of the company's business, offering opinions on the most relevant social operations.

387 Id.

Mariane Portella Garcia draws attention to the fact that even in Decree No. 2,627 of September 26, 1940,[388] the existence of a fiscal council in companies was mandatory; however, with the entry into force of the Corporate Law, further requirements emerged, such as the faculty of its permanent formation, with a minimum composition of three members and a maximum of five, shareholders or not, with the general assembly being competent for its election. The cited author also affirms that "*Thus, in being a necessary Organ to the company, the statute must regulate its performance; permanent or only in the exercises in which its installation is requested.*"[389]

On the same subject, Fábio Ulhoa Coelho explains that "*The fiscal council is a mandatory body, but with an optional function, composed of at least three, and at most five members, shareholders or not.*" He also adds that, as it is an organ that, under the constitutive act of the company (bylaws), is granted an optional function, its effective operation can only be promoted through a deliberative act of the general meeting and may propose the holding of the shareholder representing 10 % of the voting shares or 5 % of the shares lacking the right to vote (Article 161, § 2 of the Brazilian Corporate Law); in public companies, the required percentage is lower and is fixed by the Securities Commission according to the share capital.[390]

It is known that the regime of impediments and duties applicable to directors are also applicable to members of the fiscal council. Pursuant to paragraph 2 of Article 162 of the Brazilian Corporate Law, in regards to the election of a member of the board of directors, the employee of the public limited company or of a controlled company or of the same group, as well as the spouse or relative up to the third degree of company administrator, may occupy a position on the fiscal council. Holders of preferred shares without voting rights, or with restrictions on that right, may elect, separately, a member of the fiscal council. Minority shareholders have equal rights with a minimum representation of 10 % or more of the voting capital. Thus, if the fiscal council had three members, the body will have five if both minority groups exercise their rights to elect a separate fiscal council member, pursuant to the provisions of al. (a), § 4, of Article 161 of the Brazilian Corporate Law.

388 Decree on companies by shares; it is a decree partially repealed by Law No. 6,404 of December 15, 1976.

389 Mariane Portella GARCIA, op. cit., 33.

390 Fábio Ulhoa COELHO, *Manual de Direito Comercial: Direito de Empresa*; op. cit., 236.

Like the administrators, the fiscal council member acts individually, therefore having the same duties. This is because paragraph 1 of Article 165 of the Brazilian Corporate Law establishes that the members of the fiscal council are bound to carry out the functions entrusted to them by the social interest; the performance of functions in order to cause damage to the company, or to shareholders or administrators, or to acquire, for itself or for a third person, a benefit that contradicts the company's interest or results in damage to the company will be considered abusive.

Mariane Portela Garcia,[391] commenting on the aforementioned legal precept, understands that "*the director who exercises his functions with the purpose of causing damage to the company, its shareholders or administrators, or with the purpose of obtaining, for himself or for others, an advantage that does justice and that results, or could result* [in] *loss for the company, its shareholders or managers will be acting in an abusive way. They will thus respond in isolation for unlawful acts committed personally, with joint and several liability of those who are conniving with it.*"

References

- AMANNCIO, A. W. *Cessão de quotas nas Sociedades Limitadas,* available at http://www.wamancia.com.br/cessao-de-quotas-nas-sociedades-limitadas/ accessed on August 4, 2019.
- BARROS, Carla Eugenia Caldas. 2014. *Manual de Direito Empresarial Multifacetado*, Voll. III – Direito Falimentar e Recuperacional. Aracaju: Edição do Autor | PIDCC.
- BULHÕES PEDREIRA, José Luiz and Alfredo LAMY FILHO. 1992. *A Lei as S.A. – Pressupostos – Elaboração – Aplicação.* Rio de Janeiro: Renovar.
- BULHÕES PEDREIRA, José Luiz and Alfredo LAMY FILHO. 2017. *Direito das Companhias*, 2ª ed. Rio de Janeiro: Editora Forense.
- CARVALHO FILHO, José dos Santos. 2018. *Manual de Direito Administrativo*; 32ª ed. São Paulo: Atlas.
- CARVALHO, Maria Miguel and Sónia MOREIRA. 2013. *Das Sociedades Comerciais (Capítulo I) Sumários desenvolvidos das aulas de Direito para Economia e Gestão*; Universidade do Minho: Escola de Direito.
- CARVALHO, Raphael Franco Castelo Branco. 2013. *Falência: uma análise jurídica e histórica do instituto, desde a antiguidade aos dias de hoje.* In Mara Vidagal Darcanchy (org). *Direito Empresarial – Florianópolis.* FUNJAB, v. ún.
- CASTRO, Rodrigo R. Monteiro de and Leandro Santos de ARAGÃO. 2009. *Direito Societário: Desafios Actuais.* São Paulo: Quarier Latin.

391 Mariane Portella GARCIA, op. cit., 33.

- CINTRA, António Carlos de Araújo, Ada Pelligrini GRINOVER and Cândido Rangel DINAMARCO. 2009. *Teoria Geral do Processo,* 25ª Edição, Revista e Actualizada. São Paulo: Malheiros Editores.
- COELHO, Fábio Ulhoa. 2009. *Curso de Direito Comercial: Direito de Empresa,* Vol. 1, 13 Edição. São Paulo: Editora Saraiva.
- COELHO, Fábio Ulhoa. 2009. *Curso de Direito Comercial: Direito de Empresa – Contratos e Recuperação de Empresa;* 10ª ed. São Paulo: Saraiva.
- COELHO, Fábio Ulhoa. 2011. *Manual de Direito Comercial: Direito de Empresa,* 23ª ed. São Paulo: Saraiva.
- COELHO, Fábio Ulhoa. 2012. *Curso de Direito Civil.* Parte Geral, Vol. 1, 5ª ed. São Paulo: Editora Saraiva.
- CORREIA, António Arruda Ferrer. 1948. *Sociedades Fictícias e Unipessoais.* Livraria Atlântida, Coimbra.
- CORREIA, Miguel J. A. Pupo. 1996. *Direito Comercial,* 4ª ed, revista e aumentada. Lisboa: Universidade Lusíada.
- CORREIA, Miguel J. A. Pupo. 1999. *Direito Comercial,* 6ª Edição. Lisboa: Ediforum.
- CRUZ, André Santa. *Aquisição de quotas pela própria sociedade,* available at http://genjurid ico.com.br/2016/04.27/aquisicao-de-quatas-pela-propria-sociedade/, accessed in 4th August 2019.
- DAMASCENO, Maria Helena and Silva MEGALE. 1980. *Transformação, Fusão e Cisão de Sociedades,* Revista da Faculdade de Direito, Universidade de Minas Gerais, ISSN: 0304-2340.
- DINIZ, Maria Helena. 2008. *Curso de Direito Civil brasileiro,* Vol. 8. São Paulo: Editora Saraiva.
- DINIZ, Maria Helena. 2015. Curso de *Direito Civil Brasileiro: Teoria Geral do Direito Civil.* São Paulo: Saraiva.
- FAZZIO JÚNIOR, Waldo. 2010. *Manual de Direito Comercial,* 11ª Edição. São Paulo: Editora Atlas.
- FRAN MARTINS. 1978. *Comentários à Leis das Sociedades por Acções,* Vol. II. Rio de Janeiro: Forense.
- GARCIA, Mariane Portella. 2005. *Administração da Sociedade Anónima e suas relações jurídicas,* Curitiba.
- GUIMARÃES, Márcio. 2013. *Direito das Empresas em dificuldades.* Fundação Gentúlio Vargas: Direito Rio, Graduação.
- JÚNIOR, Manuel Guilherme. 2022. *Manual de Direito Comercial Moçambicano,* Vol. 1. 2ª Edição, Maputo: Escolar Editora.
- LACERDA, J. C. Sampaio de. 1996. *Manual de Direito Falimentar,* 13ª ed. revisto e actualizado por Jorge de Miranda Magalhães. Rio de Janeiro: Freitas Bastos.
- MORREIRA, Welliton Luiz. 2016. *A Sociedade Unipessoal e a Limitação da Responsabilidade Patrimonial do Empresário Individual,* Coimbra.
- NEGRÃO, Ricardo. 2010. *Manual de Direito Comercial e de Empresa, Volume 1,* 7ª Edição, São Paulo: SARAIVA.
- PAULA, Luiz Gonzaga Modesto de. 2015. *Sociedade Limitada,* 1ª.ed. São Paulo: Saraiva.
- REQUIÃO, Rubens. 1984. *Curso de direito comercial;* 14ª ed. São Paulo: Saraiva.
- REQUIÃO, Rubens. 1995. *Curso de Direito Comercial,* 22ª ed. São Paulo: Saraiva.

- REQUIÃO, Rubens. 2003. *Curso de Direito Comercial,* Vol. I, 25ª ed. São Paulo: Saraiva.
- REQUIÃO, Rubens. 2005. *Curso de Direito Comercial, Volume 1.* São Paulo: Editora Saraiva.
- RIBEIRO, Cláudia and Priscila MENEZES. 2014. *Teoria do Direito Empresarial,* FGV, Direito Rio, Graduação.
- RODRIGUES, Luiz António Barroso. 2016. *Direito Empresarial,* 3 ed. rev. Actual – Florianópolis: Departamento de Ciências da Administração/ UFSC, Brasília: CAPES: UAB, p. 47.
- SILVA ALVES, Itálo Miqueias da. *A Personalidade Jurídica no Direito Civil,* available at https://jus.com.br/artigos/61828/a-personalidade-juridica-no-direito-civil, accessed in 5th July 2019.
- WALDEMAR ZVEITER. 1991. *Sociedade por Quotas de Responsabilidade Limitada – Aspectos polémicos;* Conferência dos Advogados Catarinenses – Criciúma –SC.

5

Bankrupcty and Recovery of Companies under Brazilian Law

1. Bankruptcy of Companies

1.1 Historical Evolution of Bankruptcy under the Brazilian Legal System

The historical evolution of bankruptcy under the Brazilian legal system refers to a distant past whose characteristics are reflected and understood in our times.

1.1.1 Antiquity

Default refers to a state of a debtor or defaulter who are deprived of their liberty and, in some, even leads to situations where the defaulter chooses to take his own life on account of their inability to pay back the loan—a reality, though rare today, that has been in existence for the past several centuries and continues to prevail in contemporary times. The obligation to pay falls on the debtor's "person" and not on his "patrimonial" sphere; thus, the debtor was configured as an exclusive guarantee before his creditors.[1]

1 Raphael Franco Castelo Branco CARVALHO, *Falência: uma análise jurídica e histórica do instituto, desde a antiguidade aos dias de hoje.* In Mara Vidagal Darcanchy (org). *Direito Empresarial – Florianópolis* (FUNJAB, 2013), v. ún. 350–55.

The antiquity was a historical age marked by the validity of the Code of Hammurabi; this reveals itself as a perfect foundation for the situation explained in the previous paragraph. Articles 115–118 of the said Code are frequently cited as the basis for the content in question, as Raphael Carvalho[2] does.

> Article 115—"*If someone has a grain or money credit to another and makes the execution, and the detainee in the house of detention dies a natural death, there is no place for the penalty.*"
>
> Article 116—"*If the detainee in the house of detention dies of beatings or bad treatment, the prisoner's protector must convince his dealer before the court; if he was a free born man, the dealer's son must be killed, if he was a slave, the dealer must pay a third of the mine and lose everything he gave.*"
>
> Article 117—"*If someone has a due debt and sells his wife, son and daughter for money, or they give him a discount with work, they must work three years in the house of the buyer or of the master, in the fourth year he must release them.*"
>
> Article 118—"*If he grants a slave (woman or man) to work for the debt and the dealer grants them in turn, sells them for money, there is no place for opposition.*"

An interpretation of the above articles leads to the conclusion that in this historical period, the nonfulfillment of the bond complex by the respective debtor led to their enslavement by the creditor until the payment of debts was verified. In the event of debts not being paid, the creditor was given the right to "*sell the debtor*" as a slave. It is in this context that Article 58 of the same Code established that "*If the debtor cannot reimburse the wheat, it must be sold for money together with its goods and the farmers from whom the wheat was destroyed will divide it among themselves.*"

The predominant view about insolvency or loan default in traditional antiquity societies deems insolvency as an act of irresponsibility that warrants severe punishment.

LUIZ INÁCIO VIGIL NETO quoted by ANDRÉ FERNADES ESTEVEZ posits that by and large in classical antiquity the concept of insolvency remained in force throughout; it warranted punitive measures such as austerity, slavery, imprisonment, or even torture and humiliation, which aligned in perfect harmony with Roman attitude toward insolvency—"*verbatim: decoctus sempre*

2 *Id.*

culpposos praesumiter donec contrarum probetur." Initially, this idea came to fore in the medieval culture; gradually it was abandoned for the need to achieve greater systematic efficiency with the aim to protect the rights of the creditor.[3]

1.1.2 Ancient Greece

One cannot speak of true bankruptcy as a concept in the context of ancient Greece as one speaks of it these days.

As Rafael CARVALHO[4] pointed out, even though there was no legal instrument regulating bankruptcy under the Greek legal system, the concept of personal responsibility that had existed since ancient times was still widespread among the Greeks. Thus, if a man were in debt and did not have sufficient means to pay the debt he, as a debtor, his wife, children, or employees could be coerced into "*debt slavery*" until the creditor financially recovered his losses through physical labor of the debtor and his people.

Still, given the views of the same author, we can state that until 621 BC it was a common practice in many of the cities in ancient Greece to adopt debt slavery for a maximum duration of five years. With the assumption of Athens' governance by Solon, there was a massive promotion of intense socioeconomic and political changes that brought with them the enactment of legal provisions that abolished slavery as a means of coercive compliance with obligations (for debt) on Greek territory, a fact that would demarcate a truly important event in the culture of debt execution throughout the world.[5]

It is along these lines that Andre Fernandes Estevez adds that the Greek legal system would serve as a basis for compiling Law of the Twelve Tables, this in a context in which the rule was *the servitude of the debtor to the creditor for nonpayment of debts, and it was admitted that the creditor could alienate or even kill the debtor.* The Solon reforms brought humanitarian principles that in turn led to the release of all prisoners for debt and the consequent prohibition of making prisoners' bodies responsible for their commitments. The maximum punishment to be imposed was that if the debtor's assets existed, such assets should be absorbed

3 Luiz Inácio VIGIL NETO, *Teoria falimentar e regimes recuperatórios. apud* André Fernandes ESTEVEZ, "Das origens do Direito Falimentar à Lei nº 11.101/ 2005," *Revista Jurídica Empresarial* 15 (Julho/ Agosto, 2010): 13–14.

4 Raphael F. C. B. CARVALHO, *Falência: Uma Análise Jurídica e Histórica do Instituto, desde a Antiguidade aos dias de hoje.* Available at http://www.publicadireito.com.br/artigos/?cod=761a0c714 184cab2. Access on 25th April 2020.

5 Id.

for payment, and the creditor who presented them should have preference in that payment.[6]

1.1.3 In Ancient Rome

It is in Ancient Rome where the slow process of replacing personal and corporal execution with patrimonial execution took place; therefore, it is believed that the roots of the institute of bankruptcy are strictly connected with Roman Law; however, one cannot speak of a proper institute of bankruptcy in ancient Greece, as one speaks of it today, since at that time there was no proper commercial law and there was no clear distinction between how laws applied to merchants and non-merchants.[7]

Roman Law, like other legal systems, existed in albeit its most primitive form even before the codification of the *Lex Duodecim Tabularum* itself,[8] this in a phase in which obligations were answered by the debtor with his liberty or even with his own life, something that has been verified on several occasions.

As Perin Junior points out, "*Under the Law of the Twelve Tables, execution for debts was instituted against the debtor's own person, reflected into the possibility that the creditor could arrest him in chains (manus iniectio), sell him as a slave beyond the Tiber river (trans Tiberium), or simply kill him, with Praetorian authorization.*"[9]

As can be seen, in this period there was a scrupulously criminal enforceability, which was exclusively focused on the person of the debtor and led to physical torture or death of the defaulter. There was an extreme concern about enforcing sanctions on the individual who failed to meet his obligations to his creditors, since the complex of obligations contracted had the consequence of giving the creditor the *addicere*, or by other means, the adjudication of the insolvent, and the debtor was sent to prison for a period he was to remain as the servant of his creditor. After such time lapse without the payment of the debt or if the *videx* (family member of the debtor or another person who settled his debt to his creditors) did not appear, the creditor had the right to sell the debtor as slave in a foreign territory including the right to kill him and divide the body[10].

6 André Fernandes ESTEVEZ, "Das origens do Direito Falimentar à Lei nº 11.101/ 2005," *Revista Jurídica Empresarial* 15 (Julho/ Agosto, 2010): 15.

7 Ecio PERIN JUNIOR, *Curso de Direito Falimentar e Recuperação de Empresa;* 3ª ed. ver., atual. e ampl. (São Paulo: Editora Método, 2006), 28–29.

8 The Law of the XII Tablets.

9 Ecio PERIN JUNIOR, op. cit., 29.

10 Raphael Franco Castelo Branco CARVALHO, op. cit., 356

The Law of the Twelve Tables reflected the personal execution in regard to the debtor in the following terms: *"If there are many creditors, it is permitted, after the third day of the fair, to divide the debtor's body into pieces as many creditors as there are no matter how many to cut; if the creditors prefer, they may sell the debtor to a foreigner, beyond the Tiber."*[11]

The personal execution of obligations became a potential source of abuse in the service of creditors (within the scope of the application of the Law of the Twelve Tables) and led to the adoption by the Roman dome of the *Lex Poetelia Papiria* in 428 BC, introducing patrimonial execution as a substitute for personal execution in Roman Law. It was the birth of a new era, in which the debtor's sphere of assets would serve as a guarantee to answer for the obligational complex that he had contracted. Therefore, the private enforcement of obligations by the intervention of the magistrate was limited. The possibility of killing the debtor (capital punishment) or selling him to slavery or applying the penalty of restriction of liberty was revoked, and personal execution was the punishment prescribed in most such loan defaults.

Amador Paes de Almeida postulates that under enforcement of *bonorum venditio* instituted by the praetor Rutilio Rufo, debtor's assets could be dispossessed, as long as the praetor so determined. The latter, in turn, had to proceed with appointment of a trustee (curator bonorum) whose task was to administer the assets. Later, as a result of *Lex Julia Bonorum* dated 737 BC, the creditors were allowed to dispose of the debtor's assets through *cessio bonorum*, including the possibility of selling them separately, for the satisfaction of their rights. It is believed that it was at this stage the conditions for the existence of bankruptcy institute were created.[12]

1.1.4 Middle Ages

This historical age is characterized by a significant evolution in the creation of a complex mechanism of regulation of the bankruptcy procedure, and its improvement and systematization, granting it a body and a structure of its own that reflect many features similar to that of modern bankruptcy law.

It was the Italians who were at the forefront of the organization and systematization of Bankruptcy Law, following the process of compilation of recurrent uses and commercial practices, which would give rise to the emergence of

11 Raphael Franco Castelo Branco CARVALHO, op. cit., 356.

12 Amador Paes ALMEIDA, *Curso de Direito Falimentar e Recuperação de Empresa.* 23ª ed. (São Paulo: Saraiva, 2007), 5.

Commercial Law. At the doctrinal level, peculiar rules are identified for the execution of insolvent debtors, which can be seen as precursors of the current Bankruptcy Law. It is important to point out that such rules were applied without distinction to any kind of debtor, merchant or not, and which maintained their excessively repressive character.[13]

In this historical period, significant state intervention was evident, with the state playing a preponderant role, making judicial discipline a condition of creditor's activities and thus pushing the creditor's own initiatives to the margins.

The collective enforcement proceedings had severe repercussions on the person of the debtor, who, acting in good faith, could be subject to a penalty of infamy commensurate with other vexatious penalties. In another strand, if the debtor had acted fraudulently or in bad faith, more serious would be the punitive measures, with the possibility of bankruptcy commissioner taking over the person of the debtor and proceeding with the disposal of his assets. Bankruptcy was perceived and typified as a reprehensible offense.[14]

In this context, the decree of bankruptcy could be enforced based on three circumstances: (i) when the debtor was hiding without having left assets that were responsible for his debts, (ii) upon the request of the debtor, and (iii) upon the petition of the creditor.[15]

In the said three circumstances, facets of the first decree could be found, by virtue of which it was incumbent on the consul to authorize the creditors to take possession of the debtor's assets, forcing him to make payment; as for the second decree, if the term had elapsed and the debtor had not paid his debt, the second decree would take place, which consisted of the actual delivery of assets for their respective disposal and subsequent apportionment of dividends which were paid to the creditors, with due regard to the trustee's prerogatives.

It is important to point out that, in that historical period, the institute of bankruptcy was extended to any kind of debtor, merchant or non-merchant. Later, with the appearance of credit and commerce, different legal systems began to establish a limitation on the institute of bankruptcy, in the sense that it was only applied to merchant debtors (Italy, France, and Portugal). This measure was not incorporated in other states, however (Austria, Denmark, Hungary, England,

13 Raphael Franco Castelo Branco CARVALHO, op. cit., 359.

14 Ecio PERIN JUNIOR, op. cit., 31–32.

15 J. C. Sampaio de LACERDA, *Manual de Direito Falimentar,* 13ª ed. revisto e actualizado por Jorge de Miranda Magalhães (Rio de Janeiro: Freitas Bastos, 1996), 33.

and Norway), as they continued to apply bankruptcy on any defaulter regardless of whether the defaulter was a merchant or non-merchant.

1.1.5 Contemporary Age

With regard to this historical age, it is worth mentioning that Luiz XIV sought inspiration in recurrent norms and practices in the commercial area and introduced in France a concrete ordinance for commerce—a measure that resulted in the creation of the French Commercial Code two centuries later and provided an extremely significant development in the institute of bankruptcy.

ARNOLDI states that *"bankruptcy has become eminently commercial in France, which has served as an inspiration for the bankruptcy laws of a large part of the countries of Continental Europe and Latin America."*[16] This highlights the fact that in mid-1807, the Napoleonic Code—an instrument of extreme value for the development of bankruptcy institute—was edited and was equally denominated as *Code de Commerce*. It was part of its essence to limit the application of the institute of bankruptcy to the merchant debtor, and to the defaulting debtor (non-merchant) was simply referred to as a criminal agent.

The Napoleonic phase had as its striking feature the reduction of legislative persuasion; thus, bankruptcy became a socioeconomic imprint. Although it imposed strict limitations on the insolvent debtor, the said legal diploma was only restricted to the merchant debtor. Raphael Carvalho emphasizes the need to make a distinction between honest and dishonest debtors, in which the former had the right to choose the favors of the moratorium, with the improvement of the concordat. However, Napoleon Bonaparte, through the *Code de Commerce, would demonstrate that the bankrupt would be judged regardless of his intent or guilt, creating a penalty of detention with corrective effect.*[17]

With time and the consequent end of Napoleon's phase in 1832, legal diplomas emerged whose essence was to reduce the severe treatment applied to the defaulting debtor. After 1837, a long process of bankruptcy law reform was initiated, with emphasis on the following: (a) Law of 1838, which restricted expenses with the bankruptcy process by simplifying its terms; (b) Law of 1865, which regulated the commercial liquidation preserving the debtor's name and honor.[18]

16 P.R.C. ARNOLDI, *Falências e Concordatas*. 2ª ed. (São Paulo: Ledi – Livraria e Editora de Direito, 1999), 29.

17 Raphael Franco Castelo Branco CARVALHO, op. cit.

18 Gleick Meira OLIVEIRA, "Falência: Conhecendo a História para se Construir um Futuro Pautado na Certeza," *Revista Dat@venia* 2, Nº2 (jul./dez. 2010), 52. DOI:10.20887/rdtv.ccj.2010.v2i2p49-56.

Gleick Oliveira also highlights that in this contemporary period there were two modalities of understanding about the institute concerned: *(i) The Italian Franc System, where the Laws were conferring bankruptcy an exclusively commercial character; (ii) the Anglo-Saxon System, which did not differentiate the scope of bankruptcy, making it affect any debtor.*[19]

1.1.6 Brazilian Legal System—Brazil Colony

It is important to take into account that Brazil was a Portuguese colony. Obviously, since Brazil was a Portuguese colony at that time, Portuguese laws and Alfonsino Ordinances were in full force.

It is believed that the origins of Brazilian Bankruptcy Law are linked to the time of the discovery, a time characterized by the validity of Alfonsino Ordinances, which in turn were promoters of the regulations of solvency relations through a scrupulous Roman legal content.

A fundamental characteristic of the Alfonsino Ordinances was the mixing of different rules of Commercial Law and Civil Law; such mixing was lacking any systematic rigor, and among them, Title LXVII which dealt with those who could be restricted to freedom by civil debts. Ricardo Negrão points out a curious rule in the third section of the aforementioned title:

> And if any debtor promises his creditor to pay his debt on time, and not paying it to him, that he will be arrested in our or the Council's prison until he pays it, if he does not pay the debt on time, he should be arrested by court order until he pays it: the court should have him arrested and he should be required to do so. And if the debtor and the creditor agree that if the debtor does not pay his debt to the creditor in due time, he can arrest him by his own authority, we order that such an agreement should not be valid, and that the creditor cannot arrest his debtor by his own power, but he should request justice and the court should order him to be arrested. But if the creditor finds his debtor running away because he has not paid his debt, in such a case we order that if the creditor cannot have a copy of the presence of the judge to have him arrested, he himself may arrest him or have him arrested in any case, immediately taking him to the prison of the Council, recounting to justice by the pigeon who arrested him, and requesting him to have good custody over him, so that he may be lawfully executed.[20]

19 Id.

20 Ricardo NEGRÃO, *Manual de direito comercial e de empresa: Recuperação de Empresas e Falência.* Vol. 3; 5ªed. (São Paulo: Saraiva,2010), 43.

The Alfonsino Ordinances were replaced in 1521 by the Manueline Ordinances, and these in turn were ordained by King Dom Manuel. These ordinations were strongly influenced by principles derived from Roman Law. Their provision was that, in the event of bankruptcy, the debtor would be sentenced to prison until he fulfilled his obligations to the creditors.

Besides being influenced by the Roman law, the Brazilian Bankruptcy Law (colony) was also influenced by Italian Law; it is in this perspective that the debtor could assign his assets to the creditors in order to avoid his arrest. That said, it should also be added that in the event of debtor being taken to prison and sentenced by final judgment, it was determined, with fulcrum in the Ordinances, that his assets would be executed and, if the debtor did not possess them, his arrest was determined until the payment of the amount due.[21]

The Philippine Ordinances, which were instituted in Spain in 1603 and applied in Portugal, due to the Kingdom of Castile, also had a great influence in Brazil-Cologne, due to growing interest in developing commercial and mercantile activities.[22] One main feature of Bankruptcy Law at this stage was that if there was a sentence passed through final judgment, the debtor's assets were automatically executed and pawned. If there were no assets, the debtor would remain arrested until the debt was paid, without prejudice to being able to choose the assignment of his assets as a way to remain free.[23]

However, it was with the expiration of Philippine Ordinances and the coming into force of Permit of November 13, 1756, promulgated by Marquês de Pombal—through which it was possible to visualize an original and authentic bankruptcy process, in the face of commerce—that the Brazilian Bankruptcy Law was considered to have emerged, since it regulated not only the criminal punishment toward bankruptcy crime but also the criminal bankruptcy and the innocent. This permit necessitated bankrupt individuals to present themselves before the Board of Trade and declare before the Board of Trade the true cause of bankruptcy and handover keys of their trade, together with books of commercial bookkeeping, and also make a declaration of their assets. This made it possible to distinguish between merchants who gave cause for their bankruptcy and those who bankrupted without fault.[24] Once the inventory of bankrupt's assets was completed, creditors were called in. It should be noted that 10 % of the proceeds

21 Ecio PERIN JUNIOR, op. cit., 35.
22 Gleick Meira OLIVEIRA, op. cit., 53.
23 Raphael Franco Castelo Branco CARVALHO, op. cit., 361.
24 Ecio PERIN JUNIOR, op. cit., 35–36.

of collection was assigned to the bankrupt for his own sustenance and that of his family and the rest was divided among creditors. Even if bankruptcy was not fraudulent, the merchant in question was ordered to be arrested and later made to undergo the criminal procedure.[25]

1.1.7 Independent Brazil

The independence of Brazil on September 7, 1822 did not immediately bring to an end the Portuguese laws in the country, since the law of October 20, 1823 determined that until April 25, 1821, the ordinances, regiments, permits, decrees, and resolutions promulgated by the kings of the former Portuguese colonial power and by which Brazil, as the former Portuguese colony, was governed.[26]

However, it was with the enactment of Commercial Code[27] in 1850 that the first historical phase of bankruptcy was instituted under Brazilian Law and was extended to be in force until the emergence of the republic regime, characterized by the nonexistence of a preventive concordat, with only a suspensive concordat being applied and only in cases in which the bankrupt had not acted maliciously or with fault. It is important to point that the role played by the institute of the moratorium was important *in situations where the merchant approved the unfeasibility of ensuring the fulfillment of the obligations assumed due to extraordinary accidents or due to force majeure.*[28]

1.1.8 Republican Period

It is in this period that intense legislative activity in bankruptcy in Brazil was witnessed, where the following legal diplomas were actively in force[29]:

1.1.8.1 Decree 917 October 24, 1890

In view of the various republican ideals raised in Brazil's political intricacies, this legal diploma marks the beginning of the second phase of bankruptcy institute in Brazil and led to several innovations in Commercial Law, with emphasis on the institutionalization of preventive agreements, assignment of assets, and

25 Amador Paes ALMEIDA, op. cit.

26 See article 1 of the Law 20 of October 1823.

27 Influenced by French Law—*Promulgated the independence of Brazil, it was applied in the Brazilian legal order the French Commercial Code: as imposed by the Lei da Boa Razão. It was given a holistic preference to the application of the Napoleonic Commerce Code of 1807, deriving a deep influence of French law in the evolution of Brazilian law, including in the bankruptcy-related activities*— Gleick Meira OLIVEIRA, op. cit., 54.

28 Raphael Franco Castelo Branco CARVALHO, op. cit. p. 362.

29 *Vide*, Raphael Franco Castelo Branco CARVALHO, op. cit., 362 and following.

moratorium as preventive means of decreeing bankruptcy, which were responsible for the frauds that were taking place.

However, some negative aspects that it presented led to its discredit, and, most notably, one of the main issues was the ease with which debtors could remove the decree of bankruptcy by the use of preventive means as well as the excessive autonomy of creditors and the removal of the system from the application of the law due to the cancellation of principles that inspired it.

Decree 917 of October 24, 1890 reformed sections in part III of the Commercial Code of 1850. Manoel Deodoro da Fonseca, Head of the Provisional Government of the United States of Brazil, constituted by the Army and Navy, on behalf of the Nation, having heard the Minister of Justice Affairs, decided to decree the following[30]:

ABOUT BANKRUPTCIES:

TITLE I

The nature and declaration of bankruptcy

Art. 1: The merchant, under an individual or corporate name, which, without any relevant reason of law (art. 8), ceases to pay in maturity any liquid and certain commercial obligation (art. 2), is considered bankrupt.

§1. The state of bankruptcy is also characterized, although there is no lack of payments, if the debtor,

a) Make payments using ruinous and fraudulent means;
b) Transfer or assign assets to one or more persons, creditor or not, with an obligation to settle past due and unpaid debts;
c) Conceal himself/herself, sneak away, change his/hers domicile without the knowledge of the creditors, or attempt to do so, revealing this purpose by unequivocal acts;
d) To alienate, without the consent of the creditors, the assets he owns, by making donations, incurring extraordinary or simulated debts, placing the assets on behalf of third parties or committing some other fraudulent artifice;

30 *Id.*, 362–65.

- *e) Dispose of immovable property, hypothecate it, give them in antichresis or pawn it, without keeping any or some equivalent to debts, free and disbursed, or try to perform such acts, revealing such purpose by unequivocal acts;*
- *f) Closing or abandoning the establishment, divert all or part of the assets;*
- *g) Hide property and furniture from the house;*
- *h) Carry out rash liquidations;*
- *i) Not to pay, when executed by commercial debt, or not to appoint assets to be pawned within 24 hours after the initial summons of the execution;*
- *j) Refuse, as an endorser or drawer, to bail in the case of art. 390 of the Commercial Code;*
- *k) Not to avoid the bidding of preference in commercial execution (art. 609, §2 of Reg. N. 737 of November 25, 1850).*

§2. Civil debts can compete with commercial obligations o constitute the state of bankruptcy; but they alone do not authorize the declaration of bankruptcy.

Although the result of a very quick legislative movement, the legal framework presented proved to be very efficient and emerged as the driving force behind a new Brazilian Bankruptcy Law order. Ecio Perin Junior quotes Spancer Vampré's views on Decree 917/1890 in the following terms: *"Magnificent work although written within fifteen days, Dec. 917 laid the foundation of the new bankruptcy legislation, replacing the third part of the Commercial Code. Many of its fundamental features are preserved in the current law and, if defects were noticed, it was mainly due to the tightness of the crisis that followed the ignorance, or dubiousness, of the judges, and the absence of traditions, and unity of views, among the merchants."*[31]

1.1.8.2 Law No. 859 of August 16, 1902

It was created with the intention of putting an end to the fraud that had been patented in the period before it, the one in which Decree No. 917/1890 appeared. Its main objective was to prevent the abuses that occurred, especially with regard to the moratoria that caused abuses between debtors and creditors, but it did not provide the expected scope for the resolution of conflicts in the bankruptcy process, a deception that emerged from its failure in its implementation. It was

31 SPENCER VAMPRÉ, *Tratado elementar de direto comercial, Apud,* Ecio PERIN JUNIOR, *Curso de Direito Falimentar e Recuperação de Empresa;* 3ª ed. ver., atual. e ampl. (São Paulo: Editora Método, 2006), 38.

immediately submitted for a review, as a well-established regulation for bankruptcy process was lacking.[32]

1.1.8.3 Law No. 2.024, of December 17, 1908

Law No. 2.024 of December 17, 1908 was authored by Cravalho de Mendonça and represented the beginning of the third stage of bankruptcy institute in the Brazilian legal system. One of its main goals was to not allow frauds through procedural postponements, which were a common form of misuse to evade sanctions. This law contributed greatly to the improvement of legal interpretations, since it allowed for the simplification of the procedural mechanisms of the law, aiming at not hindering the regular functioning of the system.

This law introduced positive innovations to the laws that preceded it, among which the following stand out:

> (a) submission of public limited companies to bankruptcy; (b)introduction of a brief rite for so-called small liability summary bankruptcies; (c) regulation of the bankruptcy of construction or public service concessionaries; (d) introduction of the Public Prosecutor's Office as Trustee of the bankrupt estate, determining its notifications of all the proceedings when its assistance became usual in favor of the public order; (e) prohibition of the Public Prosecutor's office to request the bankruptcy; (f) prohibition for the Public Prosecutor's Office to receive commissions or percentages on account of the bankrupt estate; (g) establishment of the criterion of lack of punctuality and of some acts indicative of bankruptcy as characterizing the breach, as occurs in the system of the current Decree-law nº 7.661, of June 21, 1945; (h) the establishment of the invalidity of certain debtor's acts prior to bankruptcy, as provided in arts. 52 and 53 of the Law of 1945; (i) the establishment of two periods for processing the bankruptcy: that of information and that of liquidation, giving the judge freedom in the choice of liquidators when there was no creditors accepting the charge; (j) the unification of the procedure for verification and classifications of claims into a single act, defining the inclusion and classification of the claim, as drafted in the current Decree-Law 7.661/45; (k) establishment of two concordats: the preventive concordat and the concordat in bankruptcy; (l) establishment of principles for granting concordat, such as the non-validity of the concordat 'that brings to the creditors greater sacrifice than liquidation of the bankruptcy', and the possibility of embargoes of dissenting creditors and their rescission .[33]

32 Gleick Meira OLIVEIRA, op. cit., 54.

33 Ricardo NEGRÃO, op. cit., 49.

Successful in having been elaborated in all its content, the law in reference has been in force for a long time in the Brazilian legal system to discipline the institute of bankruptcy. Its main point was the verification and classification of credit, abandoning the focus on fraud, collusion, bad faith, and captious subtleties. However, it would not achieve the objectives for which it was created—a result of the action of an energetic and illustrious judiciary.

1.1.8.4 Law No. 5.746 of December 9, 1929

The need to revise some parts of Law No. 2.024 of December 17, 1908 led to the appearance of Law No. 5.746/1929; therefore, this latter law was very close to the former. This revision of contents was due to the fact that they lacked precision. However, specific features were introduced, such as reduction of number of liquidators from 3 to only 1 and the institution of a percentage on the credits for granting concordat. It was in force in the Brazilian legal system until mid-1945, when Decree-Law No. 7.661/1945 came into effect.[34]

1.1.8.5 Decree-Law No. 7.661 of June 21, 1945

Due to dissatisfaction with the then prevalent bankruptcy regime, on June 21, 1945, Decree-Law No. 7.661/45 came into force. Among the main changes that were brought about, the powers of the magistrate were strengthened and the influence of creditors was reduced by the consequent abolition of creditors' meeting. It should be known *that the concordat became a state recognition, whereby the judge granted it to the honest and unsuccessful debtor no longer constituting a contract as before*; that is, the concordat ceased to be a contract to become a benefit granted by the state.

A novel feature introduced by the legal diploma in question was that concordat was granted by the judge and not by the traditional consensus of creditors as was done previously. While previous laws were *"privately inspired"* and sought to protect the interest of creditors, the new law considered more suitable the *"official impulse"* for the protection of creditors' own common interest and elevated it to be a part of the public interest plan. In this regard, Afonso Neto[35] adds that "*breaking with the general concordat regime, maintained by recent foreign laws, such as the Italian of 1942, under which concordat is deemed approved by consensus of creditors with voting rights, representing at least two third of the sum of the credits, and like the French Law of 1955, under which concordat will only be entered into*

34 Gleick Meira OLIVEIRA, op. cit., 55.

35 Augusto AFONSO NETO, *Princípios de Direito Falimentar* (São Paulo: Max Limonad, 1962), 59–60.

by means of the contest of a majority in number of creditors admitted definitely or provisionally and representing two thirds of the total credit- Decree-Law nº 7.661, created the concordat without bankrupt's agreement with the creditors, with the same traditional name, but emptied of the meaning."

Trajano De Miranda Valverde is considered to be the author of the original draft of Decree-Law 7.661/1945; he was not in favor of creditor's meeting and conveyed the need to remove it from the concordat and, more specifically, stated the following in this context: *"Due to the manifested disinterest of creditors in the body that, according to the old legal regime, should act in defense of their rights, the creditors' meeting has always worked badly, playing a secondary role in the bankruptcy process. The law in force nullified, it can be said."*[36]

In the same vein, it was stated in the explanatory memorandum of Decree-Law No. 7.661/1945:

> According to the classic concept, the formation of the concordat depends on the free expression of the creditors' will, through the quorum of voting, reserving to the judge, simply, the ratification of the agreement with the debtor.
>
> The law considers only the conditions under which the majority's decision forces the minority. The system, however, does not produce the results one would wish. The preponderance of the majority in collective deliberations is only legitimized when all the deliberative wills are manifested; having in view the common interest that brought them together.
>
> Now, in concordats formed by a majority of votes, the creditors deliberate under the pressure of their individual interest, distorting the collective sense of the deliberation and, therefore, making the subjection of the minority illegitimate.
>
> And truth is that, in the validity of this system, the constancy of this anomaly has been verified, through the external understandings of the process, which is important in the breach of the equal treatment of creditors, an informative principle of the bankruptcy process. In view of these considerations, the project establishes the concordat as a favor granted by the judge, whose sentence replaces the manifestation of the creditor's will in the formation of the contract, reserved, however, to them, the examinations and discussion of the conditions of the debtor's application in view of the requirements of the law.

36 Trajano de Miranda VALVERDE, *Comentários à Lei de Falência*. 2ª ed. (Rio de Janeiro: Forense, 1955), V. III, 35.

It is important to consider that the logic of the decree in vogue was to withdraw from the market a company harmful to the economy, either because of its bad administration or because of unfeasibility of its business. In practice, the old bankruptcy law was strictly used for simple debt collection and creditor satisfaction. The new socioeconomic and political situation of the decades following the 1940s, including the increased development of industrial activity, accelerated economic globalization, and a growing Brazilian population, saw the need to create a law that would facilitate the continuity of company and not its disappearance.

It in this context that Rubens Requião highlights that in view of the new socioeconomic and political reality, the commission was constituted to review the bankruptcy law and, therefore, the emergency reform was approved and converted into Law 7.274 of December 10, 1984. Decree law 2.279/85 was later published to correct serious misunderstandings in the wording.[37]

1.1.8.6 Law No. 11.101 of February 9, 2005

Like other legal diplomas, the Decree-Law No. 766/45 called for a series of reforms of a structural nature, as it needed to be updated in order to be in line with the new economic order of the company and its subsistence in the social context. Such reform would end the understanding that bankruptcy was a simple liquidation mechanism, whose purpose was to close down business activities, and would demonstrate greater concern over the social function of the company before the society, and, with the foundation of the novel Competition Law, would make it possible to obtain that function relative to any private property, in the objectives sought by Law 11.101/2005.

1.2 Concept of Bankruptcy

Before we attempt to define the concept of bankruptcy itself, it becomes pertinent to understand the semantics of the bankruptcy institute in question or its etymological origin.

First of all, it should be noted that the word "bankruptcy" comes from the Latin words—*fallo, fefelli, falsum, fallere*—which, translated into the usual English meaning, are close to the meaning of the verb "to fail."

In the legal world, it has come to mean the impossibility of the debtor to pay his debts for the reason that he does not have sufficient resources to satisfy his credits. It is in this perspective that Ecio Perin Junior[38] states that that the word

37 Rubens REQUIÃO, *Curso de Direito Falimentar.* 17ª ed. (São Paulo: Saraiva, 1998), 24–25.

38 Ecio PERIN JUNIOR, op. cit., 48–49.

bankruptcy was introduced into legal language with a specific meaning, that is, the financial and economic state of the debtor. This is a situation in which there is a lack of exact fulfillment of the commercial obligation due on the day of its maturity or the practice of ruinous acts that may lead the merchant to such a lack.

Given the semantics associated with bankruptcy institute, it is opportune to bring the concept of the institute that is the object of our study.

There is a profusion of concepts formulated around the institute of bankruptcy in the doctrine. Carvalho De Mendonça[39] conceptualizes the legal institute "bankruptcy" by highlighting the genesis of the verb "to fail" whose roots can be traced back to the Latin word of the most remote origin—*falece*—because it would express the same thing as "*to fail with the promised, with the word, to deceive; hence bankruptcy, bankruptcy,* its derivate meaning *failure, lack, omission.*"

The approach to the concept of bankruptcy can be made from two perspectives—economic and legal. From the economic perspective, Carla Barros advances the view that bankruptcy means the patrimonial situation insufficient for the resolution of defaulted debts and without complete perspectives of compliance. In legal terms, bankruptcy is defined as the process of collective execution, decreed by a court decision in front of the company (debtor) with the aim of satisfying the creditor's credit.[40]

For J.C. Sampaio de Lacerda, "*bankruptcy is, therefore, the condition of the person who, having received a credit installment does not have at his disposal, for the execution of the consideration, a sufficient amount, realizable at the time of the consideration. Bankruptcy is therefore a state of imbalance between the realizable values and the required instalments.*"[41]

Thus, the position prevails that bankruptcy is first and foremost an economic phenomenon before it is a legal phenomenon.

Ricardo Negrão understands that bankruptcy is a process of collective execution, in which all the assets of a businessperson declared bankrupt, regardless of whether they belong to a natural or a legal person, are collected with a view to pay his creditors in a complete or proportional manner. It is, therefore, a complex judicial process that comprises the collection of assets and claims for the subsequent liquidation of assets and apportionment among creditors.[42]

39 Cited by Ricardo NEGRÃo, op. cit., 39.

40 Carla Eugenia Caldas BARROS, *Manual de Direito Empresarial Multifacetado*, Voll. III – Direito Falimentar e Recuperacional (Aracaju: Edição do Autor | PIDCC, 2014), 10.

41 J. C. Sampaio de LACERDA, *Manual de direito falimentar;* 13ª ed., revista e actualizada (Rio de Janeiro: Freita Bastos, 1996), 28.

42 Ricardo NEGRÃO, op. cit,. 249.

From a legal standpoint, Spencer Vampré teaches that bankruptcy "*is a collective execution of the merchant debtor's assets, to which all creditors compete for the purpose of collecting the available assets, verifying the credits, liquidating the assets, settling the liabilities, in apportionment, observing the legal preferences.*"

For Maximilianos Führer, bankruptcy is a collective execution procedure in which all the bankrupt's assets are collected for a forced judicial sale to proportionally distribute such assets among the bankrupt's creditors.[43]

While Law 11.101 of February 9, 2005 describes bankruptcy technically as a judicial means of resolving the legal situation of the businessperson or business and financial companies of the creditor, in the event the debtor, in the wording of Article 94, without any relevant reason of law, does not pay at maturity a net obligation materialized in bound or protested executive titles whose sum exceeds the equivalent of the sum of forty (40) minimum wages on the date of the petition for bankruptcy[44] and executed for any net amount, not paying, not depositing, and not appointing sufficient assets to be seized within the legal term.[45]

Also under Article 94, III, bankruptcy may involve any of the following acts, unless it is part of a judicial reorganization plan:

> (a) proceeds with the hasty liquidation of its assets or uses a ruinous or fraudulent means to make payments; (b) performs or, by unequivocal acts, tries to perform, with the purpose of delaying payments or fraud of creditors, simulated business or disposal of part or all of its assets to a third party, creditor or not; (c) transfers the commercial premises to a third party, creditor or not, without the consent of all the creditors and without remaining with sufficient assets to settle its liabilities; (d) simulates the transfer of its principal establishment with the purpose of circumventing legislation or supervision or to injure the creditor; (e) gives or reinforces a guarantee to the creditor for debt contracted previously without remaining with free and clear assets sufficient to settle its liabilities; (f) absents itself without leaving an authorized representative and with sufficient resources to pay the creditors, abandons the commercial premises or tries to hide from its domicile, the place of its headquarters or its principal establishment.

It should the noted that the above-mentioned events cannot be considered as acts of bankruptcy if the debtor has entered into a judicial reorganization plan.

43 Maximilianus Cláudio FÜHRER, *Roteiro das Falências e Concordatas,* 18ª ed. (REVISTA DOS TRIBUNAIS).

44 See Item I, Article 94.

45 See Item II, Article 94.

With regard to the aforementioned article, Ricardo Negrão postulates that the situations therein, as they characterize bankruptcy *status*, do not present insolvency as their assumption or mere default; however, only the unpunctuality or acts and situations of fact are defined in the very wording of Article 94 of the Bankruptcy Law.[46]

Certainly, the starting point of the study of the bankruptcy institute is commercial law; however, that institute is not limited to this area of legal knowledge; it is in this context that Carvalho De Mandonça states that the bankruptcy institute intervenes in the areas of civil law, public law, private and public international law, and judiciary law, in order to seek rules, precepts, and teachings to apply them with necessary adaptations in the scope of the collective enforcement that it intends to pursue. And because bankruptcy can be seen from an economic point of view, it is envisaged in the economic science; viewed from an economic perspective, bankruptcy is not only of interest to the private economy but also of interest to the public economy, since it inevitably disturbs public credit and produces the dispersion of capital, bringing damage to the general economy.[47]

1.3 Preconditions of Bankruptcy

The characterization of the state of bankruptcy is legal; therefore, the positive law determines three preconditions for its verification, namely:

1.3.1 Corporate Debtor

This is a subjective material precondition. In principle, debtors who carry out the business or economic activity in a corporate manner are subject to bankruptcy. This follows from Article 1 of Law 11.101 of February 9, 2005, which states: *"This law governs the judicial reorganization, out-of-court reorganization and bankruptcy of the business person and the corporation, henceforth referred to simply as debtor."*

Certainly, the interpretation and application of the aforementioned legal precept should gravitate around Articles 966 and 982 of Law 12.406 of January 10, 2002 of the Brazilian Civil Code in force.

Under Article 966 of the Civil Code, a businessperson is considered to be one who exercises a professionally organized economic activity for the production or circulation of goods or services. And under Article 982, with the exception of

46 Ricardo NEGRÃO, op. cit., 248.

47 J. X. CARVALHO DE MENDONÇA, *Tratado de Direito Comercial Brasileiro;* Apud, Ricardo NEGRÃO, op. cit., 248.

express exceptions, the company whose object is to carry on its own activity as an entrepreneur subject to registration is considered to be a corporative, and, simple, the others.

It is of interest to approach bankruptcy in cases of irregular or in fact company, and Ecio Pern Junior[48] is categorical in this context, stating that irregular and in fact companies, from the formal point of view, do not have legal personality, since their instruments of incorporation are not filed with the commercial companies' registry body. However, they do exercise in fact business activity, which leads to the conclusion that they acquire legal personality under a real identification criterion.

This is a qualified situation of formal absence of legal personality; even so, the aforementioned author understands that the companies in question may litigate in court to substantiate their position; the aforementioned author invokes subsection VII of Article 12 of the Brazilian Code of Civil Procedure, which infers that the irregular company or in fact company may play an active role in procedural relations as well as a passive pole. In the same way, that bankruptcy of irregular companies may be declared.

Based on Article 105, subsection II of the Bankruptcy and Corporate Restructuring Law, it is stated that *"A debtor in economic and financial crisis that believes it does not meet the requirements to petition for its judicial recovery shall petition the court for its bankruptcy, stating the reasons for the impossibility of continuing the business activity, accompanied by the following documents. '(IV)' proof of businessperson's status, articles of association or bylaws in force, if there is not the indication of all partners, their addresses and the list of their personal assets."*

Interpreting the above-described article, Ecio Perin Junior understands that it constitutes an express authorization for the irregular company to request its own bankruptcy. Considering that irregular companies or in-fact companies do not have formal legal personality, their partners are liable in an unlimited manner (unlimited liability) with all theirs assets for meeting corporate obligations.

It is imperative in this context to bring the contents of Article 81 of the Bankruptcy and Reorganization of Companies Law; as a result of this, the decision that decrees the bankruptcy of the company with partners with unlimited liability also implicates them (partners with unlimited liability), and they are subject to the same legal effects produced in relation to the bankrupt company.

48 Ecio PERIN JUNIOR, op. cit., 93–94.

Around this assumption Fábio Ulhoa Coelho[49] states that it is necessary to exploit economic activity in an entrepreneurial way to be subject to bankruptcy. As a result, those who do not exploit any economic activity without entrepreneurialism cannot be subject to bankruptcy.

In view of this, the sole paragraph of Article 966 of the Civil Code states that those who exercise an intellectual, scientific, literary, or artistic profession, even with the competition of assistants or collaborators, are not considered businessperson, unless the exercise of the profession constitutes a business element; in principle, those who exercise activities of such nature may not be subject to bankruptcy; however, the last part of the aforementioned paragraph must be taken into account, since it makes an exception (in determining that *"unless the exercise of the profession constitutes a business element"*).

Even if the exercise of profession constitutes a business element, it must be borne in mind that certain legal persons, although characterized as businessperson, cannot be subject to bankruptcy. Therefore, the Bankruptcy and Business Restructuring Law is applicable to a variety of business activities; yet, it has certain exceptions, which means that not all businesspersons are subject to bankruptcy.

In this sense, Article 2 of the Bankruptcy Law states that it does not apply to (i) public companies and mixed economy companies; (ii) public or private financial institutions, credit unions, consortia, supplementary pension funds, health care plan companies, insurance companies, capitalization companies, and other entities legally equivalent to the above.

The non-applicability of the Bankruptcy Law to certain business entities may be of absolute and relative nature.

The cases of absolute non-applicability can be summarized in three hypotheses, namely those provided for in subsection I, Article 2 of the above-mentioned law:

Public Enterprise—qualified with private law legal personality, the public enterprise is private although its capital is public. As Ricardo Negrão teaches,[50] a public company is a kind of *"governmental company"* or public enterprise in the broad sense of which the mixed-economy company is also part. The public enterprise, in the strict sense, is exclusively constituted by capital of a public nature and has the faculty to adopt any form admitted by law, from sole proprietorship to

49 Fábio Ulhoa COELHO, *Curso de Direito Comercial: Direito de Empresa – Contratos e Recuperação de Empresa;* 10ª ed. (São Paulo: Saraiva, 2009), 247.

50 Ricardo NEGRÃO, op. cit., 69.

simple or entrepreneurial company. In turn, mixed-economy company can only adopt the form if it is a public limited company.

In current doctrine, the term "*state-owned companies*" is used to refer to public companies, mixed-economy companies, and their subsidiaries. Being legal entities under private law and constituted by public capital, they must comply with the provision of subsection XIX of Article 37 of the Constitution of the Federative Republic of Brazil, according to which the creation of the public company and mixed-economy company warrants the indirect public administration of the respective federative entity.

Mixed-economy company—the mixed-economy company is provided for and regulated under Articles 235–240 of Law 6.404 of December 15, 1976 (Joint Stock Company Law). Under the terms of subsection II, paragraph 1 of Article 173 of the Constitution of the Federative Republic of Brazil, the object of mixed-economy companies is to exploit the economic activity of producing goods to be marketed or providing services, with a view to fulfilling a social function while being subject to the legal regime proper to private companies.

In general, the legal regime of these entities is characterized as hybrid and, therefore, includes a mix of private and public law rules. From this point of view, José Dos Santos Carvalho Filho's observation regarding the peculiar normative hybridity of entities in vogue should be taken into consideration:

> The analysis of the legal regime of public companies and of mixed economy companies and their subsidiaries should be based on two preconditions—one of them, considering the fact that they are private law persons, and the other, the circumstance that they are part of the Public Administration. Undoubtedly, these are aspects that usually enter in a collision course, but in turn, inevitable before the nature of the entities. In view of this, the inevitable consequence is that their legal regime is characterized by normative hybridity, in which the influx of public law and private law rules is presented. Such a peculiarity, as it could not be otherwise, gives rise to numerous perplexities and divergences.[51]

In its turn, Ricardo Negrão teaches that by virtue of this hybrid regime, the mixed-economy company is subject to the principles of public administration, including the contracting of works, services, purchases, and sales. He also

51 José dos Santos CARVALHO FILHO, *Manual de Direito Administrativo;* 32ª ed. (São Paulo: Atlas, 2018), 561.

postulates that such a company is obliged to maintain boards of directors and fiscal councils, as a rule, as optional bodies for public limited companies in general.[52]

The possibility of bankruptcy of state-owned companies is controversial. Traditionally, there was a serious debate over the interpretation of Article 242 of the Brazilian Limited Companies by Shares Law, which kept mixed-economy companies out of bankruptcy, a provision that was repealed by Law 10303 of October 31, 2001.[53] The current Bankruptcy and Corporate Restructuring, in its subsection I, of Article 2, excludes public companies and mixed-economy companies from bankruptcy. Despite the laterality of the rule, the doctrine has presented several interpretations around this subject.

As Ecio Perin Junior claims, the discussion about the legitimacy of excluding the mixed-economy company from the bankruptcy regime, by virtue of the provisions of subsection I, Article 2 of the Bankruptcy and Corporate Restructuring Law hovers around the constitutionality of Article 242 of the Limited Companies by Shares Law, which was revoked by Law 10.303/2001.[54]

The conflicts between the positions enumerated in the above discussions are summarized as follows:

(i) Public companies and mixed-economy companies are subject to bankruptcy; therefore, Article 2, subsection I, of Law 11.101/2005, should be considered unconstitutional, due to its offense against Article 173, paragraph 1, Item II of the Constitution of the Federative Republic of Brazil. Here are the wordings in the aforementioned Article 173:

> Except in the cases provided for in the constitution, direct exploitation of economic activity by the State will only be permitted when necessary for the imperatives of national security or the relevant collective interest, as defined by law (§ 1): The legal status of the public company, of the mixed economy company and of the subsidiaries that carry out economic activity of production or provisions of services shall be established, with provisions on: (II) the submission to the proper legal regime of private companies, including civil, commercial labor and tax rights and obligations.

52 Ricardo NEGRÃO, op. cit., 69.

53 Amends and adds provisions to the Law 6.404, of 15th December 1976, on the Limited Companies by Shares.

54 Ecio PERIN JUNIOR, op. cit., 70–71.

(ii) The second understanding, defended, among others by José Dos Santos Carvalho Filho, advocates an interpretation in harmony with the constitution, based on Article 2, subsection I of Law 11.101/2005 which unfailingly conjugated with Article 173, paragraph 1, item II, of the Constitution of the Federative Republic of Brazil—only state-owned companies, that is, public service providers, can be removed from bankruptcy, since the state-owned economies are submitted to the same legal regime of private companies that vests in them the rights as well as obligations of commercial nature.

(iii) The third understanding, according to Marcos Juruena Villela Souto and Marcos Bemquerer, defends that public companies are not subject to bankruptcy; this is derived from the literal interpretation of Article 2, subsection I, of Law 11.101/2005.

All the three positions presented are valid and of great merit, but the predominant position is the third. This is because the *ratio legis* of the legislator in bankruptcy when approving the new Bankruptcy and Reorganization Law (Law No. 11.101/2005), expressly in subsection I, Article 2, excludes the mixed-economy company and the public company from the possibility of bankruptcy.[55]

In this perspective, it is understood that public companies and mixed-economy companies cannot go bankrupt, in view of the inadequacy of the bankruptcy process when applied to administrative entities. State-owned companies are created, as we have already said, by legal authorization to meet relevant social interest that could not be removed by the judiciary to satisfy private (economic) interests of creditors; in the event that the state company is unable to meet the obligations, there will be subsidiary responsibility of the controlling federal entity.

Another reason that leads to the non-bankruptcy of a state enterprise arises from the fact that it is only created by a specific law and, thus, its dissolution or extinction can only be determined by law. Bankruptcy presupposes that control of the bankrupt entity is transferred to the judiciary, the latter being responsible for designating a private individual (trustee) to direct the terminal acts. There is a suspension of the power of control of the partners of the bankrupt company. This situation is incompatible with the condition of the existence of a state entity.

Supplementary pension entities—provided for in subsection II, Article 2 of the Bankruptcy and Reorganization Law. They may take the form of close-ended entities that have as their object the administration and execution of social

55 Id., 79.

security plans[56]; they may also take the form of open-ended entities, constituted solely in the form of public limited companies, and their purpose is to institute and operate social security benefit plan provided in the form of continued income or single payment that is accessible for any individual.[57]

Under Article 47 of the Supplementary Law, close-ended entities may not apply for concordat and are not subject to bankruptcy but only to extrajudicial liquidation. Therefore, no creditor of such entity may request in court the decree of its bankruptcy. It may execute the credit it held by attachment of debtor's assets. Attention should be paid to the fact that open supplementary pension entities, whose plans are accessible to any individual, are excluded from bankruptcy.[58]

In turn, the cases of relative non-applicability are summarized in the cases provided for in subsection II, Article 2, with the exception of the supplementary pension entity. Cases of relative non-applicability are considered because, even though the legislator has determined that the new law will not apply the hypotheses described in that legal provision, such affirmative proposition is not absolute since the Bankruptcy and Reorganization of Companies Law is in force until the vast legislation that regulates the extrajudicial liquidation of companies provided for in the Bankruptcy Law is repealed.

It is in this line that Ricardo Negrão postulates that in the current legislative stage the companies listed in subsection II, Article 2, are not authorized to request recovery in court, either judicial or extrajudicial, since it is up to the Executive Branch, in administrative intervention procedure, to pursue the reorganization of its activity, authorizing the liquidator to request bankruptcy, if necessary, for cases as may be applicable under law. Meanwhile, when the bankruptcy is decreed, the rules of Law 11.101/2005 shall apply.[59]

1.3.2 Insolvency

Insolvency is known as the second precondition of the state of bankruptcy. It is an objective material precondition—a non-rebutted presumption of insolvency.

From the moment a businessperson in debt becomes a patrimonial insolvent and can no longer proceed to the regular satisfaction of the complex of demandable, absolute, and mandatory obligations to which he is bound or begins to

56 See article 32 of the Complementary Law—Law 109 of 29 May 2001.
57 See article 36 of the Complementary Law 109 of 29 May 2001.
58 Fábio Ulhoa COELHO, op. cit., 249.
59 Ricardo NEGRÃO, op. cit., 71.

proceed in his patrimonial *status*, conditions are created for the materialization of insolvency.

While bankruptcy is characterized as a state of law that is only characterized by issuing of the declaratory sentence by the judicial magistrate, this sentence characterizes a *de facto* situation. Insolvency can take two forms: real and apparent.

Insolvency is considered real *"when the asset is less than the liability and is apparent when, even though the asset is less, the debtor does not have, even if eventually, financial or credit resources, to fulfil, at maturity, a net obligation assumed."* The declaration of bankruptcy of a businessperson in debt waives the presentation of evidence of insolvency on the economic side or by other evidence that his debts exceed his assets. It is quite a characterization of insolvency from a legal point of view.[60]

As can be noted, insolvency can be understood both from the economic point of view (patrimonial state of insufficiency of assets of a subject of law to be fully liable for his complex of obligations), and from the legal point of view—that insolvency must be understood based on the parameters of the new bankruptcy law. In order for the debtor businessperson to submit to bankruptcy proceedings, proof of the inferiority of the assets in relation to the debts is dispensable.

Based on the Bankruptcy and Corporate Recovery Law (Law 11. 101/2005) the insolvency precondition is not characterized by a certain patrimonial state, but by the verification of one of the facts foreseen in the law as drivers of breakage. Such understanding is derived from Article 94 of the referred law, which provides that bankruptcy will be decreed for the debtor who, without relevant reason of right does not pay, at maturity, a net obligation materialized in a bond or protested executive titles whose sum exceeds the equivalent of forty (40) minimum wages on the date of the petition for bankruptcy.

The wording of Article 94, subsection I, shows *"unjustified unpunctuality"* as the primary and most common criterion for measuring insolvency.

Unpunctuality is spoken of when the businessperson in debt, for no plausible legal reason, fails to pay the net obligation due and as contained in the instrument of credit legitimating the executive action. Unpunctuality must be evidenced by protest. The minimum amount of debt for action will be 40 minimum wages on the date of request. It follows from this that those creditors with lower claims who

60 Ecio PERIN JUNIOR, Op. Cit., 99–100.

seek resort to the judicial mechanism will have to meet in litigious proceedings until they reach the said minimum value for the action.

The second criterion for assessing insolvency is found in Article 94, subsection II—*"frustrated execution"* or *"omission in execution."* In the context of the aforementioned article, bankruptcy will be decreed for the debtor who, executed for any net amount, does not pay, does not deposit, and does not appoint sufficient assets to be seized within the legal term.

From the wording of the aforementioned article, it is noted that the frustrated execution occurs when the business debtor fails to make the payment or the deposit and does not appoint assets to be seized. In this regard, Waldo Fazzio Júnior[61] adds that the aforementioned legal provision does not require a minimum amount, since it is an execution that, regardless of the value of the security, does not require the petition for bankruptcy to be filed.

The situation regulated in Subsection II of Article 94 is also called *"presumed bankruptcy,"* as already pointed out in the previous paragraph, takes place when the debtor for whom bankruptcy has been executed by any net quantum and the debtor does not make payment or deposit the amount in court and does not make provisions for sufficient assets to be seized within the legal terms. These are, therefore, acts of omission adopted by the businessperson in debt and which carry with them the probability of triggering legal action. Consequently, it will be incumbent upon those who have a right to credit before the debtor to request a certificate of full content, in which the execution *quantum* will be stated, and which has not yet occurred as per any of the hypotheses listed in the subsection in question (§ 4, Article 94). It is not necessary, in this context, to submit any protest, with the certificate being enough to ensure the application for the opening of the debtor's bankruptcy

In the perspective of Professor Fábio Ulhoa Coelho,

> The debtor company that, when executed, does not pay, does not deposit or appoint assets to be seized within the legal term incurs in frustrated execution (LF, art. 94 II). This is the most usual hypothesis of bankruptcy petition, apart from the foundations in the unpunctuality. If an individual execution is being filed against a company, this means that the company has not paid the net, certain and due obligation (CPC, art. 586). On the other hand, if it has not appointed assets to attachment, it is a sign that it may not even have the means

61 Waldo FAZZIO JÚNIOR, *Manual de Direito Comercial,* 11ª edição (São Paulo: Atlas, 2010), 642.

> to guarantee the execution. These facts denounce the insolvency of the foreclosure and make it possible to declare bankruptcy.[62]

The summons of debtor in an individual execution process give him a time lapse of three days to make the payment, the deposit, or the appointment of goods to be attached. The attachment starts from the time defendant initiates filing for action of embargo. In the context of individual execution, in the event that the debtor does not make payment or deposit the amount requested or does not proceed with the appointment of assets to be attached within the time period established by law, the creditor has the right to make an application with the purpose of closing the individual execution and file a petition for bankruptcy of the respective debtor, in a proper process, in the main forum of the establishment of the latter.

In this context, the plaintiff is exclusively responsible for filing a petition for bankruptcy and for presenting evidence that, even though he has been summoned to regular execution, the debtor has not proceeded with the payment, not even made the deposit of the amount required, and has not made the appointment of assets to be seized. In these situations, the protest is dispensable, since the state of insufficiency of assets has already been established.

The Bankruptcy and Corporate Recovery Law does not require in these situations the submission of other different protests in order to prove the cessation of payments. Likewise, the possibility of specifying a minimum amount for the request for liquidation is ruled out, which means that any amount is enough to give rise to the presumption of insufficient assets, as long as it is derived from frustrated execution.

Once the bankruptcy petition has been filed by the creditor, the singular execution, which was previously taken to court but was unsuccessful, will at least incur the suspension and the acts performed by the debtor from the moment of suspension will be affected by the default.

Individual execution is inadmissible at the same time, as the bankruptcy petition deals with the same title and debtor as a result of the principle *"electa una via, non datur rescursos ad alterum."* The modification of request in the same filing for execution process (novelty of the case) is also unfounded, due to the common procedural complex, since the coincidence of competent courts does not always occur, either for singular execution or for collective execution.

62 Fábio Ulhoa COELHO, *Curso de Direito Comercial: Direito de Empresa; contratos e recuperação de empresas.* 10ª ed., Vol. 3 (São Paulo: Saraiva, 2009), 254.

"The bankruptcy petition of the executed one on the basis of article 94, II of the LF is not made in the individual execution records." The individual execution must be subject to suspension or even extinction, in certain cases, for the bankruptcy petition to be processed; the magistrates require the presentation of evidence that the execution has been definitively extinguished. It is the duty of executor, in view of this, to proceed with the request for an evidentiary certificate of the fact that the businessperson in debt has not paid, has not deposited, or has not appointed assets to be seized, which then leads to the filing of bankruptcy petition based on that document before the competent Judicial Magistrate.[63]

The holder of credit right before debtor no longer intends to proceed with the satisfaction of his intention to promote execution. Once the debtor's assets are deficient, the person entitled to credit before them proceeds to request the judicial liquidation of their assets, thus opening a new process. At this stage, the creditor, in addition to being provided with the enforcement order, will have the liquidation order.

In summary, in the individual execution process, within the 24-hour period, the businessperson on whom the execution will take place will adopt the following: to make payment, make deposit, or make appointment of assets to be seized for discussion of the title. In the event of not adopting the measures under judgement, *"the executor will have the right to file for bankruptcy, and the LRF will not require the bailiff to certify that no assets have been found for attachment."*[64]

1.3.2.1 Acts of Bankruptcy

The Law 11.101/05, in the wake of subsection II and III of its Article 94, deals with acts that do not depend on unpunctuality to give rise to the characterization of bankruptcy state, which means that the consideration of the acts in question, as such, occurs through presumption (the so-called absolute presumption) and indicates the status of insolvency. The indication of acts of bankruptcy must be made in the initial petition, and the plaintiff must gather all the evidence he has and indicate those he still intends to produce; furthermore, in any event, it will be up to the plaintiff to make a detailed description of the facts that characterize the state of bankruptcy, and to this end he must gather the evidence and specify those he intends to produce in the course of action.

According to Ricardo Negrão, the characterization of bankruptcy acts is firmly established in the Bankruptcy Law and leads to the presumption of

63 Fábio Ulhoa COELHO, op. cit., 254.
64 Waldo FAZZIO JÚNIOR, op. cit., 643.

existence of financial difficulties in the life of the businessperson, under subsection III of Article 94.[65]

The above-described thought is not far from that presented by Professor Fábio Ulhoa Coelho,[66] in the sense that he understands that one speaks of bankruptcy acts when a business corporation finds itself with a higher liability in relation to assets (negative net worth); that is to say that the company is in a situation of economic insolvency. In the same way that the businessperson in debt who is affected by unpunctuality is not necessarily in a situation of insolvency, the law determines the decree of his bankruptcy status because it connotes unpunctuality as a type of legal insolvency; this falls under one or more stipulations of Article 94, subsection III of the Bankruptcy and Corporate Recovery Law. The businessperson may eventually find himself in a balanced patrimonial situation; however, he is exposed to the decree of bankruptcy because the law defines it as another form of legal insolvency. In conclusive terms, it is of little interest whether the business corporation has a positive net worth, if it executes through its legal representative an act of bankruptcy, as there will be room for the interposition of compulsory execution.

The acts of bankruptcy described in subsection III of Article 94 of the aforementioned law are configured in seven hypotheses capable of removing the debtor entrepreneur from the market.

Under the terms of paragraph (a), subsection III, Article 94, it is determined that the decree of bankruptcy of debtor will be based on the practice of *"(. . .) hasty liquidation of its assets or uses ruinous or fraudulent means to make payments."* In doctrinal thinking, the act of bankruptcy described in this paragraph is the "*hasty liquidation*"; in this context, Fábio Ulhoa Coelho understands that it is a legal hypothesis that will affect the business corporation that puts as an object of legal business of sale the assets in circulation and essential to the development of economic activity (machinery, technological resources, among others), without replacing them and not being guided by the observance of rules regarding dissolution.

Regarding the adoption of *"ruinous or fraudulent means to make payments,"* that author presents as an example of this conduct the act whose purpose is to contract new loans to pay off previous ones, without immediate prospect of economic recovery of the company or accepts to pay excessive interest compared to those practiced in the market.

65 Ricardo NEGRÃO, op. cit., 250.
66 Fábio Ulhoa COELHO, op. cit., 255.

It follows from paragraph (b), III, Article 94 that a simulated legal transaction shall be considered an act of bankruptcy, in the context in which the businessperson in debt *"performs or, by unequivocal acts, tries to perform, with the purpose of delaying payments or fraud to creditors, a simulated transaction or disposal of part or the totality of its assets to a third party, creditor or not."*

The third legal hypothesis of the act of bankruptcy, along the lines of Article 94(c)(III), is that the businessperson in debt transfers the *"(. . .) establishment to a third party, creditor or not, without the consent of all the creditors and without remaining with sufficient assets to settle the liabilities."*

It is an act of bankruptcy, under paragraph (d), III, Article 94, that the debtor simulates *"(. . .) the transfer of his principal establishment with the purpose of circumventing or supervising or to harm the creditor."* As a general rule, the reality is that the business corporation is free to transfer its main establishment in the time and space of its preference, if the same is based on reasons of business rationality, the need to bring the establishment closer to consumers or suppliers, better logistic infrastructure, among others; it is therefore a legally permitted transfer and not capable of constituting any act of bankruptcy. But if the transfer of the establishment, in time and space, is done with an intention to deceive the law, frustrating supervision or harming those who have the right to credit before the company, creating difficulties for them to exercise their rights, in such cases, the transfer is disguised and constitutes an act of bankruptcy.

From the moment the businessperson in debt *"gives or reinforces a guarantee to the creditor for a debt contracted previously without remaining free and clear enough assets to settle his liabilities,"* we are faced with an act of bankruptcy by force of paragraph (e), subsection III of Article 94. Around this hypothesis, we are interested in bringing up the interpretation presented to us by Fábio Ulhoa Coelho, first of all, to say that the essence of the legal hypothesis is the "*in rem guarantee*," and, for its consummation, the real guarantee (granting of titles, mortgage, pledge, among others) must be instituted by the business corporation, after it has been constituted, for the benefit of its creditors. Therefore, there will be no room for an act of bankruptcy if the obligation is set up simultaneously with the granting of *in rem* guarantee. The occurrence of these two phenomena at different times (first the constitution of the obligation and then the granting of *in rem* guarantee) is pure manifestation of the interest in *fraud par conditio creditorum,* in the sense that it is in the interest of assigning a more favorable condition to those who already have the right to credit before the company, in the event of a breach (in the order of payments, the holder of the *in rem* guarantee is given preference over unsecured creditors). Under normal conditions, the *in rem* guarantee is not granted to the creditor who has already agreed to grant credit without it.

There are cases in which the businessperson in debt may be absent *"(. . .) without leaving a qualified representative with sufficient resources to pay the creditors, abandon the establishment or try to hide from his domicile, the place of his headquarters or his main establishment."* If he does so, such acts will be held as eligible for invoking the act of bankruptcy, pursuant to paragraph (f), III, Article 94 of the Commercial Companies Code. However, there will be no room for bankruptcy if the business corporation establishes a proxy with the powers and resources necessary to satisfy the bond complex it has undertaken.

The seventh and last legal hypothesis of the act of bankruptcy is enshrined in paragraph (g), subsection III, Article 94 of the Civil Code. Under the terms of this hypothesis, there will be room for an act of bankruptcy if the businessperson in debt *"fails to comply, within the established term, with the obligation assumed in the judicial reorganization plan."* The fact that the company is benefiting from judicial reorganization does not exempt it from complying with the obligation complex contracted in the reorganization plan. The verification of default causes the bankruptcy act to be characterized at all times.

1.3.3 Declaration of Bankruptcy

The bankruptcy state becomes effective by means of its judicial decree; without this legal phenomenon, one cannot consider bankruptcy or judicial liquidation, but only insolvency or economic and financial crisis can be spoken of and whether this means the bankruptcy state consists of a judicial process and bankruptcy consists of a set of economic facts.

The Judicial Magistrate does not have the authority to decree the state of bankruptcy on his own initiative; the condition for this is the procedural impulse on the part of those legitimized. These are characteristic traits of the dispositive principle, according to which the judge is dependent, in the examination of the case, on the initiative of the parties as to the evidence and allegations on which the decision will be based: *judex secundum allegata et probata partium indicare debit.*[67]

As Andrea Torrente and Piero Schlesinger,[68] state that in Brazilian law, unlike in other legal systems, such as Italian law, bankruptcy cannot be decreed

67 António Carlos de Araújo CINTRA/ Ada Pelligrini GRINOVER/ Cândido Rangel DINAMARCO, *Teoria Geral do Processo,* 25ª Edição, Revista e Actualizada (São Paulo: Malheiros Editores, 2009), 70

68 Cited by Ecio PERIN JUNIOR, op. cit., 141.

of its own motion; it can only be decreed at the request of the debtor or of anyone who has a right to credit before the debtor. In Italian law, the decree of bankruptcy may be made *ex-officio* by the Judicial Magistrate without the need for a procedural impulse by the parties. This form of decree of bankruptcy is called *"ufficialitá dell'impulso processuale, perchè il processo fallimentare puo essere iniziato anche di ufficio."*

The unofficial declaration of bankruptcy in the Brazilian legal system is a general rule, but there are two hypothetical exceptions*:*

> (i) "when the debtor, having filed for judicial reorganization, does not fulfill the legal conditions for its granting"; and (ii) "when the judicial reorganization is terminated."

In both situations, the Judicial Magistrate proceeds with the transformation of the petition for reorganization into bankruptcy, issuing a declaratory sentence. However, *"in spite of dissonant positions arguing to the contrary, the duty imposed on the judge to declare bankruptcy when the petition for judicial reorganization does not meet the legal requirements always depends on provocation."*[69]

Fazzio Júnior adheres to the understanding that there is no officious decree of bankruptcy in Brazilian law, but the judge is allowed to convolute judicial reorganization into bankruptcy. Such convolution should not be understood as a synonym of a bankruptcy state sentenced unofficially, since these are hypotheses in which the debtor confessed to being insolvent in the request for judicial reorganization that was not feasible or in the nonfulfillment of the reorganization in progress.[70]

1.4 Bankruptcy Procedure

The bankruptcy procedure consists of three essential phases: (i) *Pre-Bankruptcy Phase*—its purpose is to file for bankruptcy and verify the material preconditions of bankruptcy status; they are the corporate debtor or the corporate character of the debtor, that is, a corporate entity, and legal insolvency; now, the purpose mentioned is a way to reach the decision period, within which the Judicial Magistrate may proceed to decree bankruptcy or deny it; (ii*) Administration Phase*—it is an informative phase. It is in this phase that those who have the right to credit before the debtor are qualified—the definition of the liability; in turn, the phase in

69 Ecio PERIN JUNIOR, op. cit., 141.

70 Waldo FAZZIO JÚNIOR, op. cit., 648.

question integrates the sub-phase of collection of assets—definition of the asset; and the sub-phase of ascertainment—judicial inquiry; (iii) *Liquidation phase* is the phase of satisfaction of the asset—sale of the assets and closure.

1.4.1 Pre-Bankruptcy Phase

The pre-bankruptcy phase is triggered by the filing of a lawsuit for the bankruptcy of business debtor, and it is at this stage that the Judicial Magistrate will verify the material precondition of bankruptcy, as already described in the previous paragraph; depending on these preconditions, it will be up to the Judicial Magistrate to decide in favor of the declaration of bankruptcy or its denial.

1.4.1.1 Judicial Request

1.4.1.1.1 Active Legitimacy

To speak of active legitimacy is to speak of the subject who can file the lawsuit to request the declaration of bankruptcy. Article 97 of the Bankruptcy and Reorganization of Enterprises Law has taken care of filing the subjects with legitimacy before judicial instances to request or demand the petition for the opening of bankruptcy, and we will analyze it next.

(a) The Businessperson in Debt

This is a legitimacy conferred under Article 97, subsection I. As it is a type of bankruptcy requested by the debtor himself, it is called self-bankruptcy and its processing occurs based on the parameters provided in Articles 105–107 of the aforementioned law.

Self-bankruptcy can only be asked for by the debtor's person, and the term is no longer established, as was done in Article 8 of the abrogated 1945 Decree Law (Bankruptcy Law). In the current law (Bankruptcy and Reorganization Law), the referred article corresponds to Articles 105–107 of the Bankruptcy Law.

There is room for self-bankruptcy when the debtor entrepreneur concludes that the business entity he is exploring no longer meets the minimum conditions to be recovered.[71]

The businessperson in debt, guided by the virtue of honesty, when he feels that he no longer gathers resources for the development of his economic activities, adopts the bankruptcy petition as a convenient procedural mechanism to put an end to the said activities, in order to avoid giving rise to property damages to

71 Ecio PERIN JUNIOR, op. cit., 121.

those who have the right to credit before him. As soon as the debtor applies for self-bankruptcy, he is assisted by the right to transfer to the state the liquidation of his company, which is in a situation of frustration.[72]

The power granted to the debtor to apply for the opening of bankruptcy proceedings becomes operational when he is in a situation of circumstances reflecting an imminent state of insolvency or foreseeable lack of liquidity. Certainly, the power in question can only be used as a last resort, from the moment the debtor feels unable to answer for the bond complex by which he is attached to the creditors. In this logic, the suspension of payments or a simple confession of insolvency accompanied by a declaration that the debtor will cease to pay, at maturity, its charges will serve as the basis for the request.[73]

Under Article 105 of the Bankruptcy and Corporate Recovery Law, the debtor in economic and financial crisis, aware of the fact that he does not meet the requirements to petition for his judicial recovery, has the duty to proceed with the petition for his bankruptcy; for this purpose, he must make a statement of the reasons that make it impossible to proceed with the exercise of the company and must attach a list of necessary documents. See, *ipsis litteris*, the documents required under the above-mentioned article:

I. Accounting statements referring to the last three (3) fiscal years and those drawn up especially to instruct the request, prepared in strict compliance with the applicable corporate legislation and obligatorily composed of
   a) balance sheet,
   b) accumulated income statement,
   c) income statement since the last fiscal year,
   d) cash flow report,

II. Nominal list of creditors, indicating address, amount, nature, and rating of respective claims.

III. List of assets and rights that comprise the asset, with the respective estimate of value and documents evidencing ownership.

72 Fábio Ulhoa COELHO, *Comentários a nova Lei de Falências e de Recuperação de Empresas* (São Paulo: Saraiva, 2005), 256.

73 Waldo FAZZIO JÚNIOR, op. cit., 652.

IV. Proof of the status of businessman, articles of association or bylaws in effect or, if there are none, the indication of all partners, their addresses, and the list of their personal assets.
V. The mandatory books and accounting documents required by law.
VI. A list of its managers in the last 5 (five) years, with their addresses, their functions and corporate participation.

The failure to present part of the documents required in the context of Article 105 does not bring consequences of a sanctioning nature and does not constitute any kind of illegality or fraud. However, it is revealed as an irregularity in the investigation of the bankruptcy petition, which can be remedied by a decision of the Judicial Magistrate, within the period he deems convenient, since the law does not rule on the deadlines in this regard. Even if the businessperson in debt, in the scope of the petition to open bankruptcy, has not presented the entire list of documents required, or has committed other irregularities of this nature, within the period that the Judge orders to remedy such irregularities, the institution of any other petition to open bankruptcy against the businessperson in debt will be null and void. This is because a petition of bankruptcy has already been filed by the debtor, and, as long as it is not unsealed, there is no need to promote a parallel petition for the same purpose.[74]

(b) The Surviving Spouse, Any Heir of the Debtor, or the Inventor
According to item II, Article 97 of the Bankruptcy and Business Reorganization Law, the surviving spouse or any heir of the debtor or the inventor may request the bankruptcy petition. The item in question refers to the superfluous spouse, the heir, or the inventor of the estate of the natural/physical person, or if we wish, the individual or individual businessperson, in the context of Article 966 of the Civil Code. There is no doubt about the fact that the item in question applies to the natural person, since only the natural person can have spouse or heirs.[75] The bankruptcy petition, in the event in question, can only be formulated within a time period of one (1) year which is to be counted from the date of the death of the corporate debtor (§ 1, Article 96, LFRE), and if the bankruptcy petition is not initiated within this one-year period, it is considered to be of decadence, as

74 Id., 654.
75 Carlos Roberto CLARO, *Do procedimento para a decretação da falência, in* Comentários à Lei 11.105/05: Recuperação Empresarial e Falência (Curitiba, Paraná: OAB, 2017), 217.

it must be observed not only by the superfluous spouse, heir, or inventor but also by the creditors.[76]

(c) Shareholder of the Company

In the wordings of Article 97, III, "*The bankruptcy of the debtor may be petitioned for: the shareholder of the debtor in the form of the law or of the memorandum of association.*" This is a legal precept that applies to the partner or shareholder of the legal entity whose insertion falls under Private Law. The partner or shareholder, as the case may be, in the capacity of legitimate agents for the propulsion of the action to open bankruptcy, does not need to present judicial or extrajudicial executive title. Furthermore, the partner or shareholder is not required to have a right to credit before the debtor, but they must be aware that the legal entity to which they belong pursues actions that are not in keeping with their corporate purpose or that they are performing acts of a fraudulent nature, since such data are essential for a court to require the decree of bankruptcy.[77]

An important fact that should be highlighted here is that for the bankruptcy petition to proceed, the partner or shareholder (as the case may be) must present evidence that they have that *status* in the company against which they propose the decree of bankruptcy.

(d) Any Creditor

In bankruptcy proceedings, the application for bankruptcy by the person holding the credit right (creditor) before the debtor company (debtor) is considered the most prevalent hypothesis. Unlike the hypothesis seen in the preceding paragraph (petition in bankruptcy by the partner or shareholder—in which no judicial or extrajudicial title is required), in the hypothesis in question (Article 97, Subsection IV—opening of bankruptcy at the request of any debtor), it is essential that proof of the existence of the credit right be provided, taking into consideration Article 94 of the Bankruptcy and Reorganization of Companies Law.

It is important to clarify that the creditor to which the item under analysis refers may or may not be a businessperson, as the same is valid for the title legitimating his right to credit before the courts, which may or may not be of a commercial nature. The creditor not endowed with the businessperson status is also granted the right to file an application for the opening and decreeing of the bankruptcy of its debtor in the same manner as the creditor is endowed with the

76 Ecio PERIN JUNIOR, op. cit., 124.
77 Carlos Roberto CLARO, op. cit., 217.

businessperson status (entrepreneur creditor). The background to such legitimacy is the protection of the right to credit, as well as the protection of the creditor, being of little importance the commercial, civil, or fiscal nature of the debt.[78]

It must be considered that according to §§ 1 and 2, subsection IV of Article 97, certain peculiarities must be observed.

Businessperson as creditor. As to § 1, it determines that if the holder of the credit right before the debtor company is a businessperson, he has the duty to present the certificate of the Public Registry of Commercial Companies (Board of Trade), which will serve as proof of the commercial activities that he carries out. Confirmation of the regular nature of the said activities requires the presentation of the said certificate. In the event that the business creditor does not attach the certificate to the petition, the Judicial Magistrate shall have no other option but to determine the amendment of the petition, and failure by the business creditor to comply with such determination shall result in the rejection of the petition.

From what has been said in the above paragraph, the restrictive nature of Bankruptcy and Corporate Recovery Law is notorious, in relation to the entrepreneur legitimized to request the decree of bankruptcy of another businessperson, in the sense that only the regular businessperson has such legitimacy; in relation to the irregular or in-fact businessperson (the one who exercises the commercial activity without the due filing of constitutive acts in the Public Registry of Commercial Companies), he does not enjoy such legitimacy. It follows from this that, in addition to being restrictive, the said law has a sanctioning nature, since the irregular businessperson is forbidden to file for bankruptcy of another businessperson, but there is nothing to prevent bankruptcy being filed against him.

Creditor domiciled abroad. The § 2 is presented in the following terms: *"Creditors not domiciled in Brazil shall post bond related to the costs and payment of the indemnity referred to in art. 101 of this law."* The bail referred to in the paragraph in question may be paid in cash or goods (regardless of their nature), and the goods must be reduced in the records themselves. A bank guarantee may also be presented. Although the law mentions the provision of the bail, it fails to establish its limits. The rule in Article 101 states that losses and damages shall be ascertained in settlement of sentence. In the meantime, at no time is it pronounced as to the value of the bail.[79]

78 Ricardo NEGRÃO, op. cit., 254.
79 Carlos Roberto CLARO, op. cit., 218.

(i) Creditor Public Treasury

As far as the Public Treasury Creditor is concerned, the jurisprudence is not unanimous.

As Ricardo Negrão well teaches, in the previous system (Decree Law No. 7.661 of June 21, 1945—Bankruptcy Law) as well as the one in force (Law No. 11.101 of February 9, 2005—Bankruptcy and Corporate Reorganization Law), regarding the Fiscal Creditor, certain doctrinaire and jurisprudential guidelines were established.

On the one hand, some legal scholars, including Fábio Konder Comparato, Fazzio Júnior, and Amador Paes de Almeida, were in favor of the idea that the origin of the bankruptcy petition was not out of question when tax authorities (tax creditors) function as active subjects. Their reasoning was that the credit with a real right of guarantee should be distinguished from the tender privilege of the Public Treasury and, therefore, it would not be covered by the limitation determined by Article 9, subsection III, al. (b) of Decree no. 7.661 of June 21, 1945 (previous system of bankruptcy); it can be concluded thus that it would not be much of a help to understand the said issue in a restrictive interpretative sense and in an exclusive manner.

For a better understanding, we think it is pertinent in the present context to discuss the wording of Article 9: *"Bankruptcy may also be requested: III.—by the creditor, showing title to his claim, even if not overdue, observing, as the case may be, the following conditions: b. the creditor with in rem guarantee if he resigns or, wishing to keep it, if he proves that the assets do not reach the solution of his claim, this proof shall be made by expert examination, pursuant to the procedural law, in preparatory proceedings prior to the bankruptcy petition if the petition is based on Article 1, or within the term of Article 12 if the petition is based on Article 2."*

On the other hand, the opposite current of thought, defended by Rubens Requião and Minister Cláudio dos Santos, rules out any possibility of filing for bankruptcy by the Treasury.

Justice Cláudio Santos[80] of the Supreme Court of Justice, in a vote that he won in Special Appeal No. 10. 660—MG, j. 12-12-1995, presented the following position:

> (. . .) I do not intend to reduce the faculty of the Treasury to discuss in court its credit, exclusively, in tax executions. In any action proposed against it the discussion can be held, but it is unquestionable that the collection of the public

80 Cited by Ricardo NEGRÃO, op. cit., 257.

> debt must be made in the singular tax foreclosure, without prejudice to its right to the precautionary measures assured in the subsidiary applicable procedural statute. On the other hand, it is inaccurate to argue that the Public Treasury may waive its rights and privileges, as a tax creditor, in order to assume the position of a common, unsecured creditor, in competition with the other creditors, and with this affirm the right to file for bankruptcy of the debtor. The tax is collected by means of administrative activity fully bound, according to the definition contained in art. 3 of the National Tax Code, complementary law of the National Tax System, and, thus, there is no other way for the administrator, except to forward the debt certificate for collection through tax execution, because it is in the competent court that the matter must be discussed and not in the bankruptcy court. These legal arguments are not unrelated to others of an economic, moral and political nature. It is well known that our constitutional system gives priority to equality, freedom of initiative and free competition, and it is not compatible with these principles to grant the State the right to destroy the company, according to the free determination and choice of its administrative agents, due to the unpunctuality in the payment of the tax. The Brazilian bankruptcy legislation is in mismatch with the social economic reality, it is backward and iniquitous, by considering a case of simple or late payment or mere unpunctuality to be presumed insolvent for the creditor's benefit. Its new discipline in progress in the National Congress softens a little the rigor of the law in force and wraps up a principle of great significance that is the interest in the recovery of the company and not the liquidation of its assets to pay its debts. To grant the State a judicial measure of this potential annihilating is undoubtedly contrary to those guiding principles of the economic order in the country, and consecrates a reprehensible coercion for morality and politics.

This is a position to which Ricardo Negrão subscribes, and he adds that the fact of giving the state employee the decision to file for bankruptcy at his discretion, deciding in which cases he will or will not do so, is an offense to the principle of impersonality, constitutionally enshrined in Article 37 (Federal Constitution), safeguarding the hypotheses in which the request for the decree of bankruptcy by the Public Administration was linked to objective criteria legally established. Impersonality as a constitutional principle revolves around the idea that the actions of the Public Administration cannot be in the sense of causing losses or benefits to certain persons but must only be defined according to the interest of the community. As regards the criteria established by law, it cannot be ignored that in the previous system of bankruptcy, the petition for the opening of bankruptcy would occur when the impossibility and acts of bankruptcy are verified. In this context, in a situation in which the taxpayer executed by the Public

Treasury did not pay or deposit the amount or did not appoint assets to be seized within the legally established time limit, the state would assume the obligation of requesting the opening of bankruptcy, deviating from causing losses to certain merchants, leaving others out of the execution of the bid. The actions of the tax authorities to this extent would force greater state intervention in economic activity. Another fact that should not be ignored is the functions of the state, as enshrined in Article 174 of the Federal Constitution, do not include the state's action in bankruptcy matters.

In view of the positions presented in relation to the previous bankruptcy system, it is now appropriate to present the understanding of certain authors regarding the bankruptcy system in force (Law No. 11101 of February 9, 2005—Bankruptcy and Corporate Recovery Law).

In legal terms, the Treasury is not prevented from applying for judicial guardianship, which may prove to be lacking in the interest to act. It is pertinent in this situation to state that, once the bankruptcy is decreed, the tax credit will not be part of it; thus, there is no logical basis that allows the tax authorities to file the petition for bankruptcy of the debtor.[81]

Fazzio Waldo Junior is of the view that the law does not restrict the Public Treasury from filing for bankruptcy, since the Bankruptcy and Corporate Reorganization Law itself determines that *"any creditor"* may file for bankruptcy of the debtor. Assuming that the tax authorities are in possession of the executive title, and verifying the legal reasons necessary for the decree of bankruptcy, the tax authorities have the faculty and the duty to enforce their right.[82]

In order to strengthen his aforesaid view, the author cites Article 187 of the National Tax Code (Law No. 5172 of October 25, 1966), which is a law that disciplines the National Tax System and establishes the general rules of Tax Law whose applicability is on the Union, States, and Municipalities, and presents the following wording (given in Complementary Law No. 118 of 2005):

> **Art. 187.** The judicial collection of the tax credit is not subject to the contest of creditors or habilitation in bankruptcy, judicial reorganization, concordat, inventory or enrollment.
>
> Single Paragraph. The preferential bidding only takes place among legal entities of public law, in the following order:

81 Carlos Roberto CLARO, op. cit., 218.
82 Waldo FAZZIO JÚNIOR, op. cit., 655.

I— Union
II— States, Federal District and Territories together and pro rata.
III— Municipality, jointly and pro rata.

The strengthening that is referred to is presented in the following forms:

> Art. 187 of the CNT grants a privilege to the tax credit, not an imposition. The Public Treasury can choose between singular fiscal execution and the qualification of its credits in bankruptcy. If it were not so, the legislator, establishing the insolvency of the tax credit, would be reducing the spectrum of possibility of its collection, when, in its reality, its intention was to increase such possibilities, extending the guardianship of the treasury. Finally, if the extreme measure of bankruptcy is also a form of protection to the public credit, and not a mere judicial means of collection, if it aims at cleaning up the market by eliminating the insolvent and unviable economic agent, it is clear that it brings, in its bulge, the protection to the public credit par excellence.[83]

(ii) Creditor with *in rem* Guarantee
In the event that the creditor holds in its legal sphere the *in rem* guarantee, he is obliged to waive such guarantee. In the meanderings of jurisprudence, an understanding prevails that the application for bankruptcy by the creditor with *in rem* guarantee drags with it the implicit consequence of the spoiling of that guarantee. The basis of this spoiling lies in the fact that the holder of the credit right with *in rem* guarantee is certain to pay his credit in an asset earmarked for this purpose. Under these conditions, the creditor lacks the interest to file for bankruptcy of the debtor and, therefore, lacks the interest to act, which is one of the preconditions of the action. If the creditor opts to file for bankruptcy, he must divest himself of that guarantee, which will lead him to be in the same position as the other unsecured creditors.[84]

(iii) Labor Creditor
The law allows the labor creditor to file for bankruptcy against his debtor (patronage). Such permission is based on the fact that it precludes any possibility of the insolvent employer's assets being squandered as a result of individual actions brought against him.[85] No circumstance prevents the labor creditor from

83 *Id.*
84 Ecio PERIN JUNIOR, op. cit., 126.
85 *Id.*, 127.

petitioning for bankruptcy, not least because the Brazilian legislator has shown emphasis by using the expression "*any creditor,*" elucidating that any type of creditor can file for bankruptcy of the debtor, regardless of the type of credit they hold (which may be labor, civil, or commercial).

1.4.1.1.2 Passive Legitimacy

The institute of bankruptcy is exclusive to debtor entrepreneurs, whether constituted in the form of a legal person (Business Corporation) or a natural person (individual businessperson).[86]

1.4.1.1.3 Competent Court

To speak of the competent court is to seek to know to whom the action whose object the petition to open bankruptcy is should be directed. Article 3 of the Bankruptcy and Reorganization Law provides that the local court of the debtor's main establishment or the branch of the company that has its headquarters in Brazil is responsible for declaring bankruptcy. The provision in question is a mandatory rule and, for such reason, any and all statutory or contractual provisions provided for in the company's memorandum of association that aim to determine the jurisdiction shall not be liable to produce any effects.

The Bankruptcy Law in force is silent on the definition of the "*main establishment of the debtor.*" The same can be said in relation to Law No. 10,406 of January 10, 2005 (Brazilian Civil Code), which, in its system, does not present a legal definition of the debtor's main establishment but only defines the business establishment, which under the terms of Article 1142 of the referred legal diploma corresponds to the "*(. . .) complex of assets organized, for the exercise of the company, by entrepreneur or by business company.*"

In the face of such omission, the indoctrinators took action, seeking in this context to define what should be understood by the reality in question. Certainly, the controversy surrounding what is to be understood as "*main establishment*" proves to be unnecessary when the businessperson carries out his activities in one establishment and in one physical space; however, it proves to be pertinent when the activities are carried out through more than one establishment and in more than one physical space.

In Rubens Requião's[87] perspective, the main establishment is "*the place where the company's leadership is fixed, where the businessperson effectively acts in the*

86 For better understanding of the legitimacy, we recommend the reading of Section 1.2 above, on the bankruptcy requisites.

87 Cited by Ecio PERIN JUNIOR, op. cit., 115.

government or in the command of his business, from where the orders and instructions emanate, in which the commercial and financial operations of greater volume and in mass are carried out, where the general accounting is found." It is due to this understanding that Rubens Requião maintains that the determination of the competent jurisdiction is not made in the company's memorandum of association (bylaws for the statutory companies and contract for the contractual companies) but is made according to the place where the most relevant administrative activities are performed (administrative headquarters), where the accounting books of the corporate entity are kept, not least because the books are essential in the bankruptcy process, in the concordat, and in the justice.

Fábio Ulhoa Coelho[88] offers the definition that the main establishment *"is the one in which the greatest turnover of the company is concentrated; it is the most important from the economic point of view."* It is a definition that guides the said author to conclude that the determination of the competent court in bankruptcy proceedings is made according to the establishment that presents greater prominence in the economic perspective. Ecio Perin Junior, who quotes the decision of the Supreme Court of Justice— *"STJ_ 2nd Section; Confl. De Comp. 21.896—MG; Rel. Min. Sálvio de Fegueiredo Teixeira; j. 10.06.1998, vu."* to support his understanding, where the said court considered that *"the main establishment is the place where the activity is kept centralized, not being, on the other hand, the one to which the statutes confer the title of main, but the one that forms the living body, the vital center of the debtor's main activities."* And he adds that one cannot ignore the fact that the purpose of bankruptcy proceedings is to liquidate the assets of the bankrupt in order to restore the rights of creditors who, by means of a tender, execute the bankrupt; in this respect, more than just, it is logical that the competent jurisdiction be set according to the place where the majority of the bankrupt's assets are located.

Maximilianus Cláudio Américo Führer[89] states that in bankruptcy proceedings the incompetence of the forum is absolute and can be decreed unofficially by the judge.

In the event the debtor is a foreign legal person, the definition of competent jurisdiction will also be made at the discretion of the main establishment, taking into account, however, only the subsidiaries headquartered in Brazil. In the universe of the respective branches, the one that calls itself a prominent turnover will be verified.[90]

88 Fábio Ulhoa COELHO, op. cit., 261.

89 Apud Ecio PERIN JUNIOR, op. cit., 117.

90 Fábio Ulhoa COELHO, op. cit., 261.

The possibility that in a certain district there is more than one court with jurisdiction to hear the matter of bankruptcy is not ruled out; in these situations, it is necessary to take into account the rule contained in paragraph 8 of Article 6 of the Bankruptcy and Reorganization Law, which reads as follows: *"The distribution of the petition for bankruptcy or judicial reorganization prevents jurisdiction for any other petition for judicial reorganization or bankruptcy, relating to the same debtor."* Interesting is the example brought by Fábio Ulhoa Coelho about the cited norm. This author posits that *"In the District of São Paulo, for example, the regional courts do not have jurisdiction for bankruptcy, but the 44 Civil Courts of the central court are all competent for bankruptcy. The distribution of the first bankruptcy petition against a certain limited company, for example, to the 28th Civil Court, makes it competent, by prevention, for all bankruptcy petitions later filed against that same company."*

(a) Universality of the Competent Court

From the moment the bankruptcy of the businessperson in debt is decreed, whether natural or legal person, the bankrupt estate is constituted, which consists of all the rights and obligations. The doctrine divides the bankruptcy estate into two parts: (i) objective—this is constituted by the debtor's assets and is the object of the collection and (ii) subjective—constituted by the creditors. Rubens Requião[91] adds that the purpose of bankruptcy proceedings is collective execution and is guided by the *par conditio creditorum* principle, which in turn advocates that creditors of the same category should be treated equally and should, therefore, compete in the indivisible court of bankruptcy, regardless of whether they are traders or civilians. Creditors are, consequently, grouped together in a collectivity called the subjective bankruptcy estate.

Article 76[92] of the Bankruptcy and Reorganization Law raises two characteristics regarding the bankruptcy court, namely (i) indivisibility and (ii) universality, which means that the bankruptcy court is indivisible and vested with competence that gives it the knowledge of the totality of the bankrupt's actions over assets, interests, and business. This property of attraction that characterizes the bankruptcy court is called *vis atractiva* (force of attraction). Attention should therefore be paid to the exception made in the last part of the article herein, referring to labor, tax, and other cases not governed by that law, in which the bankrupt appears as the plaintiff of the bankruptcy petition or active litigation

91 Rubens REQUIÃO, *Curso de direito comercial*; 14ª ed. (São Paulo: Saraiva, 1984), 137.

92 In the previous bankruptcy system corresponds to § 2, article 7.

With regard to labor lawsuits, in constitutional terms, it is the competence of the Labor Courts to proceed with the processing and judgment of actions arising from legal-labor relations, covering the external public law entities of the direct and indirect public administration of the Union, the States, the Federal District, and the Municipalities (Article 114, item I, Federal Constitution).[93] The Judicial Administrator shall be responsible for verifying the credit constituted within the scope of labor relations, in accordance with Article 6, paragraph 2 in conjunction with Article 7, both of Law No. 11.101/2005.

Another part of the exceptions includes tax executions, which must be processed in the court with jurisdiction to do so. In the meantime, Law 11.105/2005, in paragraph 7, Article 6, states that *"Tax executions are not suspended by the granting of judicial reorganization (. . .)"*; it is, therefore, a provision that does not pronounce on the non-suspension of tax executions, in a bankruptcy situation; some doctrines argue that, *contrario sensu*, with the decree of bankruptcy verified, it is necessary to suspend the tax execution.[94][95]

93 Consideration must be taken to the Constitutional Amendment number 45, of 30th December 2004.

94 Manoel Justino BEZERRA FILHO, *Nova lei de falências e de recuperação e falências comentada; apud* Rafael Martins BORDILHÃO, op. cit., 177.

95 Different opinions are adopted in the jurisprudential domain, in the sense that the declaration of the bankruptcy does not imply the suspension of the fiscal execution. Such opinions are presented in the Parana's Court of Justice Decision, whose enactment results from the Motion for the Declaration of Interlocutory Appeal Proceedings No. 932.982—2/01: "And even if the appellant asserts that all discipline dealing with the continuity of the tax foreclosure would relate exclusively to the judicial recovery—with which the bankruptcy itself would not apply—it is certain that the reading of such provision must be carried out in conjunction with what prescribes in article 29, of Law 6.830/80, namely: [. . .] Thus, even if the bankruptcy of the company has been decreed, the tax foreclosure has its normal procedure, there being no way to talk about the suspension or its attraction by the universal judgment of bankruptcy. This is because one of the privileges enshrined in Law 6,830/1980 consists in the exclusion of the execution of tax credits by universal judges, that is, one of the concerns of the rule contained in art. 5 of the aforementioned legislation is to release the Treasury from being subject to any bankruptcy court, among which the universal bankruptcy court stands out. Thus, the competence to assess the tax foreclosure does not change in the event of a bankruptcy decree. If there is an express rule in the sense that the tax foreclosure jurisdiction remains in the face of universal courts, in particular that of bankruptcy, upon a court decision that decrees the bankruptcy of the business debtor, the foreclosure promoted by the treasury entity will continue in the jurisdiction where it was located before the bankruptcy decree, it cannot exist, there can be no change of competence or stoppage. In the same vein follows article 76, and its sole paragraph, of Law 11.101/2005, which provides: [. . .] In other words, the provision is quite clear to the disciplinary that not all demands will be analyzed by the universal bankruptcy court, among them, the tax foreclosures, showing such a situation of objective exclusion. That is, such legal discipline corroborates the reasoning of the judgment that there will be no suspension of the fiscal executive process by the simple decree of bankruptcy of the company."—TJPR—3ª C. Cível—932982-2/01-Curitiba-Rel.: Themis Furquim Cortes—Unânime - - J.03.03.2015—On this Rafael Martins BORDILHÃO, *op. cit.*, 177–78.

To explain the exception in question, Fábio Ulhoa Coelho calls Article 187 of the National Tax Code, which presents the following normative content: "*The judicial collection of the tax credit is not subject to the contest of creditors or habilitation in bankruptcy (. . .)*"; the author further adds that the same normative command suppressing the character of the competent court is applicable to the needy credits of a tax nature registered in the active debt, in accordance with Law 6.830 of September 22, 1980 (the said law provides for the judicial collection of the active debt of the Public Treasury).[96]

The "*actions claiming the gross amount regardless of the position of the bankrupt estate in the relationship*" are an integral part of the exceptions provided for in Article 76 of the current bankruptcy system and, therefore, escape the appreciation of the bankruptcy court in the event that at the time of the decree of bankruptcy they were already being processed. In this case, their processing will continue in the court where they were distributed, pursuant to Article 6, paragraph 1 of the Bankruptcy and Reorganization Law.[97]

Another exception is based on the Constitution, precisely on Article 109, subsection I of the Federal Constitution: "*Bankruptcy judges are responsible for prosecuting and judging: cases in which the Union, autarchic entity or public or federal company are interested as authors, defendants, assistants or opponents, except those of bankruptcy, accidental labor and those subject to Federal and Labor Justice.*"

1.4.1.1.4 Instruction

Speaking of the investigation of the case includes addressing the evidential means of the facts enrolled in the action of petition for bankruptcy.

The evidentiary means that guide the instruction of the petition to open bankruptcy are listed in paragraphs 3, 4, and 5 of Articles 94–96 and 98 of the Bankruptcy and Reorganization Law. In this legal situation, the bankruptcy petitioner must align his actions with that of the creditor or minority partner and seek the satisfaction of his petition within the framework of the judicial process (contentious nature). A different situation occurs in cases of self-bankruptcy petitions, where the instruction of the process is not contentious in nature and occurs according to the legally pre-established procedures in Articles 105–107 of the Bankruptcy and Reorganization Law.[98] Also in the petition for the opening of bankruptcy on the debtor's own initiative (self-bankruptcy), it is important to

96 Fábio Ulhoa COELHO, *Curso de Direito Comercial: Direito de Empresa.* op. cit., 263.

97 Fábio Ulhoa COELHO, *Comentários à nova lei de falências e recuperação de empresas.* 4ª ed. (São Paulo: Saraiva, 2007), 199.

98 Fábio Ulhoa COELHO, *Curso de Direito Comercial: Direito de Empresa.* op. cit., 264.

point out that the failure to investigate the petition, in the wake of Article 105, will lead to the Judicial Magistrate recommending the plaintiff to proceed with the amendments of the action. Once the amendments have been made or even if the amendments have not been made, the Judicial Magistrate must anyway proceed with the decree of bankruptcy, except when the withdrawal is presented before the passing of the decree of bankruptcy.[99]

The instruction of the petition pursuant to paragraph 3 of Article 94, as already discussed, applies to cases where the petition for opening of bankruptcy is based on the unjustified[100] unpunctuality of the businessperson in debt (see subsection I, Article 94, Bankruptcy and Reorganization of Companies Law). The debtor who holds the right to credit before the debtor must proceed to examine the petition by presenting evidence of his *status* as a creditor and must also, before the Judicial Magistrate, exhibit the title legitimating the execution he is attempting against the businessperson, pointing out that the respective title, by obligation, must be overdue, even in a situation when the presentation of the protest certificate is not dispensed.[101]

An application for bankruptcy by the creditor on the grounds that the debtor is not punctual can only be granted if the debtor has a reduced net obligation in the title legitimating the enforcement action. The unjustified impossibility of the debtor will be proved by protest, which in turn is exclusive as proof of the lack of punctuality by the entrepreneur in debt (paragraph 3 of Article 94). Article 96, which provides that "Bankruptcy filed on the basis of Article 94, Section I, of this law shall not be decreed if the defendant proves: defect in protest or in its instrument," reinforces such understanding.

According to Article 1 of Law No. 9492 of September 10, 1997,[102] the protest is defined as *"the formal and solemn act by which one proves default and non-fulfillment of an obligation originated in bonds and other documents in debt."* Around this legal definition it is important to mention that the figure of protest

99 Etiane Barbi KÖHLER, *DIREITO FALIMENTAR E DA RECUPERAÇO DA EMPRESA* (Rio Grande do Sul, Brasil: Editora Unijui, 2011), 16.

100 It should be added that the lack of punctuality without a plausible legal reason becomes evident from the moment the debtor does not pay the due net obligation reduced by the protested executive title(s) upon maturity in exchange terms, the amount of which is above 40 (forty) minimum wages on the date on which the action whose object is to file for bankruptcy of the debtor is brought. On this, Amador Paes ALMEIDA, *Curso de Falência e de Recuperação de Empresa.* 21ª ed. (São Paulo: Saraiva, 2005), 26.

101 Ecio PERIN JUNIOR, op. cit., 128.

102 Defines the competence, regulates the services related to titles and other debt documents protests, and gives other provisions.

configures a duality of functions: (i) It serves as a probative element; it reflects the late payment status of the businessperson in debt, due to nonpayment, for not accepting the security or for refusing its return; it is a characterization of lack of punctuality, which is a prerequisite for the creditor to exercise its right to file for the debtor's bankruptcy; (ii) it is a conservatory function—it opens space for the exercise of the right of return of the security holder against the endorsers and respective guarantors.

Around what was said in the paragraph above, it must always be kept in mind that the bankruptcy petition based on lack of punctuality does not exempt the existence of executive title(s) whose sum is above the corresponding to forty (40) minimum wages (subsection I, Article 94 of the Bankruptcy Law).

The right and the liquid and enforceable nature of the executive martyrdom are a *sine qua non* condition for triggering a bankruptcy action; the regular nature of the protest, which implies the lack of vice in its instrument, competes with the same condition, and, in this perspective, it must observe the requirements contained in the rule of Article 22 of Law No. 9492 of September 10, 1997, namely:

> I—Date and protocol number; II—name of the presenter and address; III—reproduction or transcription of the document or the indications made by the presenter and the statements inserted in it; IV—certificate of the subpoenas made and the answers eventually offered; V—indication of the voluntary interveners and the firms honored by them; VI—the bearer's acquiescence to the honorable acceptance; VII—name, debtor's identification number and address; VIII—date and signature of the Notary of Protest, his substitutes or of an authorized writer.

Interesting is the comment made by Waldo Fazzio Junior around these requirements, in the following terms: "*the instruments of protest that do not identify the person who received the letter of intent to serve the debtor, absent any document that positivates the existence of a real and effective summons, remain viscerally tainted with irregularities, not authorizing the reception of the postulation of bankruptcy, in the absence of an essential presupposition to the valid and regular constitution of the procedural relationship.*"[103] As can be seen, the regularity of the protest is configured as a fundamental presupposition of the opening and origin of the bankruptcy action; therefore, without regular protest, the request for bankruptcy will be based on unpunctuality.

103 Waldo FAZZIO JUNIOR, 1999. *Lei de falências e concordatas comentadas* (São Paulo: Atlas, 113.

According to Ecio Pern Junior, *"It is simple to glimpse the institute of protest when we focus on the titles of credit, since it is a necessary element for the exercise of the right of credit in the face of co-obligors in the event of non-payment, by the main debtor, of the amount mentioned therein."* This is an explanation that leads to the inference that the protest regarding the credit titles is indispensable regardless of the purpose of having the decree of breach issued. Meanwhile, it must be taken into account that there are credits whose representation does not materialize in credit titles; even so, they are considered executive titles, of a judicial or extra-judicial nature and, therefore, capable of substantiating the bankruptcy petition based on clauses II and III of Article 94 of the Bankruptcy and Reorganization of Companies Law, and they dispense with the figure of the protest.[104]

It is on this line that under paragraph 4 of Article 94 of the said law, the bankruptcy petition based on subsection II shall be filed with a simple certificate issued by the court through which the execution is processed. Another situation that does not require a protest is one that is set forth in paragraph 5 of Article 94, which states that the petition for bankruptcy based on subsection III shall include a description of the facts that characterize it, attaching the evidence that exists and specifying the evidence that will be produced.[105]

In order to talk about the bankruptcy petition instruction in the parameters of paragraphs 3 and 4 of Article 94 of the Bankruptcy and Corporate Recovery Law, it is important, first of all, to emphasize that it is an instruction that focuses on subsections II and III of the aforementioned article, especially for cases in which the exercise of the act of presumed insolvency is verified, and certainly that, in these cases, as in others, the plaintiff must have a right to credit before the defendant, and the existence of such right can only be proved by attaching a title.

It should be emphasized that it is not mandatory that the evidence of existence of right of credit be overdue, and in this chaos the figure of protest is dispensable.

In the instruction of petition for opening of bankruptcy, made pursuant to paragraphs 4 and 5 of Article 94, the entrepreneur in debt shall be summoned to present his defense within ten (10) days, as established in Article 98 of the Bankruptcy and Corporate Recovery Law, indicating the list of evidence he intends to generate.

The nonexistence of the acts of bankruptcy listed in the petition must be the basis for the defense of the debtor entrepreneur concerned by the bankruptcy. The

104 Ecio PERIN JUNIOR, op. cit., 129.
105 *Id,* 130.

nonappearance of the person concerned, duly cited, shall cause the proceedings to take place in his absence. In the event that the subject is not found, the Judicial Magistrate shall proceed with the appointment of the trustee to defend him. Unlike the bankruptcy petition filed under section I, of Article 94, in conjunction with section 4, in the instruction under review (sections 4 and 5, of Article 94, in conjunction with sections II and III, all of the Bankruptcy and Corporate Recovery Law), there is no legal requirement for the citation of the businessperson in debt by means of a public notice, and for this reason it is the duty of the Judicial Magistrate to appoint a trustee.

Rubens Requião[106] states that, if there is evidence of presumed bankruptcy, the Judicial Magistrate has the power to proceed with the judicial seizure of the books and assets of the businessperson in debt. Rejection of the petition to open bankruptcy causes the entrepreneur debtor to regain full availability of his assets; with the granting or decree of bankruptcy, there is absorption of the seizure (judicial seizure of assets) by the new status of the debtor's assets, which will form the bankrupt estate.

If the Judicial Magistrate decides to deny or decree the judicial seizure of assets (seizure of assets), the appeal is against his decision (Article 54, paragraph 4 of the Bankruptcy Law).

In view of the bankruptcy petition filed by the creditor, it is opportune to analyze, at this stage, the petition filed by the debtor himself; it is the so-called self-bankruptcy, and it runs according to the legally pre-established terms in Articles 105–107 of the Bankruptcy and Corporate Recovery Law.

One of the preconditions for the debtor's application for bankruptcy is the obligation of the debtor to present the evidence that he is engaged in business activity and that he is in a situation of insolvency (economic and financial crisis), or by other, when he considers he is not in a position to file for judicial recovery, and to do so, he must disclose the causes that do not allow him to continue with the exercise of the company, showing in this case the list of necessary documents.

See *in literis* the wording of Article 105 of the Bankruptcy and Corporate Recovery Law.

> **Art. 105.** The debtor in economic and financial crisis that deems it does not meet the requirements to petition for its judicial reorganization shall petition the court for its bankruptcy, stating the reasons for the impossibility of continuing the business activity, accompanied by the following documents:

106 *Apud* Ecio PERIN JUNIOR, 138.

I— accounting statements referring to the last three (3) fiscal years and those drawn up especially to instruct the request, prepared in strict compliance with the applicable corporate legislation and obligatorily composed of
  a) balance sheet,
  b) accumulated income statement,
  c) income statement since the last fiscal year,
  d) cash flow report.

II— nominal list of creditors, indicating address, amount, nature, and rating of respective claims.

III— list of assets and rights that comprise the asset, with the respective estimate of value and documents evidencing ownership.

IV— proof of the status of businessman, articles of association or bylaws in effect, or if there are none, the indication of all partners, their addresses, and the list of their personal assets.

V— the mandatory books and accounting documents required by law.

VI— a list of its managers in the last 5 (five) years, with their addresses, their functions, and corporate participation.

On the one hand, the initial petition whose object is to request the opening of bankruptcy on the debtor's own initiative, presenting itself duly instructed, incurs in the granting by the Judicial Magistrate. On the other hand, the Judicial Magistrate has no right to issue a decree of bankruptcy if the petition is not amended after the time limit has elapsed, without the petitioner having made a statement, even if the petition is not properly processed.

The decree of bankruptcy instructed by the debtor himself cannot occur if there is a timely withdrawal; logically, the withdrawal must be presented before the Judicial Magistrate issues the breaking sentence. The businessperson in debt, self-bankruptcy petitioner, has the option of withdrawing the petition for the instauration of the contest of those who have the right to credit before him (creditors), even in a situation of legally valid assumption of self-bankruptcy, that is, the status of insolvency of those who do not meet recovery conditions (judicial recovery). Any act of manifest retraction after the issuance of the decree of bankruptcy is unlikely to produce any effect that is, therefore, ineffective. In any case, in the event of a timely withdrawal, the Judicial Magistrate must proceed with the decree of breach requested by the company in debt.[107]

It should be noted that the application for the opening of self-bankruptcy may be objected to by partners who have not signed the petition for confession

107 Fábio Ulhoa COELHO, op. cit., 265–66.

of bankruptcy. In the case of a joint stock company, the objection must be made at a general meeting.[108]

1.4.1.2 Defense

Once the bankruptcy proceedings have been initiated and the debtor who is in a state of insolvency is duly cited, he may adopt certain attitudes: (i) inertia during the analysis of facts enrolled in the initial petition as grounds for the presumed insolvency; (ii) presentation of the defense based on plausible legal reasons, within 10 (ten) days, with no deposit of elisive; (iii) presentation of the defense based on plausible legal reasons, within 10 (ten) days, with deposit of elisive; (iv) presentation of the defense, with only deposit of elisive. It is of utmost importance to emphasize that, once the elisive realization is verified, the decree of bankruptcy can no longer occur; thus, the judicial magistrate will issue a judgment denying the bankruptcy that will determine the destination of the deposit.[109]

Furthermore, even if it proves to be an unsafe mechanism, the entrepreneur in debt may proceed with the presentation of his defense without making the elisive deposit, in which situation he will be subject, in the event of the dismissal of his defense, to the probable decree of bankruptcy.

In another situation, the elisive deposit is made in cash that corresponds to the claimed credit, with the addition of the respective interest, monetary correction, attorney's fees, procedural costs, and so on. In view of this, with the elisive deposit, the decree of breach cannot be issued, since the unpunctuality will have been remedied.[110]

In the event that the unjustified unpunctuality serves as a basis for the petition for declaration of bankruptcy before the Judicial Magistrate, having the protest as evidential element, the defendant has a period of 10 (ten) days to present his defense (Article 98 of Law No. 11. 101/2005); within this time period, he has the faculty to make the elisive deposit or file the petition for judicial reorganization (a possibility that did not exist in the previous bankruptcy law). The period of ten days, now referred to, runs as soon as the business debtor is duly served (with the attached writ of summons).

Having added the petitioner to the title legitimating the enforcement action duly protested in the initial petition whose object is a petition for a declaration of bankruptcy of the defendant (debtor businessperson), based on the unjustified

108 Ecio PERIN JUNIOR, op. cit., 139.

109 Márcio GUIMARÃES, *Direito das Empresas em dificuldades* (Fundação Gentulio Vargas: Direito Rio, Graduação, 2013.2), 34.

110 *Id.*

unpunctuality, the defense may focus exclusively on matters of a procedural nature or reasons not constituting the claim, the title, or deal with extinction or suspensive reasons of the obligation to pay, or even on matters qualified as prominent.

Article 337 of the new Brazilian Civil Procedure Code (Law No. 13. 105 of March 16, 2015)[111] establishes the matters of a procedural nature that can be presented by the debtor to support his defense: I—nonexistence or nullity of the summons; II—absolute and relative incompetence; III—incorrectness of the value of the cause; IV—ineptitude of the initial petition; V—preemption; VI—lis pendens; VII—res judicata; VIII—connection; IX—incapacity of the party, defect of representation, or lack of authorization; X—arbitration agreement; XI—absence of legitimacy or procedural interest; XII—lack of bail or other performance that the law requires as a preliminary condition; XIII—undue granting of the benefit of free justice.

Article 96 of the Bankruptcy and Reorganization Law makes an exemplary consecration of those considered prominent matters; in line with the aforementioned legal provision, any decree of bankruptcy requested on the grounds of unjustified unpunctuality will be unfounded if the defendant proves it: I—falsity of title; II—prescription; III—nullity of obligation or title; IV—payment of the debt; V—any other fact that extinguishes or suspends an obligation or does not legitimize the collection of a title; VI—defect in protest or in its instrument; VII—presentation of a request for judicial reorganization within the term of the defense, in compliance with the requirements of article. VIII—termination of business activities more than two (2) years prior to the bankruptcy petition, as evidenced by a capable document from the Company Public Registry, which shall not prevail against evidence of exercise subsequent to the registered act.

Dismissal of the decree of bankruptcy can happen based on a protest carried out by a third party (protest by loan), requiring the entrepreneur in debt to present evidence that any of the defenses enshrined in Article 96 of the Constitution could be utilized to oppose the protestor's request. Another type of dismissal is the dismissal of the declaration of the bankruptcy of the joint stock company after the liquidation and distribution of its assets and of the estate after one (1) year from the termination of the debtor's legal personality.[112]

111 In the previous Civil Procedure Code (Law 5.869 of 11 January 1973), part of those procedural matters were listed in the Article 301.

112 Cfr. § 1º do artigo 96 da Lei de Falências e de Recuperação de Empresas.

In the event the businessperson in debt substantiates his defense based on the prominent matter, the Judicial Magistrate may grant a period of five (5) days to present evidence supporting his defense; after the said period, the case file will be concluded for sentencing. Pursuant to paragraph 2 of the said Article 96, *"The defenses provided for in items I to VI of the main section of this article shall not prevent the decree of bankruptcy if, at the end, there are obligations not met by the defenses in an amount exceeding the limit provided for in that provision."*

1.4.1.3 Decision

Under Article 100 of the Bankruptcy and Corporate Recovery Law, the court decision is the means by which the Judicial Magistrate decides the petition to open bankruptcy; in turn, the decision may be favorable to the petition, and in these situations we are faced with a declaratory sentence of bankruptcy; it may not be favorable if the petition is unfounded and in such conditions it is said that the sentence is denial of bankruptcy.

1.4.1.3.1 Declaratory Sentence of Bankruptcy

The granting of bankruptcy petition by means of a court decision is the third assumption of bankruptcy status. It is a decision that introduces into the legal system a legal situation that brings with it a diversity of extremely serious results about the person, property, and contractual relations of the businessperson in debt. Two stages can be identified in the bankruptcy proceedings: (i) cognitive—it starts with the opening of bankruptcy petition and ends with the respective decree; (ii) tender executive—it is the phase that marks the beginning of real bankruptcy, a phase that introduces the universal tender execution.

Until bankruptcy is decreed judicially, the situation of insolvency is considered factual and will only become legally effective as soon as the Judicial Magistrate issues a decree of bankruptcy; such issuance marks the transition from a situation of fact to one of law. It should be added that the situation becomes more extensive, in addition to involving the debtor and the creditor; it becomes a situation of connecting claims over a deficient patrimonial sphere, of a new legal connection involving creditors, employers, and public authorities.

Once a new legal situation has been established—contest of creditors, and collective enforcement falling on the debtor's assets—the court sentence declaring the bankruptcy status of the businessperson in debt *"is a judicial acknowledgement in the constituent form, producing the legal state of bankruptcy."* These last words identify the legal nature of the sentence declaring bankruptcy.

Ricardo Negrão[113] stated that the sentence declaring bankruptcy is not merely a declaratory condition but one that is constitutive in nature. Pontes de Miranda, for his part, points out that

> The procedure from the petition for a decree to open bankruptcy to the sentence granting it is not in declaratory action, nor in executive action, it is in constitutive action. The decision that is made constitutes and initiates the execution, with a charge that is not the preponderant one. Note that the particularity: it is not the initial order that initiates; it is the action for enforcement of the sentence and in the action for enforcement of extrajudicial titles; it is the final sentence. What precluded were the constitutive effect and the executive; it was not the postponement of the execution, nor the execution after full cognitio. With the opening of the contest of creditors, civil or bankrupt, is that the execution is constituted and begun.[114]

From this point of view, it is understood that the decree opening the bankruptcy status of the businessperson in debt is considered essentially constitutive, since it generates a new legal situation; with regard to the debtor's assets, there is abstract pawn and integration of the bankrupt estate (subjective and objective) in the legal sphere, among other various phenomena; in this logic, the sentence cannot be deemed as being made under an executive or declaratory condition.

(a) Requirements of the Sentence

The essential requirements of the declaratory sentence of bankruptcy are common to those of the other sentence and are established in Article 489 of the new Code of Civil Procedure[115]: (I) the report, which will contain the names of the parties, the identification of the case, with the summary of the request and defense, and the record of the main events that occurred in the course of the proceedings; (II) the grounds, in which the judge will analyze questions of fact and law; and (III) the provision, in which the judge will resolve the main questions that the parties submit to him.

113 Ricardo NEGRÃO, *Manual de direito comercial e de empresa: Recuperação de Empresas e Falência; op. cit.*, 341.

114 Francisco Cavalcanti PONTES DE MIRANDE, *Tratado de Direito privado; Apud*, Ricardo NEGRÃO, *Manual de direito comercial e de empresa: Recuperação de Empresas e Falência; op. cit.*, 341.

115 The new Code of Civil Procedure is approved by Law no. 13,105 of March 16, 2015 and revokes the previous Code of Civil Procedure (Law no. 5,869 of January 11, 1973); in the new Code the essential requirements of the sentence, as mentioned above, are listed in Article 489 and in the previous one they were listed in Article 458.

(b) Elements of the Sentence

In addition to the requirements required by procedural law, Article 99 of the Bankruptcy and Corporate Recovery Law requires that the decision declaring bankruptcy contains elements whose specificity and peculiarity are inherent to bankruptcy itself. Therefore, the Judicial Magistrate, when issuing the decision of bankruptcy, must do so in compliance with the aforementioned article and its respective clauses, which include the following:

> Article 99[116] The sentence that decrees the bankruptcy of the debtor, among other provisions:
>
> (I) shall contain the summary of the request, the identification of the bankrupt and the names of those who will be its administrators at that time;
> (II) it shall fix the legal term of the bankruptcy, without being able to retroact it for more than ninety (90) days as from the petition in bankruptcy, the petition for judicial recovery or the first (1st) protest for lack of payment, excluding, for this purpose, protests that have been cancelled;
> (III) order the bankrupt to submit, within a maximum period of five (5) days, a nominal list of the creditors, stating their address, amount, nature and classification of their claims, if the latter is no longer on the file, on pain of disobedience;
> (IV) shall specify the term for credit qualifications, with due regard for the provisions of Article 7, paragraph 1 of this law;
> (V) shall order the suspension of all actions or executions against the bankrupt, except in the cases provided for in Article 6, paragraphs 1 and 2 of this law;
> (VI) prohibit any act of disposition or encumbrance of the bankrupt party's assets, subjecting them preliminarily to judicial and Committee authorization, if any, with the exception of assets whose sale is part of the debtor's normal activities if provisional continuation is authorized under the terms of the main Section, XI, of this article;
> (VII) shall determine the steps necessary to safeguard the interests of the parties involved, and may order the preventive detention of the bankrupt or his officers when requested on the basis of evidence of a crime defined in this law;
> (VIII) order the Company Public Registry and the Special Secretary of the Brazil Federal Revenue to record the bankruptcy in the debtor's registry

116 As amended by the Law nº 14.112 of 2020.

so that the expression "Bankrupt," the date of the decree of bankruptcy and the disqualification referred to in art. 102 of this law may appear;

(IX) appoint the judicial trustee, who shall perform his duties pursuant to Article 22, main Section, III, hereof, without prejudice to the provisions of Article 35, main Section, II (a), hereof;

(X) order the dispatch of letters to public bodies and offices and other entities to inform of the existence of assets and rights of the bankrupt;

(XI) rule on the provisional continuation of the bankrupt party's activities with the judicial trustee or the sealing up of establishments, with due regard for the provisions of Article 109 of this law;

(XII) shall decide, when it deems convenient, to call a general meeting of creditors to form a Committee of Creditors, and may also authorize the maintenance of the Committee, if any, in operation during judicial reorganization at the time the bankruptcy is decreed;

(XIII) shall order the electronic summoning, under the laws into force and repected the functional prerrogatives, respectively of the Public Attorney's Office and the Federal Public Treasury and of all states, federal District and Municipalities where the debtor has an establishment, so that they may become aware of the bankruptcy.

Regarding the normative content reflected in the above article, it should be noted that there is no impediment as to whether the Judicial Magistrate should designate a day and time to seek to reconcile the parties involved in the bankruptcy process, if the behavior proves to be beneficial. In the event that the parties choose to have a deal, there will be no further merit in the regular continuation of the proceedings and the proceedings will therefore be extinguished, as a result of which the proceedings cannot be suspended. In the event of failure to comply with the agreement, nothing can be done in the proceedings, since the object of an application for bankruptcy is not to collect the debt but to drive the outstanding businessperson out of the market. If there is a defense, nothing will remain with the Judicial Magistrate, if not strict compliance with the complex rules contained in the Code of Civil Procedure, until the end of the sentence, whether or not the request for the opening of bankruptcy against the debtor is favorable.[117]

Also in the context of the aforementioned article, it is interesting to comment on item XI, which deals with *"provisional continuation of the activities of the bankrupt"*; it is understood that there is no room for such a phenomenon to be verified, because the Bankruptcy and Corporate Recovery Law establishes

117 Carlos Roberto CLARO, op. cit., 221.

mechanisms, both of an economic and legal nature, for the possible restructuring of the company. Since it is impossible to restructure the company, bankruptcy is compulsory, which will lead to the bankrupt's withdrawal from the market, since he does not have sufficient conditions to continue the business activity. If the bankrupt is unable to continue to operate the business, the crisis will multiply, and so it is inconceivable that the bankrupt's assets will continue to be provisionally wound up. Certainly, continuity would generate much higher liabilities with responsibility falling on the bankruptcy estate and on the Judicial Administrator, in a personal way, according to the dictates of the National Tax Code.[118]

If in practical terms the *"provisional continuation of the bankrupt's activities"* were to be considered, difficulties of a practical nature would be encountered; the current Bankruptcy and Corporate Recovery Law (Law No. 11.101/2005) does not establish procedures to be followed in this regard, unlike Article 74[119] of the abrogated Bankruptcy Law (Decree-Law No. 7.661 of July 21, 1945). The hypothesis that is within consideration, taking into account the specificities of each case, is the continuity of the operation of machinery and equipment for a certain period of time, as a means of preserving production. If this is the case, the Judicial Administrator must be prudent and guided by common sense in order to determine whether or not the activity should be immediately halted, as well as the machinery disconnected.[120]

118 *Id.*, 221–22.

119 *This legal provision was worded as follows: "Art. 74: The Bankrupt may request the continuation of his business; after hearing the receiver and the Public Prosecutor's Representative on the convenience of the request, the judge, if he accepts, will appoint a suitable person proposed by the receiver to manage it. § Paragraph 1. The continuation of business, except in exceptional cases and at the discretion of the judge, may only be granted after the collection has been completed and the inventories have been added to the bankruptcy record. § Paragraph 2. The manager, whose salary, like that of the other two officers, shall be hired by the liquidator upon approval by the judge, shall be subject to the immediate supervision of the liquidator and shall enter the seats of the transactions in special books, which shall be opened, numbered and initialed by them; Paragraph 3. The manager shall sign, in the records, an instrument as depositary of the assets of the estate delivered to him, and shall perform his duties well and faithfully, reporting to the liquidator. § 4 Purchases and sales shall be in cash; in special cases, with the agreement of the liquidator and the representative of the Public Prosecution Service, the judge may authorize purchases for payment within thirty days. Sales may not be made at a lower price than that stated in the valuation, unless the judge authorizes it. § 5 The manager shall collect, on a daily basis, from the establishment designated to receive money from the dough (art. 209), the amounts received on the preceding day and, at the end of each week, shall submit, to be attached to the records that shall be formed separately: I—the list of goods acquired and sold and their respective prices, characterizing the business that, in accordance with the preceding paragraph, has been done on time; II—the statement of general expenses corresponding to the week, including rent and salary of proposals. § Paragraph 6. The judge, at the request of the receiver or creditors, after hearing the representative of the Public Prosecution Service, may terminate the authorization to continue the bankrupt party's business. § 7 Authorization shall cease if the bankrupt does not request concordat within the period provided for in Article 178, or, if he has done so, when his request is decided in the first instance."*

120 Carlos Roberto CLARO, *op. cit.*, 222.

The sentence declaring bankruptcy must obey the principle of publicity. This principle is established in the sole paragraph of Article 99 of Law 11.101/2005. From this perspective, it is up to the Judicial Magistrate to order the publication of a notice covering the complete context of the declaratory decision and the relationship of the creditors, for the knowledge of the creditors themselves as well as any third person (or persons).

With regard to the list of creditors, in accordance with item III of Article 9, a period of five (5) days is determined for the businessperson declared bankrupt to join the list of creditors; if the bankrupt does not observe such a legal command, he will incur on a legal type of crime, that is, disobedience. The above-mentioned inclusion of the nominal list is a fundamental assumption for the publication of a public notice; without such a list, it does not occur. If the public notice is not published, the period established in paragraph 2 of Article 7 of the Bankruptcy and Corporate Recovery Law does not begin to run. Paragraph (a), item I of Article 22 of the same law states that, as far as creditors are concerned, the term may start to run as soon as they receive the correspondence from the Judicial Trustee; however, the prevailing understanding is that, in the absence of a list of creditors, the publication of the notice cannot be made due to the consequent noncompliance with the sole paragraph of Article 99 of the Act.[121]

The necessary elements in the bankruptcy sentence include the legal term of the bankruptcy. It is subsection II of the present judgment that requires such an element.

Legal term should be understood as the time lapse in which the bankruptcy status of the businessperson in debt is seen, with the aim of establishing the revocation of acts that prove to be detrimental to the interests of creditors or acts that the law presumes to be fraudulent. Based on this understanding, the legal term of bankruptcy is configured as a complex of guarantees and efficient mechanisms, which assist creditors in obtaining payment of their credit rights; hence, it is in this context that Law 11. 101/2005, in its Article 124, states that *"Interest accrued after the decree of bankruptcy, provided for by law or by contract, shall not be payable against the bankrupt estate if the assets ascertained are not sufficient for the payment of the subordinated creditors"*; however, it must take into account the sole paragraph of the aforementioned article, since it makes exceptions to the interest on debentures and secured claims.[122]

121 *Id.*

122 Márcio GUIMARÃES, *op. cit.*, 53.

It is well known that one of the behaviors that can be undertaken by a businessperson in debt in order not to have his bankruptcy decreed is the use of acts of a cunning nature, of means vested with unlawfulness, of fraudulent acts or harmful acts against creditors, in order to obtain his own benefit. It is for this reason that this period of time is likely to be break if any unlawful or fraudulent acts are carried out by the bankrupt that result in damage to the bankrupt estate; it is within the framework of the doctrine known as the *"suspect period."* In the meanderings of the doctrine, with certain exceptions, the period of the suspect period is considered to be much more comprehensive than the period of the legal term since it is preexists the legal term.[123]

A warning is issued by Giorgio de Semo[124] regarding the manner in which the said *"suspect period"* is determined, and there is a duality of systems for this: (i) a judicial determination system, in which the judge, either of his own motion or through a court of the interested parties, proceeds with the determination of the "suspect period" in relation to the declaratory sentence or other successive sentences, without in the meantime losing the limit previously established in relation to the beginning of the insolvency *("precedent Italian system")* or without a maximum limit (French system) and (ii) a legal determination system; here, it is the legislator who establishes the duration of the *"suspect periods"* in relation to the nature of the different categories of acts (German-type legislation).

In view of what has been said in the above paragraph, the suspect period would correspond to the moment when the indebted businessperson begins to carry out acts that are likely to create harm to creditors, a fact that indirectly reflects the situation of insolvency that has not hitherto entered the legal world of bankruptcy and which would be typified by the decree of bankruptcy. These are therefore acts that were carried out before the sentence was issued and whose effects are already creating damage in the sphere of third parties.

For Tavares Paes, *"the suspect period is the time before the bankruptcy, assuming the practice by the debtor of desperate or fraudulent acts. In the case of donations, or renunciation of inheritance, for example, the bankruptcy law set the suspect period at two years before the declaration of bankruptcy. The legal term is the last part of the suspect period before the declaration of bankruptcy and is set by the judge in the declaratory breaking sentence."*[125]

123 Carla Eugénio Caldas BARROS, *Manual de Direito Empresarial: Direito Falimentar e Recuperacional;* Multifacetado; Vol. III (Arcaju: PIDCC, 2014), 31.

124 *Apud* Carla Eugénio Caldas BARROS, op. cit., 30.

125 P. R. Tavares PAES, *Curso de Falências e Concordata; apud* Carla Eugénio Caldas BARROS, op. cit., 30–31.

It is now appropriate to comment on Article 99(II), and this time the focus is on the part where the retroactive nature of the legal term of bankruptcy is referred to has the limit of 90 (ninety) days prior to the first protest suffered by the bankrupt; this means that the judge may proceed to determine this time lapse already starting from the first protested title, considering that the financial crisis of the company, under normal conditions, does not know an immediate installation; however, it occurs through a chain of events that follow.

(c) Appeals against the Judgment Declaring the Bankruptcy

In accordance with Article 100 of Law No. 11101/2005, and in objection to the sentence declaring bankruptcy, an appeal may be lodged. It should be noted that the bankruptcy procedure adopted in this law is a peculiar system of appeal and therefore differs from that established in the Code of Civil Procedure in force, given that under the terms of the bankruptcy law, while there is an interlocutory appeal against the sentence, under the Civil Procedural Law (Article 1009),[126] there is an appeal and an interlocutory appeal against interlocutory decisions (Article 1015).[127]

When the decree of opening of bankruptcy has been passed, the debtor businessperson, the creditors, third parties suffering damages, and the Public Prosecutor's Office are assisted by the legitimacy to appeal against the bankruptcy decision and may, as previously seen, file an interlocutory appeal within the time limit provided for in the Code of Civil Procedure, since the bankruptcy law does not rule on the time limits for appeals, in which case the application of procedural law is shown to be a force of the principle of subsidiarity. It should be noted that the sentence declaring bankruptcy lacks suspensive effect and therefore does not prevent it from being complied with immediately; however, it may be possible to suspend its immediate effect, by being successful in this regard, before the rapporteur of the appeal before the court.[128]

If the court rejects the appeal against the interlocutory appeal, the debtor himself, the creditors who have not been satisfied, and third parties who have suffered damage may lodge an appeal with double effect. If the appeal is known and well-founded, the court may order the opening of the bankruptcy and will comply with the sentence by the judge of the first degree, strictly observing the

126 In the revoked Civil Procedure Code (Law No. 5.869 of 11 January 1973), it corresponded to Article 513 of the Civil Procedure Code.

127 In the revoked Civil Procedure Code (Law No. 5.869 of 11 January 1973), it corresponded to Article 522 of the Civil Procedure Code.

128 Carlos Roberto CLARO, op. cit., 223.

elements of Article 99 of the EC Treaty. There is no impediment to the declaration of the second degree of jurisdiction, and there is no room to speak of a suspension of the instance.[129]

(d) Effects of the Declaratory Sentence of Bankruptcy

The sentence declaring bankruptcy has a variety of legal effects, affecting those who, in the eyes of the bankrupt, are entitled to credit (creditors) on the person of the bankrupt himself, his assets, acts, and contracts.

- **Legal Effects on the Person of the Bankrupt**

First of all, it must be made clear that the legal effects on the person of the bankrupt are projected to the partners who are answerable to the company without limit.

It should be noted that, with regard to the civil capacity of the bankrupt (aptitude to exercise his rights and obligations of a civil nature), this remains intact; however, in the context of the bankruptcy proceedings, there are limitations, as will be seen below—he loses the right to administer and dispose of the assets that he had in his possession and which become an integral part of the objective bankruptcy estate.[130]

The debtor businessperson, now declared bankrupt, shall be prevented from administering his assets or disposing of them, by virtue of Article 103 of the bankruptcy law and, as a result, shall be disqualified from developing the company (corporate activity); this can be seen in Article 2 of the same law; the aforementioned effects of disqualification shall be felt by the director or manager convicted of a bankruptcy crime.

The limitation of freedom of movement is also one of the legal effects on the person of the bankrupt, whether this means that, under the law, the bankrupt must remain in the physical space where the processing of the bankruptcy takes place; however, they may be absent with the express authorization of the magistrate, and this in turn must be based on a plausible reason, which derives from Article 104, item III, of the Constitution. The permanence of the bankrupt at the place where the bankruptcy is processed is justified by the fact that at any time he may be called upon to provide clarifications before the bankruptcy court, and

129 *Id.*
130 Etiane Barbi KÖHLER, *op. cit.*, 19.

if, as a result, he fails to observe such normative command among others of the same nature, he may be held liable for the crime of disobedience.

With regard to the civil capacity of the bankrupt (aptitude for the exercise of his rights and fulfilment of obligations of a civil nature), this remains intact; however, in the context of bankruptcy proceedings, his capacity is subject to limitations; as can be seen below, he loses the right to administer and dispose of his assets, since they become a bankrupt estate.

- **Legal Effects on Creditors**

The interpretation of Article 115 of the Bankruptcy and Corporate Recovery Law reveals that the universality of creditors, without discrimination as to the nature of their credit, whether commercial or civil, has the duty to apply to the bankruptcy court; hence, they must plead and present evidence of their right to credit before the judge. To this end, they benefit from the habilitation of creditors (free of procedural costs), as a procedural means, and have a period of 15 (fifteen) days from the publication of the public notice containing the entire decree of bankruptcy, pursuant to paragraph 1 of the article, in conjunction with the sole paragraph of Article 99, all of the aforementioned law, in strict compliance with the normative content contained in Article 9 of the same law.

In accordance with paragraph 2 of Article 7 of the current law, upon expiry of the above-mentioned period, the person in charge of the judicial administration of the bankruptcy (trustee) shall be assisted for a period of 45 (forty-five) days to publish the notice containing the list of creditors that is going to be based on the information and documents gathered. After this stage, the time limit for the session of the impugnations in the parameters of Articles 8, 11, 12, 13, 15, 16, and 17 of the bankruptcy law begins.

If there are no oppositions, nothing is left for the Judicial Magistrate to decide, except to approve the general framework of creditors, based on the list (of creditors) previously published in the public notice. The Judicial Administrator shall be responsible for consolidating the general framework of creditors, whereby the homologation of which shall be made by the magistrate; therefore, the framework shall require the signature of both the magistrate and the judicial trustee and shall contain the importance of the claims and the classification of each one according to its nature.

The condition for creditors to compete with the proceeds of the estate (the complex of assets collected from the bankrupt) is that the estate should be qualified within the time limit set by the magistrate. Creditors subject to the habilitation must be deemed to constitute the subjective bankruptcy estate (complex of creditors of the bankrupt).

If the creditor does not submit to the empowerment process within the time limit laid down, there is no obstacle for the creditor to submit to a subsequent empowerment process; however, if a certain claim has already been paid for, he will have no right to it and only the claim that remains. A creditor under these conditions, in accordance with paragraphs 2–6 of Article 10, is called debtor in arrears.

For bankruptcy reasons, the Bankruptcy and Corporate Recovery Law was cautious in including in its system, in Articles 83 and 84, the classification of creditors; such classification should serve as a basis for making payments, subject to certain situations. The payment of claims should follow the sequence of classes; this means the creditors of a particular class will only receive their claims when the creditors of the previous class have been paid.

Under the terms of Article 77 of the Bankruptcy and Corporate Recovery Law, *"The decree of bankruptcy determines the early maturity of the debts of the debtor and of the partners who are unlimited and jointly and severally liable, with the proportional reduction of interest, and converts all credits in foreign currency into the currency of the country, at the exchange rate on the day of the judicial decision, for all purposes of this law."* It should be noted that there are exceptions to this legal provision, in the sense that debts resulting from obligations dependent on the suspensive condition, joint and several obligations contracted with third parties and obligations that have their source in unilateral and bilateral contracts that the trustee decides to fulfill in the interest of the masses will not be due in advance.

Under Article 6 of the Bankruptcy Law, the issuing of a sentence declaring bankruptcy suspends the course of the limitation period and the universality of the actions and executions brought against the debtor (now declared bankrupt), including those of the private creditors of the joint or multiple partners.

- **Legal Effects on the Assets of the Bankrupt**

The complex of assets that is an integral part of the bankrupt's estate, which is the subject of the declaratory sentence of bankruptcy, is subject to collection and becomes an objective bankrupt estate.[131] That complex of assets will be liquidated, so that with the proceeds of the sale, those who have the right to credit (creditors) will be paid by the bankrupt. The collection also extends to the books

131 See Article 108 of Law 11. 101/2005.

and all the documentation of the bankrupt. In accordance with paragraph 4 of Article 108 of the bankruptcy law in force, there is no collection of assets whose unseizability is absolute.

In the wording of Article 110, *"The tax assessment record, composed by the inventory and the respective valuation report of the assets, shall be signed by the trustee, by the bankrupt or his representatives and by other persons assisting or witnessing the act."* With regard to this legal provision, it should be noted that the bankrupt continues to have the right of ownership over his assets; however, he loses the right to administer them, even though that right lasts until the liquidation takes place, or by other means, until the assets are judicially sold. Article 111, on the other hand, makes room for the acquisition or adjudication of assets by creditors, as well as for the order of preference of creditors, taking into account the value of the evaluation of the assets; in the meantime, the authorization of the judge and the hearing of the committee of creditors are required.

Due to the perishable or deteriorative nature, or the easy propensity to depreciate certain assets, or even to the expenditure or risks that may result from their conservation, it is possible, by means of the magistrate's authorization, hearing the committee of creditors and the bankrupt, to bring forward the sale of the assets of the nature described, after having been collected and evaluated, within 48 hours.[132]

- **Legal Effects on the Bankrupt's Acts and Contracts**

The Bankruptcy and Corporate Recovery Law was cautious in establishing a distinction between the acts performed by the bankrupt, the ineffectiveness,[133] and the acts that may be revoked[134]; around these types of acts, it should be noted that none of them produce effects of the bankruptcy estate.

As a general rule, acts of ineffectiveness have as their fundamental characteristic the fact that their ineffectiveness is conditioned by the execution of the act within a certain period of time—a suspect period prior to the declaration of bankruptcy, a legal term of bankruptcy established by the judicial magistrate in the decision declaring bankruptcy—and fraud does not characterize them. The declaration of ineffectiveness may be declared *ex-officio* by the magistrate, or defendant in defense through his own action or by incidental proceedings.

132 See Article 113 of Law 11.101/2005.
133 See Article 129 of Law 11.101/2005.
134 See Article 130 of Law 11.101/2005.

With regard to acts that can be revoked, they are identifiable by the fraud and by the presentation of evidence that the bankrupt and the third person with whom he has contracted have proceeded fraudulently. The time at which the act was carried out, near or far from the issuing of the sentence declaring bankruptcy,[135] does not have such importance. The revocation action brought by the judicial trustee, by any person who has a claim on the bankrupt (creditor), or by the Public Prosecutor's Office is the precondition for the revocation of the fraudulently executed acts.[136]

The revocation or ineffectiveness regime will not be applicable against acts performed by the bankrupt within the parameters provided for in Article 131 of Law 11.101/2005.

Contracts. In the wordings of Article 117, *"Bilateral contracts are not rescinded by bankruptcy and may be performed by the trustee if performance reduces or prevents an increase in the liabilities of the bankrupt estate or is necessary for the maintenance and preservation of its assets, subject to the Committee's authorization."* With regard to this legal command, it should be noted that the decree of bankruptcy carries with it the consequence of terminating bilateral contracts in which neither party has begun to comply with the complex of obligations.[137]

Regarding to unilateral contracts, in which the bankrupt becomes a debtor, a sentence declaring bankruptcy is issued in advance.[138] In the meantime, it is convenient to make room for the performance of the due instalment and the authorization of the Committee of Creditors is essential.[139] In cases where the bankrupt becomes a creditor, the unilateral contract remains intact, and the judicial trustee, in the event of nonperformance by the debtor, must proceed to find a satisfactory means of credit.

There is no termination of employment contracts with the issuing of the sentence declaring bankruptcy; however, the termination takes place with the cessation of corporate activities.

The bankruptcy law in force, in its Article 119, establishes a series of rules around various contractual relations. *In litteris,* the provisions of the article in question are set out below.

135 See Article 130 of Law 11.101/2005.
136 See Article 132 in conjunction with Article 130, both of Law 11.101/2005.
137 Etiane Barbi KÖHLER, op. cit., 20.
138 See Article 77 of Law 11.101/2005.
139 See Article 77 of Law 11.101/2005.

Article 119: The following rules shall prevail in the contractual relations mentioned below:

I. the seller may not obstruct the delivery of goods dispatched to the debtor and still in transit, if the buyer, before filing for bankruptcy, has resold them, without fraud, in sight of the invoices and bills of lading, delivered or remitted by the seller;
II. if the debtor has sold composite goods and the trustee terminates the contract no longer, the buyer may make the goods already received available to the bankruptcy estate, claiming loss and damages;
III. if the debtor has not delivered a movable item or provided a service that he had sold or contracted on installments, and if the trustee resolves not to perform the contract, the claim relating to the amount paid shall be entitled in the proper class;
IV. the trustee, after hearing the Committee, shall return the movable item purchased by the debtor with the seller's retention of title if he resolves not to continue the performance of the contract, demanding the return, pursuant to the contract, of the amounts paid;
V. in the case of things sold for a term, which are quoted on the stock exchange or market, and if the contract is not performed by actual delivery of the same and payment of the price, the difference between the quotation on the day of the contract and that at the time of settlement on the stock exchange or market shall be provided;
VI. the respective legislation shall apply to the promise of purchase and sale of real estate;
VII. the bankruptcy of the lessor shall not terminate the lease contract and, in the bankruptcy of the lessee, the trustee may, at any time, terminate the contract;
VIII. if there is an agreement for the clearing and settlement of obligations within the national financial system, under the terms of the legislation in force, the non-bankrupt party may consider the contract due in advance, in which case it will be settled in the form established by regulation, with the possibility of offsetting any credit that may be established in favor of the bankrupt with credits held by the contractor;
IX. the segregate estates, constituted for the performance of a specific purpose, shall comply with the provisions of the respective legislation, their assets, rights and obligations remaining separate from those of the bankrupt party until the advent of the respective term or until the performance of their purpose, at which time the trustee shall collect the balance in favor of the bankrupt estate or register the remaining credit against it in the proper class.

In adherence to Article 120 of the Bankruptcy Law, the decree of bankruptcy implies the cessation of the effects of the mandate granted by the bankrupt for the execution of acts of negotiation, and it is the responsibility of the judicial trustee to account for his management.[140] The mandate for judicial representation shall remain effective until it is expressly revoked by the trustee. With regard to the mandate granted to the bankrupt, except for matters outside the company's object, it is ineffective with the decree of bankruptcy.

The matter relating to the offsetting of the bankrupt's debts and claims is governed by Article 122 of the Bankruptcy Law, under which *"the debts of the debtor that have fallen due up to the day of the decree of bankruptcy shall be offset, with preference over all other creditors, whether or not they fall due, in accordance with the requirements of civil legislation."* However, claims whose transfer occurs after the declaration of bankruptcy are not offset, except in cases of succession by merger, incorporation, division, or *mortis causa* (sole paragraph, I); nor is offsetting of claims, even if they are due before the declaration of bankruptcy and whose transfer is made when the condition of the debtor's economic-financial crisis is already known or claims transferred fraudulently or willfully (sole paragraph, II).

The requirement of accrued interest is untenable on the bankruptcy estate after the declaration of bankruptcy—the provision for which is laid down by law or in the contract—if the assets established are insufficient to satisfy the claims of the creditors and subordinates.[141] An exception to the rule of this legal command is the interest on debentures and secured claims, but the proceeds of the assets constituting the guarantee are the exclusive responsibility of the debenture holders.[142]

1.4.1.4 Sentence Denying Bankruptcy

There are two distinct factors that can lead to denial of bankruptcy (through the denial sentence): (i) the rejection of the application on the basis of the deposit of the arrears by the debtor (defendant)—the prevailing consideration is that there is succession, on the assumption that if he did not make the deposit, he would inevitably go bankrupt and (ii) the merits of the grounds put forward in the defense—in this case, the succession falls on the applicant (plaintiff in the bankruptcy proceedings). As can be seen, the two cases differ in the succession.[143]

140 See § 1 of Article 120 of Law 11.101/2005.
141 See Article 124 of Law 11.101/2005.
142 See Sole paragraph of article 124 of Law 11.101/2005.
143 Fábio Ulhoa COELHO, *op. cit.*, 271.

The party (plaintiff/defendant) to whom the succession relates will be liable for the procedural costs and lawyer's fees established by the magistrate for the benefit of the lawyer of the party who wins the case. In certain cases, the succession fees will be established in settlement of denial sentence, which will be processed in accordance with the provisions of the Code of Civil Procedure, followed by enforcement, as in the case of other sentences of a condemnatory nature.

If the defendant, at the same time, proceeds with the defense and proceeds with the deposit of the elisive, nothing remains for the magistrate if he does not proceed with the assessment of the two mechanisms used by the debtor businessperson. The effect of the deposit is to prevent creditors from taking part in the invitation to tender, but it is essential to check whether the applicant's intention was well-founded in order to define the succession. If the sentence denouncing the claim is issued with a reason that is not an elision but acceptance of the merits of the defense, the amount of the deposit will be withdrawn by the defendant himself and not by the claimant.[144]

Finally, it should be noted that the plaintiff who brought the action for which the application to open bankruptcy was made is guilty of a conviction and that if he did so intentionally, the conviction will be made effective in the judgment dismissing the application.[145] Joint and several liability arises in the event of a plurality of claimants.[146] Third parties who suffer damage caused by the wrongful applicant will also have a right to compensation, and for that right to become effective they must demand it in their own proceedings.[147]

It must be taken into account that compensation in the context of Article 100 of Law No. 11.101/2005 is only admitted when the denial of the bankruptcy petition is based on the examination of the merits.[148]

1.4.2 Administration Period

The administration period is the phase in which the creditor's entitlement to verification of claims takes place and the frame of those who is entitled to credit (creditors) from the bankrupt begins to be formed; it is still at this stage that the debtor's complex of assets and documentation is collected and the illegalities are ascertained.

144 *Id.*

145 See Article 101 of Law 11.101/2005.

146 See § 1 of article 101 of Law 11.101/2005.

147 See § 2 of Article 101 of Law 11.101/2005.

148 "Civil Appeal 246.063 – 1 – São Paulo, 9.º Câmara de Direito Privado, Repporteur Brenno Marcondes, 04.06.1996, v.u.; on this, Ecio PERIN JUNIOR, op. cit., 153.

The Judicial Magistrate, the Public Prosecutor's Office (well-represented), and the bankruptcy bodies (judicial trustee, creditors' meeting, and the creditors' committee) are the three actors in charge of administering bankruptcy. The role of the magistrate is to preside over the administration of the bankruptcy, the Public Prosecutor's Office (well represented) assumes the role of supervising the law in the context of the bankruptcy procedure, and the Judicial Administrator's role is to assist the magistrate and the representative of the communion of interests of those who have a right to credit before the bankrupt (subjective mass).

As for the bankruptcy bodies, at this stage it is convenient to talk about the Judicial Trustee, because he has a fundamental role in the bankruptcy process and the others (the creditors' meeting and the creditors' committee) take on a greater role in the business recovery process.

It is the magistrate who issues the declaratory sentence, who makes the appointment of the Judicial Trustee in the respective sentence, pursuant to item IX, Article 99 of Law 11.101/2005. The Judicial Trustee may be a natural person as well as a legal person, appointed by the judge, and they may be chosen from among professionals of the legal sphere, accounting, economics, business administration, or specialized legal person; this is derived from Article 21 of the aforementioned law.

Also under the terms of Article 33 of the aforementioned law, the appointment of a director by a judge presupposes their immediate appearance in the bankruptcy court, by means of a summons, to sign within 48 hours the term of commitment indicating that they will exercise the office faithfully and assume the responsibilities pertaining to the office. The system of impediments relating to the exercise of the office of trustee is listed in Article 30 of the current legislation.

The Judicial Magistrate shall fix the remuneration of the trustee and in doing so shall take into account the debtor's capacity to pay, the level of complexity of the work, and the values practiced in the market for carrying out similar activities.[149] As a general rule, a maximum limit of 5 % of the amount due to the creditors or of the amount established shall be paid in full by the trustee.[150]

It should be noted that the bankruptcy law makes room for the replacement of the judicial trustee; such replacement may be based on supervening civil incapacity, duly justified resignation, bankruptcy, or even *mortis causa*. Even if the replacement of the judicial trustee is based on these reasons, he will be paid in the respective proportion of the work he will have done. It is essential to point out

149 See Article 24 of Law 11.101/2005.

150 See § 1, Article 124 of Law 11.101/2005.

that the judicial trustee's remuneration cannot be paid if his replacement is based on his resignation without a plausible reason or on his dismissal from office due to indolence, guilt, malice, or failure to comply with the obligations arising from the bankruptcy law.[151] The disapproval of the trustee's accounts shall also constitute grounds for his non-remuneration.[152]

The magistrate shall be granted the power of his own motion or at the request of any interested party to order the removal of the trustee from office if the trustee fails to comply with the legal requirements arising from the bankruptcy law, fails to fulfil the duties inherent to his office, or if, by his omission, indolence, or execution of acts, harms the debtor's activities or third parties.[153] And any appointment of the trustee in another bankruptcy proceeding may only take place after five (5) years have elapsed since the time of his dismissal. Certainly, the removal of the judicial trustee from office implies the appointment of another by the judge; this follows from the first part of paragraph 1 of Article 31 of the Bankruptcy Law.

The consequence of the behavior prior mentioned, on the part of the trustee, is not only limited to his dismissal; it may also lead to the civil liability of this bankruptcy officer, and it is in this context that Etiane Köhler offers the view that

> A trustee who has caused damage to the bankrupt estate, the creditors or the debtor by intent or recklessness in the performance of his duties, after having been dismissed, during the bankruptcy proceedings, may only be sued for civil liability by the new trustee appointed. If this does not occur, after the bankruptcy has been closed, the creditor who has been individually injured, if he has requested the removal of the trustee, may seek to hold him liable for the losses suffered.[154]

As a duty of the role, the judicial trustee shall verify the claims—with such duty accruing from the normative content contained in Articles 7–20 of the bankruptcy law—and proceed with the collection of assets, books, and documentation of the bankrupt; proceed with the initial report, pursuant to paragraph (e), item III of Article 22 of the same law; shall proceed to present every month the administration's statement account, pursuant to paragraph (e), item III of Article 22 of the same law and item 22 of the current law; make the final report within

151 See § 3, article 124 of Law 11.101/2005.
152 See § 4, article 124 of Law 11.101/2005.
153 See Second part of § 3, article 24 of Law 11.101/2005.
154 Etiane Barbi KÖHLER, op. cit., 22.

10 (ten) days after the judgement of its accounts; the respective report shall indicate the value of the liabilities, the payments made to the creditors, and shall make a justified specification of the responsibilities with which the bankrupt will continue, in accordance with Article 155 of the Bankruptcy Law.

1.4.3 Liquidation Period

The liquidation period is the final stage of the bankruptcy procedure. The aim of this phase is to perform the assets through the sale of the assets collected and the payment of the liabilities and, thus, to satisfy the creditors admitted, in accordance with the respective distribution by classes.

In the context of liquidation, it should be noted that the credit class of a labor nature, as it is strictly linked to the principle or values of human dignity and is still of a maintenance nature, is prioritized over the other bankruptcy estate expenditures and still over those considered essential for the temporary continuation of the bankrupt's activities. This understanding results from the interpretation of Article 151 of the Bankruptcy Law, which reads as follows: *"Labor claims of a strictly wage nature that fall due in the 3 (three) months prior to the decree of bankruptcy, up to a limit of 5 (five) minimum wages per worker, shall be paid as soon as cash is available."*

This is a legal provision that does not allow an extensive interpretation, in the sense that it only includes the credit class of a labor-related nature that is restricted to wages; therefore, this concept does not include, for instance, overdue holidays, the 13th (thirteenth) salary, prior notice, and others of this kind. These credits must be qualified in bankruptcy, where they will participate in the apportionments.[155]

In the bankruptcy system (Decree-Law 7.661/1945) preceding that in force (Law 11.101/2005), it contained a provision of disposal of assets collected, either as a whole or separately, but this was a provision of a singular nature, lacking the comprehensive and dynamic character of the current system.[156]

The Bankruptcy Law in force establishes alternative means of disposal of the assets of the businessperson now declared bankrupt and makes room for the agents of the bankruptcy to choose the most convenient alternative for the interests of the bankrupt estate and, consequently, the creditors (subjective bankrupt

155 Luiz Marcelo Souza ROCHA, "Do pagamento aos créditos", in *Comentários à Lei 11.101/05: Recuperação Empresarial e Falência* (Curitiba, Paraná: OAB, 2017), 293.

156 Under the current bankruptcy law, under the terms of Article 140, the assets collected may be sold singly or in their entirety and such sale may be made by auction, closed bidding, or trading, in accordance with the method that best satisfies the interests of creditors (see items I, II, and III of Article 142).

estate). Such alternatives are commonly referred to as *"ordinary forms of alienation of assets"*: (i) *disposal of the company with the sale of its premises en bloc*—this tends to be characterized by a higher degree of profitability, since it is assumed that it can generate more monetary value for the bankruptcy estate. However, such a presumption does not always coincide with reality, since it is rare for the purchaser to take an interest in all the premises, and it is in this context that the bankruptcy law was cautious in proposing a second alternative means; (ii) *sale of the company with the sale of its subsidiaries or production units separately.*[157]

If the two alternative means were not successful in the past, the bankrupt's assets will be sold, preferably *en bloc* and at the end individually.

It is of utmost importance to highlight that in the process of the sale of the company, the assets that are essential to the development of the economic activity by its successor, as well as the maintenance of contractual legal relations established by the bankrupt with third parties, must be an integral part of the sale.

Special attention should be paid to Article 141(II) of the Bankruptcy Law, which expressly removes any burden on the object of disposal and does so in the following terms: *"the object of the disposal shall be free of any encumbrances and there shall be no succession of the winning bidder to the debtor's obligations, including those of a tax nature, those deriving from labor legislation and those arising from occupational accidents."*

Once the sale of the scheduled assets has been concluded and payment of the creditors has been made, the trustee must submit his accounts to the courts within 30 (thirty) days.[158] Once the judge has judged the respective accounts, the trustee shall produce and submit the final report on the bankruptcy within ten (10) days, and in this report he shall indicate the value of the assets and the proceeds from their realization, the value of the liabilities, and the value of payments made to creditors.[159] Once these facts have been verified, the Judicial Magistrate will be responsible for issuing the sentence declaring the conclusion or closure of the bankruptcy proceedings, culminating in its publication in the public notice.

The businessperson, now declared bankrupt, must apply for the declaration of the extinction of the bond complex to which he was bound.[160] If the bankrupt is not responding to criminal proceedings or is not being prosecuted in this regard or has been acquitted by a final sentence, with the extinction of his

157 Filipe de POLI, "Da realização do ativo," in *Comentários à Lei 11.101/05: Recuperação Empresarial e Falência* (Curitiba, Paraná: OAB, 2017), 281–82.

158 See Article 154 of Law 11.101/2005.

159 See Article 155 of Law 11.101/2005.

160 See Article 158 of Law 11.101/2005.

bond complex, space is opened for him to proceed once again with the exploration of the economic activity of a corporate nature; in the meantime, if he is in the opposite situation, he must also apply for his criminal rehabilitation, which can only be granted after 5 (five) years have elapsed since the extinction of the punishment.[161]

2. Corporate Recovery

It is of great relevance to note that in this day and age bankruptcy and recovery legal institutes are disciplined under the Bankruptcy and Corporate Recovery Law (Law No. 11. 101/2005), which revokes Decree-Law No. 7.661 of June 21, 1945 (the former Bankruptcy Law).

In the revoked law—Brazilian Bankruptcy Law—the legal institute of concordat was in force, which in the system of bankruptcy law in force was replaced by the legal institute of Corporate Recovery. The respective law divides the above institute into two modalities: (I) Judicial Recovery: (a) ordinary or common judicial recovery[162]—in this case, by means of legal action, toward judicial bodies, the businessperson seeks to put an end to his economic and financial crisis with a view to lifting his economic and financial condition; (b) special judicial recovery (for micro and small companies)[163]; and (II) extrajudicial recovery[164]—the mechanisms adopted to avert the economic and financial crisis occur outside the judicial sphere and are therefore the result of an agreement between the debtor and the creditors (extrajudicial recovery that can be ratified and therefore ratified by the judicial authorities), or an agreement between the parties, creditors, and debtor, which does not require ratification by the judicial authorities (judicial recovery that cannot be ratified).

In the light of the above, it should be added that the current Bankruptcy Law has two main features: (i) *"to facilitate the recovery of companies and, consequently, to maintain the level of employment, to maintain the collection of taxes and finally to maintain the possibility of circulation of assets and services"*; and (ii) *"to provide greater agility so that creditors can recover, with minimum legal security, their assets and rights. As they will have more guarantees on the credit granted, it is also expected that the charges levied to compensate for default will be reduced."*[165]

161 Etiane Barbi KÖHLER, op. cit., 23.
162 See Article 47 to 69, of Law 11.101/2005.
163 See Article 70 to 72, of Law 11.101/2005.
164 See Article 161 to 167, of Law 11.101/2005.
165 Ecio PERIN JUNIOR, op. cit., 330.

3 Characteristics of the Institute of Corporate Recovery

3.1 In the Brazilian Legal System

In the Brazilian legal system, the study of the legal institute of recovery presupposes the analysis of the law that this institute disciplines, Law No. 11.101/2005.

This is a legal diploma repealing Decree No 7.661 of June 21, 1945. It brings with it considerable changes with the aim of avoiding the bankruptcy of the corporate entity that is in crisis; it was in this context that the preventive and suspensive concordats were extinguished in order to give rise to a single recovery process that is divided into judicial and extrajudicial.

The essence of the recovery institute is to undo the economic and financial crisis of the debtor businessperson and, consequently, to restore the respective economic and financial stability and assets of the business entity and, in this way, to preserve economic activity and maintain the source generating employment and its workers and the satisfaction of credit rights, with the aim of guaranteeing the fulfilment of the social function of corporate activity.

The insertion of the legal institute in question, in the system of bankruptcy law (Law No. 11. 101/2005), is based on maintaining the activities of corporate entities facing difficulties but with considerable economic viability, seeking to remove bankruptcy from them and in return promote their recovery.

3.2 In Other Legal Systems

The study of the historical aspects of the company's recovery has as its starting point, the Ancient Rome, where two fundamental characteristics stand out: (i) ***inductia quinquinallis***—which means the act of extending the period of time by no more than five years for the debtor to satisfy the complex of obligations to which he had been bound up to then and (ii) ***pactum ut minus salvatur***—a belief prevailed that when the legal personality of the debtor ceased (or when he died) without having settled his debt, his soul became grieved and his salvation presupposed the gathering of his heirs to proceed with the force of the inheritance and with the formulation of a proposal to the deceased person in whom they had a right to credit (creditors) so that the debt in question would be satisfied. Failure by the heirs to settle the debt left by the deceased person would have insulted the memory of the deceased person.[166]

166 Carla Eugénio Caldas BARROS, op. cit., 100.

In the Middle Ages in the cities of Italy, there was a complex of municipal statutes that positivized the concordat that opened space for the trader to deviate from his bankruptcy or even oppose its course. The concordat, irrespective of the concordat in Italy, served as a basis for the recovery of corporates. Today, in the Italian legal system, the institute of controlled administration is in force, and its main feature is that the magistrate appoints a commissioner whose task is merely to direct and supervise the management of the reorganization of the economic activities of corporate entities. This system has been criticized on a number of occasions, as it has proved ineffective in preventing bankruptcy and concordats.[167]

In the Spanish legal system, the distinction between the corporate entity (company) that definitively settles its debts and the one that fails to respond to the bond complex due to financial embarrassments has always been clear.

In the Anglo-Saxon legal system, bankruptcy was seen more as an economic fact and less as a procedural phenomenon, what is called a separation between the fate of the debtor and the discharge of of his assets—discharge.

In the Portuguese legal system, in 1993 there was a code regulating the special procedures for the Recovery of the Company and Bankruptcy, and the prerequisite for the opening of the procedure, whether recoverable or bankrupt, was insolvency.

Among the French, the separation between the human person and the legal person (company) only came into effect with the *"1967 law."* The year 1984 was marked by the promulgation of a new law—*"Law 84.148"*—which created a complex set of rules to prevent and regulate, of an amicable nature, the difficulties of corporate entities—an agreement signed between the debtor and the creditor before a conciliator whose appointment was made by the President of the Commercial Court, with the intention of extending the time limits for debts and their pardon.

As can be seen, since 1980, there has been a concern in France to prevent the economic and financial crisis of the corporate entity. A reform launched in 2005 treats companies in difficulty in a divided manner: (i) preventive treatment—the President of the Commercial Court uses two institutions of the convocation as a means of resolving the difficulties of companies and making progress in their recovery: *mandat ad hoc* and the *concilicion*; (ii) judicial treatment—there are mechanisms for the recovery of the corporate entity implemented with the intervention of the judicial authorities, and they are: the *sauvergard* and the

167 Márcio GUIMARÃES, op. cit., 102.

redressement, and there remains the *liquidation judiciaire* for the closure of activities without any form of salvation (this is the old bankruptcy system in France).

In the United States of America (USA), precisely in 1979, the Bankruptcy Act was promulgated, and it is forked into a competitive perspective: Bankruptcy Liquidation and Bankruptcy Reorganization or Rehabilitation Bankruptcy. In this context, it should be noted that the Bankruptcy Code is in force in these States, through Title I (Bankruptcy Act), which introduced the system of company reorganization. A series of reforms to bankruptcy were carried out in 1929 because of the crisis this year which were aimed at improving the economic situation in the United States. Given the fact that bankruptcy law took place at the individual State level, the intervention of the judiciary was mostly limited to ensuring fair treatment among the credit classes (class of creditors). The U.S. bankruptcy system is guided by the principle of freedom as regards the treatment that the creditor and debtor seek for the solution of business difficulties, considering that these more than anyone else are in a better position to seek a solution to such difficulties. The Bankruptcy Abuse Prevention and Consumer Protection Act (BAPCPA) was approved in 2005.[168]

In the English legal system (England), there is a peculiar treatment of the bankruptcy legal institute, the so-called *administration*, as well as *liquidation* or *winding up*. Due to the legal complex of the legal Enterprise Act and the Insolvency Act, the legislation of 2000 and 2002 as a whole currently presents a legal design of the recovery.

In Germany, the reorganization mechanisms of the company are lacking a preventative condition, as the reorganization of the company is based on the issuance of the bankruptcy sentence. In legal terms, there is room for the insolvent or trustee to present, in the course of the bankruptcy proceedings, a plan for complying with the bond complex to which he is attached.

It is an undeniable reality that the legal institute of recovery is treated differently and varies according to each legal system. On the one hand, some seek mechanisms of a preventive nature (as is the case with the French legal system); on the other hand, some limit themselves to dealing with the activity of the bankrupt (in particular Germany). In the United States, recovery mechanisms are based on the principle of freedom of negotiation between the parties—creditor and debtor. Other

168 Fábio Ulhoa COELHO, *Curso de Direito Comercial: Direito de Empresas: contratos e recuperação de empresas*. op. cit., 380–81.

legal systems give the judicial authorities the task of dealing with the recovery of companies.[169]

4 Judicial Recovery

4.1 Introductory Aspects and Concept of Judicial Recovery

The insertion of the legal institute of judicial recovery in the Brazilian legal system, replacing the concordat,[170] by Law No. 11.101/2005 (Articles 47–74), has as its main objective to provide a more convenient solution for the businessperson or trade companies to overcome the economic and financial crisis that affects them for a certain period of time. The basis of this legal institute is to prevent the possible extinction of the company in the midst of the company, which serves as a source of production of assets and services essential to meeting collective needs, a source of employment for citizens, and also a source of tax collection.

The legal mechanism for the removal of the crisis, referred to herein, is the judicial recovery plan that must be submitted to the courts for examination by those who have credit rights (creditors) vis-à-vis the businessperson in crisis. The judicial recovery plan in the context of Law 11.101/2005 assumes the legal nature of a contract between the parties (debtor and creditors); in this sense, the judicial magistrate will be responsible for the homologation of the agreement entered into by the parties.

The status of business, in itself, is incapable of conferring to the businessperson the legitimacy to proceed with the petition for recovery; such understanding results from the interpretation of Article 48 of the bankruptcy law in force, which presents a list of indispensable requirements for the granting of the petition for recovery of the company before the court; they are, therefore, requirements that legitimize such a request and, above all, they are cumulative in nature: the regular exercise of the corporate activity for a period of more than two (2) years, at the time of the petition,[171] not to have incurred bankruptcy, if declared bankrupt, must have a declaration certifying the extinction of the bond complex to which it was attached[172]; not to have obtained the grant of judicial recovery in the last five (5) years preceding the petition for recovery[173]; not to have been the beneficiary

169 Fábio Ulhoa COELHO, *Comentários à nova lei de falências e de recuperação de empresas;* 4ª ed. (São Paulo: Saraiva, 2005), 183.

170 The Bankruptcy and Corporate Recovery Law (Law No. 11. 101/2005) replaced the legal institute of preventive concordat with the institute of judicial recovery and abolished the suspensive concordat.

171 See Article 48, of Law 11.101/2005, in its body.

172 Cf. Subsection I of Article 48 of Law 11.101/2005.

173 Cf. Subsection II of Article 48 of Law 11.101/2005.

of the grant of judicial recovery based on a special plan, in the last eight (8) years preceding the petition for recovery[174]; not to have incurred the conviction of a bankruptcy crime, in the context of bankruptcy law.[175]

A comparative study between Decree-Law 7.666/1945 and Law 11.101/2005 shows that the latter, in the body of its Article 48, has faithfully reproduced subsection I of Article 158 of that decree, with regard to the requirement of regularity in the exercise of corporate activity for a period of more than two years. This is a provision that seeks to prevent the extension of the benefit of recovery by a person who has not yet established himself on the market, bearing in mind that in the first two (2) years, there is a higher risk of the closure of activities, due to lack of experience or poor business administration. It is based on the assumption that, after two years of carrying on the company's business, the businessperson acquires capacity and experience for the development of corporate activity, becoming, in this context, worthy of benefiting from the prerogatives of judicial recovery and, in this way, carrying out the administrative and economic reorganization of his company.[176]

By the terms of the sole paragraph of Article 48, the legitimacy to apply for judicial recovery is not exclusive to the businessperson and is therefore extended to the surviving spouse, the heirs of the debtor businessperson, and the inventor (this legitimacy will certainly be based on *mortis causa*—individual businessperson), while in the case of the corporate company, this legitimacy is extended to the remaining partner, the other being, for some reason, unable to do so.

Having said this, it is appropriate to present the lesson brought to us by the author Etiane Barbi Köhler around the legal institute under analysis, and according to her:

> Judicial recovery implies the socialization of losses, in the final analysis, with company as a whole, because the creditors of the businessperson or collectivity of the businessperson tend to pass on such losses to consumers, as costs of their products or services. That is why it is necessary that the Judiciary be prudent in allowing recovery, granting it when there was a market solution to the crisis that was not possible in the face of the idiosyncrasies of the debtor or controlling holder of the debtor company.[177]

174 Cf. Subsection III of Article 48 of Law 11.101/2005.

175 Cf. Subsection IV of Article 48 of Law 11.101/2005.

176 GIOVANA TAVARNARO, "Da Recuperação Judicial", in *Comentários à Lei 11.101/05: Recuperação Empresarial e Falência*(Curitiba, Paraná: OAB, 2017), 281–82.

177 Etiane Barbi KÖHLER, op. cit., 26.

This lesson gravitates around the justification of the insertion of judicial recovery in the system of Law No. 11.101/2005 (such justification may be extracted from Article 47 in conjunction with Article 48, which deal, respectively, with the objective and requirements of the institute in vogue). In order to be a beneficiary of the prerogatives of the institute in question, the debtor businessperson must prove to be economically powerful in order to overcome the crisis that has affected him until then, not least because, in the context of the presentation of the judicial recovery plan, he must also carry out the economic and financial feasibility study and demonstrate the importance that his recovery can generate within the company.

It is of utmost importance to understand the reality that the *sub judice* institute assumes a social cost whose justification is the continuity of the exercise of corporate activity, in the social context, in the time in which it serves as a source of production of assets and services, a source of job generation for citizens, and a generator of taxes for the public treasury.

Due to the importance that the company represents within the society, the law has attempted to establish a diversity of means of recovery to which the debtor businessperson may resort in order to avert the crisis that affects him; such a list is set out in Article 50 of the law disciplining judicial recovery (Law No. 11.101/2005). It is crucial to note that the means listed in the aforementioned legal provision are merely illustrative. This is an innovative provision in the Brazilian legislative context, because Decree-Law 7.661/1945 did not provide for such means, which, using the concordat, in its Article 156, provided for the possibility of extending the deadline for payment and partially redeeming debts and, in this way, was limited to providing a solution to temporary liquidity crises and, consequently, preventing or suspending bankruptcy.

Having made these introductory remarks, we believe that it is more than appropriate to present the concept of judicial recovery. It should be made clear from the outset that there is no legal concept of the institute in question. Law 11.101/2005, in its Article 47, limits itself to presenting the objectives and the foundation of that institute and does so in the following terms:

> Article 47. The purpose of judicial recovery is to enable the debtor to overcome the situation of economic and financial crisis, in order to allow the maintenance of the production source, the employment of workers and the interests of creditors, thus promoting the preservation of the company, its social function and stimulating economic activity.

Although this legal precept does not present a concept of judicial rehabilitation, it serves as a starting point for the elaboration of a concept of the institute in question; in this context, that institute is defined as the procedure disciplined by a complex set of rules designed for the benefit of the debtor businessperson, whether an individual or a company, for it to move away from the economic and financial crisis that is affecting it and, in return, to bring about its (economic and financial) situation and, in this way, to guarantee the continuity of the company's business or business activity, which proves to be a source of production of assets and services that are essential to satisfy the public interest, a source that generates jobs and protects the interests of creditors. In short, they are rules that preserve the company.[178]

4.2 Recovery Bodies

When, in the context of bankruptcy, precisely in the period of liquidation, we dealt with the subject of bankruptcy bodies (creditors' council, creditors' committee, and judicial trustee), we confined ourselves to talk about the trustee and proposed dealing with the others (creditors' council and creditors' committee) in the context of judicial recovery, since here they take on a greater role than in bankruptcy proceedings. It should be noted that the action of these bodies is not limited to the bankruptcy procedure and judicial recovery procedure; their actions also aim at the extrajudicial recovery procedure. It is now time to comply with our proposal.

4.2.1 General Meeting of Creditors

The general meeting of creditors is a collegial and, therefore, deliberative body. As the nomenclature itself suggests, it is a body made up of the creditors of the debtor businessperson for the defense of his interests. Due to the importance they represent in the recovery process, the law gives them the deliberative prerogative on matters relating to overcoming the economic and financial crisis that affects the corporate entity.

The provision and discipline of this body, in the system of the Bankruptcy and Corporate Recovery Law, is made under Articles 35–47; its characteristic aspects originate from Corporate Law, and its function is to promote the expression of the will and communion of those who before the debtor enjoy credit rights, with such will expressed by means of a vote. It therefore assumes an essentially

178 Carla Eugénio Caldas BARROS, op. cit., 109.

deliberative function that cannot be exercised outside the right of the members to an adversarial hearing, as set out in the aforementioned Article 35.[179]

The setting-up and operation of the general meeting of creditors are optional under these conditions, and it is certain that, in the event of lack of opposition to the recovery plan, in the context of Article 55, for example, the granting of recovery must be made by the magistrate, even if the general meeting is held.

Among the deliberative powers conferred on the general meeting of creditors in the recovery procedure,[180] as well as in the bankruptcy procedure,[181] is the power to set up the creditors' committee, choose its members, and replace them when necessary. It may also, by means of a deliberative act, appoint the judicial trustee.[182] Depending on the duties of such a nature, it is considered correct to state that they confer on the meeting a hierarchical superior position, in the organic structure of the recovery; however, this hierarchical superiority does not subordinate the trustee, since the subordination of the latter falls exclusively on the magistrate.

The fact that the judicial trustee is not subordinated to the general meeting of creditors is justified on logical grounds and consists in a way to make the trustee impartial in the exercise of his duties and thus promote a fair recovery process. Impartiality is based on the fact that the trustee does not only protect the interests of the creditors; this protective function also contributes to the interests of the debtors, to the preservation of the company as a source of goods and services, of jobs, and of the public interest.

It is true that there is no hierarchical relationship between the assembly and the magistrate, but the deliberative act of that body is of supreme force and the magistrate must comply with it. As is well known, every rule has exceptions; it is in this context that Ecio Perin Junior[183] points out that *"(. . .) there is an exception to the cram down institute, provided for in art. 58, § 1, by which the judge is authorized (may force) to grant judicial recovery even in the face of the contrary resolution of the AGC, provided certain requirements are met."*

4.2.1.1 Convocation of the General Assembly of Creditors

Pursuant to Article 36 of the Bankruptcy and Corporate Recovery Law, the magistrate shall be empowered to convene the general meeting and shall do so by

179 Ecio PERIN JUNIOR, op. cit., 239.
180 See subparagraph b), Item I, Article 35 of Law 11.101/2005.
181 See subparagraph b), Item II, Article 35 of Law 11.101/2005.
182 See subparagraph e), Item I, Article 35 of Law 11.101/2005.
183 Ecio PERIN JUNIOR, op. cit., 239.

means of a public notice to be published in the official gazette *(Official Journal)* and in newspapers with a large circulation in the localities of the head office and branches with a minimum period of 15 (fifteen) days in advance, in compliance with the following requirements: *"place, date and time of the meeting on the 1st (first) and 2nd (second) convocation, which may not be held 5 (five) days after the 1st (first)"*[184]; *"agenda"*[185]; *"place where creditors may, if appropriate, obtain a copy of the recovery plan to be submitted to the meeting for deliberation"*[186]; *"a copy of the notice convening the meeting shall be fixed in an extensive manner at the debtor's head office and branches"*[187].

Pursuant to paragraph 2 of the above-mentioned legal provision, creditors representing at least 25 % of the total value of the claims of a certain class may apply for the general meeting to be convened before the magistrate. It is undeniable that convening the general meeting and holding it entails costs; it is in this context that § 3 of the legal provision in question recommends that, unless an extraordinary request is made, such costs be borne by the debtor or the bankrupt estate (in the bankruptcy proceedings).

It should be added that the magistrate's convening of the meeting may be based on hypotheses legally provided for, for example, in the hypothesis established in Article 56, in which case the magistrate convenes the general meeting of creditors to issue a decision on the recovery plan objected to by one or more creditors. In the light of Article 22(g)(I) of the Disciplinary Law of the Recovery Process, the call may also be based on a request addressed to the magistrate by the judicial trustee. It has the same prerogative to request that the meeting be convened before the judge and the Committee of Creditors, in the parameters of Article 27(e)(I) of the same law.

The judicial trustee shall preside over the general meeting of creditors, if the latter is removed or if there is any incompatibility between the duties of chairman and those of administration, the latter may not chair the meeting, but the creditor with the largest claim shall chair it.[188]

The rule is that the vote of the creditor shall be proportional to the value of his claim.[189] The exception to this rule results from the combination of Article 38 and paragraph 2 of Article 45, from which the class of holders of labor claims

184 See item I, article 36 of Law 11.101/2005.
185 See item II, article 36 of Law 11.101/2005.
186 See item III, article 36 of Law 11.101/2005.
187 See § 1 of article 36 of Law 11.101/2005.
188 See Article 37, *Caput* and § 1 of Law 11.101/2005.
189 See Article 38 of Law 11.101/2005.

shall be considered by a simple majority of those present at the meeting convened for the approval of the judicial rehabilitation plan.[190]

4.2.1.2 Composition of the General Meeting of Creditors

The composition of the general meeting of creditors is made according to the credit classes; it is in this context that, under Article 41 of Law 11.101/2005, the general meeting is composed:

> "I—Holders of claims derived from labor legislation or arising from accidents at work"[191]; "II—holders of credit with in rem guarantee[192]; "III—holders of unsecured credits, with special privilege, with in rem privilege or subordinated"[193]; "IV—holders of credits framed as micro-company or small business"[194].

By virtue of the Special Appeal known and provided (STJ. 3rd T. Rel. Min. Nancy Andrighi. R.Esp. No. 1377764/MS. Judgement 20/08/2013. DJe 29/09/2013), the claims referred to in item I are not limited to direct employment relationship derivatives. Thus, the Superior Court of Justice has recognized, as claims falling within Class I, lawyer's fees.[195]

The inclusion of item IV in the above-mentioned article was made by Supplementary Law No. 147/2014, an item that represents a real inconvenience whose clarification is to be made in the meantime in case law. It is in this context that Rodrigo Shirai[196] provides an example of the inconvenience derived from the item in question and does so in the following terms: *"An example is the hypothesis of cram down, in the terms of § 1, since subsection II presupposes, as one of the requirements, that there has been approval in at least two classes (assuming that the original wording of the law contained only three classes) or, if there were only*

190 Both articles are from Law 11.101/2005.

191 See item I, article 41 of Law 11.101/2005.

192 See item II, article 41 of Law 11.101/2005.

193 See item III, article 41 of Law 11.101/2005.

194 See item IV, article 41 of Law 11.101/2005.

195 *"SPECIAL APPEAL. EVICTION AND RENT COLLECTION ACTION. ENFORCEMENT OF SENTENCE. ATTORNEY LAW FEE. FOOD NATURE. EQUALIZATION TO LABOR CLAIMS. SUBMISSION TO JUDICIAL RECOVERY. (...) 2—The treatment of lawyer's fees—with regard to the effects of judicial recovery—must be the same as for labor claims, since both are food-related. 3—The Legal Profession Bylaws, a legal diploma prior to the current Bankruptcy and Corporate Recovery Law, in its art. 24, provide for the need for qualification of claims arising from attorney's fees when dealing with tender execution proceedings.* In this sense, RODRIGO SHIRAI, "Assembleia-Geral de Credores", in *Comentários à Lei 11.101/05: Recuperação Empresarial e Falência*(Curitiba, Paraná: OAB, 2017), 82–83.

196 *Id*; 83.

two classes, that there has been approval in at least one of them." That author adds that the Complementary Legislator forgot to make changes to this legal precept (Article 58).

Still in line with the inconvenience presented herein, one question does not remain silent: *"If a judicial recovery contains four classes, what will be the criteria for judicial recovery in the form of § 1?"* Bearing in mind that Article 46 is at issue, in response to the question raised, it is important to point out that the exception under paragraph 1 is appropriate, therefore, in the field of bankruptcy proceedings, ensuring only preference in the order of payment for claims arising from labor legislation or arising from accidents at work up to a limit of 150 minimum wages, in accordance with the provisions of subsection I of Article 83, the balance being considered an unsecured claim.[197]

Article 49(2) of the Bankruptcy and Recovery Law states that a creditor whose right has been acquired (whose obligation is constituted) after the date of distribution of the request for judicial recovery may not take part in the general meeting of creditors. Still with regard to Article 49, precisely in paragraphs 3 and 4 of the interpretation brought by Etiane Barbie Köhler,[198] it follows that the trustee, the real estate dealer, if there is an irrevocability or irrevocability clause, does not have a seat at the general meeting, as well as the seller with a purchase and sale contract with reserve of ownership—this is because they are not subject to the results of judicial recovery and in bankruptcy they are almost unaffected; however, within a time period of 180 (one hundred and eighty) days in which recovery is granted, they cannot deprive the debtor of the assets essential to the development of the company.

The combination of § 4, Article 49 and subsection II of Article 86, both of the bankruptcy disciplinary law, states that the exclusion from participation in the general meeting of creditors is planned for the creditor banks by means of advances to exporters.

4.2.1.3 *Quorum* for the Approval of the General Meeting of Creditors

A simple majority (51 %) is the normal *quorum* for issuing a deliberative act at general meetings of creditors, in accordance with the value of the claims. In accordance with Article 45 of Law No.11.101/2005, for the issue of the deliberative act concerning the approval of the judicial recovery plan, the quorum shall be qualified according to what is defined therein.

197 *Id.*
198 Etiane Barbi KÖHLER, op. cit., 27.

The stipulations in both Article 46 and Article 145 lead to the conclusion that the *quorum* qualified to approve the *alternative form of realization of the asset* shall be at least two-thirds (2/3) of the claims present at the general meeting of creditors.

In doctrine, on the subject of the quorum for approval of the general meeting of creditors, Fabio Ulhoa Coelho[199] states that:

> For most matters, the meeting of creditors deliberates by simple majority, that is, by the vote of the majority of the creditors present at the meeting counted in proportion to the value of the claims. In voting on the recovery plan, however, the law requires that two conditions be fulfilled concomitantly: a) the majority of creditors in each of the three classical instances must vote in favor, counted only on the number of those present at the meeting; b) the majority of creditors present in the classes of non-employees must vote in favor, counted only on the basis of the value of their claims.

4.2.1.4 Committee of Creditors

The inclusion of the Committee of Creditors in the judicial recovery or bankruptcy procedure is not mandatory; it is therefore an optional insertion body. In accordance with Article 28 of Law 11.101/2005, the noninclusion of the committee in the judicial recovery proceedings leads the judicial trustee to exercise the trustee's powers, and there are incompatibilities between the rights of the trustee and those of the committee of creditors, the latter being exercised by the magistrate.

4.2.1.5 Constitution and Composition of the Committee of Creditors

The composition of the Committee of Creditors results from a legal provision. According to Article 26 of the law governing bankruptcy and recovery proceedings, the following shall form part of the committee of creditors: *"I—1 (one) representative appointed by the class of labor creditors, with 2 (two) substitutes; II—1 (one) representative appointed by the class of creditors with in rem guarantee rights or special privileges, with 2 (two) substitutes; III—1 (one) representative appointed by the class of unsecured creditors and with general privileges, with 2 (two) substitutes."*

The Committee of Creditors is set up by a deliberative act of any of the classes of creditors *("labor creditors, creditors with* in rem *guarantee rights or special privileges and unsecured creditors and creditors with general privileges and general*

199 Fábio Ulhoa COELHO, *Curso de Direito Comercial: Direito de Empresa*; op. cit., 400.

privileges") mentioned above at the general meeting. As was seen, in the paragraph above, the appointment of a representative in each class of creditors is a precondition for the composition of the Committee of Creditors; however, the failure of any of the classes to appoint one will not jeopardize the composition and functioning of the committee, a conclusion that follows from paragraph 1 of the aforementioned Article 26.

The magistrate, at the request of the defaulting class of creditors, endorsed by the majority of the claims of that class, irrespective of the general meeting, shall appoint representatives of alternates of the same class not yet represented on the committee[200] and replace the representative or substitutes of the respective class.[201]

It follows from Article 33 of Law 11.101/2005 that the appointment of members of the Committee of Creditors implies the immediate and personal summons of these members to sign the deed of good and faithful exercise of the office and the assumption of all responsibilities related to it, within 48 (forty-eight) hours, at the seat of the court.

It should be noted that any alleged member of the Committee of Creditors must take into account the system of impediments set out in Article 30 of the Bankruptcy and Corporate Recovery Law. In this sense, a member of the committee is barred from serving as a judicial trustee or member of the committee in the last 5 (five) years of bankruptcy or previous recovery proceedings, who has either been dismissed or has not complied with the legal time limits for rendering accounts or has still failed to render accounts.[202]

Anyone who is related to the debtor, the committee's administrators, the committee's supervisors, or the committee's legal representatives up to a third (3rd) degree, and anyone who has a friendly or hostile relationship or a relationship of dependency with these individuals is also barred from being a member of the creditor committee.[203] The debtor businessperson, any creditor, or the Public Prosecutor's Office, when members of the Committee of Creditors appointed are not complying with the legal requirements, shall be assisted by the legitimacy to apply for the replacement of these members toward the magistrate.[204] Once the request has been addressed to the magistrate, the latter will have 24 (twenty-four) hours to issue his decision.[205]

200 See Subsection I, paragraph 2 of Article 26 of Law 11.101/2005.
201 See Subsection II, paragraph 2 of Article 26 of Law 11.101/2005.
202 See Article 30, *Caput,* Law 11.101/2005.
203 See § 1, Article 30 of Law 11.101/2005.
204 See § 2, Article 30 of Law 11.101/2005.
205 See § Paragraph 3, Article 30 of Law 11.101/2005.

4.2.1.6 Responsibilities of the Committee of Creditors

The responsibilities of the members of the creditors' committee are laid down in Article 32 of the Bankruptcy and Corporate Recovery Act. According to the legal provisions in force it follows that *"(. . .) the members of the Committee shall be liable for damages caused to the bankruptcy estate, the debtor or the creditors through willful misconduct or fault, the dissident in deliberation of the Committee having to record his disagreement in the minutes in order to exempt himself from liability."* It should be noted that the responsibility of the Committee of Creditors is higher because it is responsible for administering the assets of third parties. It has the duty to exercise due diligence and to take the necessary measures to preserve assets and rights, subject to liability for any action or omission that gives rise to damage. This is a liability with personal property.

Though the Committee of Creditors is a collegiate body, the system of joint and several liability does not apply there, which means that its members are not jointly and severally liable. It is assumed that joint and several liability does not result from presumption but is the result of legal provision thus established by Article 265 of the Brazilian Civil Code. This is also because the aforementioned Article 32 makes room for any component part (member) of the Committee of Creditors not to agree with the decision and to record their disagreement in the minutes in order to exempt themselves from liability.[206]

4.2.1.7 Powers of the Committee of Creditors

The powers of this body result from legal provision. Law 11.101/2005, whereby it took care to insert in its systematic list of competencies of the Committee, precisely in its Article 27, as it can be seen, is projected both in the sphere of the bankruptcy process and that of the recovery process.

In both cases (bankruptcy and recovery), in the wake of Article 27(I)(a), (b), (c), (d), (e), and (f), the committee's powers are summarized: (i) to supervise the activities and examine the accounts of the judicial trustee; (ii) to take care of the due course of the process and compliance with the legal provisions inherent therein; and (iii) to request the convening of the general meeting. In the context of recovery, the legal provision in question has taken care to reserve a clause dealing with the competence that only falls to the committee in the recovery process and is not therefore intended for the bankruptcy process, under the terms of als. (a), (b), (c), and (d) of clause II (Article 27), and consists of proceeding with the

206 Ecio PERIN JUNIOR, op. cit., p. 237.

supervision of the activities of the debtor businessperson and implementing the recovery plan.

This legal instrument gives creditors fundamental powers in both the bankruptcy and the recovery proceedings. The main aim of these attributions is to allow more attention to be paid to the bankrupt estate or to the company being recovered, so that both processes do not serve as fraudulent instruments, as was significantly the case when Decree-Law 7.66/45 was revoked, so that they become social means aimed at satisfying the rights of creditors and overcoming the economic and financial crisis of the company (in judicial recovery) and the rapid liquidation and takeover of assets and business by effective companies (in bankruptcy).[207]

Pursuant to paragraph 1, Article 27 of Law 11.101/2005, the decisions of the Committee of Creditors shall be taken by a majority and shall be recorded in a register of minutes, signed by the judge, which shall be at the disposal of the judicial trustee, the creditors, and the debtor.

4.2.1.7.1 Judicial Trustee

In the process of company recovery, the powers of the trustee are established in items I and II of Article 22 of Law 11.101/2005. These clauses set out the wide range of powers granted to the body under analysis, due to its importance in recovery. In view of the matter of attributions in vogue, Fábio Ulhoa Coelho[208] states that

> The trustee always has the task of supervising the applicant company, chairing the Assembly of Creditors and verifying the claims. If there is no committee, he also performs the functions of that body. Finally, if the judge has ordered the removal of the administration from the company under recovery, it will be for the trustee to manage it until the creditors choose the trustee.

207 Luiz Eduardo VACÇÃO DA SILVA, "Do Administrador Judicial e do Comitê de Credores", in *Comentários à Lei 11.101/05: Recuperação Empresarial e Falência* (Curitiba, Paraná: OAB, 2017), 65.

208 Fábio Ulhoa COELHO, *Curso de Direito Comercial: Direito de Empresa: Contratos e recuperação de empresas.* op. cit., 405.

4.3 Judicial Recovery Procedure

4.3.1 Request Phase

In the Brazilian legal system, specifically in the system of Law 11.101/2005 (Bankruptcy and Corporate Recovery Law), there is no concept of request or petition for judicial recovery, even so, Chapter III (which has the epigraph, *"Judicial Recovery"*), in its Section I (General Provisions), precisely in Article 48, proves to be very helpful, because it is where the requirements of the initial petition regarding the recovery process are listed.

Based on the content of the above-mentioned legal provision, a petition shall be understood to mean the request that the businessperson, in the regular exercise of corporate activity for a period of more than two (2) years, who has not been condemned to bankruptcy, or with a complex of obligations declared extinct by a judgment that has the force of res judicata and that in a period of less than five (5) years has not benefited from judicial recovery, or in a period of less than eight (8) years has not benefited from recovery based on a special plan. In addition, the debtor businessperson, his directors, or his supervisory partner may not have incurred a conviction for a bankruptcy crime. Such a request must certainly be filed with the court of the debtor businessperson's main premises, in compliance with the rules seen in the context of the bankruptcy court's approach.[209]

In addition to the debtor businessperson, those whose are given legitimacy to instruct the request of judicial recovery include the surviving spouse of the businessperson, their heirs, and their inventor (legitimacy based on *mortis causa*—individual businessperson); in the case of a corporate company, legitimacy is conferred on the remaining partner, within the parameters of the sole paragraph of Article 48, referred to above.[210]

4.3.1.1 Requirements of the Application Originating Proceedings / Application

Law 11.101/2005 took care to present in its Article 51[211] a list of requirements that must be included in the petition whose object is to request judicial recovery:

> Article 51. The initial petition for judicial recovery shall be instructed with:

209 Etiane Barbi KÖHLER, op. cit., 29.
210 See Sole paragraph, article 48 of Law 11.101/2005.
211 As amended by 14.112 of 2020.

I. a statement of the concrete causes of the debtor's patrimonial situation and the reasons for the economic and financial crisis;
II. accounting statements for the last three (3) financial years and those drawn up especially to support the petition, prepared in strict compliance with applicable corporate law and consisting necessarily of
    a) the balance sheet;
    b) accumulated income statement;
    c) income statement since the last financial year;
    d) management report on cash flow and its projection;
    e) description of the companies of the by fact or by law company group.
III. the complete nominal list of creditors, subject or not to judicial recovery, including those by obligation to make or give, with the indication of the physical or electronic address of each one, the nature, as provided to in articles 83 and 84 of this Law, and the updated value of the credit, detailing its origin, and the regime of the maturities;
IV. the full list of the employees, including their respective duties, salaries, indemnities and other amounts to which they are entitled, with the corresponding accrual month, and a breakdown of the amounts pending payment;
V. the certificate of regularity of the debtor at the Company Public Registry, the updated memorandum of association and the minutes of appointment of the current officers;
VI. the list of the private assets of the supervisor partners and of the debtor's managers;
VII. updated statements of the debtor's bank accounts and of any financial investments of any kind, including those in investment funds or stock exchanges, issued by the respective financial institutions;
VIII. certificates from protest offices located in the district of the debtor's domicile or headquarters and those where it has a branch;
IX. a list, signed by the debtor, of all legal actions and arbitration proceedings to which he is a party, including labor actions, with the estimate of the respective amounts claimed.
X. the detailed fiscal debt report; and
XI. the list of assets and rights that are part of non-current assets, including those not subject to judicial recovery, concurrent with the legal transactions entered into with the creditors referred to in § 3 of art. 49 of this Law

§ 1. The bookkeeping documents and other ancillary reports, in the form and format prescribed by law, shall remain at the disposal of the court, the trustee and, upon judicial authorization, any interested party.

§ 2. With respect to the requirement under the main Section II, of this article, micro companies and small companies may submit simplified books and bookkeeping in accordance with specific legislation.

§ 3. The judge may order that the documents referred to in paragraphs 1 and 2 of this article, or a copy thereof, be deposited at the registry.

§ 4. In the event that the court recovery if filled before the final date of delivery of the balance sheet corresponding to the previous year, the debtor will present a prior balance sheet and attach the final balance sheet within the period of the applicable company law;

§ 5. The judicial proceedings' value will be the total amount of the credits subject to judicial recovery;

§ 6. Regarding the period referred to in § 3 do art. 48 of this Law:

i. The exposure referred to in caput of section I of this article must prove the insolvency crisis, characterized by insufficient financial or equity resources with sufficient liquidity to settle its debts;
ii. The requirement of the caput of section II of this article will be substituted by the documents mentioned in § 3 of article 48 of this Law corresponding to the last two years.

The instruction of the request for judicial recovery must comply with the requirements listed in the legal precept described above; such requirements are called specific, and those contained in the procedural law (Brazilian Civil Procedure Code of 2015) are called generic and are established in Article 319 of the Brazilian Civil Procedure Code. In this context, the instruction of the cause of action, in addition to complying with the provisions of the procedural law, must take into consideration the rules of the substantive law, in line with item I of Article 51 of Law 11.101/2005; the plaintiff must, in the petition, provide a detailed description of the history of the company, of the area of activity operated, of its patrimonial situation, and of the causes that gave rise to the economic and financial crisis.

Although there is no express legal provision, it is understood that under Article 47 of the Disciplinary Law on judicial recovery, it is necessary, in the application originating proceedings, to demonstrate the viability of the company and the suitability of judicial recovery as an instrumental means chosen by the debtor to prevent it from being declared bankrupt, in accordance with the guiding principles of the recovery process. By virtue of the rule that special law takes precedence over general law, Article 319(VII) of the Civil Procedure Code requires *"The application initiating the proceedings shall state: The plaintiff's choice whether or not to hold a conciliation or mediation hearing,"* thus derogating from the general rule of procedural law by the special rite of Law 11.101/2005.[212]

There is a remarkable complementarity of Article 320 of the Civil Procedure Code, which, on the one hand, states that the examination of the application must be made with the documentation essential to the filing of the action, with items II to IX of Article 51 of Law 11.101/2005, which, on the other hand, took care to enroll the documentation necessary for such filing. In accordance with Article 321 of the procedural law, failure to comply with the formal requirements in the examination of the application and/or failure to submit the necessary documents shall lead the magistrate to determine the amendment and/or order the submission of the missing documents within 15 (fifteen) days, specifying the corrections to be made and the missing documents.

It must be stated that the application originating proceedings will be rejected if the plaintiff (in this case, the businessperson debtor, or the surviving spouse, his heirs, his inventor, or remaining partner) does not diligently comply with the determinations and orders of the magistrate, as stated in the sole paragraph of Article 321 above.

4.3.2 Processing Phase

According to Article 52 of Law 11.101/2005, the magistrate will grant the processing of the judicial recovery if the application originating proceedings is duly instructed. It should be noted that the magistrate's decision—granting of processing—pursuant to paragraph 2, Article 203 of the Civil Procedure Code, takes effect from an interlocutory decision and may be appealed against. In turn, the dismissal of the processing of the claim for recovery has as a consequence the extinction of the procedure in the first degree and against it an interlocutory appeal will be possible, with protection for the injured third party, in accordance with Article 1009 of the said Civil Procedural Law.

212 See ELTON BIAOCCO, "Do Pedido e do Procedimento de Recuperação Judicial", in *Comentários à Lei 11.101/05: Recuperação Empresarial e Falência* (Curitiba, Paraná: OAB, 2017), 123.

The decision on the processing of the judicial recovery by the magistrate shall be issued in a public notice (considered as the first public notice) that shall be published in the official body and shall contain the following elements[213]: (I) a summary approach to the decision providing for the processing of judicial recovery[214]; (II) a list of the names of the creditors with the respective breakdown of the updated value and classification of each claim[215]; and (III) an admonition on the time limits for the habilitation of claims and for the presentation of the objection to the recovery plan by the creditors.[216]

The provision of judicial recovery process suspends the course of actions and executions on the recovered company, with the exception of those demanding gross amounts, those of a labor nature, tax executions, and credits that cannot be recovered in the context of paragraphs 3 and 4 of Article 49 of Law No. 11.101/2005, and such suspension is intended to prevent the expropriation of assets essential to the continuity of business activities and thus ensure that the recovery plan is successful.[217]

4.3.3 Qualifications

Clearance of claims is the procedure by which creditors are admitted to the judicial recovery procedure after the initial verification of claims. This is an obligation of a procedural nature that is carried out after the verification of claims originating from the granting of judicial recovery proceedings, in accordance with the provisions of Article 52, paragraph 1, item III of Law 11.101/2005—*"Being in terms of the documentation required by article 52, paragraph 1, of the Law 11.101/2005. 51 of this law, the judge shall grant processing of the judicial recovery and, in the same act: the judge shall order the dispatch of a notice, for publication in the official body, which shall contain: a warning about the time limits for qualification of claims, pursuant to article 7, paragraph 1 of this law (. . .)."*

As can be seen from the legal section described above, the entitlement must gravitate around Article 7 and in adherence to the legal diploma in vogue.

After the time lapse of qualifications (the period of qualifications corresponds to 15 days from the date of publication of the first notice), the judicial trustee shall have 45 (forty-five) days to proceed with the publication of the notice (second notice) that shall contain the list of creditors and an indication of the place

213 See § Paragraph 1, Article 52 of Law 11.101/2005.

214 See Subsection I, Paragraph 1, Article 52 of Law 11.101/2005.

215 Subsection II, Paragraph 1, Article 52 of Law 11.101/2005.

216 See Subsection III, Paragraph 1, Article 52 of Law 11.101/2005.

217 See Article 52, *caput,* subsection III.

and the common period in which the committee, any creditor, the debtor, and its partners or the Public Prosecutor's Office shall have access to the documentation supporting the relationship in question. From this moment on, the public notice may be contested; in the event of challenge, another one will be published with a consolidated general framework, formulated by the trustee and approved by the magistrate.

4.3.4 Phase of the Recovery Plan

It follows from the legal provision in Article 53, *caput,* of Law 11.101/2005, that the presentation of the recovery plan by the businessperson debtor must be made within the time limit of sixty (60) non-extendable days, whereby the counting begins from the date of publication of the decision that provided for judicial recovery processing; if the debtor fails to comply with that time limit, his petition for recovery will go bankrupt.

The non-extendable condition of the period of 60 (sixty) days attributes to Article 53 the character of a mandatory rule and is therefore not subject to a settlement procedure, reinforcing this character of Article 73, item II, by determining that the magistrate will order bankruptcy in the course of the judicial recovery procedure on the grounds that the debtor has not submitted the recovery plan within that period.

In doctrinal terms, it is believed that the normative content of the two aforementioned legal precepts (Articles 53 and 73, item II of Law 11.101/2005) is justified in the importance that the recovery plan represents in the judicial recovery process, the plan being considered a fundamental part of the respective process.

Fábio Ulhoa Coelho[218] illustrates the importance of the plan in the following terms:

> The most important piece of the judicial recovery process is, without a shadow of a doubt, the judicial recovery plan (or "reorganization of the company"). It depends exclusively on it whether or not the goals associated with the institute are achieved, which are the preservation of economic activity and the fulfillment of its social function. If the recovery plan is consistent, there is a chance that the company will restructure and overcome the crisis into which it has been plunged. In this case, the sacrifice imposed directly on the creditors and indirectly on all the paperwork aimed at fulfilling a mere procedural formality would have been worthwhile, so the future of the institute is complete

218 Fabio Ulhoa COELHO, *Comentários a nova Lei de Falências e de Recuperação de Empresas* (São Paulo: Saraiva, 2005), 154–55.

> demoralization. It should be noted that a good recovery plan is not in itself an absolute guarantee that the company in crisis will be re-established. Global or national macroeconomic factors, stiffer competition in the market segment concerned or even inefficiency in its implementation may jeopardize the desired reorganization. But a bad plan is an absolute guarantee of a failed judicial recovery.

The recovery plan should contain the following elements: (I) a detailed description of the means of recovery to be employed and a summary of each act comprising them[219]; (II) a demonstration of the company's economic viability[220]; and (III) an economic and financial report and evaluation of the debtor's assets and liabilities, signed by a legally qualified professional or specialized company.[221] It is crucial to add that the recovery plan must be consistent and qualitative; otherwise, the judicial recovery will go bankrupt.

It follows from the combination of Articles 53, sole paragraph and 55 of Law 11.101/2005 that, upon submission of the recovery plan to the court, the magistrate will order its publication in the public notice containing notice to the creditors of its receipt and will set the deadline for the expression of possible objections. Objections, in turn, may be filed within 30 (thirty) days from the date of publication of the list of creditors referred to in Article 7(2) of the same law. The period of 30 (thirty) days for the objection starts to run from the date of publication of the second notice containing the list of creditors, if the first notice announcing the presentation of the plan has already been published. If, however, at the time of publication of the second notice containing the list of creditors, the notice of submission of the plan has not yet been published, that period shall run from the date of publication of the plan.

In accordance with Article 56, if one or more creditors express their objection to the judicial recovery plan, the magistrate will convene the meeting of creditors to decide on the recovery plan. In legal terms, consensus is required for the resolution approving the recovery plan, but Article 45 establishes a qualified *quorum* for the issuing of the resolution: for the class with *in rem* guarantee and for the class of unsecured creditors, with special privilege, with general privilege, or subordinated, approval is dependent on the favorable resolution of the creditors representing more than half of the total number of the creditors present at the meeting and, cumulatively, by the simple majority of the creditors present[222];

219 See Item I, Article 53 of Law 11.101/2005.
220 See Item II, Article 53 of Law 11.101/2005.
221 See Item III, Article 53 of Law 11.101/2005.
222 See § 1, article 45 of Law 11.101/2005.

for the class of creditors holding credits deriving from labor legislation or from accidents at work, approval is dependent on the favorable resolution of the simple majority of the creditors present, regardless of the value of their credit.[223]

In the event that the meeting of creditors convened by the magistrate does not approve the recovery plan submitted by the debtor, the magistrate may grant it if the provisions of paragraph 1, Article 58 of Law 11.101/2005 are complied with. In this logic, the magistrate may grant a recovery plan on the basis of the plan that did not obtain approval in the form of Article 45, provided that, at the same meeting, it was obtained cumulatively: (I) favorable vote of creditors representing more than half of the value of all claims present at the meeting, regardless of classes[224]; (II) approval of two classes of creditors pursuant to Article 45, and if there are only two classes with voting creditors, the approval of at least one of them[225]; and (III) in the class that rejected it, the favorable vote of more than one-third of the creditors pursuant to paragraphs 1 and 2 of Article 45, if there are only two classes with voting creditors.[226]

The current Article 58(2) reflects a guiding principle of the recovery procedure: *par conditio creditorum,* which advocates equal treatment between classes of creditors. Accordingly, in the context of the legal provision in question, the class of creditors who disapprove of the plan may not be treated differently. It is an appropriate mechanism for ruling out any form of collusion between the debtor and the creditors who choose to approve the plan in order to disadvantage other creditors who reject the plan.[227]

Under the terms of Article 57, if the creditors do not object to the recovery plan, or even if they object to it, it is approved under the circumstances of paragraph 1 of Article 58, the corporate debtor, by order of the magistrate, must submit negative tax debt certificates, within the context of the Brazilian Tax Code *("Código Tributário Nacional").*

Pursuant to Article 59 of Law 11.101/2005, the judicial recovery plan implies the renewal of the credits prior to the filing of the petition and binds the debtors and all creditors subject to it without detriment to the guarantees. It should be noted that in legal terms the judicial recovery plan is not allowed to provide for

223 See § 2, article 45 of Law 11.101/2005.
224 See Subsection I, paragraph 1, article 58 of Law 11.101/2005.
225 See Subsection II, paragraph 1, article 58 of Law 11.101/2005.
226 See Subsection III, paragraph 1, article 58 of Law 11.101/2005.
227 Artur Mendes LOBO and Daniel António RIBEIRO DE SOUSA, "Do Procedimento de Recuperação Judicial", in *Comentários à Lei 11.101/05: Recuperação Empresarial e Falência*(Curitiba, Paraná: OAB, 2017), 143.

a period exceeding two (2) years for the payment of labor claims whose maturity occurred prior to the filing of the petition for judicial recovery (Article 54, *caput*) or a period exceeding 30 (thirty) days for the payment of up to five (5) minimum wages of labor claims whose maturity occurred three months prior to the filing of the petition (sole paragraph, Article 54).

The normative content of Article 61 states that once judicial recovery has been granted, the businessperson debtor will remain in recovery until the complex of obligations, the provision for which is included in the plan, which fall due up to two years after the respective concession, are fulfilled. In the meantime, it is of utmost importance to bear in mind that, within the time span of two (2) years, if it is necessary to amend the recovery plan, the general meeting of creditors must be held in order to pass a resolution to this effect.

Failure to comply with any obligation under the plan will result in bankruptcy (Article 61[1]). After two (2) years, in the event of failure to comply with any obligation, any creditor may apply for specific performance or bankruptcy (Article 62).

In accordance with the provisions of Article 69, the debtor businessperson, while acting as businessperson, has the duty, in all acts that he performs, to add to his business name the expression *"in Judicial Recovery"*; this is in order to make public and transparent the situation in which the businessperson finds himself. Certainly, the means for promoting the publicity and transparency of the situation in which the businessperson finds himself is not limited to adding the expression *"in Judicial Recovery"* to the businessperson's name in the acts he performs; such promotion is also possible in the form of Article 191 of Law 11.101/2005, according to which, subject to the specific provisions of the said legal diploma, the ordered publications shall be preferably made in the official press, and, if the debtor includes them, in a newspaper or magazine of regional circulation, as well as in any other periodicals circulating throughout the country (Brazil). Such ordered publications shall be entitled *"judicial recovery of"* (sole paragraph of Article 191).

Under the sole paragraph of Article 60, in the event that the recovery plan provides for the transfer of the corporate premises, the acquisition for the purchaser does not entail any onus or succession for the latter; however, a succession of a labor nature is granted, meaning that the purchaser will succeed the businessperson in the responsibilities relating to the satisfaction of the labor obligation complex.[228]

228 Etiane Barbi KÖHLER, op. cit., 31.

Once the compulsory complex provided for in the plan has been fulfilled, within two years, the magistrate will order the closure of the judicial recovery process by means of a sentence. The content in question results from Article 63 of Law 11.101/2005, which deals with the closure of the judicial recovery process, the conclusion of which obliges the debtor to (I) pay the fees of the judicial trustee, the payment being subject to the presentation of the respective rendering of accounts, by the trustee, approved in due terms[229]; (II) pay the judicial costs arising from the judicial recovery process[230]; the consequences of such closure include the following: the dissolution of the creditors' committee and the dismissal of the judicial trustee[231]; communication of the closure to the Public Registry of Commercial Companies for the necessary measures; withdrawal of the expression *"in Judicial Recovery"* so that the debtor may perform legal acts with third parties in which it has not been under judicial recovery, even if its plan has not been fully complied with.[232]

5. Special Judicial Recovery for Micro and Small Companies

Micro and small businesspeople are liable to be hit by the economic and financial crisis in the development of corporate activity, and, consequently, the law gives them the right to seek judicial recovery. Such recovery is governed by a specific complex set of rules, which are different from that governing the ordinary judicial recovery process; therefore, it is in this context that it is called the special judicial recovery process.[233] The legal provision for the possibility of special judicial recovery of micro and small companies is made in chapter III, section V, Article 70–72 of the Bankruptcy and Corporate Recovery Law (Law No. 11101/2005).

Under Article 71, the presentation of the special judicial recovery plan shall be made within a non-extendable period of 60 (sixty) days as from the day on which it is decided to grant the processing of judicial recovery and shall cover only unsecured creditors,[234] which may have their claims paid in up to 36 (thirty-six)

229 See Subparagraph I of Article 63 of Law 11.101/2005.

230 See Subparagraph II of Article 63 of Law 11.101/2005.

231 See Subparagraph IV of Article 63 of Law 11.101/2005.

232 See Subparagraph V of Article 63 in conjunction with article 69, both from Law 11.101/2005.

233 Fábio Ulhoa COELHO, *Curso de Direito Comercial: Direito da Empresa: contratos e recuperação de empresas;* op. cit., 428–29.

234 See Subparagraph I, Article 71 of Law 11.101/2005.

monthly instalments, equal and successive, monetarily adjusted, plus interest of 12 % (twelve percent)[235] per year, with payment of the first instalment within 180 (one hundred and eighty) days of distribution of the request for judicial recovery.[236]

The period of 180 (one hundred and eighty) days referred to in the above article may be extended by the magistrate for a period not exceeding 1 (one) day, such extension requiring the consent of the majority of the creditors.[237]

By virtue of the sole paragraph of Article 71, a recovery request based on a special plan does not lead to suspension of the course of limitation or of actions and executions for claims not covered by the plan.

The special judicial recovery plan may be granted to the micro businessperson or small businessperson by the magistrate without the need to hold a meeting of creditors, provided that the dictates of the law disciplining the recovery process are observed.[238] The concession may not be made if creditors holding more than half of the unsecured claims object to the plan.[239]

6 Extrajudicial Recovery

The legal institute of extrajudicial recovery is the second type of company recovery affected by the economic and financial crisis, and its discipline is made under Articles 161–167 of Law 11.101 of February 9, 2005.

Through the institute in force, the Brazilian legal system (Bankruptcy Law) was significantly innovated, in the revoked Bankruptcy Law (Law 7.661/1945) if the debtor called his creditors to issue them the proposal for an extension of the time limit to satisfy the bond complex, such act would be considered as bankruptcy based on the presumption of his generated insolvency; Law 11.101/2005 did not characterize the assumption of insolvency of the debtor and businessperson and introduced the agreement as a means by which the debtor and creditors seek to resolve the economic and financial crisis and thus prevent the debtor from going bankrupt.

235 See Subparagraph II, Article 71 of Law 11.101/2005.

236 See Subparagraph III, Article 71 of Law 11.101/2005.

237 Ecio PERIN JUNIOR, op. cit., 353.

238 See Article 72 of Law 11.101/2005.

239 See Sole paragraph of Article72 of Law 11.101/2005.

6.1 *Inapplicability of Extrajudicial Recovery to Certain Creditors*

By authority of Article 161 of Law 11.101/2005, the institute of judicial recovery is inapplicable to certain creditors, precisely the labor tax creditors[240]; the combination of the legal provision herein mentioned, with paragraphs 3 and 4 of Article 49 of the same law, leads to the conclusion that the inapplicability of the institute in question is also projected to the commercial lessor, fiduciary creditor, the seller of property with contracts with an irrevocability or irreversibility clause, the seller with reserve of control, and the bank granting credit for the export exchange contract.

6.2 *Approval of the Extrajudicial Recovery Plan*

Type approval of the Extrajudicial Recovery Plan may be optional or compulsory.

Extrajudicial recovery is said to be optional when all the business debtor's creditors adhere to the recovery plan, and, in this sense, ratification is not necessary. This has, in the case *sub judice*, genuinely formal effects; however, if the debtor is interested, he may request the ratification of the plan within the parameters of legal precepts 162 and 162, for which he will have to fulfil cumulatively the requirements provided for in Article 48 of Law 11.101/2005 (we have already dealt with them in the study of judicial recovery).

In the situation of Article 163 (mandatory ratification), the ratification of the plan will oblige the universality of the creditors covered by it, even if they have only agreed for three-fifths (3/5) of all the credits of each species covered by it. On the other hand, not all creditors agree with the plan but if creditors with a minimum representation of three-fifths (3/5) of all the credits of each class sign it (agree with it), it will oblige everyone, even those who disagree.

6.3 *Instruction of the Application for Approval*

The approval of the extrajudicial recovery plan, pursuant to Article 163(6), requires the debtor to examine the application containing the following documentation: (i) the recovery plan[241]; (ii) the justification for the recovery[242]; (iii) an account of the debtor's assets[243]; (iv) accounting statements relating to the last

240 See § Paragraph 1 of Article 161 of Law 11.101/2005.
241 See Article 162 of Law 11.101/2005.
242 See Article 162 of Law 11.101/2005.
243 See Article 163, item I, § 6 of Law 11.101/2005.

financial year and those drawn up especially to deal with the petition[244]; (v) the documents proving the subscribers' powers to renew or compromise, a complete nominal list of the creditors, with an indication of each one's address, the nature, classification, and updated value of the credit, detailing its origin, the regime of the respective maturities, and an indication of the accounting records of each pending transaction.[245]

6.4 Procedure

Under the terms of Article 164 of Law 11.101/2005, if the petition for approval of the extrajudicial recovery plan is duly filed, the bankruptcy court shall receive it. The magistrate having received it, by means of a public notice, shall proceed to summon the creditors, as well as to do so by means of correspondence sent by the businessperson debtor, for the manifestation of the objections within 30 (thirty) days, on the part of the creditors.

The above-mentioned legal provision, in paragraph 3, presents a list of the allegations that may be presented for the objection of the ratification of the extrajudicial recovery plan; they are: (I) failure to comply with the minimum three-fifths (3/5) proportion for approval of the plan; (II) practice, by the debtor, of any act denouncing the state of bankruptcy or of acts revealing the intention to create losses to the creditors; (III) failure to comply with any legal requirements or dictates.

If one or more creditors exercise their right to object to the approval of the plan, the businessperson debtor will be given 5 (five) days to present their objection.[246] After this period of time has elapsed, the magistrate will be immediately summoned to consider any objections, and a further period of 5 days will be opened, within which the magistrate will issue his decision, by means of a sentence, whether or not he is in favor of the plan's ratification, that is, granting or rejecting it.[247]

Finally, it should be noted that in accordance with paragraph 7 of Article 164 of Law 11.101/2005, an appeal may be lodged against the ratification decision of the recovery plan, without suspensive effect.

244 See Article 163, item II, § 6 of Law 11.101/2005.
245 See Article 164, item III, § 6 of Law 11.101/2005.
246 See § paragraph 4 of article 164 of Law 11.101/2005.
247 See § paragraph 5 of article 164 of Law 11.101/2005.

6.5 *Effects of the Homologation of the Extrajudicial Recovery Plan*

As a general rule, the extrajudicial recovery plan starts to take effect after it has been approved by the courts. In the meantime, there is a legal provision according to which it is liable to generate effects even before being ratified, but this happens only in the situation referring to the modification of the value or form of payment of the signatory creditors; this is an exception deriving from paragraph 1, Article 165 of Law 11.101/2005.

The exception provided for in paragraph (1) of the above-mentioned article must take into account the normative content established in paragraph (2) of the same legal provision, according to which, if the plan is subsequently rejected by the magistrate, the signatory debtors must be given back the right to demand the claims on the original terms, deducting the amounts actually paid.

6.6 *Extrajudicial Recovery Not Subject to Ratification*

Provided for and disciplined under Article 167 of Law No. 11.101/2005, this is a form of recovery made effective by means of private arrangements between the parties, debtor, and his creditors; such arrangements do not require ratification by the courts.

References

- AFONSO NETO, Augusto. 1962. *Princípios de Direito Falimentar.* São Paulo: Max Limonad.
- ALMEIDA, Amador Paes. 2005. *Curso de Falência e de Recuperação de Empresa.* 21ª ed. São Paulo: Saraiva.
- ALMEIDA, Amador Paes. 2007. *Curso de Direito Falimentar e Recuperação de Empresa.* 23ª ed. São Paulo: Saraiva.
- ARNOLDI, P. R. C. 1999. *Falências e Concordatas.* 2ª ed. São Paulo: Ledi – Livraria e Editora de Direito.
- BARROS, Carla Eugenia Caldas. 2014. *Manual de Direito Empresarial Multifacetado,* Voll. III – Direito Falimentar e Recuperacional. Aracaju: Edição do Autor | PIDCC.
- BULHÕES PEDREIRA, José Luiz and Alfredo LAMY FILHO. 1992. *A Lei as S.A. – Pressupostos – Elaboração – Aplicação.* Rio de Janeiro: Renovar.
- CARVALHO FILHO, José dos Santos. 2018. *Manual de Direito Administrativo*; 32ª ed. São Paulo: Atlas.
- CARVALHO, Raphael Franco Castelo Branco. 2013. *Falência: uma análise jurídica e histórica do instituto, desde a antiguidade aos dias de hoje.* In Mara Vidagal Darcanchy (org). *Direito Empresarial – Florianópolis.* FUNJAB, v. ún.

- CINTRA, António Carlos de Araújo, Ada Pelligrini GRINOVER and Cândido Rangel DINAMARCO. 2009. *Teoria Geral do Processo,* 25ª Edição, Revista e Actualizada. São Paulo: Malheiros Editores.
- CLARO, Carlos Roberto. 2017. *Do procedimento para a decretação da falência, in* Comentários à Lei 11.105/05: Recuperação Empresarial e Falência, OAB, Curitiba, Paraná.
- COELHO, Fábio Ulhoa. 2005. *Comentários a nova Lei de Falências e de Recuperação de Empresas.* São Paulo: Saraiva.
- COELHO, Fábio Ulhoa. 2007. *Comentários à nova lei de falências e recuperação de empresas.* 4ª ed. São Paulo: Saraiva.
- COELHO, Fábio Ulhoa. 2009. *Curso de Direito Comercial: Direito de Empresa,* Vol. 1, 13 Edição. São Paulo: Editora Saraiva.
- COELHO, Fábio Ulhoa. 2009. *Curso de Direito Comercial: Direito de Empresa – Contratos e Recuperação de Empresa;* 10ª ed. São Paulo: Saraiva.
- ELTON BIAOCCO. 2017. *Do Pedido e do Procedimento de Recuperação Judicial.* In *Comentários à Lei 11.101/05: Recuperação Empresarial e Falência*; OAB, Paraná, Curitiba.
- ESTEVEZ, André Fernandes. *Das origens do Direito Falimentar à Lei nº 11.101/ 2005;* Revista Jurídica Empresarial 15, Julho/Agosto, 2010.
- FAZZIO JÚNIOR, Waldo. 2010. *Manual de Direito Comercial,* 11ª Edição. São Paulo: Editora Atlas.
- FÜHRER, Maximilianus Cláudio. 2002. *Roteiro das Falências e Concordatas,* 18ª ed. REVISTA DOS TRIBUNAIS.
- GUIMARÃES, Márcio. 2013. *Direito das Empresas em dificuldades.* Fundação Gentúlio Vargas: Direito Rio, Graduação.
- KÖHLER, Etiane Barbi. 2011. *Direito Falimentar e da Recuperação Da Empresa.* Rio Grande do Sul, Brasil: Editora Unijui.
- LACERDA, J. C. Sampaio de. 1996. *Manual de Direito Falimentar,* 13ª ed. revisto e actualizado por Jorge de Miranda Magalhães. Rio de Janeiro: Freitas Bastos.
- LOBO, Artur Mendes and Daniel António RIBEIRO DE SOUSA. 2017. *Do Procedimento de Recuperação Judicial.* In *Comentários à Lei 11.101/05: Recuperação Empresarial e Falência*; OAB, Paraná, Curitiba.
- NEGRÃO, Ricardo. 2010. *Manual de Direito Comercial e de Empresa, Volume 1,* 7ª Edição, São Paulo: SARAIVA.
- OLIVEIRA, Gleick Meira. 2010. *Falência: Conhecendo a História para se Construir um Futuro Pautado na Certeza,* **Revista Dat@venia V.2**, Nº2 (jul./dez.), p. 52. DOI:10.20887/rdtv.ccj.2010.v2i2p49-56.
- PERIN JUNIOR, Ecio. 2006. *Curso de Direito Falimentar e Recuperação de Empresa;* 3ª ed. ver., atual. e ampl. São Paulo: Editora Método.
- REQUIÃO, Rubens. 1984. *Curso de direito comercial*; 14ª ed. São Paulo: Saraiva.
- ROCHA, Luiz Marcelo Souza. 2017. *Do pagamento aos créditos.* In *Comentários à Lei 11.101/05: Recuperação Empresarial e Falência*; OAB, Paraná, Curitiba.
- RODRIGO SHIRAI. 2017. *Assembleia-Geral de Credores.* In *Comentários à Lei 11.101/05: Recuperação Empresarial e Falência*; OAB, Paraná, Curitiba.

- VACÇÃO DA SILVA, Luiz Eduardo. 2017. *Do Administrador Judicial e do Comitê de Credores.* In *Comentários à Lei 11.101/05: Recuperação Empresarial e Falência*; OAB, Paraná, Curitiba.
- VALVERDE, Trajano de Miranda. 1955. *Comentários à Lei de Falência.* 2ª ed. Rio de Janeiro: Forense, V. III

Further Reading

- BULHÕES PEDREIRA, José Luiz and Alfredo LAMY FILHO. 2017. *Direito das Companhias,* 2ª ed. Rio de Janeiro: Editora Forense.
- CARVALHO, Raphael F. C. B. *Falência: Uma Análise Jurídica e Histórica do Instituto, desde a Antiguidade aos dias de hoje.* Available at http://www.publicadireito.com.br/artigos/?cod=761a0c714184cab2. Accessed on 25th April 2020.
- CASTRO, Rodrigo R. Monteiro de and Leandro Santos de ARAGÃO. 2009. *Direito Societário: Desafios Actuais.* São Paulo: Quarier Latin.
- COELHO, Fábio Ulhoa. 2011. *Manual de Direito Comercial: Direito de Empresa,* 23ª ed. São Paulo: Saraiva.
- COELHO, Fábio Ulhoa. 2012. *Curso de Direito Civil.* Parte Geral, Vol. 1, 5ª ed. São Paulo: Editora Saraiva.
- DAMASCENO, Maria Helena and Silva MEGALE. 1980. *Transformação, Fusão e Cisão de Sociedades,* Revista da Faculdade de Direito, Universidade de Minas Gerais, ISSN: 0304-2340.
- GIOVANA TAVARNARO. 2017. *Da Recuperação Judicial.* In *Comentários à Lei 11.101/05: Recuperação Empresarial e Falência*; OAB, Paraná, Curitiba.
- REQUIÃO, Rubens, 1998, *Curso de Direito Falimentar,* 17ª ed., São Paulo: Saraiva.
- REQUIÃO, Rubens. 2003. *Curso de Direito Comercial,* Vol. I, 25ª ed. São Paulo: Saraiva.
- REQUIÃO, Rubens. 2005. *Curso de Direito Comercial, Volume 1.* São Paulo: Editora Saraiva.
- RIBEIRO, Cláudia and Priscila MENEZES. 2014. *Teoria do Direito Empresarial,* FGV, Direito Rio, Graduação.
- RODRIGUES, Luiz António Barroso. 2016. *Direito Empresarial,* 3 ed. rev. Actual – Florianópolis: Departamento de Ciências da Administração/ UFSC, Brasília: CAPES: UAB, p. 47.

About the Authors

Dan WEI is Full Professor and Associate Dean of the Faculty of Law, at University of Macau. Wei obtained a Bachelor of Law at Peking University, a Master of Law and PhD in Law at University of Coimbra. She is the first (and still the only) Chinese person to obtain a PhD in Law in Portuguese language.

Wei is a Member of the Economic Development Council of the Macau Special Administrative Region Government. She is Vice-President and Titular Member of the International Academy of Comparative Law (IACL, Paris), Rapporteur of the Committee on International Protection of Consumers of International Law Association (ILA, London).

She served as an Invited Expert of Ascertainment of Foreign Law of the Center for Ascertainment of Foreign Law of the Supreme People's Court of Republic of China.

She is Arbitrator and Mediator of China International Economic and Trade Arbitration Commission (CIETAC), Arbitrator of Arbitration Center of World Trade Center of Macau, Arbitrator of Shenzhen Court of International Arbitration, Arbitrator of Zhuhai Court of International Arbitration, Arbitrator of Jiangsu (Nanjing) International Commercial Arbitrator Center, Member of Governing Board of Macau Mediation and Arbitration Center for Consumer Disputes of Macau Government Consumer Council.

Professor Dan Wei is also an expert of China – Portuguese Speaking Countries relations (in particular, Brazil-China and Portugal-China). She is the General Director of Macau Association for Brazilian Studies and Co-Editor-in-Chief of Macau Journal of Brazilian Studies. Prof. Dan Wei accompanied the Brazilian President Lula da Silva in a series of activities during his State Visit in Beijing in 2004 and participated in some Brazil-China ministerial level technical negotiations on bilateral trade, upon invitation of the Brazilian government. She served as a consultant for the Brazilian government in the WTO ministerial conference in Hong Kong during the Doha Round (2005) and in the same year participated in Brazil-China bilateral ministerial negotiations in Beijing and in Hong Kong. Prof. Dan Wei was also invited by the Brazilian President Dilma Rousseff to participate in a series of activities of the State Visit of Chinese President Xi Jinping in Brasilia in 2014. She has been invited by the Ministry of Justice of Brazil to act as an expert-collaborator. Wei was in charge of several consultancy projects (e.g. Brazilian Legal Systems of Foreign Trade and Investment) of the Ministry of Commerce of China (primarily through the Department of American and Oceanian Affairs which is directly responsible for Chinese economic and commercial relations with the USA, Brazil and other Latin American countries).

She is Visiting Professor of various universities in Portugal and in Brazil. Wei's specialties include international trade law, international investment law, competition law, consumer protection, arbitration, commercial law, legal systems of Portuguese-speaking countries and BRICS. She has authored/edited several monographs including *China and the WTO* (2001), *Globalization and National Interests: China's Perspectives* (2006), *The Portuguese-speaking Countries and China in a Globalized World* (2009), *Contingent Protection Measures of Brazil (2012)*, and *Settlements of Trade Disputes between China and Latin American Countries (2015)* and has published numerous articles in top-tier journals such as Oxford Journals and Cambridge Journals. Wei is the Series Editor of the Book Series "Laws of Emerging Countries" of Springer-Verlag GmbH.

Almeida MACHAVA, is Assistant Professor and Deputy Dean for Research of the Faculty of Law at University Eduardo Mondlane. Obtained his PhD in Law (Economic Juridical Sciences) and Master of International Business Law at University of Macau, and the Bachelor of Law at University Eduardo Mondlane, in Mozambique.

As responsible of the research activities, Almeida is a member and President of the Scientific Council and Editor of the Law Journal at Faculty of Law,

University Eduardo Mondlane. He is also member of the Intellectual Property Management Committee of the University Eduardo Mondlane.

As Professor, Almeida teaches Commercial Law, International Economic Law, International Trade Law, Consumer Law, Regional Integration and SADC Law, Company Law, Commercial Contracts Law, Energy Law and Regulation and Oil and Gas Contracts. He is visiting Professor in several Universities in Mozambique.

His research areas of interest include commercial and company law, international economic and trade relations, harmonization of commercial law in the African Portuguese speaking countries, China – Africa relations (in particular, China – African Portuguese speaking countries) investment law, consumer protection, and alternative dispute settlement mechanisms, and has several studies published in those research areas. Almeida has been engaged in collaborative research in South Africa, Portugal and Brazil.

www.ingramcontent.com/pod-product-compliance
Ingram Content Group UK Ltd.
Pitfield, Milton Keynes, MK11 3LW, UK
UKHW020259051026
15470UKWH00021B/1432

9 781433 197697